The Milošević Trial

When Slobodan Milošević died in the United Nations Detention Unit in The Hague over four years after his trial had begun, many feared – and some hoped – that international criminal justice was experiencing some sort of death itself. Yet the Milošević case, the first trial of a former head of state by a truly international criminal tribunal and one of the most complex and lengthy war crimes trials in history, stands for much in the development and the future of international criminal justice, both politically and legally. This book, written by the senior legal adviser working for the Trial Chamber, analyses the trial to determine what lessons can be learnt that will improve the fair and expeditious conduct of complex international criminal proceedings brought against former heads of state and senior political and military officials, and develops reforms for the future achievement of best practice in international criminal law.

GIDEON BOAS is Senior Lecturer in Law at Monash University Law Faculty and an international law consultant. He was, until October 2006, a Senior Legal Officer of the International Criminal Tribunal for the former Yugoslavia (ICTY) and the Senior Legal Adviser to the Chamber on the Milošević case.

The Milošević Trial: Lessons for the Conduct of Complex International Criminal Proceedings

GIDEON BOAS

CAMBRIDGE
UNIVERSITY PRESS

CAMBRIDGE UNIVERSITY PRESS
Cambridge, New York, Melbourne, Madrid, Cape Town, Singapore, São Paulo

Cambridge University Press
The Edinburgh Building, Cambridge CB2 8RU, UK

Published in the United States of America by Cambridge University Press, New York

www.cambridge.org
Information on this title: www.cambridge.org/9780521700399

First published 2007

Printed in the United Kingdom at the University Press, Cambridge

A catalogue record for this publication is available from the British Library

ISBN–13 978-0-521-87699-5 hardback
ISBN–13 978-0-521-70039-9 paperback

To Pascale

CONTENTS

FOREWORD

This book makes an important contribution to the development of global justice. It is the most authoritative post mortem on the proceedings against Slobodan Milošević, which were hailed as the first 'trial of the century' of the twenty-first century. When Justice Jackson observed, *apropos* of Nuremberg, that 'courts try cases, but cases also try courts' he accurately described the *Milošević* case, a test for whether international courts can today deliver on the Nuremberg legacy that political leaders who mass-murder their own people can be made subject to human justice. In Mr Boas's expert verdict, it was a test that our fledgling system of international criminal justice only narrowly managed to pass.

Others, more prejudiced and less informed, regard the trial as a total failure. The White House, for example, has cited its inordinate length, its massive cost, and its inconclusive end as an argument against producing any kind of fair trial by an international court for the prisoners in Guantanamo Bay. Its short-comings were much in mind when the Iraqi Special Tribunal was set up to try Saddam Hussein: there were no international judges, no right of self-representation, no 'friends of the court' allowed to show friendship with a defendant whose death sentence was predetermined rather than self-inflicted. Those of us who champion international justice, and the International Criminal Court in particular, have winced and shuddered in disbelief as this showcase trial went on, and on, and on. It began in February 2002, but the prosecution case alone took three years. By 24 November 2005 this 'whale of a trial' had produced 46,639 pages of transcript and 2,256 separate written filings amounting to 63,775 pages. The prosecution had introduced 930 exhibits, amounting to 85,526 pages, as well as 117 videos. The material disclosed to Milošević amounted to over 1.2 million pages of documentation – material he would never have the time to read, let alone absorb. In answer to all this, he initially submitted a list of 1,631 witnesses. By the end of 2005, 75 per cent of the way through the time allocated for his defence, he had introduced 50 videos and 9,000 pages of exhibits but had led only

40 witnesses and had barely touched on the indictments relating to Croatia and Bosnia. These statistics alone show just how unmanageable this trial really was, during the four years in which both Trial and Appeal Chambers tried to manage it.

When Milošević died and the trial had to be aborted, there was no shortage of instant journalistic hindsight. In contrast, Dr Boas's criticism proceeds from an analysis that is both expert and from the inside: he was the senior legal adviser to the trial judges, sitting in court for four years, from the day on which the prosecution opened to the day on which the trial collapsed. He shows the trial's failings, precisely and irrefutably, and his insight must inform and instruct the future development of international justice. The lessons he draws will be pondered in other courts trying truculent defendants, most notably in the International Criminal Court now taking shape in The Hague. The prosecution mistake of 'throwing the book' at those charged with crimes against humanity must not be repeated: gargantuan indictments are unmanageable and unnecessary. Criminal trials are not truth commissions – the adversary system is a process for determining whether an individual accused committed a particular criminal act, and is not a means for retrospectively testing the morality of a political policy. Just as national courts have abandoned dragnet conspiracy charges in favour of indictments containing sample or representative charges of substantive offences, so international prosecutors must concentrate on specific events – usually specific massacres – for which they have evidence to prove that the defendant bears command responsibility. Prosecutors do not (as many of them think) owe a duty to victims to charge a political leader for every conceivable consequence of his brutal policies: they must observe a sensible divide between facts that can be proved by admissible evidence in court and opinions that must be left to the conjectures of historians.

Dr Boas rightly seeks to shake the complacency of what might be termed the international justice industry – the lawyers and human rights activists who behave as if the struggle to establish a global justice system has been won, just because the ICC and other instrumental courts have been established. Unless these courts achieve measurable improvements in efficiency and expedition in the conduct of their trials, the enterprise will founder, as its high ideals and hopes collapse through delay and massive expense. The symbolic importance of Milošević on trial – the alleged architect of mass murder and genocide in the Balkans denied impunity and brought to justice – was largely squandered by the mistakes that are so rigorously analysed in this book. Dr Boas identifies the principal mistakes as the prosecution's incoherent case strategy, the Appeal Chamber's decision to combine three overloaded indictments, the trial chamber's failure to cope with the defendant's malevolent tactics, and the consequences of his self-inflicted harm.

Hindsight, of course, is generally the prerogative of the armchair critic. Dr Boas had to suffer these problems in silence and in person for the years in which he was Senior Legal Adviser to the trial court. It is important to remember that the prosecution and the Appeal Chamber, and indeed the trial judges he advised, were acting in good faith and coping as best they could with unprecedented situations and problems. Nonetheless, he argues that the prosecution was over-zealous and over-expansive, trying to impute too much to Milošević and to attribute too much to his 'Greater Serbia' policy. This is borne out by the fact that it failed, at the close of its case, to establish over 1,000 of the allegations it made at the outset – a massive indictment, by judgement of the court, of the prosecution's own massive indictment. In retrospect, the trial court should have ordered the prosecution to close in September 2002 after its evidence on Kosovo was complete and when the consequences of the defendant's severe heart condition first became clear. Had it ordered Milošević then to proceed with his defence to that separate indictment, a verdict upon it could have been delivered a year before his death.

Paradoxically, however, what also emerges from Dr Boas's critique is that in respects other than its length, the trial was fair. The court, indeed, bent over backwards to help the accused, providing him with the three expert *amici* counsel and ample facilities for his own research team – so ample that he was able to participate in Serbian politics under the guise of preparing his defence.

The adversary system in Anglo-American courts has grown up in the context of defendants who co-operate with court procedures in the hope of achieving acquittals, even on technical grounds. Milošević had no interest in an acquittal: his object was to undermine the court and to exploit its procedures to attack his political enemies and to publicise his own victimhood. This is a common enough phenomenon now in international courts, and the problem is how to adjust procedures to limit such grandstanding whilst retaining an acceptable level of fairness. *Amici* counsel cannot be friends both of the court and of the accused, and it makes no professional sense to order a lawyer to 'represent' a client who refuses all communication with him. Various expedients were attempted by the long-suffering *Milošević* judges, and others have been attempted in other international tribunals, but with little success. It may be necessary to opt for a more radical solution: to deny the right of adversary trial to an unco-operative defendant, and shift instead to a civil inquisitorial process in which a judge examines the evidence and presents his findings to the Court, at which point the defence may challenge them.

It is certainly true that the adversary trial procedure offers the best guarantee for the rights of defendants, but they are only entitled to it if they accept the jurisdiction and the rules of the court that provides it. If they refuse all co-operation or offer it in a form which entails persistent disruption, they should be made subject to an inquisitorial process whether they like it or not – a process recognised as fair in many countries of the world and which does not depend upon the defendant's co-operation.

The *Milošević* prosecution produced no 'smoking gun' although late in its case it was permitted to introduce an amateur video shot at Srebrenica, showing young Muslims being taken out of a truck by Serb paramilitaries who – after a blessing from a Serb orthodox priest – tied them up and murdered them. These grainy, black-and-white images, so reminiscent of the Second World War film of the SS slaughter of Jews in Eastern Europe, did not directly implicate Milošević but had a similar impact to the film of concentration camp victims shown in the Nuremberg courtroom in legitimating the process of putting him on trial. Other evidence pointed to his control over Serb paramilitaries. These bloodthirsty groups – 'Arkans Tigers' and 'Frankie's Boys' – were linked to Milošević through documents found on the bodies of their fighters proving they had drawn pay as well as arms and ammunition from the Yugoslav army. His long-denied backing for Karadžić was demonstrated by electronic intercepts. In respect of the deportations in Kosovo, the prosecution evidence showed Albanians fleeing from the pillaging, raping, and murder instigated by the Serb forces, who made co-ordinated and planned attacks from village to village and even laid on special trains to take the inhabitants to the border after their homes had been looted and burned.

Slobodan Milošević deserved to stand trial: he was no brain-damaged Pinochet or cancer-ridden Honecker, but a defendant suffering from high blood pressure which he brought on himself by insisting on being his own advocate and by not taking medical advice or prescribed medication. He was not an ignorant soldier or an isolated hereditary ruler: he trained as a lawyer and became President of Yugoslavia's biggest bank before becoming President of the Communist Party and of the country. He was the hands-on commander of its army and police force, and the self-confessed architect of the mass extirpation of 800,000 Albanian Kosovars, uprooted from homes where their families had lived for centuries.

International law now says that the person in ultimate command is responsible for crimes committed by soldiers, police, and paramilitaries if he knows about them yet fails to take necessary and reasonable steps to stop or to punish them. Although the *Milošević* trial ended without a verdict, and many victims felt robbed of the satisfaction they would otherwise have obtained from his conviction and lengthy imprisonment, the very fact that he was put on trial by the international community stands as a landmark in the struggle for global justice. True, there was no written and reasoned judgement to confound those who deny Serb war guilt: they turned up in their thousands to bid farewell to his coffin with their 'Slobo the Hero' banners. But mourners were predominantly elderly and mostly from redneck provinces: their lost leader was denied all state honours and his wife and son stayed away, as did all national and international dignitaries. His chief mourners were fellow indictees, on bail from The Hague, and the release of white doves over his grave provided a surreal, if unintended, promise that his burial might bring peace at last to the Balkans.

PREFACE

The trial of Slobodan Milošević got under way on 12 February 2002 with the grand words of the ICTY Prosecutor, 'Today, as never before, we see international justice in action.' Four years and one month later, Milošević lay dead in his cell in the United Nations Detention Unit in The Hague, the trial unconcluded and the grand project of international criminal justice apparently in jeopardy.

What had brought international criminal law to this point and what would be the legacy of the *Milošević* trial? This question is the background and motivation for this book. The prosecution, the court, and Milošević himself, had all played a part in the course this trial had run, for better and for worse. The monstrously broad case pressed by the prosecution and the pathological behaviour and ill health of the accused persistently plagued the trial. Yet the complexities faced by the court and its responses to them have yielded profound lessons that should serve the development of best practice in the conduct of fair and expeditious international criminal trials.

These lessons are not just important for the limited remainder of the *ad hoc* Tribunals' work. As the newly created flagship of international criminal law – the International Criminal Court – stumbles at the first hurdle of its daunting mandate, it is essential that the Court heeds the lessons learnt by the *ad hoc* Tribunals, not the least those from the *Milošević* case, or risk dealing the greatest of blows to the development and continued viability of international criminal justice. The danger staring those of us who care in the face is complacency born of the successful long-term institutionalisation of international criminal law. Having pursued such an institution since the ineffective Treaty of Versailles following the First World War, and more recently and vigorously following the relatively successful post-Second World War trials, those involved in the momentous achievement of creating an International Criminal Court risk – if they do not achieve measurable improvements in the conduct of international criminal trials – frustrating the political and financial masters of international criminal law to the point of despondency and, worse, withdrawal of crucial political and financial commitment.

I sat in the courtroom listening to Del Ponte's words at the opening of the *Milošević* trial. I was there throughout most of the following four years as the senior legal adviser to the judges of the Trial Chamber and I was there on the day Judge Robinson formally closed the proceedings at 9.06 am on 14 March 2006. This book was conceived and evolved from this experience, as I realised that for the most part there was little in the way of precedent to assist in the determination of the myriad legal and practical problems raised. This book is therefore coloured by my intimate experience of the case and its characters and, while it is first and foremost an objective legal and factual analysis, it is no doubt affected by my particular experience of the issues confronted.

Finally, some acknowledgements are warranted. This work is a revision of my Ph.D. thesis undertaken at the University of Melbourne. To Professor Tim McCormack, my chief supervisor, sagely *amicus* on the *Milošević* case and good friend, I owe a debt of considerable gratitude for his intellectual and practical advice throughout. To Dr Carolyn Evans, my co-supervisor, for whose advice, relentless and speedy attention to my drafts and, mostly, for pushing me outside of my intellectual comfort zone I am profoundly appreciative. To Pascale Chifflet I owe a great deal, for her extraordinary intellectual clarity that helped dig me out of conceptual holes in which I frequently found myself during this process, and for much more. I am grateful also to Natalie Reid, my friend and former colleague, who painstakingly reviewed drafts and offered sound advice. To Geoffrey Robertson, who agreed to write the Foreword to this book, I would like to express my gratitude, not just for this task but also for the inspiration that his own work has had upon my decision ever to take up the law and to stick at the area of international criminal justice. To Finola O'Sullivan at Cambridge University Press, for her enthusiasm and encouragement for this project, and others, much thanks. Finally, I would like to acknowledge the trial judges and lawyers with whom I had the great privilege to work throughout the years of the *Milošević* trial. The myriad of stories and events that can now never be told were shared with some of these people and I am grateful for their enormous commitment to this one great project of international criminal justice.

Gideon Boas
October 2006

Introduction

On 11 March 2006, Slobodan Milošević died in his bed in the UN Detention Unit in The Hague.[1] At the time, he had been on trial for 66 count of genocide, crimes against humanity, grave breaches of the Geneva Conventions and violations of the laws and customs of war. The alleged conduct encompassed more than 7,000 allegations of wrongdoing over eight years of conflict in the former Yugoslavia. Milošević's death left a significant hole in the fabric of the development and solidification of international criminal justice. An emblem of a challenge to the impunity of tyrannical heads of state who commit such atrocities ended lamentably. The trial had lasted over four years and, despite *ex post facto* statements by the prosecution that its end was only weeks away,[2] in reality it was some months away from being concluded, and yet many more months from a judgement being rendered. The reasons for the trial lasting so long lay in a number of factors, chief among which were the scope of the prosecution case and the refusal to adjust its case strategy; the Appeals Chamber's ruling to join the three indictments (Croatia, Bosnia, and Kosovo) into one gargantuan indictment; issues relating to the self-representation; and the ill health of the accused, which caused interruptions to the trial and required a reduced sitting schedule.

With the passing away of Milošević, many feared – and some hoped – that international criminal justice was experiencing some sort of death itself. For the victims of the wars in the former Yugoslavia, the people and communities of the region, the family and supporters of the accused, the international community and those dedicated to the process, it was a heavy blow.

[1] See *Prosecutor v. Milošević*, 'Order Terminating the Proceedings', Case No. IT-02-54-T, 14 March 2006; 'Report to the President: Death of Slobodan Milošević', Judge Kevin Parker, Vice-President, 31 May 2006 LM/MOW/1081e www.un.org/icty/milosevic/parkerreport.pdf at 15 August 2006.

[2] Statement by the ICTY Prosecutor, 11 March 2006, FH/OTP/1051e www.un.org/icty/latest-e/index.htm at 15 August 2006.

Yet the trial stands for much in the development and the future of international criminal justice, both politically and legally. In developing principles for the best practice of international criminal trials, the *Milošević* trial is a pre-eminent source for the conduct of such trials, in both positive and negative ways.

The Purpose and Content of this Book

The key purpose of this book is to analyse what lessons can be learnt from the *Milošević* trial that would improve the fair and expeditious conduct of complex international criminal trials of senior political and military officials. Critical to this question is the challenge of striking an appropriate balance between the sometimes competing obligations on a court to guarantee an accused person's right to a fair trial and to bring trial proceedings to a conclusion with reasonable expedition. A common feature of the trials of senior political and military leaders accused of violating international criminal law is that they rarely physically perpetrate the alleged crimes themselves. Instead, individual criminal responsibility for these accused is either based on some involvement in planning, ordering or instigating the crimes, or on a failure to act to prevent or punish the crimes occurring (superior or command responsibility). In such circumstances, the prosecution has the double challenge of proving the crimes themselves as well as the accused's responsibility for those crimes. More often than not, senior political and military leaders are charged not with responsibility for a single isolated incident, but with the design or implementation of a policy encompassing numerous incidents in various physical locations, or with the failure to act to stop patterns of conduct involving multiple incidents of atrocity. These factors usually render such trials exceedingly complex and very long.

Thanks to a war in Iraq and some good luck in digging a cowering former dictator out of a hole in the ground, as well as an apparent change of political will in Nigeria, Milošević did not remain for long the only former head of state to be tried for atrocities on a vast scale against his own and others citizens. At the time the door was closing on the writing of this book, the trials of Saddam Hussein abruptly concluded with his execution, ordered by the Supreme Iraqi Criminal Tribunal in Iraq for his involvement in the Dujail massacre (the Anfal genocide trial obviously being abandoned) and Charles Taylor, charged with crimes against humanity and other serious violations of international humanitarian law, was taken into custody by the Special Court for Sierra Leone and transferred to The

Hague where the Sierra Leone Court will make use of the facilities of the International Criminal Court.

However, the place of the *Milošević* trial remains unique for several reasons. It was the first trial of a former head of state by an international criminal tribunal and one of the most complex and lengthy war-crimes trials in history. It spawned problems and lessons that no other trial had necessarily confronted or contemplated. Despite early hopes for the trials of Saddam Hussein and other former Iraqi leaders, the Iraqi Tribunal has been profoundly plagued with fair trial and impartiality issues that will tarnish any judgement it renders[3] and it is not, at any rate, an international criminal tribunal.[4] Differently placed, the Taylor trial is poised to impact upon some of the fundamental issues considered in this book but will take some time yet to begin and conclude.

In analysing the *Milošević* case, I will seek to identify the criteria for determining what constitutes fairness and what constitutes expeditiousness in international criminal trials. I will also explain how these concepts interact and, on occasion, conflict. I will argue that best practice in the conduct of such trials requires, first and foremost, that the trial be fair, and second, but also extremely important, that the trial be expeditious. I will analyse how these concepts must sometimes be balanced to arrive at criteria of best practice for such trials. This will lead to recommendations for reform concerning the future conduct of international criminal trials.

[3] See Diane Marie Amann, '"The Only Thing Left is Justice": Cherif Bassiouni, Saddam Hussein, and the Quest for Impartiality in International Criminal Law' in David E. Guinn (ed.), *Coming of Age in International Criminal Law: An Intellectual Reflection on the Work of M. Cherif Bassiouni* (forthcoming); report by Human Rights Watch on the removal of Judge Abdullah al-Amiri, the presiding judge of the Hussein trial by a decision of the Prime Minister and Cabinet because, according to a Government spokesman, 'he ha[d] lost his neutrality after he made comments saying Saddam is not a dictator': 'Removal of Judge a Grave Threat to Independence of Genocide Court', Human Rights Watch, 19 September 2006 http://hrw.org/english/docs/2006/09/19/iraq14229.htm at 4 October 2006.

[4] For information about the Iraqi Special Tribunal, how it is structured and will operate and the revocation of the initial statute and transition to the Iraqi High Criminal Court (including rebuffing the notion that the tribunal should be international in nature), see generally Michael J. Frank, 'Justice for Iraq, Justice for All' (2004) 57 *Oklahoma Law Review* 303; Michael P. Scharf and Curtis F. J. Doebbler, 'Will Saddam Hussein Get a Fair Trial?' (2005) 37 *Case Western Reserve Journal of International Law* 21 (recorded debate); Human Rights Watch, 'The Former Iraqi Government on Trial: A Human Rights Watch Briefing paper', 16 October 2005; Diane Marie Amann, '"The Only Thing Left is Justice": Cherif Bassiouni, Saddam Hussein, and the Quest for Impartiality in International Criminal Law', above n. 2; Eric Stover, Hanny Megally, and Hania Mufti, 'Bremer's "Gordian Knot": Transitional Justice and the US Occupation of Iraq' (2005) 27 *Human Rights Quarterly* 830, 838–43.

My use of the reference to best practice in the context of this book is one that requires some explanation. Although the development of modern international criminal law is in many profound respects incipient in nature, some important work has begun to flesh out or suggest meaningful solutions to the myriad problems facing the conduct of complex international criminal trials. The *Milošević* case proved a crucial source for this work, and other cases have followed or have taken different approaches. All of this suggests that the process of determining and defining best practice in the conduct of such trials, while in the early stages of development, is not purely aspirational.

Furthermore, in discussing best practice in the context of this book, I am expressing a clear preference for the view of international criminal trials that their purpose is primarily forensic in nature – that is, to determine the guilt or innocence of individuals for their role in atrocities. I acknowledge that this is not the only view of the purpose and nature of international criminal trials, and that some scholars reason that they should be legitimately viewed as broader sociological and/or political exercises fulfilling a purpose beyond the determination of the guilt or innocence of the accused being tried – whether that be a commemorative or didactic function.[5] However, while these may be legitimate derivative outcomes of international criminal trials (outcomes that are profoundly subjective in nature), I do not believe that these trials can operate effectively or – far more importantly – fairly outside of the forensic trial paradigm. Therefore, when I discuss best practice throughout this book it is in measurement against the more traditional view of a criminal trial as a forensic process.

The *Milošević* trial was a fair trial, although some fair trial rights were challenged by its conduct, the responsibility for this resting with the court, the prosecution, and the accused himself. The trial was not concluded expeditiously. The predominant reasons for the lack of expeditiousness in the *Milošević* case were the prosecutorial approach taken, the approach of the accused to the trial and his health, as well as some key trial and appellate decision-making. In discussing these issues, it will not be the purpose of this analysis to disparage those involved in the trial and decision-making process, although inevitably criticism will be made so as to extract

[5] See Gerry J. Simpson, *Law, War and Crime* (forthcoming), chapter four. See also, Laurence Douglas, *The Memory of Judgment: Making Law and History in the Trials of the Holocaust* (2001); Shoshana Felman, The Juridical Unconscious: Trials and Traumas in the Twentieth Century (2002); Hannah Arendt, *Eichmann in Jerusalem: A Report on the Banality of Evil* (1994).

lessons for the future conduct of these important trials. In fact, the struggle to conduct and to conclude this trial provides crucial primary source material for the future achievement of fair and expeditious international criminal trials of senior political and military accused, including that of Charles Taylor.

While nomenclature relating to 'truly' international tribunals (composed entirely of international judges) and 'internationalised' tribunals (otherwise described as hybrid or supranational tribunals, which are composed of a mix of international and national judges) has been employed, it is equally acceptable – and has been said to be preferable by some scholars – to describe all such courts or tribunals as 'international'.[6] The reason for this is that, while the composition, structure, and constitutional framework of such institutions may vary, each tribunal falls at a different point in the 'spectrum of internationality' and each serves the same end of international criminal justice.[7] Differing terminology will be used throughout this book to refer to these courts and tribunals depending on context, sometimes distinguishing their character but often speaking generically of them as 'international', particularly when referring to generally accepted practice or procedure in international criminal law.

The Structure of this Book

The first substantive chapter of this book discusses the principles of a fair and expeditious trial. The analysis focuses on the interpretation and application of such rights in international criminal law, as developed in the jurisprudence of the ICTY and other international criminal tribunals

[6] See Diane Marie Amann, '"The Only Thing Left is Justice": Cherif Bassiouni, Saddam Hussein, and the Quest for Impartiality in International Criminal Law' in David E. Guinn (ed.), *Coming of Age in International Criminal Law: An Intellectual Reflection on the Work of M. Cherif Bassiouni* (forthcoming), where Amann claims that, although useful for some purposes, the distinction between 'international' and 'internationalised' 'obscures that each forum rests at a different point on a spectrum of internationality; that is, each is one of several judicial mechanisms available to serve the international criminal justice project'. See also Jacob Katz Cogan, 'International Criminal Courts and Fair Trials: Difficulties and Prospects' (2002) 27 *Yale Journal of International Law* 111, 127–8; Laura A. Dickinson, 'Using Legal Process to Fight Terrorism: Detentions, Military Commissions, International Tribunals, and the Rule of Law' (2002) 75 *South California Law Review* 1407, 1411; Mark A. Drumbl, 'Collective Violence and Individual Punishment: The Criminality of Mass Atrocity' (2005) 99 *Northwestern University Law Review* 539, 542–4; Patricia M. Wald, 'Accountability for War Crimes: What Roles for National, International, and Hybrid Tribunals?' (2004) 98 *American Society of International Legal Proceedings* 192.

[7] Diane Marie Amann, above n. 5, 2.

(all of which operate within the same fundamental rights framework) and, in particular, the *Milošević* trial. While fair trial issues emerge and are discussed throughout this book in their context, this chapter focuses on some broad principles and rights, such as the principle of an expeditious trial, the right to a trial without undue delay, the principle of equality of arms, the right to a public trial, the right to confront witnesses, defence representation and particularly the right to self-representation, as well as the interpretation and application of human rights in international criminal law. These issues are of fundamental importance to the framework in which international criminal law is created, interpreted, and applied, and form the basis for any prescriptive discussion about how to conduct international criminal trials.

Chapter 2 turns to the logical first step in an analysis of the *Milošević* trial – the prosecution's indictments, its case strategy, and the substance of its case. The role of the prosecution is extremely significant in international criminal trials. In the adversarial structure of international criminal law, it is the prosecution that conducts investigations, makes decisions about who to indict, and prepares the indictments which determine the nature, scope, and structure of the case. The purpose of this chapter is to examine the prosecution's approach to the *Milošević* case to determine criteria for best practice in the conduct of such trials. This chapter will establish that important strategic and policy aspects of the prosecution case in *Milošević* were far from best practice, and seriously threatened the fair and expeditious trial framework within which international criminal proceedings are to be conducted. The prosecution approach to its case was zealous and overly expansive, creating a trial that was unmanageably complex and long. The factors which contributed to this are examined, as are some of the considerations which motivated the prosecution to approach its case in this way. There are tensions and competing interests in the presentation of complex international criminal trials, which encompass forensic, historical, political, and sociological issues. The prosecution, while seeking in good faith to satisfy the interests it considered significant, made it impossible to conduct an expeditious trial and put at risk its fairness, requirements that are not only the responsibility of the court but also – to a lesser but significant extent – the responsibility of a prosecutor in international criminal proceedings.

Chapter 2 examines the three indictments against Milošević. An analysis of the prosecution indictments reveals significant defects, and these will be identified and discussed in some detail. The prosecution case revolved around a theory that Milošević espoused the notion of a Greater

Serbia and implemented policies to realise the notion – a case theory which remained unclear until well into the defence case. This theory is discussed in the context of the prosecution's case to better understand its approach and the overall effect on the length and complexity of the trial. The pleading requirements for indictments before the ICTY and the indictment review process in this and other cases is discussed, as is the relevant content of the three *Milošević* indictments. The prosecution application for joinder of the three separate indictments – one of the most important issues in the trial because of its consequent impact on issues of fairness and expedition – is explored. Finally, the ruling of the Trial Chamber on the motion for judgement of acquittal will be analysed. The Decision is important because it dismissed over one thousand individual allegations against the accused and is the only pre-Judgement determinative ruling of the Chamber on aspects of the indictments.

Chapter 3 first considers case management challenges experienced in the *Milošević* trial. The prosecution and defence cases in the *Milošević* trial and how the Trial Chamber managed them are analysed, as are the innovative case management techniques developed and applied, or considered and dismissed, during that trial. Measures for managing complex international criminal law cases are considered and a framework for best case management practice in international criminal law is developed. The scope of the prosecution case in *Milošević* had a direct impact on the scope of the defence case. The Trial Chamber tried several techniques to manage the case, ultimately determining that limiting the time allocated to the parties was the preferable approach. Other radical case management approaches were considered, and these alternatives are analysed in the context of the management of international criminal trials.

The case management experience of the *Milošević* trial is not, however, entirely unique. There is a body of practice in national law as well as developing experience in international law relevant to developing best practice for the conduct of international criminal trials. This chapter will also examine the development and application of case management in domestic criminal law systems and then in modern international criminal law, in particular before the ICTY (where most of the regulatory and jurisprudential developments have occurred). Given the circumstances of Milošević's death, these considerations take on a particular importance in the case management analysis. Lessons abound in the *Milošević* case in how to manage complex international criminal trials to a satisfactory conclusion. Again, balancing a Trial Chamber's commitment to a fair and expeditious trial is central to this analysis.

An issue of developing importance and complexity in the conduct of these cases is the assertion by accused of a right to represent themselves. Chapter 4 commences with a discussion of Milošević's insistence on a right to self-representation. After two and a half years of trial, following the completion of the prosecution case, the commencement of his defence case, and after having upheld on several occasions his right to represent himself, the Trial Chamber imposed court-assigned defence counsel on Milošević. In doing so, the Chamber initiated an important legal development concerning how an accused's right to a fair trial is to be interpreted in international criminal law. The operation of the right to self-representation, and its treatment in the common law, civil law, and regional human rights systems having already been discussed in chapter 1, the development and treatment of self-representation in all the international criminal courts and tribunals that have dealt with this issue will be analysed.

Chapter 4 will then consider the issues related to representation and resources in international criminal law. These matters were some of the most contentious of the *Milošević* trial, and have plagued other international criminal trials of high-ranking accused. In the brief existence of modern international criminal law, there has been significant development of different representation models, ranging from standard defence counsel representation to innovative use of *amici curiae*. Closely related to representation is the issue of adequate resources for an accused to prepare and present an effective defence. In complex cases of this nature, representation and resources issues go to the core of fair trial rights, in particular those of adequate time and facilities for the preparation of a defence; the right to communicate with counsel of an accused's own choosing; the right of defence in person or through legal assistance, and the equality of arms. The application of these principles in the complex international criminal trial process already discussed in chapter 1 is considered with particular reference to the way these principles were applied in the *Milošević* case.

In chapter 5, the conclusions and outcomes of the analysis in this book are discussed and proposals for reforms to the conduct of complex international criminal trials are made. Fairness and expeditiousness in such trials must be considered in light of the competing interests and issues discussed throughout this book. The *Milošević* trial was fair but it was not expeditious. The lessons learnt from the analysis of this and other international criminal trials considered in this work form the basis for reaching important conclusions about how such trials must be conducted to achieve best practice. Obligations on the prosecution to exercise restraint, focus their cases, and act responsibly are of paramount concern. Where such restraint is not exercised, courts must act in a measured but firm manner to ensure fairness and reasonable expeditiousness. Courts must themselves develop or have developed for them (depending on the applicable system) their regulatory framework to optimise the procedural and substantive environment in which the goals which make up best practice can be achieved. Courts must also develop and apply consistent and balanced jurisprudence to attain these goals. Within this framework, development of innovative and well-considered case management must occur. Again, the *Milošević* trial created a basis from which this important area of procedural law can – and already has started to – develop. Proposals for future reform and perimeters within which case management principles can be applied are discussed and concrete proposals are made for how to manage these cases. Conclusions relating to the management of resource and representation issues in complex international criminal law cases are made, as are proposals concerning the future conduct of these trials where the right to self-representation is asserted. The tension in the application of common law and civil law principles is an issue that re-emerges throughout this book. It is argued that while these tensions were instrumental in the development of important aspects of international criminal law, it is now time to abandon the preoccupation of international criminal courts and tribunals with this dichotomy and embrace the newly created system of international criminal law as a jurisdiction in its own right. This chapter will then consider problems in the appellate structure, particularly flowing from the *ad hoc* Tribunals, but also more generally the structure of appellate review in international criminal courts and tribunals and propose an appropriate way in which to provide for appellate review in international criminal law. In tying these conclusions together, I will discuss the crucial lessons from the *Milošević* trial and what potential reforms emerge that will contribute materially to the achievement of fair and expeditious international criminal trials of senior officials in the future.

The Context of this Book

One of the critical analyses of the *Milošević* case is an understanding of what worked, what did not work, and why, so that lessons can be drawn for future trials of this kind. Complex international criminal trials are fraught with difficulties, requiring the existence and application of a well-structured legal process that respects the fundamental rights of the accused. However, as can be seen from the *Milošević* trial, the modern international criminal trial process, with its well-articulated fair trial guarantees for accused persons, is not strictly speaking designed to deal with intelligent and manipulative accused, who do not accept the legitimacy of the judicial process to which they are subjected and who have a political agenda to pursue, using the forensic trial process as their stage. Milošević was exactly such an accused, and he exploited the niceties of the criminal legal process and the weaknesses inherent in a prosecution and a court trying someone of this stature for the first time. Milošević made his position clear from the outset. At his initial appearances and early on in the trial, he adopted a robust rejection of the Tribunal's legitimacy – accusing it of being the puppet of NATO, and the indictments against him another farcical extension of the international community's persecution of the Serbs in general, and of him in particular.[8] At Milošević's initial appearance, he predictably rejected the legitimacy and legality of the Tribunal, and the purpose for which it sought to try him:

> I consider this Tribunal a false Tribunal and the indictment a false indictment. It is illegal being not appointed by the UN General Assembly, so I have no need to appoint counsel to [an] illegal organ . . . This trial's aim is to produce false justification for the war crimes of NATO committed in Yugoslavia.[9]

Milošević continued to stress this position in subsequent hearings prior to the commencement of his trial, and at times – although with diminishing frequency – during his trial.[10] Exemplifying his use of the forensic trial process for political purposes, Milošević stated at the pre-trial conference for the Kosovo part of the case:

> [A]n operation is under way to reverse the scene and the culprit and accused, and all this is geared towards a construed justification for the crimes committed during the NATO aggression on my country and my nation. Even the indictment represents proof that what I say is true, that is, further evidence of it, because all the alleged misdeeds committed in conformity of that indictment by the armed forces of Yugoslavia, which I had the honour to be at the head and command, were precisely put into a time framework which is the time framework during which the NATO air campaign and aggression against my country was committed.

[8] See e.g., *Prosecutor v. Milošević*, Hearings, 3 July 2001, at Transcript, 2; 30 August 2001; 12 November 2001; 9 January 2002.

[9] *Prosecutor v. Milošević*, Hearing, 3 July 2001, Transcript, 2, 4.

[10] See e.g., *Prosecutor v. Milošević*, Hearings, 30 August 2001; 12 November 2001; 9 January 2002.

> It is quite obviously the intention to explain how those who defended their families, who defended their children and their thresholds and homes and home country are criminals, are evil people, whereas those who travelled thousands and thousands of kilometres to destroy their houses in the course of the night and to kill innocent people and to destroy maternity wards, hospitals, bridges, railways, that those are the people who, in cooperation with the Albanian terrorists, are responsible for the vast number of victims and for enormous material damage. And with this reversal of thesis, it would appear that they are the good guys and that they should be given the support of international public opinion.[11]

There are some interesting analogues to the events surrounding the trials of Milošević and Saddam Hussein. Hussein's arrest, confinement, and the commencement of his trial have certain similarities to Milošević. At his appearance before the Iraqi Special Tribunal on 20 October 2005, Hussein stood in defiance:

> 'I do not recognize the body that has authorized you and I don't recognize this aggression. I do not respond to this so-called court, with all due respect', and when identified by the Judge as the 'former president', Hussein snapped, 'I said I'm the president of the republic of Iraq. I did not say deposed.'[12]

The personality of the deposed dictator/accused is an interesting factor in the conduct of international criminal proceedings against them. Milošević's initial defiance, like that of Hussein, really mirrors the dictatorial personality-type when trapped and subjected to a civilised legal process. As Geoffrey Robertson noted in respect of the Nuremberg trial:

> In retrospect, the most astonishing feature of Nuremberg was how the adversary dynamics of the Anglo-American trial sucked in the defendants, who played an earnest and polite, at times desperate, part in making it work. Their leader, Goering, had initially advised them to confine their evidence to three words, 'Lick my arse' – the defiant catchcry of one of Goethe's warrior heroes. But as months passed they became flattered by the fairness (at least fairishness) of the procedures and rose to the bait of making their excuses to posterity.[13]

These accused have a particular personality profile that makes the management and conduct of their cases difficult – a theme that re-emerges in

[11] *Prosecutor v. Milošević*, Hearing, 9 January 2002, Transcript, 287.

[12] See CNN Report, 'Saddam Hussein Defiant in Court', 20 October 2005, http://www.cnn.com /2005/WORLD/meast/10/19/saddam.trial/ at 1 October 2006.

[13] Geoffrey Robertson, *Crimes Against Humanity* (1999), 203.

consideration of various issues in this book. Milošević, Hussein, and Taylor – all having ruled their nations with varying aggression, brutality, and manipulation – when their fortunes changed either fled their country, hid in the ground, or barricaded themselves into a luxury family compound. This combination of pathological self-belief, megalomania, and cowardice is a factor that renders the trial of these people extremely difficult.

Milošević himself had no intention of playing into the prosecution's hands and remaining mute while the case against him was laid out and determined.[14] Despite his belligerence towards the court, he engaged in a robust and, at times, competent forensic defence, while all the time maintaining at least the façade that he was interested only in telling the 'truth' to the world, a political and social truth, that placed NATO and its member States (in particular the USA and Germany), as well as the Vatican, on trial. Yet although the rhetoric gradually subsided and Milošević cooperated superficially with the trial process and the institution he had vowed to bring down, his conduct and manipulative talents continued to have an extraordinary impact on the viability of the proceedings.

However, the conduct of Milošević is only one part of this story. It is not unexpected that an accused of this nature might have the will, and some capacity, to interfere in the trial in such a way as to threaten its fair and expeditious conduct. Of greater significance to the conduct of complex international criminal trials is the manner in which the prosecution and the court approach the preparation and undertaking of all aspects of the proceedings. The *Milošević* trial is rich in lessons about what to do and what not to do in order to achieve best practice in the conduct of these cases, and this is at heart what this book is about.

[14] See e.g., *Prosecutor v. Milošević*, 'Prosecution's Position in Relation to Management of Trial Proceedings and the Regime for Presentation and Admission of Evidence with Comments on Issues Concerning the Accused's Health', Case No. IT-02-54-T, 5 April 2002, para. 7(e), which acknowledges that the Prosecution planned its case initially on the basis that 'the Accused would take little or no part in the trial process'.

1

Fair and Expeditious International Criminal Trials

Introduction

This chapter analyses the key principles of fairness and expedition, by which all international criminal trials are to be conducted, and which are defined in the constitutional instruments and the relevant jurisprudence of the major international criminal tribunals. The ICTY, as the richest source for the development of these principles in international criminal law, will be the main focus of the analysis, although appropriate reference will be made to other courts and tribunals applying them and to their origin and context in international human rights law. In analysing these principles of fairness and expeditiousness, criteria will be identified for determining what constitutes fairness and what constitutes expedition in complex international criminal trials, as well as explaining how these concepts interact and, on occasion, conflict. This problem is not new to international criminal law. Sixty years ago, Lord Wright, Chairman of the UN War Crimes Commission, commented on the conduct of the post-World War II *Belsen* trial:

> For a few days I occupied the seat marked for the British observer and could observe and admire the fairness of the trial, though I noted, as in other such cases, that fairness was not generally compatible with expedition.[1]

Complexities arise in defining the contours of these principles, how they interact and how they are to be balanced and applied in the international criminal law context. Fair trial rights, strictly speaking, belong to an accused and are applied as a guarantee to ensure he or she receives a fair trial. Expedition, on the other hand, is a consideration which reflects more the interest of the community (the international community in the case of international criminal trials) in seeing proceedings brought to a conclusion in an acceptable time. But in reality these sets of interests are composite in nature, such that both the accused and the international

[1] *Law Reports of Trials of War Criminals* (1947), volume 11, Foreword by Lord Wright.

community have a stake. An overly long trial threatens its fairness, because it can be unmanageable for an accused for a variety of reasons. Furthermore, if any aspect of a fair trial is not properly respected then the whole process of international criminal justice suffers and, therefore, the community interest in the proper functioning of the trial process. It is not simply a case of asserting that an accused wants a fair trial but that the international community wants a trial that is expeditious. For example, it was clear that Milošević did not want an expeditious trial, seeking constantly to extend the time taken to prepare and present evidence. Other accused in other international criminal tribunals evince a similar attitude, in different ways seeking to obstruct or delay the trial process.[2]

In many ways, these principles manifest as competing interests. A trial might be fair but not expeditious. A trial might be expeditious but not fair, for example if an accused were refused permission to lead highly relevant evidence because of a time limitation imposed. Of course, a trial could be neither fair nor expeditious. Obviously, international criminal trials should be both fair and expeditious. How to navigate that course in complex international criminal trials is problematic, and the myriad issues which make up the components of these interests emerge throughout this book.

These issues are further complicated by the context in which the key principles are interpreted and applied, and by the practical application of them to international criminal trials. The discussion in this chapter accentuates the difficulties sometimes experienced in appropriately defining and achieving fairness. Lord Diplock of the Privy Council once said: 'The fundamental human right is not to a legal system that is infallible, but to one that is fair.'[3] There is force in this epigrammatic statement. It is a proposition that has been reflected and reaffirmed consistently in the jurisprudence of the international criminal tribunals and it has particular application in light of the contextual and purposive interpretation of the application of human rights principles to international criminal law.[4]

[2] See discussion in chapter 4 in the context of self-representation, concerning accused Norman (before the SCSL), Baryagwiza (before the ICTR) and Šešelj and Krajišnik (before the ICTY).

[3] *Maharaj v Attorney-General of Trinidad and Tobago* (1978) 2 WLR 902 (Privy Council).

[4] See e.g., *Prosecutor v. Nyiramasuhuko et al.*, 'Decision in the Matter of Proceedings under Rule 15*bis* (D)', Case no. ICTR-98–42-A15*bis*, 24 September 2003, 'Dissenting Opinion of Judge David Hunt', para. 16: 'There may be many difficulties placed in the way of an accused in the course of applying an 'interests of justice' test in various situations, so that the trial is not a perfect one (such as the need to protect victims and witnesses) but the absence of perfection does not mean that the trial will not be a fair one. However, the

Fair Trial Rights

The right to a fair trial is a fundamental element of international human rights law as it applies to the criminal trial process at both the domestic and the international level. It would be logical that the world's first multilateral criminal tribunal since Nuremberg would strive for best practice in this area of its work. The right to a fair trial is reflected in both primary instruments governing proceedings before the ICTY: the Statute and the Rules of Procedure and Evidence.[5] In discussing the rights of the accused, the UN Secretary-General, in his Report to the Security Council on the creation of the ICTY, stated:

> It is axiomatic that the International Tribunal must fully respect internationally recognized standards regarding the rights of the accused at all stages of its proceedings. In the view of the Secretary-General, such internationally recognized standards are, in particular, contained in article 14 of the International Covenant on Civil and Political Rights.[6]

Indeed, most of the fair trial rights and minimum guarantees accorded accused persons before international criminal courts and tribunals are a largely verbatim repetition from the International Covenant on Civil and

interests of justice cannot be served where the accused is denied a fair trial.' See also *Prosecutor v. Milošević*, 'Decision on Admissibility of Evidence-in-Chief in the form of Written Statements', Case no. IT-02–54-AR 73.4, 30 September 2003, 'Separate Opinion of Judge Mohammed Shahabuddeen', para. 16: '[T]he fairness of a trial need not require perfection in every detail. The essential question is whether the accused has had a fair chance of dealing with the allegations against him.' For a discussion of the application of human rights principles to international criminal law, see Section III of this chapter below.

5 www.un.org/icty/legaldoc-e/index.htm. For a discussion of the right to a fair trial before the ICTY, see generally Judge Richard May and Marieke Wierda, *International Criminal Evidence* (2002); Salvatore Zappalà, *Human Rights in International Criminal Proceedings* (2003); Christoph Safferling, *Towards an International Criminal Procedure* (2001), at 21–30; Patrick L. Robinson, 'Ensuring Fair and Expeditious Trials at the International Criminal Tribunal for the Former Yugoslavia' (2000), vol. 11, no. 3, *EJIL*, 569; Patrick L. Robinson, 'Fair but Expeditious Trials' in Hirad Abtahi and Gideon Boas (eds.), *The Dynamics of International Criminal Justice: Essays in Honour of Sir Richard May* (2005), 169; Hafida Lahiouel, 'The Right of the Accused to an Expeditious Trial', in Richard May *et al.* (eds.), *Essays on ICTY Procedure and Evidence In Honour of Gabrielle Kirk McDonald* (2001), 197.

6 Report of the Secretary-General (S/25704), 3 May 1993, para. 106. Some commentators argue that this statement is of crucial importance to guide the approach of the ICTY as a body which is 'born' of the UN Security Council (see James Sloan, 'The International Criminal Tribunal for the Former Yugoslavia and Fair Trial Rights: A Closer Look' (1996) 9 *LJIL* 475, 501), whereas other commentators give it little weight, describing it as a political statement with no legal binding force (see Christoph Safferling, *Criminal Procedure* 29).

Political Rights,[7] as well as regional human rights conventions, such as the European Convention on Human Rights,[8] the American Convention on Human Rights,[9] and the African Charter on Human and Peoples' Rights.[10] The early view on the application of the fair trial provisions set out in these treaties was that they 'define the right to a fair trial in criminal proceedings'.[11] The extension of these principles to *international* criminal trials is both logical and appropriate.[12] Zappalà sets out several arguments in favour of such an extension. First, it is said that due process (or the package of fair trial rights) is a fundamental protection belonging to the individual, 'to be restricted only in exceptional circumstances and to a limited extent'.[13] Second, the ICTY and ICTR, as well as the ICC, were created to contribute to international peace and justice 'where the national system has collapsed or is otherwise unavailable due to an exceptional situation'. It would, therefore, be illogical that the instruments of international criminal law would not comply with due process guarantees.[14] Third, the extension of due process principles to international criminal trials allows states to cooperate with international criminal courts without the risk of non-compliance with their own human rights obligations under domestic law.[15] The final argument for this extension of fair trial rights to international criminal trials is that the fair trial rights set out in Articles 20 and 21 of the ICTY Statute (reflecting Article 14 of the International Covenant on Civil and Political Rights (ICCPR)) amount to *jus cogens*, and are binding as such on the tribunals and courts applying them.[16]

7 GA Res 2200A (XXI) 21 UN GAOR Supp. (no. 16) at 52, UN Doc. A/6316 (1966), entered into force 23 March 1976 ('ICCPR').

8 ETS no. 5, opened for signature 4 November 1950, entered into force 3 September 1953 ('ECHR').

9 OAS, Treaty Series, no. 36, adopted 22 November 1969, entered into force 18 July 1978 ('ACHR').

10 African Charter on Human and Peoples' Rights, adopted 27 June 1981, OAU Doc. CAB/LEG/67/3 rev. 5, 21 ILM 58 (1982), entered into force 21 October 1986 ('ACHPR').

11 David Harris, 'The Right to a Fair Trial in Criminal Proceedings' (1967), vol. 16, no. 2, 352, quoted in Zappalà, *Human Rights*, 5. See also David Weissbrodt and Rüdiger Wolfrum (eds.), *The Right to a Fair Trial* (1997).

12 Zappalà, *Human Rights* 5. See also Safferling, *Criminal procedure.*

13 Zappalà, *Human Rights* 5–6.

14 Ibid. 6. See also Antonio Cassese, 'Opinion: the International Criminal Tribunal for the Former Yugoslavia and Human Rights' (1997) 2 *EHRLR*, 331–2.

15 Zappalà, *Human Rights*, 6.

16 See Gerhard Hafner, 'Limits to the Procedural Powers of the International Criminal Tribunal for the Former Yugoslavia', in Karel C. Wellens (ed.), *International Law: Theory and Practice* (1998), 651, 657.

With regard to this last argument, however, it would be more accurate to distinguish between the fundamental right to a fair trial and the procedural guarantees set forth in these international instruments. While the right to a fair trial is itself a *jus cogens* norm, the provisions which make up the content or constituent parts of that right are more appropriately characterised as amounting to customary international law.[17] The distinction is an important one for international criminal proceedings: as shown by the established practice of the ICTY, ICTR, and other international tribunals, although these provisions reflect customary international law, applicable to international criminal proceedings,[18] these fair trial provisions have been subjected to contextual interpretation and, at times, derogation. For a

17 See above, n. 6 (comments of the UN Secretary-General reflecting the view that the fair trial provisions in question amount to rules of customary international law) and the statement of the Secretary-General that 'the application of the principle *nullem crimen sine lege* requires that the international tribunal should apply rules of international humanitarian law which are beyond any doubt part of customary law so that the problem of some but not all States to specific Conventions does not arise' (para. 34 of his Report); see also Theodor Meron, 'Editorial Comment: Revival of Customary Humanitarian law' (2005) 99 *American Journal of International Law* 817 in particular arguing, at 818 and 821ff. that international criminal tribunals have taken an essentially conservative and traditional approach to the identification and application of customary international law principles – an assertion with which I do not agree; Theodor Meron, *Human Rights and Humanitarian Norms as Customary International Law* (1989), 96–7; and, generally, Antonio Cassese, *Human Rights in a Changing World* (1990). For a general definition of customary international law, see *Continental Shelf (Libya v Malta)* [1985] ICJ Rep 29; Nicaragua v. USA (Merits) [1986] ICJ Rep 14, 97; Peter Malanczuk, *Modern Introduction to International Law* (7th edn 1997).

18 For the ICTY and ICTR, see e.g., *Prosecutor v. Blagojević et al.*, 'Decision on Dragan Obrenović's Application for Provisional Release', Case No. IT-02-60.PT, 22 July 2002; *Prosecutor v. Aleksovski*, 'Judgement', Case No. IT-95-14/1-A, 24 March 2000; *Prosecutor v. Furundžija*, 'Judgement', Case No. IT-95-17/1-A, 21 July 2000; *Semanza v. The Prosecutor*, 'Judgement', Case No. ICTR-97-20-A, 20 May 2005; *Prosecutor v. Milošević*, 'Reasons for Decision on the Prosecution Motion Concerning Assignment of Counsel', Case No. IT-02-54, 4 April 2003. For the Special Court of Sierra Leone ('SCSL'), see e.g., Article 17 of the SCSL Statute and Rule 33 to 46 of the SCSL Rules of Procedure and Evidence, available at www.sc-sl.org; 'Statement Issued by the Principal Defender at the Beginning of the Defence Case in the CDF Trial', www.sc-sl.org, http://www.sc-sl.org/Press/statement-012006.pdf, at 1 October 2006; *Prosecutor v. Norman*, 'Decision on the Prosecutor's Motion for Immediate Protective Measures for Witnesses and Victims for Non-Public Disclosure', Case No. SCSL-2003-08-PT, 23 May 2003; *Prosecutor v. Norman et al.*, 'Decision on the Application for a Stay of Proceedings and Denial of Right to Appeal', Case No. SCSL-2003-09-PT, 4 November 2003. For the East Timor Tribunal, see e.g., Section 2, Transitional Rules of Criminal Proceedings (UNTAET Regulation 2000/30, as amended by 2001/25), available at http://www.jsmp.minihub.org; Judicial System Monitoring Programme, *The Case of X: A Child Prosecuted for Crimes Against Humanity* (Dili, Timor Leste, January 2005), http://www.jsmp.minihub.org/Reports/jsmpreports/The%20Case%20of%20X/case_of_x_final_e.pdf at 1 October 2006; Suzannah Linton, 'Cambodia, East Timor and Sierra Leone: Experiments in International Justice' (2001) 12

customary rule to be *jus cogens*, no derogation to it would be permissible.[19] Of course, such judicial modification in the implementation of these guarantees is not itself a conclusive indication that they cannot be *jus cogens* norms which have themselves been violated. However, the treatment of these rights both in their interpretation in international criminal law, as well as within the human rights regime (as is apparent from the discussion below), embodies a pragmatic practice which reflects this view of the relationship between the right to a fair trial and the specified procedural guarantees, particularly as international tribunal jurisprudence speaks of such derogations being exercised for the achievement of the fairness of the trial overall or otherwise in the interests of justice.

It will therefore be clear that courts and tribunals applying international criminal law must apply the fair trial provisions set out in their constitutive instruments and reflected in the human rights treaties on which those provisions are based. Yet, tensions emerge in the strict application of human rights standards to the evolving international criminal law system. There is a distinct tension in the consideration of human rights principles, particularly as interpreted by some human rights bodies, to the application of substantive and procedural international criminal law. Their interpretation and application to achieve a fair and expeditious trial has and must be made in the context of this *sui generis* system of law. At the same time, there are examples of inconsistent or tentative approaches taken in some of the jurisprudence,

Footnote 18 *(cont.)*
Criminal Law Forum 185, 199, 228; *Lino De Carvalho v. Prosecutor General*, Criminal Appeal No. 25 of 2001, Judgement of Frederick Egonda-Ntende, 29 October 2001; *The General Prosecutor v. Joni Marques and 9 Others*, Case No. 09/2000, Judgment, 11 December 2001; Suzannah Linton, 'Unravelling the First Three Trials at Indonesia's Ad Hoc Court for Human Rights Violations in East Timor' (2004) 17 *Leiden Journal of International Law* 303. For the Cambodia Tribunal, see e.g. Suzannah Linton, 'Cambodia, East Timor and Sierra Leone: Experiments in International Justice' (2001) 12 *Criminal Law Forum* 185, 198; Janet Lee and Karen Yookung Choi, 'Introduction to the Khmer Rouge Tribunal', *Cambodian Genocide Group*, 2 November 2005, http://www.cambodiangenocide.org/khmerrouge_tribunal.htm at 1 October 2006. See, generally, Håkan Friman, 'Procedural Law of Internationalized Criminal Courts', in Cesare P. R. Romano, André Nollkaemper, and Jann K. Kleffner (eds.), *Internationalized Criminal Courts and Tribunals: Sierra Leone, East Timor, Kosovo, and Cambodia* (2004).

19 See R. Y. Jennings and A. Watts (eds.), *Oppenheim's International Law* (9th edn 1992), 7-8; Malcolm N. Shaw, *International Law* (3rd edn 1995), 98-9; Antonio Cassesse, International Law (2nd edn 2004). This would mean that the international criminal tribunals either accurately interpreted these provisions as amounting to customary international law but not referring to them as *jus cogens*, or – to the extent derogation has occurred – they are in violation of them.

particularly by the ICTY and ICTR, which will be examined. This will inevitably leave some with the sense that there is randomness in the application of fair trial rights in international criminal law. However, evolving jurisprudence which reasons well the application of these principles by reference to international and regional human rights courts and bodies and domestic criminal courts in different legal systems will, and already has, given a greater sense that international criminal law is a solid and well-founded system of law, which respects fundamental rights and norms.

These issues are highly relevant to the conduct of complex international criminal trials. The analysis in this chapter concerns important underpinnings for the ascertainment of the effective and proper conduct of such trials.

Articles 20 and 21 of the ICTY Statute are the critical provisions setting out the fair trial rights before the ICTY:[20]

Article 20
Commencement and conduct of trial proceedings

1. The Trial Chambers shall ensure that a trial is fair and expeditious and that proceedings are conducted in accordance with the rules of procedure and evidence, with full respect for the rights of the accused and due regard for the protection of victims and witnesses.
2. A person against whom an indictment has been confirmed shall, pursuant to an order or an arrest warrant of the International Tribunal, be taken into custody, immediately informed of the charges against him and transferred to the International Tribunal.
3. The Trial Chamber shall read the indictment, satisfy itself that the rights of the accused are respected, confirm that the accused understands the indictment, and instruct the accused to enter a plea. The Trial Chamber shall then set the date for trial.
4. The hearings shall be public unless the Trial Chamber decides to close the proceedings in accordance with its rules of procedure and evidence.

Article 21
Rights of the accused

1. All persons shall be equal before the International Tribunal.
2. In the determination of charges against him, the accused shall be entitled to a fair and public hearing, subject to article 22 of the Statute.

[20] See e.g., Robinson, 'Ensuring Fair and Expeditious Trials, Sections (C) and (D).

3. The accused shall be presumed innocent until proved guilty according to the provisions of the present Statute.
4. In the determination of any charge against the accused pursuant to the present Statute, the accused shall be entitled to the following minimum guarantees, in full equality:
   (a) to be informed promptly and in detail in a language which he understands of the nature and cause of the charge against him;
   (b) to have adequate time and facilities for the preparation of his defence and to communicate with counsel of his own choosing;
   (c) to be tried without undue delay;
   (d) to be tried in his presence, and to defend himself in person or through legal assistance of his own choosing; to be informed, if he does not have legal assistance, of this right; and to have legal assistance assigned to him, in any case where the interests of justice so require, and without payment by him in any such case if he does not have sufficient means to pay for it;
   (e) to examine, or have examined, the witnesses against him and to obtain the attendance and examination of witnesses on his behalf under the same conditions as witnesses against him;
   (f) to have the free assistance of an interpreter if he cannot understand or speak the language used in the International Tribunal;
   (g) not to be compelled to testify against himself or to confess guilt.

The ICTY Rules also embody these fair trial rights. Under these Rules: there is a presumption of innocence in favour of an accused;[21] the accused is entitled to legal counsel, at the expense of the ICTY where he or she is indigent;[22] there is a right to a public hearing;[23] the accused has a right to test the prosecution evidence and present evidence on his or her own behalf;[24] there is a right to be protected against self-incrimination;[25] and, the Prosecutor is required to provide substantial pre-trial disclosure.[26] As already discussed, these and other rights set out in conformity with Articles 20 and 21 of the ICTY Statute, themselves based on the broader fair trial principles set out in the above international instruments, are considered reflective of customary international law.[27]

21 Rules 62 and 87. 22 Rule 42. 23 Rule 78. 24 Rule 85. 25 Rule 90.

26 Rule 66 requires extensive disclosure and Rule 68 provides for disclosure of exculpatory evidence.

27 For an expansive analysis of the fair trial rights as applied and interpreted by the ICTY, see May and Wierda, *International Criminal Evidence*, chapter VIII; Zappalà, *Human Rights*, chapter 3, III; Rodney Dixon, Karim Kahn, and Richard May (eds.), *Archbold: International Criminal Courts: Practice, Procedure and Evidence* (2002); Geert-Jan A. Knoops, *An*

The rights of an accused person in international criminal law are distinct from but interrelated with the expeditiousness of the trial process. Fairness and expedition are composite rights or interests, because they involve both the accused and the international community, although clearly to differing degrees. The fundamental rights of an accused embodied in the ICCPR, and essentially mirrored throughout the constitutional instruments of human rights bodies and international criminal courts and tribunals, belong to the accused but are also subjected to interpretation in the broader context of the international criminal trial process. Therefore, the right of an accused to cross-examine witnesses against him or her has been subjected, in some circumstances, to the discretion of a court which will determine whether that right can be exercised in the particular circumstances of the evidence in question. It is not, therefore, absolute. The right to self-representation is, likewise, not an absolute right. The right to a public trial is also subjected to exceptions or (as they have been described) derogations where the appropriately balanced interests of victims and witnesses prevail. It is with this understanding that the following rights are considered. The particular rights discussed below are not exhaustive of all rights and interests in the international criminal trial process, but rather are some of the key rights that inform the inquiry into how best to structure and conduct an international criminal trial. Other rights, such as the right to silence, the right to be informed promptly of the charges against an accused, the right to the assistance of an interpreter or the right not to be compelled to testify against oneself, are not discussed because they have thrown up less difficulty or controversy in the practice of international criminal law and, in particular in the conduct of the *Milošević* trial. Therefore these rights do not inform materially the consideration of fair trial rights in the context of this book.

Requirement that the proceedings be public

Article 21(2) of the ICTY Statute provides that '[i]n the determination of charges against him, the accused shall be entitled to a fair and public hearing, subject to article 22 of the Statute', which provides, in turn, that the Tribunal:

> shall provide in its rules of procedure and evidence for the protection of victims and witnesses. Such protection measures shall include, but shall

Introduction to the Law of International Criminal Tribunals: A Comparative Study (2003); Antonio Cassesse, *International Criminal Law* (2003).

not be limited to, the conduct of in camera proceedings and the protection of the victim's identity.

In a decision in the *Tadić* case,[28] the Trial Chamber stated that the point of a trial being public was that it assisted in ensuring that it is fair.[29] Article 14(1) of the ICCPR and Article 6(1) of the ECHR state that everyone is entitled to a fair and public hearing. The European Court of Human Rights ('ECtHR') has stated that by 'rendering the administration of justice visible, publicity contributes to the aim of a fair . . . trial, the guarantee of which is one of the fundamental principles of any democratic society'.[30] The right to a public hearing was said in *Tadić* to be a right which attaches to the accused, being a means by which fairness is achieved.[31] This proposition has been repeated persistently in the jurisprudence of the ICTY.[32] However, it has also been acknowledged, including by the *Milošević* Trial Chamber, that this is a right that is shared by the international community.[33] Furthermore, in an important decision on the public nature of the trial, the *Brđanin* Trial Chamber held that the right to a public trial did not end at the trial proceedings themselves being open, but extended to all aspects of the case, including the filings between the parties and all areas of the trial record.[34] The Trial Chamber in this

[28] *Prosecutor v. Tadić*, 'Decision on the Prosecutor's Motion Requesting Protective Measures for Victims and Witnesses', Case No. IT-94-1-T, 10 August 1995.

[29] Ibid. para. 32.

[30] *Sutter v. Switzerland* (1984) 74 Eur Court HR (ser. A) para. 26. See also *Pretto & Ors. V Italy* (1984) 71 Eur. Court HR (ser. A) 182.

[31] *Prosecutor v. Tadić*, 'Decision on the Prosecutor's Motion Requesting Protective Measures for Victims and Witnesses', Case No. IT-94-1-T, 10 August 1995, paras. 35, 36.

[32] *Prosecutor v. Milošević*, 'Decision on Prosecution's Motion for Protective Measures', Case No. IT-02-54-T, 4 January 2002 and 12 February 2002; *Prosecutor v. Milutinović et al.*, 'Decision on Prosecution's Motion for Protective Measures', Case No. IT-99-37-PT, 27 January 2004; *Prosecutor v. Halilović*, 'Decision on Prosecution's Request for Order of Non-Disclosure', Case No. IT-01-48-PT, 22 January 2004; *Prosecutor v. Rajić*, 'Order on Prosecution's Motion for Protective Measures for Victims and Witnesses and Motion to Amend Prosecution's Motion', Case No. IT-95-12-PT, 24 July 2003; *Prosecutor v. Stanišić and Simatović*, 'Decision on Prosecution Motion for Protective Measures', Case No. IT-03-69-PT, 1 August 2003; *Prosecutor v. Furundžija*, 'Judgement', Case No. IT-95-17/1-A, 21 July 2000, para. 239; *Prosecutor v. Delalić et al.*, 'Decision on the Motions by the prosecution for the Prosecution Witnesses Pseudonymed "B" Through "M" ', Case No. IT-96-21-T, 28 April 1997 (stating that 'a public hearing is mainly for the benefit of the accused and not necessarily of the public', para. 34).

[33] *Prosecutor v. Milošević*, 'Decision on Prosecution's Motion for Protective Measures', Case No. IT-02-54-T, 4 January 2002; *Prosecutor v. Brđanin and Talić*, 'Decision on Motion by Prosecution for Protective Measures', Case No. IT-99-36-PT, 3 July 2000, para. 55.

[34] *Prosecutor v. Brđanin and Talić*, 'Decision on Motion by Prosecution for Protective Measures', Case No. IT-99-36-PT, 3 July 2000, para. 55.

Decision scolded the prosecution for its practice of rendering confidential aspects of the record, and stated firmly that this was a practice which should not be permitted lightly:

> The attitude displayed by the prosecution in the present case appears to be part of an unfortunately increasing trend in proceedings before the Tribunal for matters to be dealt with behind closed doors. When the prosecution seeks to have anything dealt with confidentially, the accused does not usually object because it is in his interest that the less that is made public concerning his case the better. This trend is a dangerous one for the public perception of the Tribunal, and it should be stopped.[35]

The ICTY, like all other international criminal courts, provides for circumstances in which parts of the trial, either its hearings or other aspects of the trial record, may be closed to the public. The protection of victims and witnesses required by Article 22 of its Statute includes the conduct of *in camera* proceedings and the protection of a victim's identity. A number of Rules of the ICTY also provide for victim and witness protection. Rule 66(A)(i) provides for disclosure of material to the accused subject to the provisions of Rules 53 and 69, the latter two Rules providing for the non-disclosure to the public, or the Accused, of documents or information '[i]n exceptional circumstances . . . [and when] . . . in the interests of justice'. Rule 75(A) provides that 'appropriate measures' may be ordered for the privacy and protection of witnesses, 'provided that the measures are consistent with the rights of the accused'. Finally, while Rule 78 states that '[a]ll proceedings before a Trial Chamber, other than deliberations of the Chamber, shall be held in public, unless otherwise provided', Rule 79 provides explicitly for the exclusion of the press and the public from all or part of the proceedings for reasons of public order or morality, for safety, security or non-disclosure of the identity of a victim or witness as provided in Rule 75, or for the protection of the interests of justice. The Trial Chamber is obliged in such circumstances to make public the reasons for its order.

One Chamber has stated that these provisions evince an intention that everything to do with the proceedings 'should be done in public unless good cause is shown to the contrary'.[36] Another Chamber has held that the right to a public hearing cannot be denied 'without good reason',[37]

35 Ibid. paras. 55–6. 36 Ibid. para. 54.

37 *Prosecutor v. Delalić et al.*, 'Decision on the Motions by the prosecution for the Prosecution Witnesses Pseudonymed "B" Through "M" ', Case No. IT-96-21-T, 28 April 1997, para. 33.

and cited the US Supreme Court in support of the proposition in the following terms:

> There can be no blinking the fact that there is a strong societal interest in public trials. Openness in court proceedings may improve the quality of testimony, induce unknown witnesses to come forward with relevant testimony, [and] cause all trial participants to perform their duties more conscientiously[.][38]

The Tribunal has used the protective measures provisions liberally, seeking to strike the balance between the right to have the proceedings public and the interest in protecting vulnerable victims and witnesses in order to ensure that witnesses testify and their legitimate fear of repercussion against them or their families be properly taken into account.[39] This point was developed in a string of seminal decisions concerning the pre-trial stage of the Croatia and Bosnia parts of the *Milošević* proceedings.[40] The Trial Chamber made it clear that, even more than rendering inaccessible information from the public, to deprive the accused of access to all relevant information, the prosecution must do more than merely assert that a witness or his family is at risk: it must show an objective basis for this assertion. This onus on the prosecution was considered even more critical for the exceptional grant of non-disclosure of witness identification to the accused until some time prior to the trial or the testimony of the witness.[41]

[38] Ibid. para. 34, citing Chief Justice Warren in *Estes v. Texas*, 381 US 532 at 583 (1965).

[39] See David Tolbert and Frederick Swinnen, 'The Protection of, and Assistance to, Witnesses at the ICTY', in Hirad Abtahi and Gideon Boas (eds.), *Dynamics of Inter-national Criminal Justice*, 193; Pascale Chifflet, 'The Role and Status of the Victim', in Gideon Boas and William A. Schabas (eds.), *International Criminal Law Developments in the Case Law of the ICTY* (2002); Florence Mumba, 'Ensuring a Fair trial whilst Protecting Victims and Witnesses – Balancing of Interests?', in Richard May et al. (eds.), *Essays on ICTY Procedure*, 363.

[40] See *e.g.*, *Prosecutor v. Milošević*, 'Decision on Prosecution Motion for Provisional Protective Measures', Case No. IT-02-54-T, 19 February 2002; *Prosecutor v. Milošević*, 'Decision on Prosecution's Motion for Order of Non-Disclosure', Case No. IT-02-54-T, 19 July 2001; *Prosecutor v. Milošević*, 'Decision on Prosecution Motion for Trial Related Protective Measures (Bosnia)', Case No. IT-02-54-T, 30 July 2002; *Prosecutor v. Milošević*, 'Decision on Prosecution Motion for Trial Related Protective Measures (Croatia)', Case No. IT-02-54-T, 30 July 2002.

[41] See e.g. *Prosecutor v. Milošević*, 'First Decision on Prosecution Motion for Protective Measures for Sensitive Source Witnesses', Case No. IT-02-54-T, 3 May 2002; *Prosecutor v. Milošević*, 'Second Decision on Prosecution Motion for Protective Measures for Sensitive Source Witnesses', Case No. IT-02-54-T, 18 June 2002; *Prosecutor v. Milošević*, 'Decision on Third Prosecution Motion for Protective Measures for Sensitive Source Witnesses Testifying During the Croatia Phase of the Trial', Case No. IT-02-54-T, 30 September 2002; *Prosecutor v. Milošević*, 'Decision on Sixth Prosecution Motion for Protective

The Appeals Chamber held early on that the Statute and the Rules had to be interpreted within the context of the Tribunal's own unique framework[42] and noted in this context that 'the Statute of the international tribunal, which is the legal framework for the application of the Rules, does provide that the protection of victims and witnesses is an acceptable reason to limit the accused's right to a public trial'.[43]

Judge Stephen, in a separate opinion in the *Tadić* case, stated that, while the protection of victims and witnesses provides justification for limiting the public nature of a hearing, it does not justify measures that affect, not its public nature, but its fairness.[44] Judge Stephen identified a hierarchy of rights in the Statute, stating:

> There is a marked contrast . . . to be seen in the language of Article 20(1) between what it says about ensuring that proceedings are conducted *with full respect* for the rights of the accused and what it then says about proceedings being conducted *with due regard* for the protection of victims and witnesses. This is, if anything, given more emphasis by the further contrast between the detailed and emphatic enumeration of distinct rights of the accused in Article 21 and the rule-making direction in Article 22, which does no more than direct that provision be made in the Rules for witness protection, in particular two specific forms of such protection, in camera proceedings and protection of identity.[45]

This was a crucial point because it was made in the context of an application for a witness to testify in anonymity, that is without ever disclosing to the accused the identity of that witness and, therefore, clearly infringing on his capacity to test that witness's evidence.[46] Judge Stephen expressed

Measures for Sensitive Source Witnesses Testifying During the Croatia Phase of the Trial', Case No. IT-02-54-T, 4 October 2002.

42 *Prosecutor v. Tadić*, 'Decision on the Defence Motion for Interlocutory Appeal on Jurisdiction', Case no. IT-94-1-AR72, 2 October 1995, paras. 32–3.

43 Ibid. para. 36.

44 *Prosecutor v. Tadić*, 'Separate Opinion of Judge Stephen on the Prosecutor's Motion Requesting Protective Measures for Victims and Witnesses', Case No. IT-94-1, 10 August 1995.

45 Ibid. For a discussion of witness anonymity protection, see Tolbert and Swinnen, 'Protection . . . and Assistance', 193; Pascale Chifflet, *Role and Status*, 102; Christine M. Chinkin, 'Due Process and Witness Anonymity' (1997) 91 *American Journal of International Law* 75; Monroe Leigh, 'The Yugoslav Tribunal: Use of Unnamed Witnesses Against Accused' (1996) 90 *American Journal of International Law* 235; Natasha A. Affolder, 'Tadic, the Anonymous Witness and the Sources of International Procedural Law' (1998), 19 *Michigan Journal of International Law* 445.

46 Although the Trial Chamber did grant this measure in respect of the one witness, the witness never did testify and the procedure has never been used in proceedings since. See Tolbert and Swinnen, 'Protection . . . and Assistance', 218; Pascale Chifflet, *Role and Status*, 87.

strong reservations about the use of such measures to render the proceedings closed to the public, and his cautious approach to this question as it affects the fairness of the trial has resonated through subsequent Tribunal jurisprudence.[47]

The fundamental proposition and starting point in the jurisprudence is that the proceedings be public and open, unless the interests of justice require otherwise. As discussed, concern over the protection of victims and witnesses, if properly weighed against the accused's interest in the trial being public, is a legitimate exercise of a court's powers.[48] Furthermore, it is well established in the Rules and jurisprudence of the ICTY that the right to a public trial is not infringed by the admission of testamentary evidence in written form. The Trial Chamber in the *Milošević* case, dealing with the persistent refusal of the accused to utilise this form of evidence to enable the introduction of a greater amount of evidence (because he believed that it infringed the statutory requirement that the proceedings be public), explained that evidence 'presented in writing, subject to public scrutiny, is no less public than *viva voce* evidence'.[49] It explained that, as 'with *viva voce* testimony, written testimony may be subject to privacy to, for example, protect victims and witnesses'.[50]

The latest word on this issue comes from the same Trial Chamber, but in the context of contempt proceedings against two Croatian journalists who published the identity of a witness testifying in the *Blaškić* case in closed session and the content of some of his closed session testimony.[51] In the judgement in this case, the Chamber held that entering closed session is, in effect, 'a derogation of the right to a public trial, which is a basic right protected under international law'.[52]

47 *Prosecutor v. Tadić*, 'Separate Opinion of Judge Stephen on the Prosecutor's Motion Requesting Protective Measures for Victims and Witnesses', Case No. IT-94-1, 10 August 1995. See also ECtHR cases dealing with the issue, at times referred to as highly persuasive and generally adhered to by chambers of the international criminal tribunals: *Kostovski v. The Netherlands* (1989) 166 Eur, Court HR (ser. A); *Unterpertinger v. Austria* (1986) 110 Eur Court HR (ser. A); *Windisch v. Austria* (1989) 186 Eur, Court HR (ser. A); *Delta v. France* (1989) 191 Eur Court HR (ser. A); *Ludi v. Switzerland* (1992) 238 Eur Court HR (ser. A).

48 See also, *Prosecutor v. Tadić*, 'Separate Opinion of Judge Stephen on the Prosecutor's Motion Requesting Protective Measures for Victims and Witnesses', Case No. IT-94-1, 10 August 1995.

49 *Prosecutor v. Milošević*, 'Decision in Relation to Severance, Extension of Time and Rest', Case No. IT-02-54-T, 12 December 2005, para. 22.

50 Ibid. footnote 51.

51 *Prosecutor v. Marijačić and Rebić*, 'Judgement', Case No. IT-95-14-R77.2, 10 March 2006.

52 Ibid. para. 28.

The importance of the trial being public is emphasised in the jurisprudence of the ICTY, and the constitutional instruments of the other international courts and tribunals express the same principle.[53] In cases concerning high-level political and military accused, where important evidence may come from insiders or others with credibility or reliability issues, it is critical that the accused be provided with adequate information to challenge the witness and that the public be able to judge for itself the nature and content of the evidence and its affect on the trial process. However, such trials can only be conducted and managed effectively if victims and witnesses (particularly those in an especially vulnerable position) can also be appropriately protected. This is a balance that is important to strike to achieve best practice in trials of this nature.

The approach taken by international courts and tribunals with respect to circumstances in which the public nature of a trial may be curtailed appear to be generally consistent with human rights law, at least as it has been articulated in the ECtHR (from where most of the relevant jurisprudence emerges).[54] The non-disclosure to the public of information relating to witnesses does not suggest any infringement of accepted human rights standards, even though the quantity of non-disclosure in the international tribunals has caused chambers of the ICTY to express their own concerns. The non-disclosure of information to an accused is more controversial. It is possible that had the provision for anonymous witnesses established in the *Tadić* jurisprudence been employed beyond the one witness, the ECtHR jurisprudence may well have suggested a strong divergence in accepted principle between the human rights regime and international criminal law. However, the jurisprudence has consistently supported the proposition that, even where witness identity was undisclosed for a period of time, the accused would always be provided with full disclosure within sufficient time to enable preparation for cross-examination. In this way, international criminal courts and tribunals have managed to strike an appropriate balance between legitimate concerns of victims and witnesses and the paramount interest of according the accused a fair trial.

Adequate time and facilities to prepare a defence

Article 21(4)(b) of the Statute expresses another fair trial right of the accused – the requirement to provide 'adequate time and facilities . . . for

53 See Articles 67(1) and 64(7) of the ICC Statute; Article 20(2) of the ICTR Statute; Article 17(2) of the SCSL Statute.

54 See Judge Stephen's comments in *Tadić* and ECtHR cases cited in n. 47 above.

the preparation of [the accused's] defence' (mirroring Article 14(3)(b) of the ICCPR and Article 6(3)(b) of the ECHR). This right must be assessed according to the facts of each case. In the *Čelebići* case, the Trial Chamber held that:

> The operative phrase in the Article [Article 21], 'adequate time', is flexible and begs of a fixed definition outside the particular situation of each case. It is impossible to set a standard of what constitutes adequate time to prepare a defence because this is something which can be affected by a number of factors including the complexity of the case, and the competing forces and claims at play, such as consideration of the interests of other accused persons.[55]

The right of the accused to adequate time and facilities is one that attaches from the moment the accused is taken into custody by a court. It is something that must be balanced with the right to trial without undue delay and the requirement that the trial be expeditious.[56] These tensions have often been tested in complex international criminal trials and were stretched to breaking point during the *Milošević* trial, the accused constantly complaining that he had not been given sufficient time (or facilities) to enable him to prepare his defence.[57] The *Milošević* Trial Chamber, in considering what constituted fairness in the provision for an accused to present his case, stated that '[t]he proper test must be whether the Accused has been given a reasonable and adequate opportunity to present his case'.[58] This test, although comprehensible, gives little guidance in how the right is to be applied in international criminal law. In the context in which the Chamber made this statement in the *Milošević* case itself, the accused had referred to the more than one million pages of material served on him by the prosecution and complained that he had never been given adequate time to read and consider this material in the preparation of his case.[59] This complaint is indicative of the nature of complex international criminal trials, which invariably entail disclosure of extraordinary quantities of potential evidence that an accused or their counsel must incorporate in the preparation and conduct of a defence.

55 *Prosecutor v. Delalić et al.*, 'Decision on the Applications for Adjournment of the Trial Date', Case No. IT-96-21-T, 3 February 1997, para. 19.

56 See e.g. Zappalà, *Human Rights*, 124.

57 See e.g., *Prosecutor v. Milošević*, hearings on 29 November and 8 December; *Prosecutor v. Milošević*, 'Decision in Relation to Severance, Extension of Time and Rest', Case No. IT-02-54-T, 12 December 2005, para. 13.

58 Ibid. para. 25.

59 *Prosecutor v. Milošević*, hearing on 29 November, Transcript, 46689.

Unfortunately, there is little relevant jurisprudence to define in specific terms what is an adequate time to prepare for trial in international criminal trials. The Nuremberg and Tokyo Tribunals simply provided, in their Charters, that the accused were to be provided with an indictment and documents lodged therewith 'at a reasonable time before the Trial'.[60] The defence were usually allotted a matter of weeks to prepare for trial.[61] The application of this principle in the ICTY and in modern international criminal trials generally, is dealt with mainly in respect of procedural issues related to access to disclosure materials and capacity to cope with disclosure of large quantities of material and prepare in time for trial. These are matters taken up at length in the following two chapters of this book. It is through that analysis that concrete principles related to the adequate time and facilities to prepare a defence, and their impact on how best to conduct complex international criminal trials, will crystallise.

Trial without undue delay

Trial without undue delay, reflected in Article 21(4)(c) of the ICTY Statute (mirroring Article 14(3)(c) of the ICCPR and Article 5(3) of the ECHR), is another important fair trial right. An example of the importance placed on this right is the treatment of it in the jurisprudence of the *ad hoc* Tribunals considering requests by the prosecution to amend indictments close to trial. Trial Chamber I of the ICTY has stated that it 'considers that the Prosecutor's right to submit a request for leave to amend the indictment must not be exercised to the prejudice of the accused's right to be tried without undue delay as stated in Article 21(4)(c) of the Statute'.[62] In a decision in the *Halilović* case, Trial Chamber III concluded that an application to amend the indictment months before the proposed commencement of the trial would cause unfair prejudice.[63] In decisions on motions to amend indictments before the ICTY (and ICTR), two factors have been highlighted as relevant to the consideration of unfair prejudice: (1) the lack of 'an adequate opportunity

60 Article 16(a) of the Charter of the International Military Tribunal annexed to the London Agreement, 8 August 1945 ('IMT Charter'); Article 9(a) of the Charter of the International Military Tribunal for the Far East (1946) TIAS No. 1589, 4 Bevans 20 ('IMTFE Charter').

61 See May and Wierda, *International Criminal Evidence*, 272.

62 *Prosecutor v. Kordić and Čerkez*, 'Decision on the Prosecutor's Motion to Hold Pre-Trial Motions in Abeyance', Case No. IT-95-14/2-T, 28 January 1998.

63 *Prosecutor v. Halilović*, 'Decision on Prosecution's Motion Seeking Leave to Amend the Indictment', Case No. IT-01-48-PT, 17 December 2004.

to prepare an effective defence to the amended case';[64] and (2) undue delay in the proceedings.[65] Either factor may be sufficient to ground a finding of unfair prejudice and result in the denial of a motion to amend the indictment. The *Halilović* Trial Chamber found that, since the proposed amendment constituted a new charge, if it were granted, there would be three direct procedural consequences under the Rules, each of which would entail some delay:

> (1) the Accused would have to appear again in accordance with Rules 50(B) and 62 to enter a plea on the new charge; (2) pursuant to Rule 50(C), the Accused would have a further period of thirty days from disclosure of any additional supporting material by the Prosecution to file preliminary motions to respond to the new charge; and (3) also under Rule 50(C), the date for trial would have to be postponed, since such a delay would be necessary even if only to ensure adequate time for the submission and consideration of the preliminary motions envisaged by the Rule.[66]

The Chamber held that the potential deferral of trial for at least several months that the amendment would cause, after an extended pre-trial period of more than three years, could constitute undue delay amounting to unfair prejudice to the accused.[67] In light of this holding, the Chamber concluded that 'any benefit of allowing the amendment to the indictment could not outweigh the significant and unfair prejudice that would result from the further postponement of this trial', and therefore found that the circumstances of this case require the denial of the Motion to Amend.[68]

Even earlier than the *Halilović* ruling, the Appeals Chamber in the *Kovačević* case had referred to Article 14(3)(c) of the ICCPR and held that the answer to what constitutes undue delay turns on the circumstances of each case. In the context of the timeliness of the prosecution request to amend the indictment, it stated that this must be assessed in light of the general requirement of fairness. The Appeals Chamber in that case held that a delay of seven months caused by the amendment process did not amount to undue delay because it did not infringe the right to a fair trial.[69]

[64] *Prosecutor v. Brđanin and Talić*, 'Decision on Form of Further Amended Indictment and Prosecution Application to Amend', Case No. IT-99-36-PT, 26 June 2001, para. 50.

[65] *Prosecutor v. Brđanin and Talić*, 'Decision on Form of Fourth Amended Indictment', Case No. IT-99-36-PT, 23 November 2001; *Prosecutor v. Karemera et al.*, 'Decision on Prosecutor's Interlocutory Appeal Against Trial Chamber III Decision of 8 October 2003 Denying Leave to File an Amended Indictment', Case No. IT-99-36-PT, 19 December 2003.

[66] *Prosecutor v. Halilović*, para. 38. [67] Ibid, para. 39. [68] Ibid, para. 41.

[69] *Prosecutor v. Kovačević*, 'Appeals Chamber Decision Stating Reasons for Appeals Chamber Order of May 29, 1998', Case No. IT-97-24-AR73, 2 July 1998, paras. 28–31.

May and Wierda suggest, however, that 'such a delay for these sorts of reasons can only be justified in an exceptional case, especially when the accused is in custody'.[70]

It is not uncommon at the ICTY and other international criminal tribunals for pre-trial detention to last a matter of years. Delays in the process of commencing trial are numerous and cause collateral concern over the achievement of an expeditious trial. Many reasons exist for such delays, including challenges to the form of the indictment and jurisdictional challenges by an accused which can take some time to resolve; problems associated with preparing evidence for trial, including (sometimes substantial) delays in translations; and the need to allow the accused a reasonable amount of time to prepare a defence, itself a sometimes competing right.

An important issue that arises out of the delay of trials at the Tribunal is the right of the accused to provisional pre-trial release. Rule 65 of the ICTY Rules governs this right at the ICTY. Rule 65(B) places a presumption on pre-trial detention (not release) and a burden on the accused to satisfy the court that he 'will appear for trial and, if released, will not pose a danger to any victim, witness or other person'. The Rule initially required an accused to make an additional showing that 'exceptional circumstances' justified his or her release, a requirement now expressly removed.[71] Nonetheless, the length of pre-trial detention has generated considerable concern in the Tribunal jurisprudence itself. In an early decision of Trial Chamber III of the ICTY,[72] Judge Robinson argued in dissent that that the purpose of the amendment to the Rule to remove the 'exceptional circumstances' requirement was to bring the ICTY procedure in line with other human rights instruments making provisional release the rule rather than the exception. He referred to the obligation stated in the Secretary-General's Report that the Tribunal 'must fully respect internationally recognised standards regarding the rights of the accused at all

[70] See May and Wierda, *International Criminal Evidence*, 273.

[71] Rule 65 was amended at the 21st plenary session of the Judges, IT/32/Rev.17, 17 November 1999. For a discussion of the application of Rule 65 and issues relating to provisional release at the ICTY, before and after the removal of the 'exceptional circumstances' requirement, see Gabrielle McIntyre, 'Defining Human Rights in the Arena of International Humanitarian Law: Human Rights in the Jurisprudence of the ICTY', in Boas and Schabas, *International Criminal Law Developments*; Judge Patricia Wald and Jenny Martinez, 'Provisional Release at the ICTY: A Work in Progress', in Richard May *et al.* (eds.), *Essay on ICTY Procedure*, 231.

[72] *Prosecutor v. Krajišnik*, 'Decision on Momcilo Krajišnik's Notice of Motion for Provisional Release', Case No. IT-00-39 and 40-PT, 8 October 2001 ('*Krajišnik* Decision').

stages of its proceedings' and Article 9(3) of the ICCPR. Judge Robinson claimed that this provision reflected customary international law[73] and identified the presumption of innocence as the rationale that underpinned this customary norm.[74] Judge Robinson's reliance on ECtHR jurisprudence[75] to support his assertion that the burden must be on the prosecution to satisfy a court that the accused will not appear for trial and will pose a danger to victims, witnesses or others,[76] is at odds both with the clear appellate jurisprudence of the ICTY and ICTR,[77] its justification in the jurisprudence being described by Judge Wald as 'brisk but plausible'.[78] It is also oddly in contradiction with Judge Robinson's strongly expressed view – and one that it is asserted as correct in this book – that human rights principles must be applied contextually to international criminal law.[79] The presumption against provisional release in ICTY procedure remains and periods of pre-trial detention, particularly in the case of high level accused whose cases are complex and take time to prepare, can be extremely lengthy. Although a clear practice has emerged in the ICTY, based not upon any human rights principle but rather on a greater acceptance of the guarantees of security and return offered by governmental entities of the former Yugoslavia, involving the provisional release of accused pending trial (and sometimes post-trial and pending judgement).[80] Some high (and lower-level) accused remain in detention for considerable periods of time.

Equality of arms

Article 21(1) of the ICTY Statute (like Article 14(1) of the ICCPR) mandates that '[a]ll persons shall be equal before the International

[73] Ibid., Dissenting Opinion of Judge Patrick Robinson, para. 6. [74] Ibid. para. 6.

[75] In particular, *Ilijkov v. Bulgaria* (2001) 33 Eur Court HR (ser. A).

[76] *Krajišnik* Decision, Dissenting Opinion of Judge Patrick Robinson, para. 44.

[77] See e.g. *Prosecutor v. Brahimaj*, 'Decision on Lahi Brahimaj's Interlocutory Appeal Against the Trial Chamber's Decision Denying Him Provisional Release', Case No. IT-04-84-AR65.2, 9 March 2006; *Prosecutor v. Stanišić*, 'Decision on Prosecutor's Interlocutory Appeal of Mićo Stanišić's Provisional Release', Case No. IT-04-79-AR65.1, 17 October 2005.

[78] See Judge Patricia Wald and Jenny Martinez, 'Provisional Release at the ICTY', 234.

[79] See discussion in section IV of this chapter below.

[80] See e.g., *Prosecutor v. Milutinović et al.*, 'Decision on Second Motion for Provisional Release, Case No. IT-99-37-PT, 14 April 2005; *Prosecutor v. Milutinović et al.*, 'Decision on General Ojdanić's Fourth Application for Provisional Release', Case No. IT-99-37-PT, 14 April 2005; *Prosecutor v. Delić*, 'Decision on Defence Request for Provisional Release', Case No. IT-04-83-PT, 6 May 2005; *Prosecutor v. Milutinović et al.*, 'Decision On Joint Motion For Temporary Provisional Release During Summer Recess', Case No. IT-05-87-PT, 1 June 2006

Tribunal'. Article 21(4)(e) of the Statute further embodies the principle of equality of arms, requiring that, as a minimum guarantee, an accused shall be entitled 'in full equality . . . to examine, or have examined, the witnesses against him and to obtain the attendance and examination of witnesses on his behalf under the same conditions as witnesses against him'. Early on, Judge Vohrah wrongly expressed the view that the principle of equality of arms was intended principally to favour the accused:

> The principle is intended in an ordinary trial to ensure that the Defence has means to prepare and present its case equal to those available to the Prosecution which has all the advantages of the State on its side . . . It seems to me . . . that the application of the equality of arms principle especially in criminal proceedings should be inclined in favour of the Defence acquiring parity with the Prosecution in the presentation of the Defence case before the Court to preclude any injustice against the accused.[81]

In a separate and dissenting opinion to the same Decision, Judge McDonald considered that, in the context of the ICTY, the Prosecutor could not be presumed to enjoy inherent advantages *vis-à-vis* the defence, which the principle of equality of arms would then serve to correct. Judge McDonald questioned the validity of comparing 'the resources and powers of the Prosecution of the ICTY with that of many national entities',[82] since the prosecutor of the Tribunal has to rely on state co-operation for her investigations and prosecutions, which was often not forthcoming. This position was perhaps of more relevance at the time Judge McDonald wrote her opinion. However, even at that time – and certainly now – it is obvious that the resources at the disposal of the prosecution in any proceedings before the ICTY is substantially greater than that available to the accused (at least an accused who is funded under the ICTY legal aid system). This is not to suggest that the legal aid system is not adequate – it is largely very generous. However, the quantity of defence funding to service trials of high-level officials, when compared with the resources expended on those cases by the Office of the Prosecutor, may be considerably unbalanced. This can be seen by the

[81] *Prosecutor v. Tadić*, 'Prosecution Motion for Production of Defence Witness Statements, Separate Opinion of Judge Vohrah', Case No. IT-94-1, 27 November 1996, paras. 4, 7.

[82] *Prosecutor v. Tadić*, 'Prosecution Motion for Production of Defence Witness Statements, Separate and dissenting Opinion of Judge McDonald', Case No. IT-94-1, 27 November 1996, para. 32.

number of challenges to resource decisions by the Registry in these cases.[83] An example of the extraordinary resources available to the Prosecution can be seen in the prosecution of the *Milošević* trial, where it had more than twenty lawyers and investigators working during its case-in-chief. One filing by the prosecution concerning compliance with its disclosure obligations is interesting:

> At various times, between twenty and forty members of the OTP, including attorneys, investigators, analysts, legal interns, trial support assistants, language assistants, computer specialists and administrators were mobilised to sustain a comprehensive and reasonably expeditious review of all the materials in the OTP's possession that might be exculpatory for the Accused. Just one part of this project, electronic searches of the OTP's collections by the OTP's Information Support Unit . . . required the equivalent of twenty-six 'person years' of labour and cost nearly 1.5 million U.S. dollars. To date, the Prosecution team has reviewed nearly two million pages of documentary material (apart from hundreds of videos and other items) and has identified and disclosed (electronically and in 'hard copy') more than 441,751 pages of material pursuant to Rule 68.[84]

The extraordinary quantity of disclosure material and the impact on fairness issues is a matter that will be taken up in the context of this case in chapters 2 and 3. However, for the purposes of this discussion it is clear that no legally aided defence team (and not many privately funded defence teams) could boast these sorts of resources.

In large-scale war crimes cases, resource issues are highly relevant. The matter was the subject of dispute as early in the history of the ICTY as the *Tadić* trial. On appeal, the accused argued that the lack of cooperation by the government of Republika Srpska and local Prijedor authorities had created an imbalance in the equality of arms between the parties, and that 'this principle ought to embrace not only procedural equality or parity of

83 There have been numerous applications dealing with such issues, the vast majority of which have – for obvious reasons – been rendered confidentially. An example of one such public decision rendered by the Appeals Chamber is *Prosecutor v. Prlić et al.*, 'Decision on Appeal by Bruno Stojić Against Trial Chamber's Decision on Request for Appointment of Counsel', Case No. IT-04-74-AR73.1, 24 November 2005.

84 *Prosecutor v. Milošević*, 'Prosecution's Comprehensive Report Concerning Its Compliance to Date with Rule 68', Case No. IT-02-54-T, 20 February 2004, para. 2. Rule 68 is the provision in the ICTY Rules which deals with the disclosure of potentially exculpatory or mitigatory material. The Rule has radically changed since, but at the time read as follows: 'The Prosecutor shall, as soon as practicable, disclose to the defence the existence of material known to the Prosecutor which in any way tends to suggest the innocence or mitigate the guilt of the accused or may affect the credibility of prosecution evidence.'

both parties before the Tribunal, but also substantive equality in the interests of ensuring a fair trial'.[85] The Appeals Chamber held that the accused had not established his claim that he had not had an opportunity to present his case as a result of this, and noted that the Trial Chamber had done what it could to assist.[86] The Chamber did acknowledge that a fair trial must entitle an accused to adequate time and facilities to prepare his defence, but that under the Statute of the Tribunal a more liberal interpretation must apply to the principle than its application to domestic proceedings by human rights bodies such as the ECtHR and the Human Rights Commission ('HRC').[87]

After reviewing some contradictory jurisprudence from the ICTR on this subject, Judge May concluded:

> Although it is clear that the question of equality of arms cannot be reduced to an exact equation, there must, in the least, be an approximate equality in terms of resources. Any substantial inequality will call into question the fairness of the trial.[88]

These issues are even more critical in trials of high-level political and military accused, because access to government source documentation and other material may provide critical and direct evidence of such an accused's guilt or innocence.[89]

In an interlocutory decision in the *Čelebići* case, Trial Chamber II dealt with the view expressed by Judge Vohrah, set out above. It held that there was 'no doubt that procedural equality means what it says, equality between the Prosecution and the Defence', and to suggest an inclination in favour of the defence would achieve the result of an 'inequality of arms'.[90]

Efforts have been made in other *fora*, domestic and international, to interpret the equality of arms principle as necessitating a procedural

85 *Prosecutor v. Tadić*, 'Judgement', Case No. IT-94-1-A, 15 July 1999, para. 30.

86 Ibid. para. 53. 87 Ibid. paras. 49–51.

88 May and Wierda, *International Criminal Evidence*, 271.

89 For a discussion of issues related to the content of and access to such material in international criminal law, see Grant Dawson and Mieke Dixon, 'The Protection of States' National Security Interests in Cases Before the International Criminal Tribunal for the former Yugoslavia: A Descriptive and Prescriptive Analysis of Rule 54*bis* of the Rules and Procedure and Evidence', in Abtahi and Boas, *Dynamics of International Criminal Justice*, 95.

90 *Prosecutor v. Delalić et al.*, 'Decision on the Prosecutor's Motion for an Order requiring Advance Disclosure of Witnesses by the Defence', Case No. IT-96-21-T, 4 February 1998, para. 49. The Chamber used this rationale to order the Defence to provide the Prosecution with a list of the witnesses it intended to call at trial, because the prosecution had done likewise.

advantage to the defence in war crimes cases. In one example in Canada, the Supreme Court upheld a trial judge's ruling admitting a deceased statement, which was exculpatory in nature, on the basis that a court has 'a residual discretion to relax *in favour of the accused* a strict rule of evidence where it is necessary to prevent a miscarriage of justice'.[91] Likewise, the Supreme Court of Israel overturned a conviction for war crimes and crimes against humanity on the basis that reasonable doubt existed about the guilt of the accused, Demjanjuk, based on the admission of a hearsay statement casting doubt on the identification of the accused.[92]

Attempts to create equality for an accused by creating an inequality in the adversarial relationship was an early dysfunctional symptom in international criminal law stemming from two interrelated problems. The first is the historical context of the prosecution of war crimes cases. The stain of what has been described as 'victor's justice' left by the post-World War II trials is a reminder of the frailty of the root of the international criminal justice system.[93] Bassiouni, although supportive of Nuremberg and satisfied as to the justification of the post-World War II prosecutions, has noted that 'when Nuremberg, Tokyo, and Subsequent Proceedings are referred to as "victor's vengeance," it is not without merit to claim that this means one-sided justice'.[94] Cassese notes that the setting up of the Nuremberg and Tokyo Tribunals was the imposition of 'victor's justice' over the defeated, a point underscored by the appointment of the judges and prosecutors by and composed of the victor states.[95] McCormack refers to criticism of 'the apparently relentless pursuit of "victor's justice" '

91 *R. v. Finta* [1994] 1 S.C.R. 701, 853–4 (my italics). For a discussion of this issue, and the *Finta* case, see May and Wierda, *International Crimal Evidence*, 267.

92 See May and Wierda, *International Criminal Evidence*, 267. See also Kenneth Mann, 'Hearsay Evidence in War Crimes Trials', in Yoram Dinstein and Mala Tabory (eds.), *War Crimes in International Law* (1996), 351. In the context of discussing the failure to prosecute war crimes successfully or appropriately post-Nuremberg, Geoffrey Robertson has described the Demjanjuk trial as 'disgracefully and demonstrably unfair': Geoffrey Robertson, *Crimes Against Humanity* (1999), 203.

93 Antonio Cassese, *International Criminal Law* (2003), 332–3; Geoffrey Robertson, *Crimes Against Humainity*, 200–4; M. Cherif Bassiouni, *Crimes Against Humanity in International Criminal Law* (1999), 552–4; Timothy L. H. McCormack, 'Selective Reaction to Atrocity: War Crimes and the Development of International Criminal Law' (1997), 60 *Alb. L. Rev* 681, 717; Timothy L. H. McCormack, 'From Sun Tzu to the Sixth Committee: The Evolution of an International Criminal Law Regime' in Timothy L. H. McCormack and Gerry J. Simpson, *The Law of War Crimes: National and International Approaches* (1996), 31; Richard H. Minear, *Victor's Justice: The Tokyo War Crimes Trial* (1973).

94 M. Cherif Bassiouni, *Crimes Against Humanity*, 552.

95 Antonio Cassese, *International Criminal Law*, 332.

concerning the Nuremberg and Tokyo trials.[96] Speaking of trials before the creation of the ICTY, Simpson says that '[i]n the absence of a uniform and global approach' trials of war criminals have generally occurred where defeat and criminality coincide: 'The phrase "victor's justice" as applied to such trials is by now a truism.'[97] Disparate resources as between the prosecution and defence at Nuremberg and Tokyo, lack of time for defendants to prepare their cases before trial, to have documents translated, to receive equal treatment in the admission of documentary evidence, to maintain silence without adverse inference being drawn, among other factors,[98] were all matters which have attracted the criticism that the post-war trials were (at least in some respects) of questionable fairness. This has not been forgotten in the sixty years of development of the human rights regime. Yet, at the same time, it should be remembered that the grim alternative to the Nuremberg (and Tokyo) trials was the summary execution of German political and military leaders – a solution strongly urged in particular by the British leadership.[99] Furthermore, the overall verdict of legal scholars and jurists is that the Nuremberg trial (although the same is possibly not so in respect of Tokyo[100]) was a success.[101] It is true that Milošević himself, and Serb nationalist leaders, had good cause in their mental framework to liken the ICTY to Nuremberg and to a form of 'victor's justice'. As Scharf has noted:

> In contrast to Nuremberg . . . the Yugoslavia Tribunal was created neither by the victors nor by the parties involved in the conflict, but rather by the United Nations, representing the international community of States. . . . On the other hand, Milošević has pointed out that the decision to establish the Yugoslavia Tribunal was made by the U.N. Security Council, which cannot truly be characterized as a neutral third party; rather, it has itself become deeply involved and taken sides in the Balkan conflict. . . . Finally, as Milošević has repeatedly observed, NATO cruise missiles specifically targeted Milošević's residence in an effort to kill him and his family. . . . While both the Prosecutor and the judicial Chambers of the Yugoslavia Tribunal were conceived to be independent from the Security Council, one cannot

96 Timothy L. H. McCormack, 'Selective Reaction to Atrocity: War Crimes and the Development of International Criminal Law', 717–18.

97 Gerry J. Simpson, 'Problems Confronting International Law and Policy on War Crimes and Crimes Against Humanity' (1997), 60 *Albany Law Review* 801, 805–6.

98 See generally, May and Wierda, *International Criminal Evidence*, Chapter VII; B. V. A. Röling and Antonio Cassese, *The Tokyo Trial and Beyond: Reflection of a Peacemonger* (1993).

99 Geoffrey Robertson, *Crimes Against Humanity*, 200–4.

100 See e.g., Simpson, 'Problems Confronting International Law'.

101 See generally, sources cited at n. 93 above.

> ignore the fact that the Statute provides that the Tribunal's Prosecutor is selected by the Security Council. The Judges are selected by the General Assembly from a short list proposed by the Security Council, and they have to stand for re-election after a four-year term. Moreover, the operation of the Tribunal has been dependent on tens of millions of dollars in contributions from the United States and its Western allies and most of the staff of the Office of the International Prosecutor are on loan from NATO countries.[102]

However, it is clear that, political rhetoric aside, the ICTY is not a form of 'victor's justice'.[103] As has been rightly noted, even if one conceived the ICTY as being essentially directed at the Serbs,[104] 'it is impossible to conceive of them as vanquished'.[105] Neither Milošević nor Šešelj is any longer in power, and the actions of a Tribunal created by the Security Council have changed the political make-up of the states of the former Yugoslavia, but this will be true of any international tribunal invested with authority to interfere with the sovereignty of a nation in the name of bringing contemporary war criminals to account. The fact is that the ICTY was – unlike the Special Iraqi Criminal Tribunal – created by a process entirely distinct from defeat and occupation and was an act of considerable faith and investment by the international community in a new legal order, although

[102] Michael P. Scharf, 'Symposium: The ICTY at Ten: A Critical Analysis of the Major Rulings of the International Criminal Tribunal Over the Past Decade' (2003) *New Eng. L. Rev.* 915, 921–3. An interesting article by an anthropologist supports the perspective of Milošević and some others that the ICTY delivers biased justice, 'with prosecutorial decisions based on the personal and racial characteristics of the accused rather than on what available evidence indicates the person has done. This bias is seen in the failure to prosecute NATO personnel for acts that are comparable to those of people already indicted . . . This pattern of politically driven prosecution is accompanied by the use of the Tribunal as a tool for Western countries, especially the United States, to pursue political goals in the Balkans': Robert M. Hayden, 'Commentary and Analysis: UN War Crimes Tribunal Delivers a Travesty of Justice' http://www.d-n-i.net/fcs/international_criminal_tribunal_critique.htm at 21 September 2006.

[103] In support of this proposition, See e.g., Enrique Carnero Rojo, 'The Role of Fair Trial Considerations in the Complementarity Regime of the International Criminal Court: From "No Peace without Justice" to No Peace with Victor's Justice' (2005), 18 *Leiden Journal of International Law* 829, 867–8.

[104] See responses from the Serb media to acquittals of the Bosnian Muslim, Sefir Halilović ('Judgement', Case No. IT-01-48-T, 16 November 2005), and Kosovo Albanians, Fatmir Limaj and Isak Musliu ('Judgement', Case No. IT-03-66-T, 30 November 2005), e.g., RTV B92 news report, 1 December 2005; BBC news, 'UN acquits top Kosovo rebel', 30 November 2005; Le Monde, 'Le TPIY rend son premier verdict sur l'UCK Kosovare', 1 December 2005.

[105] Gerry J. Simpson, 'Problems Confronting International Law', 808. See also Roger Cohen, 'Tribunal to Cite Bosnian Serb War Chief as War Criminal', New York Times, 24 April 1995, at A.1.

no doubt this is not accepted either by Milošević[106] nor some Serbs. Beyond issues related to the establishment of the ICTY, the clear mandate vested in that Tribunal (as with all the modern international criminal tribunals) is for the appointment of independent judges who determine the cases and issues before them free from any state political influence. These judges come from a variety of countries; some which are NATO member states and many without NATO affiliation or whose geopolitical interests are entirely disparate. Unlike the process of establishment and appointment of judges in respect of the Nuremberg, Tokyo and other post-World War II tribunals, let alone the unenthusiastic and failed attempts to create an international 'High Tribunal' following World War I,[107] the modern international criminal tribunals (as well as the ICC, created without a particular conflict in mind) have no credibly identifiable political link, affiliation or process that would reasonably attract allegations that these tribunals are a kind of 'victor's justice', despite their creation or endorsement by the Security Council.

The second reason for the attempt to establish equality through unequal treatment in international criminal law stems from the awkwardness of the adversarial criminal justice system as a basis for trying war crimes cases of massive scale. The ECtHR has held that the right to a fair trial implies an equality of arms.[108] As noted by Zappalà, this principle 'assumes enormous importance in proceedings based on the adversarial approach'.[109] The Statutes of the ICTY and ICTR, the ICC to a slightly lesser extent, and other international criminal tribunals, all have profound characteristics of an adversarial criminal law system and, in the case of the ICTY and ICTR, have certainly been interpreted as such.[110]

106 See e.g. *Prosecutor v. Milošević*, Transcript, 18 and 20 October 2005, 29 November 2005.

107 See Geo A. Finch, 'The Peace Conference of Paris 1919: Its Organization and Method of Work' (1919), 13 American Journal of International Law', 159.

108 See e.g., *Ruiz-Mateos v. Spain* (1993) 262 (ser. A) para. 63; *Bendedau v France* (1994) 284A (ser. A).

109 Zappalà, *Human Rights*, 112.

110 Robinson, 'Ensuring Fair and Expeditious Trials, *Human Rights*; Patrick L. Robinson, '*Ensuring* Fair and Expeditious Trials' Daryl A. Mundis, 'From "Common Law" Towards "Civil Law": The Evolution of the ICTY Rules of Procedure and Evidence' (2001), 14 *Leiden Journal of International Law* 367; Gideon Boas, 'A Code of Evidence and Procedure for International Criminal Law? The Rules of the ICTY' in Gideon Boas and William A. Schabas, *International Criminal Law Development*; Mirjan Damaška, 'The Uncertain Fate of Evidentiary Transplants: Anglo-American and Contemporary Experiments' (1997), 45 *American Journal of Comparative Law* 839; Françoise Tulkens, 'Main Comparable Features of the Different European Criminal Justice Systems' in Mireille Delmas-Marty (ed.), *The Criminal Process and Human Rights: Toward a European Consciousness* (1995), 5.

The adversarial/common law structure brings with it the philosophy of a trial as a battle between two parties, with complicated and restrictive rules governing the admission and application of evidence.[111] Attempts have been made to overlay the vastly more flexible evidential rules applicable in inquisitorial criminal law systems. Thus, there is no best evidence rule before the Tribunal;[112] hearsay evidence is admissible,[113] documentary evidence is admissible in a more flexible manner[114] and the principle of orality in testamentary evidence has been appreciably reduced.[115] However, the adversarial structure creates the paradigm of a trial defined by two warring parties, not by the endeavour to discover the truth in an environment controlled by impartial and professional judges.[116] Thus, the perceived need to seek advantage in the battle emerges. At the same time, the flexibility permitted allows a prosecution to lead more evidence in a shorter period of time, and of a character that would not normally be admissible in a common law criminal court.

In this context, a further tension emerges from the historical criticism of the surprising flexibility applied by the Nuremberg and Tokyo Tribunals to the admission of evidence, in particular large-scale admission of

[111] See Geoffrey Nice and Philippe Vallières-Roland, 'Procedural Innovations in War Crimes Trials' in Hirad Abtahi and Gideon Boas (eds.), *The Dynamics of International Criminal Justices*, A. T. H. Smith, in Christine van den Wyngaert (ed.), *Criminal Procedure Systems in the European Community* (1993), 85.

[112] The 'best evidence' or 'primary evidence' rule requires the production by a party of the best evidence which is available and procurable under the circumstances and any lesser evidence is considered 'secondary evidence': see *Black's Law Dictionary* (6th edn 1990).

[113] *Prosecutor v. Aleksovski*, 'Decision on Prosecutor's Appeal on Admissibility of Evidence', Case No. IT-95–95-14/1-AR73, 16 February 1999. Cf. *Prosecutor v. Milutinović*, 'Decision on Evidence Tendered Through Sandra Mitchell and Frederick Abrahams', Case No. IT-05-87-T, 1 September 2006, where the Trial Chamber denied admission of hearsay evidence in the form of human rights reports on crimes committed in Kosovo: these organisations' [Human Rights Watch and OSCE] careful methods can at best assure the *accuracy* of the process for recording the information contained in the eventual report[s], not the *reliability* of the material contents. . . . Not having had the opportunity of hearing any of the persons upon whose statements these [reports] are based, the Chamber is not in a position to assess the reliability of the factual contentions contained therein', para. 21.

[114] See generally, May and Wierda, *International Criminal Evidence*; Gideon Boas, 'A Code of Evidence and Procedure for International Criminal Law? The Rules of the ICTY'; Geoffrey Nice and Philippe Vallières-Roland, 'Procedural Innovations in War Crimes Trials', *Procedural Innovations.*

[115] See e.g. Rule 92*bis* of the ICTY Rules; Rule 89(F) of the ICTY Rules, as applied by the Appeals Chamber in *Prosecutor v. Milošević*, 'Decision on Interlocutory Appeal on the Admissibility of Evidence-in-Chief in the Form of Written Statements', Case No. IT-02-54-AR73.4, 30 September 2003; Rule 92*bis* of the Rules.

[116] For a discussion of this paradigm, see Gideon Boas, 'A Code of Evidence and Procedure for International Criminal Law? The Rules of the ICTY'.

documentary evidence. Article 19 of the International Military Tribunal ('IMT') Charter stated:

> The Tribunal shall not be bound by technical rules of evidence. It shall adopt and apply to the greatest possible extent expeditious and non-technical procedure, and shall admit any evidence which it deems to have probative value.[117]

This loosening of the rules of admissibility of evidence might itself be seen as an expression of the resolve of the victor states to conclude the trials as expeditiously as possible, perhaps evincing an assumption on the part of the Allied powers that the trial process, although the option preferred to summary execution,[118] should lead as expeditiously as possible to the 'correct' result. For example, in parliamentary debates in the House of Lords of Great Britain, it was said that the rationale behind the post-World War II tribunals was that they should reflect the reality that a large number of offenders existed and a process had to be devised for trying them expeditiously.[119] The fact that there was in these cases, far more than in any subsequent international criminal prosecution, a vast quantity of contemporaneous written inculpatory evidence[120] no doubt influenced the approach, although the rules of admissibility in these tribunals were alien to the restrictive adversarial criminal process applicable in the countries of most of the judges at the time. Not all were comfortable with the expansive approach taken by the post-World War II trials, and one dissenting International Military tribunal for the Far East ('IMTFE') judge was outwardly critical:

> In prescribing the rules of evidence for this trial the Charter practically discarded all the procedural rules devised by the various national systems of law, based on litigious experience and tradition, to guard a tribunal against erroneous persuasion, and thus left us, in the matter of proof, to guide ourselves, independently of any artificial rules of procedure.[121]

The ICTY, and other international criminal tribunals, are moving more and more towards openness and flexibility in the treatment of

[117] For a discussion of the approach taken by the IMT and IMTFE, see May and Wierda, *International Criminal Evidence*, 94–8.

[118] See Geoffrey Robertson, *Crimes Against Humanity*, 200–4.

[119] Great Britain, Parliamentary Debates, House of Lords, 5th Series (Hansard), vol. 142, 1945–6, 663 at 678. See also May and Wierda, *Crimes Against Humanity*, 95.

[120] See e.g., May and Wierda, ibid.

[121] Dissenting Judgement of Justice Pal, Tokyo Judgment, in Roling and Ruter (eds.), *The Tokyo Judgment – The International Tribunal for the Far East (IMTFE) 29 April 1946–12 November 1948* (1977).

evidentiary material, and the more that information is managed in a fair and balanced manner by the chambers, the less likely it is that technical rules of evidence or other factors will influence the outcome of material issues in the proceedings. Clearly, tensions arise in the loosening of technical rules of evidence when it becomes necessary for a court to control the admission of an enormous amount of evidence by an undisciplined litigant – a point that will be discussed below at length with respect to the *Milošević* trial.

Furthermore, the application of the fundamental fair trial provisions of the human rights regime to international criminal tribunals provides the framework for equality in a more global sense – that is, instead of focussing on advantage that can be obtained in a discrete area such as admissibility of a piece or category of evidence, the bench of professional judges can use the fair trial emblem to assess individual issues that arise, and weigh them in light of all the relevant factors. This process, properly applied and monitored, might better contribute to the fairness of the trial and protect accused from a breach of their fundamental fair trial rights. It may also provide a vehicle for expediting the trial process, by reducing the time taken to lead a significant amount of evidence. This process is highly relevant in complex international criminal trials.

Ultimately, the Appeals Chamber of the ICTY, after citing a number of judgments of the ECtHR, resolved the equality of arms issue as follows:

> This application of the concept of a fair trial in favour of both parties is understandable because the Prosecution acts on behalf of and in the interests of the community, including the interests of the victims of the offence charged (in cases before the Tribunal the Prosecutor acts on behalf of the international community). This principle of equality does not affect the fundamental protections given by the general law or Statute to the accused, and the trial proceeds against the background of those fundamental protections. Seen in this way, it is difficult to see how a trial could ever be considered to be fair where the accused is favoured at the expense of the Prosecution beyond a strict compliance with those fundamental protections.[122]

The *ad hoc* Tribunals have therefore adopted the approach that the fair trial issue, as it relates to the equality of arms, is resolved by an overall assessment of the time and resources available to the parties to prepare and bring their case before the Tribunal. In light of the above discussion, it remains important to assess carefully the differing resources available

[122] *Prosecutor v. Aleksovski*, 'Decision on Prosecutor's Appeal on Admissibility of Evidence', Case No. IT-95–95-14/1-AR73, 16 February 1999, para. 25.

to the parties, particularly in the investigative and legal support areas, on a case-by-case basis, to ensure that an accused is not unfairly disadvantaged. This is a critical area in establishing fairness in international criminal trials, requiring the expenditure of considerable professional time and resources. This issue impacts considerably on the determination of how best to conduct international criminal trials and will be taken up further in respect of the *Milošević* case in chapters 3 and 4.

The right to confront witnesses

Article 21(4)(e) of the ICTY has been interpreted as an affirmation of the accused's right to confront the witnesses against him or her, a right recognised in the Statutes of other international criminal tribunals.[123] Early in the Tribunal's jurisprudence, one Trial Chamber stated:

> It is important to re-emphasise the general rule requiring the physical presence of the witness. This is intended to ensure confrontation between the witness and the accused and to enable the Judges to observe the demeanour of the witness when giving evidence.[124]

In the same decision, however, the Trial Chamber recognised exceptions to the general rule requiring the physical presence of the accused, including the possibility of video-conferencing.[125] The Appeals Chamber later articulated its view that there are four exceptions to the principle that witnesses should testify in person.[126] The principle of orality of evidence, originally encapsulated in Rule 90(A), is now incorporated in the new Rule 89(F) which, following amendment in December 2000,[127] formulates the principle differently: 'A Chamber may receive the evidence of a

[123] Article 67(1)(e) of the ICC Statute; Article 21(4)(e) of the ICTR Statute; Article 17(4)(e) of the SCSL Statute.

[124] *Prosecutor v. Delalić et al.*, 'Decision On The Motion To Allow Witnesses K, L And M To Give Their Testimony By Means Of Video-Link Conference', Case No. IT-96-21-T, 28 May 1997, para. 15.

[125] Ibid. para. 14: '[T]here are exceptions to the general rule where the right of the accused under Article 21(4)(e) is not prejudicially affected.'

[126] *Prosecutor v. Kordić and Čerkez*, 'Decision on Appeal Regarding Statement of a Deceased Witness', Case No. IT-95-14/2-AR73.5, 21 July 2000, para. 19: Deposition evidence under Rule 71; testimony via video-link under Rule 71*bis*; expert witness statements under Rule 94*bis*; and affidavit evidence under (now deleted) Rule 94 *ter*.

[127] The Rules are amended by agreement of not less than ten judges sitting in plenary (Rule 6(A)). The procedure for proposal and consideration of amendments to the Rules is set out in the 'Practice Direction on Procedure for the Proposal, Consideration of and Publication of Amendments to the Rules of Procedure and Evidence of the international Tribunal', U.N. Doc. IT/143, 18 December 1999. This document is reflected in Rule 6(C) of the Rules.

witness orally or, where the interests of justice allow, in written form.' This dramatic change in the way in which evidence is to be received by the ICTY was expanded upon by Rule 92*bis*, as well as a decision by the Appeals Chamber in the *Milošević* case on the admission of evidence-in-chief under Rule 89(F),[128] and then finally in a Rule change to Rule 92*bis* and the creation of Rules 92*ter* and 92*quater* in September 2006.[129]

To understand the use of the Rule 92*bis* provisions in the context of international criminal law, it is important to set out briefly how it operates. In December 2000, the Judges adopted Rule 92*bis*, entitled 'Proof of Facts Other than by Oral Evidence',[130] relating to the proof of facts by means *other than* by oral evidence, and covers (1) evidence in the form of a written statement (Rule 92*bis*(A)), and (2) transcripts of evidence provided by witnesses in other Tribunal proceedings (Rule 92*bis*(D)). In a subsequent and seminal decision of the Appeals Chamber on this Rule,[131] the determinations required to be made by the Trial Chamber are broken down into three categories. First, a determination is made as to whether the witness statement or transcript of evidence *is capable of admission* under Rule 92*bis*; that is to say, if it goes to proof of the acts or conduct of the accused as charged in the indictment, it is inadmissible. By acts and conduct of the accused, the Appeals Chamber clarified that this did not simply refer to the things accused did or said themselves. For example, if evidence was proposed which went to the criminal responsibility of a member of a joint criminal enterprise shared by an accused, then that would be inadmissible because the accused's responsibility could be implicated. Similarly, if the evidence went to the criminal conduct of a subordinate to the accused that would, for the same reason, also be inadmissible under Rule 92*bis*. Second, a determination is made as to whether there are any other reasons why it is inappropriate for the

128 *Prosecutor v. Milošević*, 'Decision on Interlocutory Appeal on the Admissibility of Evidence-in-Chief in the Form of Written Statements', Case No. IT-02-54-AR73.4, 30 September 2003 ('Rule 89(F) Decision').

129 These provisions, which only entered into force on 22 September 2006, regulate the circumstances in which evidence in the form of a written statement, or transcript of evidence given before the Tribunal in previous proceedings, may be admitted; whether cross-examination is required, and the content that written evidence may go to in determining the responsibility of an accused for crimes charged against him. See IT/250, 'Amendments to the Rules of Procedure and Evidence', 15 September 2006.

130 This and other amendments to the Rules made at the twenty-third plenary session entered into force on 19 January 2001, seven days after the filing of IT/184 and in accordance with Rule 6(D).

131 *Prosecutor v. Galić*, Decision on Interlocutory Appeal Concerning Rule 92*bis*(C)', Case No. IT-98-29-AR73.2, 7 June 2002.

witness statement or transcript of evidence to be admitted, such as the proximity of the evidence to an accused. This appears to be an additional protection for an accused in circumstances in which the evidence may not fall foul of the proscription on evidence going to the acts and conduct of the accused but which may nonetheless be of sufficient importance to their case that it should be heard live. Finally, if the form of proof is capable of admission, a determination is made as to whether the maker of the witness statement or transcript of evidence should appear for cross-examination.[132] Despite some strong dissenting jurisprudence and legal writing,[133] the Rule has been interpreted as allowing a chamber to admit the testimony without cross-examination over the objection of an accused who wishes to cross-examine the witness. The creation of Rule 92*bis* revolutionised the presentation of evidence in trial (particularly by the prosecution). It enabled the prosecution to admit large amounts of evidence it would otherwise have had to lead in examination-in-chief. As can be seen from the *Milošević* prosecution case, more than 50 per cent of the prosecution case was led through Rule 92*bis*, and over 15 per cent of that was admitted without cross-examination.

The ICTR, for its part, has a mirror Rule 92*bis* in the same terms (prior to the September 2006 amendments) as the ICTY; the SCSL has a less detailed Rule 92*bis* (entitled 'Alternative Proof of Facts') providing for the admission of 'information in lieu of oral testimony . . . if, in the view of the Trial Chamber, it is relevant to the purpose for which it is submitted and if its reliability is susceptible of confirmation'; and finally, while the ICC Rules contain no direct equivalent of Rule 92*bis* of the ICTY Rules, Rule 68 of the ICC Rules (entitled 'Prior Recorded Testimony'), provides that the Trial Chamber may allow the admission of previously recorded audio or video testimony of a witness, or the transcript or other documented evidence of such testimony.[134]

132 Ibid.

133 See *Prosecutor v. Milošević*, 'Decision on Prosecution Motion for the Admission of Transcripts in Lieu of Viva Voce Testimony Pursuant to Rule 92bis(D)-Foča Transcripts: Dissenting Opinion of Judge Patrick Robinson', Case No. IT-02-54-T, 30 June 2003; Patrick L. Robinson, 'Rough Edges in the Alignment of Legal Systems in the Proceedings at the ICTY' (2005), 3 *Journal of International Criminal Justice* 1.

134 Such evidence may only be introduced (a) if the witness is not present before the Trial Chamber, both the Prosecutor and Defence had the opportunity to examine the witness during the recording, or (b) if the witness who gave the testimony is present before the Trial Chamber, he/she does not object to the submission of the previously recorded testimony and the Prosecutor, Defence and the Trial Chamber have the opportunity to examine the witness during the proceedings.

Like other international criminal tribunals, the fundamental guarantees of an accused person under the Statute and the Rules of the ICTY are essential not only to the administration of justice under the ICTY's mandate, but also to the appearance that it is in full conformity with an accused's procedural rights. It is already a subject of criticism that the ICTY was created in a manner unbecoming such an important institution, and is jurisdictionally unsound.[135] The ICTY has also come under criticism for carrying out its work in a manner that disregards the rights of accused persons. One observer has even criticised the Tribunal as a 'rogue court with rigged rules'.[136]

The right to confrontation has become an issue of fundamental importance to the question of fairness in international criminal trials. It is itself an equality issue. What Article 21(4)(e) protects is the full and equal right of an accused 'to examine, or have examined, the witnesses against him and to obtain the attendance and examination of witnesses on his behalf under the same conditions as witnesses against him'. The same or similar provisions apply before the ICTR,[137] SCSL[138] and ICC,[139] and it was provided for in the Nuremberg and Tokyo Charters.[140] The right does not amount to an absolute right to cross-examine witnesses, although some important opinion has been expressed strongly to the contrary.[141] In this respect, although international criminal law is ostensibly adversarial in nature involving the crucial feature of the right of cross-examination of witnesses, many forms of non-oral testamentary evidence (such as written statements, admission of transcripts from other proceedings, depositions and admission of expert evidence in writing) are admissible.

[135] For a discussion of the creation of the ICTY, see generally Paul Tavernier, 'The Experience of the International Criminal Tribunals for the former Yugoslavia and for Rwanda' (1997), 321 *International Review of the Red Cross*, 605. Some commentators consider the creation of the ICTY under Chapter VII of the Charter of the United Nations to be an unlawful exercise of the Security Council's powers: see e.g., V. Gowlland-Debbas, 'Security Council Enforcement Action and Issues of State Responsibility' (1994), 43 *International Criminal Law Quarterly* 55; Gabriël H. Oosthuizen, 'Playing Devil's Advocate: the United Nations Security Council is Unbound by Law' (1999), 12 *Leiden Journal of International Law* 549.

[136] 'The anomalies of the International Criminal Tribunal are legion' (letter), *The Times*, 17 June 1999.

[137] Article 20(4)(e) of the ICTR Statute.

[138] Article 17(4)(e) of the SCSL Statute.

[139] Article 67(1)(e) of the ICC Statute.

[140] Article 16 (e) of the IMT Charter and Article 9(d) of the IMTFE Charter.

[141] See e.g., Patrick L. Robinson, 'Rough Edges in the Alignment of Legal Systems in the Proceedings at the ICTY'; *Prosecutor v. Milošević*, 'Dissenting Opinion of Judge Patrick Robinson' in 'Decision on Prosecution Motion for the Admission of Transcripts in Lieu of Viva Voce Testimony Pursuant to 92bis(D) – Foča Transcripts', Case No. IT-02-54-T, 30 June 2003.

Written evidence in lieu of oral testimony

The use of written testimony in lieu of oral testimony is a facility available to the prosecution and defence. The same terms and conditions must apply. In the *Milošević* case, the accused persistently refused to make use of written statements, arguing that in principle such use is a violation of the right (enshrined in the ICTY Statute under Article 21(2)) to a public trial.[142] The Trial Chamber, in a Decision refusing the accused any additional time in which to present his defence case, dealt with this proposition, stating that the accused relied on a 'misguided view of what is required for a trial to be public'.[143] However, it was argued by counsel assigned by the Chamber to Milošević that all defence teams find it difficult in relation to the resources available to them to avail themselves of this form of evidence.[144]

In international criminal law, the decision about whether evidence may be admitted when an accused has not been able to 'confront', or cross-examine, the witness giving it appears to depend on the nature and importance of the evidence given as to his guilt or innocence. The ECtHR, for its part, has recognised that admission of and reliance on certain evidence in a trial, in circumstances where the accused has not had an opportunity to confront that witness, *may* be unfair.[145] The ICTY has recognised in its Rules and jurisprudence that a witness giving direct evidence against an accused, going to their acts and conduct (at least in respect of witness testimony brought into existence for the purposes of that litigation), should be available for cross-examination.[146] Until September 2006, such evidence-in-chief was also required to be given

142 See e.g. *Prosecutor v. Milošević*, Hearing, 14 April 2005, Transcript, 38477: '[ACCUSED]In the total, as you yourself said, only one-third of the witnesses testified live, viva voce [in the Prosecution's case in chief]. I think that that goes to the detriment of the principle of the public nature of the trial and greatly so . . . However, the general public doesn't use that type of information, and it is only what is going on here live and what is stated here viva voce can truly be considered to be public and open to the public. So that you know my position full well. I would like witnesses who testify here to testify publicly.' See above discussion concerning the right to a public hearing.

143 *Prosecutor v. Milošević*, 'Decision on Severance, Extension of Time and Rest', Case No. IT-02-54-T, 13 December 2005, para. 22.

144 Ibid., para. 20.

145 See e.g. *Kostovski v. The Netherlands* (1989) 166 Eur. Court HR (Ser. A); *Windisch v. Austria* (1990) 186 Eur. Court HR (Ser. A).

146 See e.g. Rule 98*bis*, *Prosecutor v. Milošević*, 'Decision on Admission of Documents in Connection With Testimony of Defence Witness Dragan Jasovic', Case No. IT-02-54-T, 26 August 2005, para. 18. See also *Prosecutor v. Aleksovski*, 'Decision On Prosecutor's Appeal on Admissibility of Evidence', Case No. IT-95-14/1-AR73, 16 February 1999, para. 15; *Prosecutor v. Tadić*, 'Decision on the Defence Motion on Hearsay', Case No. IT-94-1-T, 5

orally on the basis that the proximity of such evidence to the criminal responsibility of the accused mandated an assessment by the Chamber not only of the witness's response to cross-examination but also to the delivery of affirmative evidence against an accused.[147] It has also recognised that although hearsay evidence is admissible, the weight to be attributed to it will depend on its probative value and any impact on the fairness of the trial.[148]

The admission of certain evidence without allowing cross-examination has the potential to interfere with an accused person's capacity to challenge an aspect of the case against them. Interference with that right has clearly been based upon an assessment of its impact on fairness weighed against the expedition of the trial. Clearly, there are qualitative differences in the deprivation of a right to confrontation; 'non-live' evidence given by video-link or closed circuit television poses less fair trial challenges than the admission of a witness's statement or transcript of evidence given in other proceedings where cross-examination is denied entirely, because in the case of the former the evidence can still be directly tested by the accused before the Chamber.

The right to confront witnesses is another example of the inherent tensions involved in balancing the sometimes competing interests of fairness and expedition. Hearing all evidence live, and allowing unfettered cross-examination on it (as suggested in some of the minority jurisprudence and literature[149]), will ensure fairness in this limited respect. On the other hand, it also ensures a longer trial. If the cross-examination conducted was not necessary, effective and – most of all – relevant, expedition has been sacrificed for no real gain in the fairness of the trial. Of course, it is

Footnote 146 *(cont.)*

August 1996, paras. 15–19 and Separate Opinion of Judge Stephen on the Defence Motion on Hearsay, pp. 2–3; *Prosecutor v. Blaskic*, 'Decision on the Standing Objection of the Defence to the Admission of Hearsay with No Inquiry as to Its Reliability', Case No. IT-95-14-T, 21 January 1998, paras. 10, 12; *Prosecutor v. Galic*, 'Decision on Interlocutory Appeal Concerning Rule 92bis(C)', Case No. IT-98-29-AR73.2, 7 June 2002, para. 35.

[147] See discussion in the *Milošević* and *Galic* Appeals Chamber decisions, in above n. 142. The amendment to Rule 92*bis* and addition of Rule 92*ter* in September 2006 changes to the rules: 'Amendments to the Rules of Procedure and Evidence', IT/250, 15 September 2006.

[148] *Prosecutor v. Aleksovski*, 'Decision on Prosecutor's Appeal on Admissibility of Evidence', Case No. IT-95-95-14/1-AR73, 16 February 1999. Rule 89(D) provides the fundamental protection in respect of these matters: 'A Chamber may exclude evidence if its probative value is substantially outweighed by the need to ensure a fair trial'. This proposition has since been repeatedly stated in Tribunal rulings on admissibility of hearsay evidence. See e.g., *Prosecutor v. Milošević*, 'Decision on Admission of Documents in Connection With Testimony of Defence Witness Dragan Jasović', Case No. IT-02-54-T, 26 August 2005.

[149] See references in n. 133 above.

difficult to calibrate the operation of these rights so as to ensure the outcome will always be consistent with best practice. Well-regulated provisions for the admission of written testimony and careful consideration of whether it is fair to foreclose the right of an accused to cross-examine on a piece of evidence is something that can only be achieved fairly on an application of the principle to the particular facts in a particular case. It requires a balanced but interventionist approach from the court. This is an important aspect of the fair and expeditious trial paradigm. If the pre-trial process is refined and the prosecution is called upon to reduce and focus its case then appropriately limiting the right to confront witnesses in cross-examination becomes part of the overall process and of achieving a fair *and* expeditious international criminal trial.

Ultimately, it is safer and more consistent with the interest of ensuring a fair trial, to limit the amount of witness testimony received by the court in written form. At the ICTY, the use of written forms of testimony has been developed clearly as a means of expediting trials, enabling the court to admit more (invariably prosecution) evidence in a limited time. In the *Milošević* case, the testimony of 54 prosecution witnesses were admitted by way of Rule 92*bis* in writing without any cross-examination – or even appearing in court. In the *Krajišnik* case, the prosecution were permitted to lead 97 witnesses in this way without cross-examination. Subsequent to Rule changes in September 2006, a principle articulated in the *Milošević* case – that evidence going to the acts and conduct of the accused must in principle be given orally[150] – it is now possible for such evidence to be admitted in writing.[151]

[150] Following the decision of the Appeals Chamber that evidence-in-chief could be admitted in writing pursuant to Rule 89(F) (Rule 89(F) Decision, above n. 126), the *Milošević* Trial Chamber applied that Decision consistently on the basis that evidence relating to the acts and conduct of the accused were to be led orally: see e.g. *Prosecutor v. Milošević*, 'Decision on Prosecution Motions for the Admission of Witness Statements Pursuant to Rule 89(F) and Protective Measures for Witnesses B-1770 and B-1619', Case No. IT-02-54-T, 9 December 2003; *Prosecutor v. Milošević*, 'Decision on Prosecution Application Under Rule 89(F) to Admit the Statement of Witnesses Hrvoje Sarinic in Evidence', Case No. IT-02-54-T, 9 December 2003; *Prosecutor v. Milošević*, 'Decision on Prosecution Motion for Admission of a Summary of the Testimony of Witnesses B-1489 Pursuant to Rule 89(F)', Case No. IT-02-54-T, 12 January 2004; *Prosecutor v. Milošević*, 'Decision on Confidential Prosecution Motion for Admission of a Transcript and Statement Pursuant to Rules 92bis(D) and 89(F) for Witnesses B-1805', Case No. IT-02-54-T, 12 January 2004; *Prosecutor v. Milošević*, 'Decision on Prosecution Application Under Rule 89(F) to receive the Evidence-in-Chief of Witnesses Diego Arria in Written Form', Case No. IT-02-54-T, 23 January 2004.

[151] Rule 92*ter*(B): 'Evidence admitted under paragraph (A) may include evidence that goes to proof of the acts and conduct of the accused as charged in the indictment'.

Admission of adjudicated facts

Another more profound challenge to the right of an accused to confront witnesses and the evidence against him comes in the form of ICTY Rule 94(B), dealing with the admission of adjudicated facts from previously determined cases. This Rule provides that a Trial Chamber 'may decide to take judicial notice of adjudicated facts . . . from other proceedings of the Tribunal relating to matters at issue in the current proceedings'.

Up until February 2003, this Rule was never applied to admit a fact which the accused had not stipulated to or which was capable of reasonable dispute. On 28 February 2003, the *Krajišnik* Trial Chamber issued a Decision allowing the admission of more than 1,000 proposed adjudicated facts that were not agreed between the parties.[152] The Trial Chamber held in relation to adjudicated facts under Rule 94(B):

> By taking judicial notice of an adjudicated fact, thus, the Chamber establishes a well-founded presumption for the accuracy of that fact, which therefore does not have to be proven again at trial – unless the other party brings out new evidence and successfully challenges and disproves the fact at trial.[153]

Shortly after this, the *Milošević* Trial Chamber issued a decision on an application to admit 482 adjudicated facts from four cases which had been the subject of final appeal decisions before the Tribunal.[154] The Trial Chamber admitted 130 paragraphs of facts and rejected the remainder. Those 130 paragraphs were ones the Chamber considered were properly characterised as historical and geographical background information and not subject to reasonable dispute. The Trial Chamber considered the remainder of the facts 'may be' the subject of a reasonable dispute and therefore refused to admit them.

The Trial Chamber noted that the *Krajišnik* Decision had the effect of creating a presumption that the fact has been established in the proceedings, thereby shifting the burden of proof to the accused. The Trial Chamber regarded this as inappropriate, considering 'a fact, if admitted, is a fact that is accepted by the Chamber and cannot give rise to a presumption'.[155]

[152] *Prosecutor v. Krajišnik*, 'Decision on Prosecution Motions for Judicial Notice of Adjudicated Facts and for Admission of Written Statements by Witnesses pursuant to Rule 92bis', Case No IT-00-39-PT, 28 February 2003 ('Krajišnik Decision'), criteria for determination set out at para. 15.

[153] *Krajisnik* Decision, para 16.

[154] *Prosecutor v. Milošević*, 'Decision on Prosecution Motion for Judicial Notice of Adjudicated Facts', Case No. IT-02-54-PT, 10 April 2003 ('*Milošević* Trial Chamber Adjudicated Facts Decision').

[155] Ibid., 2.

The Prosecution appealed the Trial Chamber's ruling and the Appeals Chamber upheld the appeal.[156] The majority of the Appeals Chamber noted that there was no definition within the Rules of 'adjudicated facts' but agreed with the *Krajišnik* Trial Decision and held that a judicially noted fact is presumed to be true and can be challenged at trial:

> **CONSIDERING** that by taking judicial notice of an adjudicated fact, a Chamber establishes a well-founded presumption for the accuracy of this fact, which therefore does not have to be proven again at trial, [citing *Krajišnik* in support] but which, subject to that presumption, may be challenged at that trial . . .[157]

The Appeal Chamber provided no further reasoning or support for its decision – this paragraph being the only dispositive paragraph in the decision – and simply returned the matter to the Trial Chamber to rule on in accordance with the decision. In fact, it is almost impossible to extract any principle or test from the Appeals Chamber's three-page ruling and, were it not for a detailed dissent by Judge Hunt which explains the apparent position of the majority, it is difficult to see how the Trial Chamber would have been in a position to apply the ruling.

Judge Hunt dissented strongly, stating that no error was made by the Trial Chamber and focused on two reasons for this. First, if an adjudicated fact is a rebuttable presumption (as determined by the majority) it places a burden of proof upon the accused, which is contrary to the presumption of innocence enshrined in the ICTY Statute. He stated that the prosecution 'must at all times establish beyond reasonable doubt that the accused did the act alleged in the indictment'.[158] Secondly, in considering how to interpret Rule 94, Judge Hunt considered the concept of judicial notice at the time Rule 94(B) was enacted. He stressed it was 'basic to the concept that, because the judicially noticed fact was one which was not the subject of reasonable dispute, evidence of the relevant fact was unnecessary'. Judicial notice is taken of that fact, not the evidence upon which that finding is based.[159]

Judge Hunt argued that it was 'manifestly unsatisfactory' for a Trial Chamber to determine whether to accept a judicially noticed finding from other proceedings in the face of other evidence refuting that finding.[160] To do so, the Chamber would have to examine the evidence on

[156] *Prosecutor v. Milošević*, 'Decision on Prosecution's Interlocutory Appeal Against the Trial Chamber's 10 April 2003 Decision on Prosecution Motion for Judicial Notice of Adjudicated Facts', Case No. IT-02-54-AR73.5, 28 October 2003 ('*Milošević* Appeal Chamber Adjudicated Facts Decision'). [157] Ibid., 2.

[158] Ibid., Dissenting Opinion of Judge David Hunt, para. 7. [159] Ibid., paras. 8 and 9.

[160] Ibid., para. 9.

which the initial finding is based. In this regard, he notes that the Prosecution should simply tender the transcripts of evidence on which those findings were based under Rule 92*bis*(D).[161]

The decision is an example of poor appellate decision-making that unhelpfully interferes with the conduct of the trial without adding materially or positively to the important legal principles upon which these issues are founded. The ICTR Appeals Chamber, composed of the same judges as the ICTY Appeals Chamber, in a recent and even more egregious decision, extended the application of Rule 94(B) by allowing an adjudicated fact establishing that genocide in Rwanda was a fact of common knowledge and holding that it is permissible for judicial notice to be taken of a fact that goes to the acts and conduct of subordinates of an accused or his co-participants in a joint criminal enterprise.[162]

The *ad hoc* Tribunal jurisprudence has persistently held that taking judicial notice of adjudicated facts under Rule 94(B) 'is a method of achieving judicial economy and harmonizing judgements of the Tribunal while ensuring the right of the Accused to a fair, public and expeditious trial'.[163] However, it is hard to see how the admission of facts which the defence must be given an opportunity to rebut will have this overall effect. My own experience with the use by the prosecution of adjudicated facts in ICTY cases is that the admission of these facts reduces marginally – if at all – the number of witnesses or scope of evidence led in its cases. On the other hand, the defence is in a position where it must rebut any such evidence that it considers harmful to an accused. If the Appeals Chamber was serious about enforcing the stated principle that the admission of adjudicated facts is to expedite the trial process, perhaps it should require the prosecution to identify in respect of every fact sought to be admitted the correlative reduction in testamentary or documentary evidence which it would otherwise seek to lead. This way a Trial Chamber would be in a position to determine whether a genuine impact on judicial

161 Ibid., para. 12.

162 *Prosecutor v. Karemera et al.*, 'Decision on Prosecutor's Interlocutory Appeal of Decision on Judicial Notice', Case No. ICTR-98-44-AR73(C), 16 June 2006 ('*Karemera* Appeals Chamber Judicial Notice Decision').

163 Ibid., para. 39. See also, *Prosecutor v. Krajišnik*, 'Decision on Third and Fourth Prosecution Motion for Judicial Notice of Adjudicated Facts', Case No. IT-00-39-T, 24 March 2005, para. 12; *Prosecutor v. Mejakić*, 'Decision on Prosecution Motion for Judicial Notice Pursuant to Rule 94(B)', Case No. IT-02-65-PT, 1 April 2004, 5; *Prosecutor v. Ntakirutimana et al.*, 'Decision on the Prosecutor's Motion for Judicial Notice of Adjudicated Facts', Case No. ICTR-96-10-T & ICTR-96-17-T, 22 September 2001, para. 28; *Prosecutor v. Sikirica et al.*, 'Decision on Prosecution Motion for Judicial Notice of Adjudicated Facts', Case No. IT-95-8-PT, 27 September 2000, 4.

economy, and therefore expedition, would be achieved by admission of a particular fact, and could then balance that with any effect on the fairness of the trial overall. As it is, notwithstanding the general comment by the Appeals Chamber in the *Karemera* case that the purpose of Rule 94(B) was expediency without compromising the rights of the Accused,[164] the law regulating the use of adjudicated facts amounts to a vague stated principle which concretely threatens the presumption of innocence and the right of an accused to confront a witness against him, and promises no measurable gains in terms of the expedition of the trial.

Great importance is placed on expediting complex international criminal trials.[165] That motivation is greater where the accused is a senior political official, very far removed from the physical perpetration of alleged crimes. However, there is a danger, one that is currently very real in international criminal tribunals, that the focus on expedition will detract from the real and perceived importance of fairness.[166] The answer to this conundrum is two-fold. First, all the stakeholders in the international criminal trial process must accept that these trials will take time to conduct and conclude, because they encompass large-scale criminality. Second, focus should be given to areas in which these trials can be more fairly (and, therefore, safely) rendered expeditious. In this respect, the discussion in particular in the following two chapters serves as something of a roadmap for achieving the conduct of fair and more expeditious complex international criminal trials. More focused and narrower indictments and prosecution cases, strong case management provisions and action taken at all stage of these proceedings, will have the effect of expediting these cases and are less likely to harm the ultimate goal of fairness.

The right to counsel and to self-representation

Issues relating to the right to counsel and the right to self-representation in the conduct of a defence in a complex international criminal law trial have a significant impact on the fair and expeditious trial paradigm, and

[164] *Karemera* Appeals Chamber Judicial Notice Decision, paras. 52 and 53.

[165] Eighth Annual Report of the ICTY, UN General Assembly, 56th sess, A/56/352–S/2001/865, 17 September 2001, para. 50: 'These changes reflect an increase in the capacity of the Tribunal to fulfil its mandate more expeditiously as well as an increase in the power of judges to control the proceedings before it.'

[166] See e.g., an article written by the presiding judge of the *Milošević* case itself: Patrick L. Robinson, 'Rough Edges in the Alignment of Legal Systems in the Proceedings at the ICTY'.

therefore upon how to achieve best practice in such trials. Article 21(4)(b) of the ICTY Statute requires that an accused be given 'adequate time and facilities for the preparation of his defence' and the right 'to communicate with counsel of his own choosing'. Furthermore, Article 21(4)(d) of that Statute provides for the right of an accused 'to defend himself in person or through legal assistance of his own choosing'. Together, these rights – which are to a large extent reflected in the constitutional instruments of other international criminal courts and tribunals,[167] and which are derived from human rights instruments[168] – caused considerable conflict and debate in the *Milošević* trial, as they have in other international criminal trials. These issues also significantly affect the equality of arms and the expeditiousness of the trial, both fundamental interests. Balancing the sometimes conflicting concerns that emerge from the application of these interests is difficult. There are limited resources available to conduct such long and complicated cases, and high level accused are more able, and appear to have a greater tendency, to manipulate the trial process and regime of rights available to them in a way that can frustrate the expeditiousness (in particular) of the trial – and can at times threaten its fairness. Furthermore, the choice of some high level accused to represent themselves in such trials has placed an enormous strain on resources and on the ability of the court to control and manage the trial in a manner that can be considered fair. It has also raised some fundamental questions about the nature and scope of a right to self-representation in international criminal law, and the extent to which a court should assist and resource an accused who elects either to appear *pro se* or to obstruct the defence representation processes put in place.

A range of representation models exists in international criminal law. Most typically, an accused is represented by defence counsel, either privately funded or remunerated through legal aid funds. Although such representation does not typically give rise to substantial difficulties in these trials, it raises concerns questions about resources and the capacity of individuals and institutions to meet the challenges of a defence to large and complex cases. The self-representation models which are emerging in international criminal law raise far greater challenges to the ability of international criminal courts and tribunals to conduct fair and expeditious trials.

[167] See e.g., Article 20(4) of the ICTR Statute and Article 17(4) of the SCSL Statute.

[168] See e.g., Article 14(3) of the ICCPR, Article 6(3) of the ECHR and Article 8(2) of the ACHR.

Defence counsel representation in international criminal courts and tribunals

The manner in which an accused obtains, or chooses not to obtain, legal assistance in matters related to cases before the *ad hoc* Tribunals is governed by each Tribunal's Statute, Rules of Procedure and Evidence, and the relevant Directives and Codes of Conduct.[169] The system of representation in these tribunals provides for three representation scenarios: (1) the accused engages counsel of their choosing, remunerated directly by the accused; (2) the accused is assigned counsel by the Tribunal under its legal aid scheme (if the accused is indigent), and (3) the accused defends himself in person. The first two scenarios encapsulate the classic defence counsel representation model.

In the *ad hoc* Tribunals, where an accused engages counsel directly, that counsel is remunerated by the accused or a third party – such as a state.[170] The chosen counsel must fulfil the requirements set out in Rule 44(A) of the ICTY and ICTR Rules, which provide for certain minimum requirements that counsel must fulfil. If accused do not have sufficient means to pay for legal assistance, they are entitled – 'where the interests of justice so require' – to have legal assistance assigned at the expense of the Tribunal. Michael Bohlander points out that the condition 'where the interests of justice so require' is effectively superfluous as the interests of justice require all persons accused of war crimes who request counsel and who are without sufficient means should be provided counsel.[171] Assignment of counsel to an accused or a suspect is governed by Rule 45 of the ICTY and ICTR Rules, as well as the procedure set out in the relevant Directive on Assignment of Defence Counsel. In the majority of cases, the accused makes a request to the registrar, who is the responsible authority in such matters, for the assignment of counsel in the prescribed form.[172] The

[169] For the ICTY, see 'Directive on the Assignment of Defence Counsel Directive', IT/73/REV 10 ('ICTY Directive') and 'Code of Professional Conduct for Defence Counsel', IT/125 REV 1, as amended on 12 July 2002 ('ICTY Code'). For the ICTR, see 'Directive on the Assignment of Defence Counsel', 9 January 1996 as amended 6 June 1997, 8 June 1998, 1 July 1999, 27 May 2003 and 24 April 2004 ('ICTR Directive') and 'Code of Professional Conduct for Defence Counsel', 8 June 1998 ('ICTR Code').

[170] For example, Dario Kordić's defence costs were met for some time by the Republic of Croatia.

[171] See Michael Bohlander, 'The Defence' in Hirad Abtahi and Gideon Boas, *Dynamics of International Criminal Justice*, 39.

[172] See Article 7, ICTY Directive (and ICTR Directive). The Office of Legal Affairs and Detention Matters ('OLAD') estimates that 80% of all accused in the past 2 years have been declared themselves indigent: interview with ICTY OLAD representative, Martin Petrov, 20 April 2006.

registrar maintains a list of persons eligible to be assigned as counsel. As articulated in both the Rules[173] and the Directives[174] of the two tribunals, persons on the list must fulfil the requirements of Rule 44(A), as well as possess established competence in criminal law and/or international criminal law/international humanitarian law/international human rights law; have at least seven years experience in criminal proceedings;[175] and must have indicated their willingness and availability to act as assigned counsel to any indigent person detained at the Tribunal.[176]

The Special Court for Sierra Leone (SCSL) is the first internationalised tribunal to create a permanent and separate organ of the Court dedicated to defence, namely the Principal Defender's Office (PDO). The PDO can assist in all three representation scenarios discussed above in respect of the ICTY and ICTR. The laws governing the system of representation and the PDO at the SCSL are the Statute, Rules of Procedure and Evidence,[177] Directive on the Assignment of Counsel,[178] and the Code of Professional Conduct for Counsel with the Right of Audience before the Special Court for Sierra Leone.[179] Rule 45 of the SCSL Rules sets up the Defence Office, which is entrusted with 'ensuring the rights of suspects and accused'. The registrar holds responsibility to establish, maintain and develop the office, which indicates it is not an entirely separate organ of the Court. The PDO is headed by the Special Court Principal Defender, who is supported by a team of lawyers, duty counsel and defence advisors.

The ICC Statute contains a representation provision in Article 67(1)(d) that is similar to that of the *ad hoc* Tribunals, but which expressly provides for some limitations on the right of the accused in regard to representation and presence in trial. The system of representation before the ICC is established by its Statute, the Rules of Procedure and Evidence[180] and the Regulations,[181] as well as by its Code of Professional Conduct for Counsel.[182] Similar to the SCSL, an Office of Public Counsel for the Defence (OPCD)[183] was established by the ICC as

[173] Rule 45B. [174] Article 14.

[175] This amendment was introduced in July 2004 – existing counsel were permitted to remain. Rule 45(A) of the ICTR Rules requires 10 years' minimum experience.

[176] Rule 45(B) of the ICTY Rules There is no equivalent in the ICTR Rules.

[177] Adopted on 16 January 2002, as amended on 7 March 2003, 1 August 2003, and 14 March 2004. [178] Adopted on 1 October 2003. [179] Adopted on 14 May 2005.

[180] ICC-ASP/1/3, adopted by the Assembly of States Parties; First session; New York, 3–10 September 2002. [181] ICC-BD/01-01-04, adopted by the Judges on 26 May 2004.

[182] ICC-ASP/4/32, adopted at the 3rd plenary meeting on 2 December 2005.

[183] Regulation 77. It is noted that the Registrar shall also develop an Office of Public Counsel for victims (Regulation 81).

a form of in-house defence counsel to provide advice and *ad hoc* representation. The OPCD has two specific functions: (1) representing and protecting the rights of the defence during the initial stages of the investigation; and (2) providing support and assistance to defence counsel and to the suspect or accused, including (where appropriate) legal research and advice as well as appearing before the Chamber in respect of specific issues.

Self-representation

The right of an accused person to self-representation is embodied in many of the regional human rights conventions. Article 21(4)(d) of the ICTY Statute is derived from Article 14(3)(d) of the ICCPR and is similar to Article 8(2)(d) of the American Convention on Human Rights, Article 6(3)(c) of the European Convention on Human Rights and Article 67 of the Rome Statute of the International Criminal Court. Its application in the human rights regime has generally yielded an interpretation of there being a right to self-representation which reposes in an accused, but that this right is and can be limited for various reasons.[184] The treatment of this important issue in international criminal law, and in particular in the *Milošević* case, will be considered in detail in chapter 4. The purpose of the discussion of self-representation in this chapter is its place in the context of the fair trial right to legal representation, the treatment of which in international criminal law has been considerably influenced by the position in the common and civil law criminal justice systems.

[184] See the jurisprudence of the ECtHR: *Croissant v. Germany* (1992) A237-B Eur. Court HR (Ser. A); *Correia de Mateos v. Portugal* (2001) Eur. Court HR, Case No. 48188/95; *X. v Norway*, Decision, 30 May 1975, DR 3, 43; *Weber v Switzerland*, (1990) 12 EHRR 508; *X v. Austria*, Case No. 7138/75, Commission decision, 5 July 1977, DR 9, 50. *Contra* one case of the Human Rights Committee: *Michael and Brian Hill v. Spain*, Human Rights Committee, Communication No. 526/1993, UN Doc CCPR/C/59/D/526/1993, 2 April 1997 (the relevance of this decision was challenged by the Trial Chamber in a decision rendered in the *Milošević* case: *Prosecution v. Milošević*, 'Reasons for Decision on Assignment of Defence Counsel', Case No. IT-02-54-T, 22 September 2004, para. 44, as well as in the *Šešelj* case: *Prosecutor v. Šešelj*, 'Decision on Prosecution's Motion for Order Appointing Counsel to Assist Vojislav Šešelj with his Defence', Case No. IT-03-67-PT, 9 May 2003, para. 18. See also, scholarly challenge to the view that Article 14(3)(d) of the ICCPR, from which the relevant provisions derive, supports a right to self-representation: Michael P. Scharf and Christopher. M. Rassi, 'Do Former Rogue Leaders Have an International Right to Act as Their Own Lawyers in War Crimes Trials?' (2004), 20 *Ohio State Journal on Dispute Resolution* 1, 11; David Weissbrodt, *The Right to a Fair Trial under the Universal Declaration of Human Rights and the International Covenant on Civil and Political Rights – Articles 8, 10, 11 of the Universal Declaration of Human Rights* (2001), 45; Manfred Nowak, *U.N. Covenant on Civil and Political Rights: CCPR Commentary* (1993), 258.

(a) Self-representation in common law jurisdictions The relevant provisions in the statutes of international criminal courts and tribunals have generally been interpreted as providing an accused with a right to self-representation, a position that is consistent with that of most common law jurisdictions.[185] For example, in the United States, where the Supreme Court has upheld the right to self-representation as a constitutional right, the treatment of the issue here is typically robust and focussed on an extravagant respect for the individual's free will. In the leading case on the matter, *Faretta*,[186] which has never been overturned and is still considered good law, the US Supreme Court held that in its federal courts, the right to self-representation had been protected since 1789.[187] In 1942, the US Supreme Court had already found that the Sixth Amendment right to the assistance of counsel implicitly embodies 'a correlative right to dispense with a lawyer's help'.[188] In *Faretta*, the US Supreme Court (by majority) went further, stating that the Sixth Amendment embodied a right of an accused person to self-representation which could not be taken away from them by a State or one of its courts.[189]

The precedent set by *Faretta* stands for the proposition that in the USA, an accused has a constitutionally sanctioned right to self-representation despite, as Justice Blackmun (dissenting) asserts, 'the obvious dangers of unjust convictions in order to protect the individual defendant's right of free choice'.[190] Justice Blackmun also observed, as have many lower courts subsequently, that while the right to counsel is 'based on the premise that representation by counsel is essential to ensure a fair trial', the recognised right to waive representation would directly undermine the right to a fair trial[191] – a right that the US Supreme Court has itself described as 'the lamp that shows that freedom lives'.[192]

[185] For the United States, see Article [VI.], Amendments to the Constitution of the United States of America; *Faretta v. California*, 422 US 806 (1975); *United States v. Farhad*, 190 F.3d 1097, 1101 (9th Cir. 1999), *cert. denied*, 529 US 1023 (2000), 1101; *Strickland v. Washington*, 466 US 668 (1984); *Mayberry v. Pennsylvania*, 400 US 455 (1971); *Estes v. Texas*, 381 US 532 (1965); *Duncan v. Louisiana*, 391 US 145 (1968); *Martinez v. Court of Appeal*, 528 U.S. 152 (2000); *Illinois v. Allen*, 397 US 337 (1970). For Canada, see Constitution Act 1982, Article 10 (incorporating the Canadian Charter of Rights and Freedoms); *R v. Swain* (1991) 1 SCR 933. For England and Wales, see *R v. Woodward* [1944] KB 118; *R v. De Oliveira* [1997] 9 *Criminal Law Review* 600; *R v. Lyons*, 68 Cr.App.R. 104.

[186] *Faretta v. California*, (1975) 422 US 806. [187] Ibid. 812.

[188] Ibid. 814, citing *Adams v. United States ex rel. McCann*, (1942) 317 US 269, 279. See also *Snyder v. Massachusetts*, (1934) 291 US 97.

[189] Article [VI.], Amendments to the Constitution of the United States of America.

[190] Ibid. 851. [191] Ibid.

[192] *Duncan v. Louisiana* (1968) 391 US 145, 155–6, n. 23, cited by Judge Reinhardt in *United States v. Farhad*, 190 F.3d 1097, 1101 (9th Cir. 1999), *cert. denied*, 529 U.S. 1023 (2000),

The right to self-representation is acknowledged in most common law jurisdictions. However, in these jurisdictions, limitations and qualifications have developed such that there is a trend towards greater judicial control of the circumstances in which the right may be exercised.[193] Even in the USA, the Supreme Court has confined its holding in *Faretta* to a defendant's right to self-representation at trial, not extending to appeal.[194] It further reasoned that, 'the right to self-representation is not absolute' and '[e]ven at the trial level . . . the government's interest in ensuring the integrity and efficiency of the trial at times outweighs the defendant's interest in acting as his own lawyer'.[195] However, it is in Scotland that the most robust interference with the right to self-representation exists. Whereas in England and Wales, Canada, Australia and New Zealand, there are statutory prohibitions on *pro se* accused cross-examining rape victims and other categories of protected witnesses,[196] in Scotland section 288C(1) of the *Criminal Procedure Act* provides that an accused 'charged with a sexual offence [. . .] is prohibited from conducting his defence in person at the trial'. Section 288D(2) provides that an accused must appoint a lawyer. If they fail to do so, dismiss the lawyer or if the lawyer withdraws, the court shall 'at its own hand' appoint a lawyer to act on behalf of the accused. A lawyer so appointed 'is not susceptible to dismissal by the accused or obliged to comply with any instruction by the accused to dismiss counsel'.[197] Subject to this, it is the duty of the lawyer '(a) to ascertain and act upon the instructions of the

1105. See also the concurring opinion of Justice Breyer, in *Martinez v. Court of Appeal*, 528 U.S. 152, 164–5 (2000): 'I agree with the Court and join its opinion. Because Justice Scalia writes separately to underscore the continuing constitutional validity of *Faretta* . . . I note that judges closer to the firing line have sometimes expressed dismay about the practical consequences of that holding.' In respect of judicial criticism, see e.g., *Martinez v. Court of Appeal of California, Fourth Appellate District* (2000) 528 US 152, 154; *United States v. Farhad*, 190 F.3d 1097, 1101 (9th Cir. 1999), *cert. denied*, 529 US 1023 (2000), 1107, 1108–9.

193 For Canada, see *Criminal Code, RS* 1985, s. 486(2.3). For England and Wales, see *Youth Justice and Criminal Evidence Act* (England) 1999, ss. 34, 36, 38. For Australia, see *Crimes Act 1914* (Cth), ss. 15YF and YG; *Criminal Procedure Act 1986* (NSW), s. 294A; New South Wales Law Reform Commission, *Questioning of complainants by unrepresented accused in sexual offences trials*, Report No. 101, 2003; *Evidence (Children) Act 1997* (NSW), s. 28; *Sexual Offences (Evidence and Procedure) Act 1983* (NT), s. 5; *Domestic Violence Act* (NT), s. 20AD; s. 21 of the *Evidence Act 1977* (Qld) (amendments introduced by *Evidence (Witness Anonymity) Amendment Act 2005*, Act No. 57/2000); *Evidence Act 1906* (WA), s. 106G. For New Zealand, see *Evidence Act 1908* (NZ), s. 23F.

194 *Martinez v. Court of Appeal of California, Fourth Appellate District* (2000) 528 US 152, 154.

195 Ibid. 161–2.

196 See sources cited in above n. 180 and n. 188.

197 *Criminal Procedure (Scotland) Act 1995*, s. 288D(3).

accused; and (b) where the accused gives no instructions or inadequate or perverse instructions, to act in the best interests of the accused'.[198]

(b) Self-representation in civil law jurisdictions In stark contrast to the varyingly limited tolerance in common law countries of the right to self-representation, the criminal codes of civil law countries routinely provide for the imposition of defence counsel on an accused charged with serious criminal offences. The consent of the accused is not required and the imposition of counsel is normally codified as mandatory in circumstances where the charges are serious in nature.

The French Code of Criminal Procedure requires that an accused charged with a serious crime must be represented by counsel. Article 274 of that Code requires that, early in criminal proceedings before the *cour d'assises*, and after the presiding judge interrogates the accused as to his identity and ascertains that he has been served with the indictment, 'the accused is [. . .] invited to choose an advocate to assist him in his defence. If the accused does not choose his advocate, the presiding judge or his delegate appoints one *ex officio* to act for him. This appointment becomes void if the accused later chooses an advocate.' In the section of the Code of Criminal Procedure dealing with the trial, Article 317 requires that the presence of defence counsel with the accused is compulsory during the hearing. If the defence counsel chosen or appointed in accordance with article 274 does not appear, the presiding judge appoints another.

Section 140(2) of the German Code of Criminal Procedure requires that '[t]he assistance of defense counsel shall be mandatory if [. . .] the accused is charged with a serious criminal offense', and Section 141 requires that counsel shall be assigned to an accused as soon as he is asked to respond to an indictment, or earlier, if so requested by the Office of Public Prosecution. The choice of defence counsel, under Section 142 of the Code of Criminal Procedure, rests with the presiding judge, and if counsel fails to appear, or leaves at an inopportune time, the presiding judge may appoint another counsel and/or suspend the hearing in order to do so.[199] At any rate, under Section 145, the hearing 'shall be interrupted or suspended if the newly appointed defense counsel declares that he does not have the time needed to prepare the defense'. According

[198] Ibid. s. 288(D)(4). See also, a pre-legislative consultation paper concerning the Sexual Offences (Procedure and Evidence) Act: Scottish Executive, *Redressing the Balance: Cross-Examination in Rape and Sexual Offence Trials* (1991), available at http://www.scotland.gov.uk/consultations/justice/rtb-05.asp#b7 at 30 August 2006.

[199] Section 145 of the *Code of Criminal Procedure of Germany*.

to the case-law of the Federal Court of Justice and the Federal Constitutional Court, '[Section] 141(1) does not preclude a court from appointing, when it holds this to be necessary in the interests of justice, one or more defence counsel for an accused who is already represented by one or more counsel of his own choice.'[200]

Of particular interest to *Milošević* and other ICTY cases is the fact that in the legal system of Serbia and Montenegro, and before that the Federal Republic of Yugoslavia and Socialist Federal Republic of Yugoslavia, it is mandatory for the accused to be represented by defence counsel in respect of serious criminal charges. Under Article 71(1) of the Criminal Procedure Act of Serbia and Montenegro, it is mandatory for defence counsel to be imposed where the offence is punishable by a term of imprisonment of more than ten years, or where the accused is otherwise 'unable successfully to defend himself'. Under Article 71(4), where the accused fails to appoint counsel, the presiding judge shall do so for him. Article 73(1) allows for the accused to later appoint counsel of his own choosing, in which case imposed counsel is released.[201]

Standby counsel

The ICTY, ICTR and SCSL have all placed reliance upon the standby counsel model in responding to some of the complexities of self-representation. The concept of standby counsel was first developed in domestic US law, and refers to an attorney who is appointed to assist a self-represented accused. The treatise *American Law Reports* states as follows:

> Where a criminal defendant chooses to represent himself or herself at trial, the judge may wish to determine, among other matters, whether the defendant has the mental capacity to present a coherent defence. [. . .] Also, the judge may find it advisable to appoint standby counsel, especially if the case is expected to be long or complicated, or if there are multiple defendants.

200 See *Croissant v. Germany* (1992) A237-B Eur. Court HR (Ser. A), para. 20.

201 Similarly, codes of criminal procedure of other European civil law countries require the assignment of counsel in circumstances where an accused is charged with serious criminal offences: see *e.g.*, section 41 of the *Austrian Code of Criminal Procedure*; section 11 of the *Zurich (Switzerland) Code of Criminal Procedure*; and section 21:3 of the *Swedish Code of Criminal Procedure*. See also Articles 62, 63 and 64 of the *Portuguese Code of Criminal Procedure*. In Spain and Norway, the accused is required to be represented by counsel unless he is charged with only minor criminal offences for which a prison sentence does not attach: Article 118 of the *Spanish Code of Criminal Procedure*; Article 94 of the *Norwegian Code of Criminal Procedure*. Outside of Europe, other civil law countries have similar provisions: See Articles 282 and 283 of the *Code of Criminal Procedure of the Republic of Korea*; Articles 463 and 467 of the *Code of Criminal Procedure of Argentina*; Article 127 of the *Code of Criminal Procedure of Colombia*.

> Counsel who has been asked by a pro se criminal defendant to aid in the defence, or who has been appointed standby counsel by the trial court without the defendant's solicitation, should be aware that the role of counsel in such a situation is a sensitive and sometimes difficult one. Thus, although counsel may expect to take part in such tasks as investigating the facts and law of the case, preparing and presenting pretrial motions, helping the defendant present the case in court, and assembling and presenting information relevant to sentencing, counsel may find it prudent to keep in mind that it is the defendant who still has the right to control all strategic decisions and speak for the defence unless the court specifically directs otherwise.[202]

The leading case on this mechanism is the US Supreme Court decision in *McKaskle v Wiggins*.[203] In that case, the appellate court had reversed the denial of *habeas corpus* relief to a petitioner inmate, finding that an accused's right to self-representation was violated by the unsolicited participation of standby counsel, and that a court-appointed standby counsel was generally appointed for advisory purposes only. The accused argued before the US Supreme Court that 'his Faretta right to present his defense *pro se* was impaired by the distracting, intrusive, and unsolicited participation of counsel throughout the trial.[204] The US Supreme Court reversed the appellate court's decision, concluding that the accused was accorded all the rights encompassed within the right to self-representation, including the right to make motions, argue points of law, and question witnesses. Furthermore, it was held that participation by standby counsel did not interfere with the accused's right to present his own defence, and that the accused was given ample opportunity to present his own positions to the trial court on every matter discussed.

Interestingly, however, for the purposes of how the operation of standby counsel might transpose into international criminal law the US Supreme Court held as follows:

> [T]he pro se defendant is entitled to preserve actual control over the case he chooses to present to the jury. This is the core of the Faretta right. If standby counsel's participation over the defendant's objection effectively allows counsel to make or substantially interfere with any significant tactical decisions, or to control the questioning of witnesses, or to speak instead of the defendant on any matter of importance, the Faretta right is eroded.[205]

[202] D. Klein, *Annotation, Right, under Federal Constitution, of accused to represent himself or herself in criminal proceeding – Supreme Court cases* (2004) 145 L. Ed. 2d 1177.

[203] *McKaskle v. Wiggins*, 465 US 168 (1984).

[204] Ibid. 176; *Faretta v. California*, 422 US 806 (1975).

[205] Ibid. 178.

Standby counsel has been enthusiastically espoused by some of the international tribunals in several key decisions.[206] The model gives the impression of allowing an accused to represent themselves, while at the same time providing the court with some comfort that counsel – acting in the interests of an accused, even if uninstructed – is present and able to step into the proceedings in some capacity, thus assisting the court in its obligation to ensure a fair trial. However, as will be seen in chapter 4, the role of standby counsel in an international criminal trial and the manner in which that counsel can and should act raises questions as to whether it is an appropriate or efficacious form of representation in international criminal law.[207]

Imposition of counsel

Another method of representation which has emerged from the increasing trend of self-representation in international criminal trials, is the imposition of defence counsel on an accused. This model of representation clearly lacks the standard and crucial ingredient of defence counsel representation – that of an accused cooperating with and instructing counsel. Like the use of standby counsel, the imposition of counsel on an unconsenting accused creates another layer of representation over the accused's self-representation. The basis upon which counsel can be imposed in international criminal trials has only been explored directly in the context of the *Milošević* case and more recently the *Šešelj* case. However, as will be argued in chapter four of this book, this more radical model of representation looms as an important remedy to manipulation of international criminal trials by accused who elect to represent themselves, has the potential when exercised properly to render trials more expeditious and accommodate crucial issues of fairness, and is an important point of discussion for the future conduct of these cases.

Expeditious Trials

The issue of the fairness of a trial intersects with its expedition. The right to an expeditious trial has been said to have its roots at the foundation of criminal proceedings, and the US Supreme Court has traced its roots

[206] See e.g. the *Norman*, *Baryagwiza*, *Šešelj* cases, discussed in detail in chapter 4.

[207] Because standby counsel is appointed primarily to assist a self-represented accused, it is possible that it is not strictly speaking a form of representation. However, because of the unique role of such counsel in the representation rubric I will consider and discuss it in these terms.

back to the twelfth century.[208] The right to an expeditious trial is reflected in the major human rights instruments (for example in Article 14(3) of the ICCPR, Article 6(1) of the ECHR and Article 7(5) of the ACHR) and is reflected in the Statutes of all of the international criminal courts and tribunals. It is generally interpreted as requiring that an accused person be tried within a reasonable period of time, although before human rights adjudicating bodies the circumstances falling within that concept of reasonableness have been given broad interpretation and extensive periods of pre-trial and pre-judgement detention have been considered reasonable.[209] The ICTY has also consistently held that extensive periods of detention and lengthy trial proceedings have not violated the right to an expeditious trial, although the obligation to provide for an expeditious trial has received considerable attention in the jurisprudence of the ICTY.[210]

The expeditious conclusion of trials has become something of an obsession of the ICTY. Since the first trial before the Tribunal, *Tadić*, the Trial Chambers have sought, to varying degrees, to expedite trials by defining the issues in dispute before trial by means of pre-trial briefs and by requesting parties to stipulate, or formally admit, any non-disputed facts. In the *Dokmanović* case, the Trial Chamber contemplated ordering the defence, pursuant to Rules 54 and 65*bis*, to make any formal admissions, or stipulations, within a certain time-limit, for the purposes of expediting the trial and defining the issues.[211] The Trial Chamber had also ordered that witness statements be presented to the Chamber before trial, not as evidence but rather to enable the Chamber to familiarise itself with the case. Both parties were ordered to file pre-trial briefs and opening statements, and the defence was further ordered to file any alibi notice and a document 'setting out those points, if any, in the . . . indictment which are admitted, those which are denied and the grounds for so doing, and

[208] *Klopfer v. North Carolina*, 386 US 213 (1967). See also Hafida Lahiouel, 'The Right of the Accused to an Expeditious Trial', above n. 5.

[209] See e.g., *Firmenich v. Argentina*, before the Inter-American Court of Human Rights, Resolution 17/89, Report Case 10037 (13 April 1989); *Maznetter v. Austria*, before the ECtHR, (1969) 10 Eur Ct HR (Ser. A).

[210] For an early but still relevant discussion of the treatment of this issue by the Tribunal, see Patricia Wald and Jenny Martinez, 'Provisional Release at the ICTY: A Work in Progress' in Richard May et al. (eds.), *Essays on ICTY Procedure and Evidence In Honour of Gabrielle Kirk McDonald* (2001), 231.

[211] *Prosecutor v. Dokmanović*, 'Scheduling Order', Case No. IT-95-13a, 20 November 1997; 'Decision on Pre-Trial Motions', 21 January 1998; *Prosecutor v. Kovačević*, 'Scheduling Order', Case No. IT-97-24, 5 March 1998; *Prosecutor v. Aleksovski*, 'Scheduling Order', Case No. IT-95-14/1, 3 December 1997.

setting out in general terms the defence to the indictment', as well as any motions, by certain specified dates.[212]

The practice of seeking agreement on material issues, requiring production of witness summaries, statements and proposed exhibits in an effort to expedite trial proceedings was subsequently codified in Rules 65*ter*, 73*bis* and 73*ter* at the eighteenth plenary session in 1998.[213] This is now standard pre-trial practice before the ICTY, although the impact of the practice on the expedition of the trial process is questionable. The admission of written evidence in lieu of oral testimony under Rules 89(F) and 92*bis* has also been aimed at expediting the trial.[214]

The fervent desire to expedite trials at the ICTY appears to have developed out of a review process of the two *ad hoc* Tribunals, and has since gathered momentum. In 1998, the General Assembly of the UN asked the Secretary-General to conduct a review of the operation and functioning of the ICTY and ICTR.[215] The Secretary-General subsequently appointed a five-member expert group and, with the objective of 'enhancing the efficient use of the resources of the Tribunals', conferred a broad mandate on the Group.[216] The Expert Group ultimately made forty-six separate recommendations relating to trial and appellate proceedings; the administration of the Office of the Prosecutor, and in particular the investigation and indictment process; Chambers practices, and the management of administrative matters under the competence of the Registrar.[217]

The Expert Group encouraged the Judges of the Tribunals to exercise greater judicial control, both through the use of existing Rules and the creation of Rules to better facilitate this. The recommendations

212 Oral ruling made on 28 November 1997. The same approach was taken by Trial Chamber I in *Prosecutor v. Aleksovski*, above n. 133.

213 See Rule 73 bis (B) (i)(ii) and (iii) and (F), and Rule 73 ter (B) (i) and (ii) prior to their amendment at the twenty-first plenary in November 1999 (U.N. Doc. IT/32/Rev. 16).

214 For a discussion of these issues, see generally May and Wierda, above n. 5, Chapter VII; Patrick Robinson, 'Ensuring Fair and Expeditious Trials at the International Criminal Tribunal for the Former Yugoslavia', above n. 5; Gideon Boas, 'A Code of Evidence and Procedure for International Criminal Law? The Rules of the ICTY', above n. 110, 1; Patrick L. Robinson, 'Fair but Expeditious Trials', above n. 5, 169; Geoffrey Nice and Philippe Vallières-Roland, 'Procedural Innovations in War Crimes Trials', above n. 5, 111. These are matters that will be taken up at length in chapters two and three of this book.

215 GA Res. 53/212 (18 December 1998); GA Res. 53/213 (18 December 1998).

216 'Report of the Expert Group to Conduct a Review of the Effective operation and Functioning of the International Tribunal for the Former Yugoslavia and International Criminal Tribunal for Rwanda', UN Doc. A/54/634 (1999) ('Expert Group Report'). For a discussion of the Expert Group and its work, see Daryl A. Mundis, 'Improving the Operation and Functioning of the International Criminal Tribunals' (2000), 94 *American Journal of International Law* 759.

217 Daryl A. Mundis, above n. 216, 760.

concerning new Rule changes involved increasing the powers of judges to question counsel and witnesses, stopping irrelevant or repetitive testimony or questioning, and excluding witnesses whose testimony is cumulative or of no material value to resolving the disputed issues.[218] However, all of these powers existed at the time in Rules 65*ter*, 85(B) and 90(G),[219] and what was in fact required – and has been seen in incremental change evident in some Benches of the ICTY – is the exercise of greater judicial intervention. This is a concept which is traditionally more alien in many adversarial systems, whereas in the civil law tradition it is the Court that controls all aspects of the proceedings, including investigations, the conduct of the trial and questioning witnesses, among other matters.[220] However, a more tangible and manifest reason for non-intervention derives from the relative lack of confidence and inexperience of individual judges, some of whom have never presided over a criminal trial (or any trial).[221]

The Expert Group went on to recommend the greater use of written testimony,[222] judicial notice,[223] and stipulations between the parties on factual matters not in dispute.[224] Furthermore, the Expert Group recommended, with respect to the Office of the Prosecutor of the ICTY, that investigations be more focused on cases for which a realistic expectation of obtaining a conviction exists, and that the prosecution be 'trial ready' at the time at which indictments are issued.

A process ensued from the Expert Group's intervention, which led to the development of the Tribunal's troubled strategy for concluding its work expeditiously: the development of a 'completion strategy'. The Security Council itself had a considerable influence on this issue by issuing resolutions to the effect that the Tribunal should adopt all possible measures to complete investigations by the end of 2004, all trial activities at first instance by the end of 2008 and all work including appeals by the end

[218] Expert Group Report, above n. 216, recommendation 7.

[219] For a discussion of these matters, see Mundis, above n. 216, 764–5.

[220] See generally, Boas, 'A Code of Evidence and Procedure for International Criminal Law? The Rules of the ICTY', above n. 110, 19–27.

[221] Such is the nature of nomination and election of international law Judges. Article 13 of the Statute of the ICTY, for example, provides: 'The judges shall be persons of high moral character, impartiality and integrity who possess the qualifications required in their respective countries for appointment to the highest judicial offices. In the overall composition of the Chambers due account shall be taken of the experience of the judges in criminal law, international law, including international humanitarian law and human rights law.' The process has yielded many academics and diplomats without judicial experience.

[222] Expert Group Report, above n. 216, para. 88.

[223] Ibid. para. 85.

[224] Ibid. recommendation 10.

of 2010 – a timetable that cannot in fact be achieved.[225] This followed a proposal made by the President of the ICTY at the time, the former French Prosecutor Claude Jorda, and was probably his brainchild.[226] The Security Council resolutions caused the Tribunal to radically review its trial process and the Prosecutor to seek wholesale referral under Rule 11*bis* of lower-level cases to be tried in the region, most notably the State Court of Bosnia and Herzegovina. Rule 11*bis*, entitled 'Referral of the Indictment to Another Court', was adopted by the Tribunal as early as November 1997 but was revised on four separate occasions.[227] The process supporting this change of focus in the way the Tribunal was to discharge its considerable workload included a strange political process of ICTY-generated strengthening of the local courts of the region of the former Yugoslavia so that they were in a position to try lesser offenders.[228] In the first referral decision of the Tribunal, *Stanković*, revision of the Rule was said to be necessary 'in order to give effect to the broad strategy endorsed by the Security Council for the completion of all Tribunal trial activities at first instance by 2008'.[229] This completion strategy has been summarised in Security Council Resolution 1503 as 'concentrating on the prosecution of the most senior leaders suspected of being most responsible for crimes within the

[225] See Security Council Resolutions, S/RES/1503 (2003) and S/RES/1534 (2004). But see speech by President Pocar of the ICTY to the Security Council, 15 December 2005 (http://www.un.org/icty/pressreal/2005/speech/pocar-sc-051215.htm): 'In May 2005, my predecessor stated that it was definitely no longer feasible to envisage an end of all trial activity at the Tribunal by the end of 2008. This was due to the large number of indictees and fugitives who had arrived at the Tribunal since the last report, as well as the filing and confirmation of seven new or amended indictments by the Prosecution involving thirteen accused. He predicted that trials will have to run into 2009 . . . Six months later, I can only confirm that prediction. Whether the growing number of trials will conclude by the end of 2009 depends upon . . . [a number of] . . . factors.'

[226] 'Report on the Judicial Status of the International Criminal Tribunal for the Former Yugoslavia and the Prospects of Referring Certain Cases to National Courts', UN Doc. S/2002/678 (2002).

[227] In its original form, Rule 11*bis* provided for transfer of an accused from the Tribunal to the authorities of the State in which the accused was arrested. Transfer required an order from the Trial Chamber suspending the indictment pending the proceedings before the national courts. Such an order necessitated findings by the Trial Chamber that State authorities were prepared to prosecute the accused in their own courts and that it was appropriate in the circumstances for the courts of that State to exercise jurisdiction over the accused.

[228] For a discussion of the impact of the 'completion strategy', see Daryl A. Mundis, 'The Judicial Effects of the "Completion Strategies" on the Ad Hoc International Criminal Tribunals' (2005), 99 *American Journal of International law*, 142–58.

[229] *Prosecutor v. Stanković*, 'Decision on Referral of Case Under Rule 11*bis*' Case No. IT-96-23/2-PT, 17 May 2005, para. 2.

ICTY's jurisdiction and transferring cases involving those who may not bear this level of responsibility to competent national jurisdictions, as appropriate . . . '.[230] As a further measure to implement the terms of the Resolution, the Judges of the ICTY amended Rule 28 of its Rules so as to require any new indictments by the Prosecutor to be reviewed by the Bureau[231] to determine whether the indictment concerns 'the most senior leaders'.

It is clear that the expedition of trials and conclusion of the Tribunal's work are matters that have impacted greatly on the Tribunal's political and regulatory work. The 'completion strategy' has placed a significant restraint on the Tribunal's work and longevity. Political will to support the trials, and the essential financial support that flows therefrom, has been capped and the Tribunal is being required to conclude all of its important work in a matter of a few years – while maintaining judicial independence and focusing only on the forensic, not the political, aspects of the trials before it. The pressures of these sometimes conflicting goals are enormous. The impact, if any, on equality or overall fairness to the proceedings, is something that will have to be assessed in time.

Interestingly, one well respected former Appeals Chamber Judge had, on a number of occasions, felt obliged to dissent and to openly criticise his colleagues on the appellate Bench for what he considered a 'destruction of the rights of the accused enshrined in the Tribunal's Statute and in customary international law', caused by reversing or ignoring previously carefully considered interpretations of the law or procedural rules on the basis of an improper contemplation of the completion strategy.[232]

Perhaps apprehensive of Judge Hunt's criticism, or desirous of distancing himself from any conduct that might be consonant with it, Judge

[230] S/RES/1503 (2003). The Security Council further noted that referral of cases to the War Crimes Chamber of the Court of Bosnia and Herzegovina was an essential prerequisite to achieving the objectives of the completion strategy. See also, S/RES/1534 (2004); S/PRST/2004/28.

[231] The Bureau is a body consisting of the President, the Vice-President and the Presiding Judges of the Trial Chambers, which '[t]he President shall consult . . . on all major questions relating to the functioning of the Tribunal' (Rule 23(B)).

[232] See *Prosecutor v. Milošević*, 'Dissenting Opinion of Judge David Hunt on Admissibility of Evidence in Chief in the Form of Written Statements (Majority Decision Given 30 September 2003)', Case No. IT-02-54-AR73.4, 21 October 2003, paras. 20–2; *Prosecutor v. Nyiramasuhuko*, 'Decision in the Matter of Proceedings Under Rule 15*bis* (D), Dissenting Opinion of Judge David Hunt', Case No. ICTR-98-42-A15*bis*, 24 September 2003, para. 17.

Robinson in a subsequent joinder decision appended a Separate Opinion containing a clear statement on this matter:

> In principle, the Security Council resolution does not impose an obligation on the Tribunal to do anything other than adopt all reasonable measures to meet the deadlines set. Certainly, it is not to be interpreted as requiring the Chambers to exercise their judicial function in a manner that enables the Tribunal to meet the deadline, but breaches the fundamental principle of fairness in the trial process.[233]

The lack of critical attention to and analysis of Judge Hunt's opinions is distressing.[234] It is critical to the proper development and maintenance of international criminal justice that the international community be satisfied as to its lack of political or other improper motivation in its decision-making processes, particularly at the appellate level. The legitimate interest in international criminal trials being expeditious is a right shared by the accused and the international community. As will become apparent in the following analysis of the *Milošević* trial in this book, scrupulous attention to fair trial rights can have the effect of lengthening the trial. The stakeholders in an international criminal trial must accept that the breadth and nature of these trials require sufficient time to be prosecuted and determined fairly. Yet, a lack of prosecutorial preparation or focus can have an unnecessarily expansive effect on a trial, as can the insistence on charging and proceeding on a large number of offences and, indeed, a court's failure to appropriately control the proceedings. Achieving a balance between fairness and expedition is critical to achieving best practice in the conduct of complex international criminal trials. A detailed analysis of the *Milošević* trial will provide the basis upon which best practice in the conduct of complex international criminal trials can be developed.

Application and Interpretation of Human Rights by the ICTY

A crucial aspect of the fair trial rights embodied in the ICTY Statute and Rules is the manner in which they are interpreted. This issue, raised at the

233 *Prosecutor v. Popović et al.*, 'Decision on Motion for Joinder . . . Separate Opinion of Judge Patrick Robinson', Case No. IT-02-57-PT, IT-02-58-PT, IT-02-63-PT, IT-02-64-PT, IT-04-80-PT, IT-05-86-PT, 21 September 2005, para. 2.

234 A rare, if cautious, exception is found in Mundis, 'The Judicial Effects of the "Completion Strategies" on the Ad Hoc International Criminal Tribunals', above n. 154, 155–6. But see Larry D. Johnson, 'Another Perspective: Closing an International Criminal Tribunal While Maintaining International Human Rights Standards and Excluding Impunity' (2005), 99 *American Journal of International Law* 159.

commencement of this chapter, is an overarching issue that impacts crucially the conduct of international criminal proceedings. It is now well established in the jurisprudence of the *ad hoc* Tribunals that the Statutes of these tribunals, and the legal system they embody, are *sui generis.*[235] The Appeals Chamber in the ICTR *Kanyabashi* case stated that although the Statute is not a treaty, it is a *sui generis* legal instrument resembling a treaty:

> Adopted by the Security Council, an organ to which Member States of the United Nations have vested legal responsibility, the Statute shares with treaties fundamental similarities. Because the Vienna Convention codifies logical and practical norms that are consistent with domestic law, it is applicable under customary international law to international instruments which are not treaties. Thus recourse by analogy is appropriate to Article 31(1) of the Vienna Convention in interpreting the provisions of the Statute.'[236]

Judge Robinson's approach to the issue of interpretation of the Statute and its broader impact on contextual interpretation is informative:

> While Trial Chambers have affirmed the achievement of a fair and expeditious trial as a fundamental purpose of the Statute and the Rules, the fulfilment of this purpose cannot, however, be separated from the broader purpose and context in which the Tribunal operates, that is, the prosecution of persons responsible for serious violations of international humanitarian law in the former Yugoslavia. As such, the transposition of domestic legal practices to the International Tribunal must be effected in a manner that takes due account of the specific context in which the Tribunal operates. In this way, a purposive approach links up with a contextual approach. A comprehensive description of the interpretive task would, therefore, be the good faith ascertainment of the ordinary meaning of the terms of the Statute and Rules in light of the purpose of achieving a fair and expeditious

[235] See *Prosecutor v. Tadić*, 'Decision on the Prosecutor's Motion, Protective Measures for Victims and Witnesses', Case No. IT-94-1-T, 10 August 1995, 10; *Prosecutor v. Erdermović*, 'Joint Separate Opinion of Judge McDonald and Judge Vohrah to the Judgement', Case No. IT-96-22-A, 7 October 1999, para. 3; *Prosecutor v. Theoneste Bagasora and 28 Others*, 'Decision on the Admissibility of the Prosecutor's Appeal from the Decision of a Confirming Judge Dismissing an Indictment Against Theoneste Bagasora and 28 Others', Case No. ICTR-98-37-A, 8 June 1998; and, most recently, in *Prosecutor v. Milošević*, 'Separate Opinion of Judge Patrick Robinson' to 'Decision on Motion for Judgement of Acquittal', Case No. IT-02-54-T, 16 June 2004, para. 7.

[236] *Kanyabashi v. Prosecutor*, 'Joint and Separate Opinion of Judge McDonald and Judge Vohrah', Case No. ICTR-96-15-A, 3 June 1999, para. 15. See generally Patrick L. Robinson, 'Fair but Expeditious Trials', *Dynamics of International Criminal Justice.*

> trial of those accused of serious violations of international humanitarian law . . . This use of contextual interpretation of this sort raises many questions. Does it result in a quality of fairness in a trial before the Tribunal that is lower than that in a domestic criminal court? Does it affect the principle that human rights are universal? Does it result in the application of a principle of relativity in the Tribunal's dispensation of justice that breaches the fair trial requirements of international human rights instruments?[237]

Discussion about the universality of human rights versus contextuality can legitimately be dealt with in terms of an esoteric philosophical debate.[238] Indeed, Zappalà asserts that the extension of human rights principles to international criminal trials is a policy issue, rather than a legal one.[239] Safferling, meanwhile, examines the origin and meaning of 'human rights' in order to ascertain their application to international criminal law, acknowledging that the philosophical origins of human rights are difficult to ascertain and are derived from a conception of natural law, most frequently referred to as 'human dignity'.[240] However, as appropriate as these peregrinations are to human rights theory, the criminal law requires a practical and graspable approach to the question of fairness. In domestic systems of criminal law, principles of fairness have evolved often over hundreds of years, whereas the development of modern international criminal law is a mere decade old, really commencing with the advent of the ICTY. In this context, Judge Robinson's conclusion is rightly pragmatic and legally sound. He asserts that a contextual approach to interpretation of the Tribunal's Statute and Rules is not only reasonable, it is essential. While concluding that such an approach cannot

[237] Ibid. 572–3.

[238] See e.g., Hirad Abtahi, 'Reflections on the Ambiguous Universality of Human Rights: Cyrus the Great's Proclamation as a Challenge to the Athenian Democracy's Perceived Monopoly on Human Rights', in Abtahi and Boas, *Dynamics of International Criminal Justice*, 1.

[239] Salvatore Zappalà, *Human Rights*, 5.

[240] Christoph Safferling, *Criminal Procedure*, 36. Safferling proceeds to set out four different philosophical bases for the development of human rights: (1) the 'Communitarian view', whereby human rights are derived as inherited ways of life and grown communities (based on Aristotle); (2) 'political liberalism, whereby basic rights derive from a social contract (based on Rawls); (3) 'discourse theory, whereby human rights are the pre-conditions for communication, resulting from a self-legislation where all free and equal parties conceive of each other as common creators of law to which each are bound (based on Habermas), and (4) the 'cosmopolitan view', whereby human rights are understood as basic rights in a world-state. Cf Salvatore Zappalà, *Human Rights*, who refers to the earliest evolution of a fair trial and due process rights being found in the Magna Carta of 1215; and, Hirad Abtahi, 'Universality of Human Rights', who traces the evolution of human rights principles back to the Proclamation of Cyrus the Great of 538 BCE.

be used to nullify rights which attach to an accused under customary international law, and does not prevent appropriate comparative law analysis, 'the Statute and Rules should be seen as establishing a legal system that is self-contained and comprehensive, and capable of providing answers to any question that arises in the work of the Tribunal . . . [the test being] whether the solution is consistent with a fair and expeditious trial'.[241]

Human rights impact upon and interact with the legal operation of the international criminal tribunals in a number of different ways. The application of the human rights provisions set out in the Statute and Rules are an obvious example. The Secretary-General's Report, approved by the Security Council in establishing the ICTY can be considered an authoritative interpretation of the ICTY Statute, for reasons set out at the commencement of this chapter. Finally, human rights principles which have attained the status of customary international law or general principles of international law may or should be binding on the international tribunals and their activities.[242] However, real difficulty lies in the interpretation of the nature and content of these principles and customs and their application to Tribunal decision-making.

The jurisprudence of international criminal tribunals is, in fact, a rich source of reaffirmation of the proposition that because of their unique structure in international law, and the nature of the subject-matter they deal with, international human rights principles are not applicable in the same way as they are to domestic jurisdictions.[243] One commentator raises some relevant concerns over the contextual approach adopted by the ICTY:

> By justifying departure from universal principles recognised by the international community, it is arguable that the Tribunal establishes a hierarchy of law to which those universal norms can be subverted. It also fragments the idea of an international community by distinguishing the internal legal order of States from the international legal order – a distinction that human rights law had hitherto denied . . . However, more importantly from the perspective of the Tribunal, by adopting a contextual

[241] Patrick L. Robinson, 'Fair but Expeditious Trials', 573.

[242] See e.g., Goran Sluiter, 'Symposium: The ICTY at Ten: A Critical Assessment of the Major Rulings of the International Criminal Tribunal Over the Past Decade: International Criminal Proceedings and the Protection of Human Rights' (2003), 37 *New England Law Review* 935.

[243] See *Prosecutor v Tadić*, 'Decision on Defence Motion for Interlocutory Appeal on Jurisdiction', Case No. IT-94-1-AR72, 2 October 1995.

approach the Tribunal raises questions about its legality as a functioning legal institution.[244]

The Tribunal has had to confront the application of human rights principles to its work in a number of ways. Often this has led to judicial determinations that are consistent with the interpretation of fair trial rights before the human rights regime.[245]

However, there are several areas in which the Tribunal has wrestled with the application of human-rights principles to its work which have been more difficult to resolve. Article 14(1) of the ICCPR requires that '[i]n the determination of any criminal charge against him, or of his rights and obligations in a suit at law, everyone shall be entitled to a fair and public hearing by a competent, independent and impartial tribunal established by law'. In the first case before the ICTY, the accused, Tadić, argued that the Tribunal had not, in fact, been 'established by law' in accordance with the ICCPR, and that the Tribunal should have been created by treaty or amendment to the Charter of the UN, not by a Resolution of the Security Council.[246] Unhelpfully, the Trial Chamber initially decided it could not determine the problem[247] – the decision to create the ICTY having been made by the Security Council – and in so deciding effectively rendered the issue of the legality of the Tribunal's creation non-justiciable. The Appeals Chamber did deal with the issue, holding that, for a tribunal such as the ICTY to be established according to the rule of law, it must be established 'in accordance with the proper international standards; it must provide all the guarantees of fairness, justice and even-handedness, in full conformity with internationally recognized human rights instruments'.[248] The Appeals Chamber, unsurprisingly, did find that the Tribunal had been established by law.[249] In the *Milošević* case,

244 Gabrielle McIntyre, 'Defining Human Rights', 194. See also Maya Steinitz, 'The Milošević Trial – Live! An Iconical Analysis of International Law's Claim of Legitimate Authority' (2005), 3 *Journal of International Criminal Justice* 103.

245 See for a general discussion, May and Wierda, *International Criminal Evidence*; Zappalà, *Human Rights*.

246 *Prosecutor v. Tadić*, 'Decision on the Defence Motion on Jurisdiction in the Trial Chamber of the International Tribunal', Case No. IT-94-1-PT, 10 August 1995. The argument has re-emerged throughout the Tribunal's existence. It even emerged in questioning by Milošević of the witness (and Accused in his own proceedings), Vojislav Šešelj, in his trial: 16 September 2005, transcript p. 44262–263, 44270.

247 *Prosecutor v. Tadić*, 'Decision on the Defence Motion on Jurisdiction', Case No. IT-94–1-T, 10 August 1995, para. 40.

248 Ibid. para. 45.

249 *Prosecutor v. Tadić*, 'Decision on Defence Motion for Interlocutory Appeal on Jurisdiction', Case No. IT-94-1-AR72, 2 October 1995, paras. 28–40.

the Trial Chamber was asked to reconsider the arguments raised by Tadić in his application challenging jurisdiction.[250] The Trial Chamber held that, while it was willing to reconsider the *Tadić* arguments, it was satisfied, on the basis of the Appeals Chamber's holding that 'the establishment of the International Tribunal falls squarely within the powers of the Security Council under Article 41 [of the UN Charter]',[251] that it was established by law. Furthermore, the Chamber held that the Tribunal genuinely afforded the accused the full guarantees of fair trial set out in Article 14 of the ICCPR and without much further consideration of the issue, dismissed Milošević's application.

The application of human rights principles to international criminal proceedings before the ICTY, including the fair trial rights set out in the ICCPR, has been a matter of some confusion. Early on, again in a decision in the *Tadić* case, the Trial Chamber held that it was not bound by universally established human rights principles as interpreted by the HRC or the ECtHR,[252] and suggested that the ICTY is 'more akin to a military tribunal which often has limited rights of due process and more lenient rules of evidence'.[253] In light of subsequent developments in the use of military tribunals by the US Government,[254] this early approach by the Tribunal is one that has a disturbing ring to it, and it is an analogy the Court would likely have the courage to draw today. The Appeals Chamber, hearing an appeal in an ICTR case four years later, tempered and clarified the position somewhat:

> The Report of the Secretary-General establishes the sources of law for the Tribunal. The ICCPR is part of general international law and is applied on

[250] *Prosecutor v. Milošević*, 'Preliminary Protective Motion', Case No. IT-99-37-PT, 9 August 2001. The arguments of the accused were set out in an untitled supporting document filed on 30 August 2001; '*Amici* Brief on Jurisdiction', 19 October 2001.

[251] *Prosecutor v. Milošević*, 'Decision on Preliminary Motions', Case No. IT-99-37-PT, 8 November 2001, para. 36.

[252] *Prosecutor v. Tadić*, 'Decision on the Prosecutor's Motion Requesting Protective Measures for Victims and Witnesses', Case No. IT-94-1-T, 10 August 1995.

[253] Ibid. paras. 27–8.

[254] See generally, Wayne McCormack, 'Military Detention and the Judiciary: Al Qaeda, the Kkk and Supra-State Law' (2004) 5 *San Diego International Law Journal* 7; Laura A. Dickinson, 'Transitional Justice in Afghanistan: The Promise of Mixed Tribunals' (2002) 31 *Denver Journal of International Law and Policy* 23; Kenneth Anderson, 'The Military Tribunal Order: What to Do with Bin Laden and Al Qaeda Terrorists? A Qualified Defense of Military Commissions and United States Policy on Detainees at Guantanamo Bay Naval Base (2002) 25 *Harvard Journal of Law & Public Policy* 591; Joan Fitzpatrick, 'Jurisdiction of Military Commissions and the Ambiguous War on Terrorism' (2002) 96 *American Journal of International Law* 345; Ruth Wedgwood, 'Al Qaeda, Terrorism, and Military Commissions' (2002) 96 *American Journal of International Law* 328; Daryl A. Mundis, 'Military Commissions: The Use of Military Commissions to Prosecute Individuals Accused of Terrorist Acts' (2002) 96 *American Society of International Law* 320.

> that basis. Regional human rights treaties, such as the European Convention on Human Rights and the American Convention on Human Rights and the jurisprudence developed thereunder, are persuasive authority which may be of assistance in applying and interpreting the Tribunal's applicable law. Thus, they are not binding of their own accord on the Tribunal. They are however authoritative as evidence of international custom.[255]

Other areas in which the application of fair trial issues to the ICTY have given rise to some confusion are the right to challenge lawfulness of arrest,[256] as well as undue delay and provisional release.[257] The position is well summed up by one commentator:

> It is apparent that the Tribunal is ambiguous about how to define its obligations under universal human rights principles as stipulated in the Secretary-General's Report . . . However, although asserting in the *Tadić* Protective Measures Decision that it had a right to adopt a contextual approach to the interpretation of universal human rights principles, the jurisprudence of the Tribunal shows that it is uncomfortable about its departures from interpretations of those principles by the human rights regime . . . As a consequence, instead of embracing the view that human rights are contextual principles, and reasoning persuasively as to why a different interpretation of human rights is warranted by the context of the Tribunal, the Tribunal often betrays in its jurisprudence an ambivalence to this issue. Claims that it adheres to the interpretation of human rights by the human rights regimes, where its framework is clearly incompatible with their requirements, discredits the legitimate interpretation of human rights . . . By taking a contextual approach to the application of human rights principles and setting the parameters for doing so, the Tribunal would make a considerable contribution to establishing how

[255] *Barayagwiza v. Prosecutor*, 'Decision', Case ICTR-97-19-AR72, 3 November 1999, para. 40.

[256] See Thomas Henquet, 'Accountability for Arrests: The Relationship between the ICTY and NATO's NAC and SFOR', in Boas and Schabas, above n. 38, 113; Susan Lamb, 'The Powers of Arrest of the International Criminal Tribunal for the Former Yugoslavia' (1999) 70 *British Yearbook of International Law* 165, 230–1; Michael Scharf, 'Prosecutor v. Slavko Dokmanović: Irregular Rendition and the ICTY' (1998) 11 *LJIL*, 376; Goran Sluiter, 'Commentary to Prosecutor v. Mrksić et al., Decision on Motion for Release by the Accused Slavko Dokmanović', in André Klip and Göran Sluiter (eds.), *I Annotated Leading Cases of International Tribunals* (1999), 151, 153.

[257] Gabrielle McIntyre, 'Defining Human Rights'; Patrick L. Robinson, 'Ensuring Fair and Expeditious Trials at the International Criminal Tribunal for the Former Yugoslavia'; Patrick L. Robinson, 'Fair but Expeditious Trials', above n. 5. See especially Dissenting Opinion of Judge Patrick Robinson in *Prosecutor v. Krajišnik and Plavšić*.

human rights are to be properly established within international criminal trials.[258]

The conclusion to this issue probably lies in the approach set out by Judge Robinson. If it is accepted that international criminal law, and the individual instruments which control its judicial institutions, are *sui generis*, then it cannot be assumed that the human rights regime automatically applies *in toto*. The application of these principles, the human rights instruments encapsulating them and the jurisprudence explaining them are, as generally accepted in the jurisprudence of the international tribunals, persuasive. But they are not, contrary to the impression given by occasional Tribunal decisions, binding. It is clear that international criminal law must, in its development and application, strictly adhere to the rights of accused persons that are fundamental to the achievement of a fair and expeditious trial. But this must be done in the context of its underlying philosophy, as well as the practical environment in which it operates. Undoubtedly, failure to do so will only lead to an undermining of its aim and purpose and, speedily, to a loss of the political and therefore financial will of the international community to support its development and sustainability.

Of course, such an approach is not uncontroversial. Even within the judiciary of the ICTY itself, there have been expressions of concern or dissent with a contextual approach to the application of human rights to international criminal law. Judge Mumba, in the context of considering how to balance the protection of witnesses with the right of the accused to a fair trial, noted that while in the *Tadić* case the Appeals Chamber had held that the ICTY Statute and its sources must be interpreted in the context of the 'object and purpose' and unique characteristics of the Statute, she favourably considered a decision in the *Delalić* case supporting the strict application of human rights principles as interpreted in the human rights regime.[259] The first President of the ICTY, Antonio Cassese, has also stated (albeit at a time before the contextual interpretation model had really developed) that the ICTY endeavours to fully apply inter-

258 Gabrielle McIntyre, above n. 71, 237–8.

259 Florence Mumba, 'Ensuring a Fair trial whilst Protecting Victims and Witnesses – Balancing of Interests?' in Richard May *et al.* (eds.), *Essays in Honour of Judge McDonald*, 363, citing *Prosecutor v. Delalic and Others*, 'Decision on the Motions by the Prosecutor for Protective Measures for the Prosecution Witnesses pseudonymed "B" through "M"', Case No. IT-96-21-T, 28 April 1997, para. 27. Judge Mumba does, however, accept that in interpreting the Statute and human rights instruments, may take into account the unique situation of the Tribunal.

national human rights standards relating to the accused, victims and witnesses in criminal trials. He cautioned against 'derogations from human rights obligations' (now clearly accepted in international criminal law jurisprudence) although he acknowledged that it was necessary to 'find novel solutions to protect the interests at stake'.[260]

Furthermore, it may be argued that the view that human rights attach to individuals and, as such, cannot be conveniently altered or derogated from except to the extent provided for in the relevant human rights treaties in which they are defined,[261] renders a contextual interpretation unacceptable. However, for several reasons it is asserted that this position is unsustainable. For a start, the Tribunal exercises its jurisdiction over individuals, while the human rights regime is concerned with the behaviour of States towards its nationals. Furthermore, as McIntyre argues, states parties under the human rights regime are already accorded a measure of flexibility in their adherence,[262] and the ECtHR has developed its own form of contextual approach with yardstick concepts such as the 'margin of appreciation' by which it defers to the specificities of the national jurisdiction.[263] Further support for this proposition is found in the context of the International Court of Justice in the *Nuclear Weapons* case.[264] Finally, international criminal courts and tribunals now routinely interpret the fair trial rights of accused persons derived from the human rights regime in a contextual manner and do so with increasing clarity and consistency.

Human rights are principles that can only have meaning in context, and this is certainly true of their application to and interpretation in international criminal law. The difficulty lies in defining appropriately and

[260] Antonio Cassese, 'The International Criminal Tribunal for the former Yugoslavia and Human Rights' (1997) 4 *European Human Rights Law Review* 329, 336. See also James Sloan, 'The International Criminal Tribunal for the Former Yugoslavia and Fair Trial Rights: A Closer Look' (1996) 9 *Leiden Journal of International Law* 475; Caroline Buisman, 'Defence and Fair Trial', in Roelof Haveman, Olga Kavran, Julian Nicholls, *Supranational Criminal Law: A System Sui Generis* (2003), 167, 181ff.

[261] See e.g., Louis Henkin, Gerald L. Neuman, Diane Orentlicher, and David W. Leebron, *Human Rights* (1999), 3.

[262] Gabrielle McIntyre, 'Defining Human Rights', 200.

[263] Ibid. References to *Handyside v. United Kingdom*, (1976) 24 Eur Court HR (ser. A) 22; *Rasmussen v. Denmark*, (1984) 87 Eur Court HR (ser. A) 15.

[264] *Legality of the Threat or Use of Nuclear Weapons (Request by the United Nations General Assembly for an Advisory Opinion)* [1996] ICJ Rep 226 (in response to an argument that the use of nuclear weapons would violate the 'right to life' guarantee of Article 6 of the ICCPR, the ICJ reasoned that 'whether a particular loss of life through the use of a certain weapon in warfare is to be considered an arbitrary deprivation of life could only be decided by reference to the law applicable in armed conflict and not deduced from the terms of the Covenant itself).

consistently what that contextual application entails in terms of the applicability of human rights in the relevant context. International criminal law has developed evolving jurisprudence which reasons well the application of human rights principles by reference to international and regional human rights courts and bodies and domestic criminal courts in different legal systems. A consistent and coherent approach will, and already has, defined international criminal law as a solid and well-founded system of law that respects fundamental rights and norms.[265] This has led to the creation and definition of a comprehensible and binding normative framework for the conduct of international criminal trials, which is the context in which this book proceeds.

[265] See generally Theodor Meron, 'Editorial Comment: Revival of Customary Humanitarian law' (2005) 99 *AJIL* 817; Mohamed Shahabuddeen, 'Does the Principle of Legality Stand in the Way of Progressive Development of the Law' (2004) 2 *Journal of International Criminal Justice* 1007; Christopher Greenwood, 'Command Responsibility and the *Hadžihazanović* Decision' (2004) 2 *Journal of International Criminal Justice* 598.

2

The Miloševič Prosecution Case: Getting Off on the Wrong Foot

In the adversarial context of international criminal law, the role of the prosecution is extremely significant. It is the prosecution that conducts investigations, makes decisions about who to indict, and prepares the indictments which determine the scope and structure of the case.[1] The purpose of this chapter is to examine the prosecution approach to the *Milošević* case, which will assist in determining criteria for best practice in the conduct of complex international criminal trials. Important strategic and policy areas of the prosecution case in *Milošević* were far from best practice, and seriously threatened the fair and expeditious trial framework within which international criminal trials are conducted. The prosecution approach to its case was zealous and overly expansive, creating a trial that was unmanageably complex and long. The factors which contributed to this are discussed, as are some of the considerations which motivated the prosecution to approach its case in this way. There are tensions and competing interests in the presentation of such a case, which encompass forensic, historical, political and sociological issues. The prosecution, while seeking in good faith to satisfy the interests it considered significant, made it impossible to conduct an expeditious trial and put at risk its fairness, requirements that are not only the responsibility of the court but also – to a lesser extent – the responsibility of a prosecutor in international criminal proceedings.

This chapter commences with an examination of the three indictments against the accused. Exploring the prosecution case against Milošević is important to an understanding of its scope and the nature

[1] See e.g. Articles 16, 18, 19 of the ICTY Statute; Articles 15, 17, 18 of the ICTR Statute; Part 5 of the ICC Statute; Articles 15, 16 of the SCSL Statute. See also Michael J. Keegan and Daryl A. Mundis, 'Legal Requirements for Indictments' in Richard May *et al.* (eds.), *Essays on ICTY Procedure and Evidence In Honour of Gabrielle Kirk McDonald* (2001), 123; Judge David Hunt, 'The Meaning of a "*prima facie* case" for the Purposes of Confirmation', in Richard May *et al.* (eds.), *Essays on ICTY Procedure and Evidence In Honour of Gabrielle Kirk McDonald* (2001), 137.

of complex cases involving senior officials in international criminal law. An analysis of the prosecution indictments reveals significant defects. The Croatia and Bosnia indictments were issued in haste shortly after the arrival of the accused, suggesting a case strategy that was reactive rather than well planned and executed. All the indictments, and in particular the Kosovo indictment, reveals some significant deficiencies. Furthermore, the prosecution case concerning Milošević's espousal of a policy of a Greater Serbia is discussed in the context of the prosecution case so as to better understand its approach and the overall effect of this on the length and complexity of the case. I examine the pleading requirements for indictments before the ICTY and the indictment review process in this and other cases. Then I review in some detail the relevant content of the three *Milošević* indictments. I explore the prosecution application for joinder of the three separate indictments into one case spanning three conflicts over eight years, all tied together by the prosecution's theory that these matters covered a single transaction under the umbrella of the creation of a Greater Serbia. Finally, I analyse the decision of the Trial Chamber on the motion for judgement of acquittal filed on behalf of the accused by (then) *amici curiae* in the case. This Decision is important because it exposed the extent to which the prosecution failed to or did not seek to establish over one-thousand allegations contained in the indictments. The Decision also clarified some attendant legal issues in the trial revealing the scope of the case and is important as the only pre-Judgement determinative ruling of the Chamber on the case.

Content and Scope of the Miloševič Indictments

There were three operative indictments in the *Milošević* case, relating chronologically to Croatia, Bosnia and Kosovo. The Appeals Chamber, in its decision to join these indictments, stated that although the three indictments had been drafted, reviewed, and confirmed separately, they should be treated as a single indictment against the accused for the purpose of the case.[2]

[2] *Prosecutor v. Milošević*, 'Decision on Prosecution Interlocutory Appeal From Refusal to Order Joinder', Case No. IT-99-37-AR73, IT-01-50-AR73, IT-01-51-AR73, 1 February 2002 ('Appeal Joinder Ruling'); *Prosecutor v. Milošević*, 'Reasons for Decision on Prosecution Interlocutory Appeal From Refusal to Order Joinder', Case No. IT-99-37-AR73, IT-01-50-AR73, IT-01-51-AR73, 18 April 2002 ('Appeal Joinder Decision')

The Kosovo indictment

The prosecution case concerning Kosovo

The first indictment issued against Milošević concerned events in Kosovo. On 24 May 1999, Judge Hunt confirmed the indictment against Milošević and four others concerning events in Kosovo.[3] On 29 June 2001, the Prosecution submitted a proposed amended indictment; the Trial Chamber approved it the same day.[4] On 3 July 2001, the accused made his initial appearance for this indictment and the Trial Chamber entered a plea of 'not guilty' in relation to all counts against him. On 29 October 2001, the Trial Chamber orally granted leave to amend the indictment again.[5]

The indictment alleged that Milošević was criminally responsible for crimes against humanity, war crimes and violations of the laws or customs of war, in that he (together with named and unnamed others) 'planned, instigated, ordered, committed' or 'otherwise aided and abetted in the planning, preparation or execution' of the crimes. The indictment asserted that the reference to 'committing' referred to participation in a joint criminal enterprise as a co-perpetrator, the purpose of the criminal enterprise being to expel a substantial proportion of the Kosovo Albanian population from the province.[6] The joint criminal enterprise was said to have come into existence by October 1998 and continued throughout the period of the crimes (1 January–20 June 1999).[7] It also alleged that the various crimes were within the object of the criminal enterprise or, in the case of the murders and persecutions, were the natural and foreseeable consequence of it; the accused was aware that the crimes were the likely outcome of the enterprise; and, despite this awareness of the foreseeable consequences, knowingly and wilfully participated in the joint criminal enterprise.[8]

[3] *Prosecutor v. Milošević*, 'Decision on Review of Indictment and Application for Consequential Orders', Case No. IT-99-37-PT, 24 May 1999.

[4] *Prosecutor v. Milošević*, 'Decision on Application to Amend Indictment and on Confirmation of Amended Indictment', 29 June 2001 (granting leave to amend the original indictment by substituting for it the proposed amended indictment, which is annexed to the Motion of 29 June 2001; and confirming the amended indictment). See also, 'Corrigendum', 2 July 2001 (correcting footnote two of the above Decision to read 'Motion to Substitute Proposed Amended Indictment, 29 June 2001').

[5] *Prosecutor v. Milošević*, Hearing, 29 October 2001, Transcript, 69. The indictment can be found in Attachment A to *Prosecutor v. Milošević*, 'Motion for Leave to File a Second Amended Indictment', Case No. IT-99-37-PT, 16 October 2001. This decision confirmed that the Second Amended Indictment was the operative indictment for the Kosovo part of the case. The final version of the indictment will be referred to hereafter as the 'Kosovo indictment'.

[6] Kosovo indictment, para. 16.

[7] Ibid. para. 17.

[8] Ibid. para. 18.

The indictment further alleged that the accused, while holding a position of superior authority, was responsible for the acts of his subordinates under Article 7(3) of the Statute.[9] As the President of the Federal Republic of Yugoslavia (FRY),[10] he was also president of the Supreme Defence Council which issued decisions concerning the Yugoslav Army (VJ); he was supreme commander of the VJ in war and peace, and as such, under the FRY Law on Defence, exercised command over the federal and republic police units subordinated to the VJ during the state of war which was proclaimed on 24 March 1999.[11] The indictment also alleged that the accused exercised *de facto* control over numerous federal and republican institutions and aspects of political and economic life, particularly the media; and was the primary interlocutor with whom the international community negotiated.[12] As President of the FRY, Supreme Commander of the VJ, President of the Supreme Defence Council and pursuant to his *de facto* authority, Milošević was also said to be responsible for the actions of his subordinates within the VJ and police, or alternatively to be criminally responsible for their actions as a superior.[13]

In its Kosovo pre-trial brief,[14] the prosecution explained that Milošević's criminal responsibility revolved around a campaign of ethnic cleansing in Kosovo, during which between 600,000 and 800,000 Kosovo Albanians were expelled from their homes and deported. In addition, hundreds of thousands of Kosovo Albanians were said to have been expelled from their homes and internally displaced.[15] This programme of ethnic cleansing was alleged to have been carried out against Kosovo Albanians based on their ethnicity and religion, as a part of a campaign of terror and violence, including murders, sexual assaults, beatings and other physical and psychological abuse of Kosovo Albanians, as well as the destruction of cultural and religious sites.[16]

The prosecution submitted that the constitutional structure of the FRY and Republic of Serbia made Milošević responsible for the VJ and the implementation of decisions by the Supreme Defence Council (composed

[9] Ibid. paras. 19, 28.

[10] Upon the break up of the Socialist Federal Republic of Yugoslavia, the remaining confederation of Serbia and Montenegro was reconstituted in 1992 as the Federal Republic of Yugoslavia. In 2002, Serbia and Montenegro came to a new agreement regarding continued co-operation. In February 2003, the federal parliament of Yugoslavia created a commonwealth of Serbia and Montenegro called Serbia and Montenegro.

[11] Ibid. paras. 21 and 22. [12] Ibid. paras. 23–6. [13] Ibid.

[14] *Prosecutor v. Milošević*, 'Prosecution's Pre-Trial Brief Pursuant to Rule 65*ter*(E)(i)', Case No. IT-99-37, 26 November 2001 (hereafter referred to as the 'Kosovo pre-trial brief'). [15] Ibid. para. 3. [16] Ibid.

of the Presidents of Serbia, Montenegro and the FRY).[17] The President of the FRY was said to command the VJ in peace and war, pursuant to Supreme Defence Council decisions, and in a state of emergency (including a state of war, which existed during the indictment period) as well as those units of the Serbian Ministry of Internal Affairs (MUP) which are subordinated to the VJ. This was the foundation for its case that Milošević had *de facto* responsibility for the crimes charged in respect of the armed forces and subordinated organs in the Kosovo indictment.[18] It also explains why Milošević spent so much time in his defence leading evidence on the formal military and chain of command structures, and seeking to establish that they had been properly followed and therefore that the alleged crimes could not have been committed by the forces of the governmental authorities.[19] He was also alleged to have wielded *de facto* authority by circumventing official chains of command for the VJ and the MUP by, for example, issuing orders directly to senior political and military officials under his control or influence, including General Pavković (commander of the 3rd Army of the VJ) and General Lukić (head of the MUP), or through Šainović (Deputy Prime Minister of the FRY) and to the VJ and MUP in Kosovo.[20]

The indictment alleged that an ethnically pure region was sought, which was part of the accused's plan to create a Greater Serbia. To achieve this, the accused – by way of either a criminal enterprise with, or command of, the Serb political and military structures – is said to have committed crimes, including persecutions, murder, detention, deportation or forcible transfer, rape, inhumane treatment, wanton destruction, and plunder of public and private property.[21]

B The Croatia and Bosnia indictments

On 8 October 2001, Judge Rodrigues confirmed the initial Croatia indictment against Milošević.[22] On 29 October 2001, the accused made his initial appearance for this indictment and the Trial Chamber entered a plea of 'not guilty' to all counts against him. On 4 November 2002, the

[17] Ibid. paras. 36–7. [18] Ibid. paras. 37.

[19] See, e.g., testimony of General Božidar Delić, 7 July 2005, Transcript, 42008; General Obrad Stevanović, 18 May 2005, Transcript, 39668; Colonel Vlatko Vuković, 27 October 2005, Transcript, 45849. [20] Kosovo pre-trial brief, above n. 14, para. 48.

[21] See Kosovo indictment, para. 16.

[22] *Prosecutor v. Milošević*, 'Order Confirming An Indictment', Case No. IT-01-50, 8 October 2001.

Trial Chamber granted the prosecution leave to amend the Croatia indictment, and later clarified that this amended instrument would be the operative indictment for purposes of the Croatia phase of the proceedings.[23]

On 22 November 2001, Judge May confirmed the Bosnia indictment against Milošević.[24] On 11 December 2001, the accused made his initial appearance for this indictment and the Trial Chamber entered a plea of 'not guilty' on all counts in the indictment. The Trial Chamber granted the prosecution leave to amend the Bosnia indictment and confirmed that the operative Bosnia indictment was the Amended Bosnia Indictment, dated 22 November 2002.[25]

The prosecution case concerning Croatia and Bosnia

The Trial Chamber denied an early prosecution application to join the three indictments, while allowing the joinder of the Croatia and Bosnia indictments into one case, with the intention of conducting the Kosovo case first. Although the Appeals Chamber subsequently granted the prosecution motion to join all three indictments, because these conflicts were temporally and geographically co-related and because they emerged from the break-up of the Socialist Federal Republic of Yugoslavia (SFRY), which pre-dated the dissolution of Yugoslavia, it makes sense to examine the case concerning Croatia and Bosnia together.

(a) The context in which the crimes were committed The prosecution alleged that from 1991 to 1995, Milošević, Croatian and Bosnian Serb leaders, high-ranking members of the Yugoslav National Army (JNA) and the MUP, along with other leading Serbian and Montenegrin figures, were key participants in the formulation, preparation and execution of a plan

[23] *Prosecutor v. Milošević*, 'Order Granting Leave To Amend The Croatia Indictment', Case No. IT-02-54-T, 4 November 2002. The sole change to the initial Croatia indictment was a reduction in the allegations contained in paragraph 36 dealing with the charge of persecution pursuant to Article 5(h) of the ICTY Statute. On 28 July 2004, the Trial Chamber issued its 'Order Modifying Second Order Granting Leave to Amend the Croatia Indictment', confirming that the second amended indictment was the operative indictment for the Croatia part of the case (hereafter referred to as the 'Croatia indictment').

[24] *Prosecutor v. Milošević*, 'Decision on Review of Indictment', Case No. IT-01-51, 22 November 2001.

[25] The Indictment can be found in Annex A of *Prosecutor v. Milošević*, 'Prosecution Motion to Amend the Bosnia Indictment with Confidential Annex B', Case No. IT-02-54-T, 22 November 2002. The status of this indictment as the operative indictment for the Bosnia case was explicitly confirmed in *Prosecutor v. Milošević*, 'Order on the Amended Bosnia Indictment', Case No. IT-02-54-T, 21 April 2004. The final version of the indictment will be referred to hereafter as the 'Bosnia indictment'.

to impose and maintain Serb control over targeted regions of the former Yugoslavia by forcibly removing Muslim, Croat, Albanian and other non-Serb inhabitants through persecutory campaigns.[26]

The prosecution alleged that Milošević exerted substantial influence over the Croatian and Bosnian Serb leaders, as well as over the leadership of the JNA, the VJ, the Republic of Serbia MUP, and several paramilitary groups.[27] According to the prosecution, not only did Milošević have communications with a number of these leaders, mainly Radovan Karadžić, but he was also given authority to represent the interests of the Bosnian Serbs and make commitments on behalf of their leadership.[28]

According to the prosecution, realising that an explicit policy of Serb unification would not be accepted by the international community or by the JNA, nationalist Serb politicians characterised their objective as the preservation of Yugoslavia, while in fact accelerating its demise.[29] Milošević and his co-conspirators are said to have embarked on two parallel paths of action designed to allow the formation of a Serb-dominated State. The first involved gaining control over the institutions of the federal government, in particular the JNA.[30] The second aimed at creating an independent Serbian armed force by transforming the JNA into the army of Serbia.[31]

Starting around mid-March 1991, senior officers of the Serbian MUP formed, trained, armed, co-ordinated and in some cases co-opted a wide array of Serbian armed groups – both special forces of the MUP and paramilitary units – in Croatia, Bosnia and Serbia proper.[32] Milošević is said to have supported and exercised influence over these groups in numerous ways, and continued doing so long after becoming aware of serious crimes that they committed.[33]

The prosecution alleged that the political structures for implementation of the plan were first set up in targeted areas of Croatia. This began in 1990 with the first 'association of municipalities' regrouping six municipalities in northern Dalmatia and Lika, and continued through other parts of Croatia: Slavonia, Baranja, Western Srem, and Western Slavonia.[34] From that point on, these associations of municipalities were transformed into 'Serb Autonomous Regions' (SAOs), holding referenda on 'joining Serbia and remaining in Yugoslavia', with the JNA intervening in favour of the Serb movements.[35] The Bosnian Serbs were alleged to have first

[26] *Prosecutor v. Milošević*, 'Prosecution's Second Pre-Trial Brief (Croatia and Bosnia Indictments)', Case No. IT-02-54-T, 31 May 2002 (hereafter referred to as the 'Croatia and Bosnia pre-trial brief'), paras. 1–4. [27] Ibid. para. 9. [28] Ibid. para. 39.
[29] Ibid. para. 15. [30] Ibid. para. 19. [31] Ibid. para. 20. [32] Ibid. para. 21.
[33] Ibid. para. 21. [34] Ibid. para. 22. [35] Ibid. paras. 22–3.

formed the communities of municipalities in three regions of Bosnia and then, progressively, transformed them into SAOs.[36] The establishment of the Serbian Assembly was followed by the proclamation of the Serbian Republic of Bosnia, a constitution and a declaration of independence.[37] The creation of the Bosnian Serb Army (VRS) ensued and was said to be another feature of the statehood sought by Bosnian Serbs.[38]

(b) Executing the plan According to the prosecution, from the formation of the Socialist Party of Serbia (SPS) and its first victory in December 1990 to its defeat in September–October 2000, Milošević enjoyed *de facto* power within the Republic of Serbia and the SFRY and thereafter the FRY, through the SPS, since that party was either the ruling or majority party in coalition governments.[39] From its inception, the SPS called for a 'Serbian nation on the territories where it constitutes the majority population', to be achieved through 'deciding to remain in a common Yugoslav state'.[40] After serving as a member of the collective presidency of the Socialist Republic of Serbia, Milošević was elected President of the Republic of Serbia on 8 December 1990 and served in that office until 23 July 1997.[41] In that position, he is said to have commanded the armed forces in peace and war, but also to have had legal authority over the police and other personnel of the MUP in some cases.[42]

Furthermore, according to the prosecution, the President of Montenegro was the political ally of Milošević.[43] Under the Constitution of 1974, the FRY Presidency was composed of eight members (six republics and the two autonomous provinces), it had supreme command over the armed forces, which included the JNA, the Territorial Defence (TO) and any other participant in armed resistance against an enemy in war and peace, which was exercised by the president of the Presidency on its behalf.[44] By March 1991, Milošević was alleged to have controlled four of the eight votes on the SFRY Presidency (Serbia, Montenegro, Vojvodina, and Kosovo) through his influence over the 'Serbian Bloc'.[45] The prosecution case was that after this bloc failed to force the Presidency to declare a state of emergency in the SFRY on 12 March 1991,[46] on Milošević's request, the Supreme Command Staff was activated as a means to control the armed forces.[47] Pursuant to this scheme, high-ranking JNA officers are said to have ignored the orders of the Croat, Stjepan Mesić

[36] Ibid. para. 41. [37] Ibid. para. 49. [38] Ibid. para. 62. [39] Ibid. paras. 65 and 69.
[40] Ibid. paras. 66–7. [41] Ibid. para. 74. [42] Ibid. paras. 75, 77–8. [43] Ibid. para. 81.
[44] Ibid. paras. 86–8. [45] Ibid. para. 93. [46] Ibid. para. 93. [47] Ibid. para. 93.

(then President of the SFRY Presidency), and denied him influence over the armed forces.[48]

The prosecution argued that, by the beginning of October 1991, the SFRY Presidency was reduced to a 'Rump Presidency', as exercised by the Serbian Bloc, which, although lacking a majority, began amending the Presidency's Rules of Procedure of 1984, allowing it to continue functioning and to assume the powers of the SFRY Presidency in relation to command of the armed forces.[49] Thus, Milošević is said to have exercised direct control not only over the Rump Presidency, but also over all major police and military organs of the Republic of Serbia and the (S)FRY.[50]

The FRY Constitution, which came into force on 27 April 1992, abolished the collective SFRY Presidency and mandated the Presidency of the FRY, the Supreme Defence Council and the VJ with primary responsibility for the defence of the country.[51] The President of the FRY commanded the army in peace and war, in compliance with decisions made by the Supreme Defence Council, composed of the President of the FRY – presiding over the Council – and the presidents of Serbia and Montenegro.[52] The prosecution alleged that, although as President of Serbia Milošević exercised limited legal authority over the Serbian MUP, his *de facto* powers over it were considerable.[53] According to the prosecution, the resources and personnel of the Serbian MUP were regularly and directly employed by him as a means to participate in the take-over of targeted areas in both Croatia and Bosnia, including through the training of paramilitary units.[54] Milošević was said to have actually created paramilitary armed forces within and associated with the Serbian MUP, as a more reliable alternative to the JNA.[55] Among those, were Arkan's Tigers[56] and Šešelj's men.[57]

The Croatian Serbian Democratic Party (SDS) was founded on 17 February 1990. The prosecution alleged that, gradually, Croatian Serbs established regional structures: the SAO Krajina, SAO Western Slavonia, SAO Slavonia, Baranja, and Western Srem, and the Republic of Serbian Krajina (RSK).[58] Parallel to the establishment of these structures, the Croatian Serb MUP was set-up.[59] The prosecution alleged that it received the support of the accused and government organs and officials of Serbia and (S)FRY, as well as the cooperation of the military forces, including the JNA, in order to establish military and police posts in the entire region of the SAO Krajina.[60]

[48] Ibid. para. 94. [49] Ibid. paras. 95–6. [50] Ibid. para. 99. [51] Ibid. para. 100.
[52] Ibid. para. 100. [53] Ibid. para. 105. [54] Ibid. paras. 105, 114–15.
[55] Ibid. para. 118. [56] Ibid. paras. 127–32. [57] Ibid. paras. 133–44.
[58] Ibid. paras. 145–77. [59] Ibid. para. 178. [60] Ibid. paras. 179–94.

The physical secession of Bosnian Serbs from Bosnia was alleged to have been realised through the Bosnian SDS, led by Radovan Karadžić, Momčilo Krajišnik, and Biljana Plavšić.[61] According to the prosecution, Karadžić's primacy over the SDS was cemented by his close working relationship with Milošević.[62] Despite their public language on the preservation of Bosnia in Yugoslavia through peaceful negotiations, the Bosnian SDS leadership are alleged to have made meticulous preparations for conflict, in collusion with Croatian Serbs and Belgrade institutions.[63]

(c) The scope of the charges The prosecution alleged the commission of crimes in six different regions of Croatia claimed by Serbs. In all of them, it was alleged that an ethnically pure region was sought. To achieve this, Milošević – either by way of a criminal enterprise with, or command of, the Croatian Serb political structure, together with their military and paramilitary formations – was said to have committed crimes of extermination, murder, torture and other forms of cruel treatment, unlawful detention, forcible transfer and deportation, wanton destruction and plunder of public and private property, some of which were said to have been committed as persecutions.

The Bosnia indictment charged Milošević with crimes committed in forty-seven municipalities. The prosecution selected fourteen municipalities in which they stated they would adduce comprehensive evidence of the criminal events therein and Milošević's participation in those events.[64] In all the crime locations enumerated in the prosecution pre-trial brief, it was alleged again that an ethnically pure region was sought. To achieve this, Milošević – either by way of a criminal enterprise with, or command of, the Bosnian Serb political structure, together with their military and paramilitary formations – committed widespread crimes, including genocide and persecutions, as well as extermination, murder, detention, forcible transfer and deportation, rape, inhumane treatment, wanton destruction and plunder of public and private property.

(d) Milošević's role and responsibility According to the prosecution, all of the acts alleged to have been committed by Milošević could be categorised as relating to one or more of the forms of responsibility prescribed by Article 7(1), while paragraph 5 of the Croatia and Bosnia indictments states clearly that by reference to commission as a form of responsibility,

[61] Ibid. para. 195. [62] Ibid. para. 196. [63] Ibid. para. 200. [64] Ibid. para. 596.

the prosecution did not intend to suggest that the accused physically committed any of the crimes charged personally, but that he participated in the crimes charged as a co-perpetrator in a joint criminal enterprise.[65] The purpose of this joint criminal enterprise was pleaded as 'the forcible removal of the majority of the Croat and other non-Serb population from the approximately one-third of the territory of the Republic of Croatia [and Bosnia] that he planned to become part of a new Serb-dominated state through the commission of crimes in violation of Articles 2, 3, and 5 of the Statute of the Tribunal'.[66] For Croatia the plan is said to have come into existence before 1 August 1991 and continued at least until June 1992, and for Bosnia it is said to have continued until at least 31 December 1995.[67]

The forced removal of non-Serbs from the territories covered by the indictments was said to be the result of a plan developed, implemented, and overseen by Milošević and his co-perpetrators, among whom Milošević was alleged to have been the leading figure.[68] Further to the allegations that he developed such a criminal enterprise, Milošević was alleged to have held positions of superior authority and exercised effective control over the individuals and institutions perpetrating crimes in Croatia and Bosnia. He was said to have had either *de facto* or *de facto* power or authority to prevent crimes or to punish them.[69] He was said to have negotiated with international organisations and at peace conferences on behalf of the JNA/VJ and the Croatian and Bosnian Serbs, showing his position of influence and power,[70] and to have had the ability to take measures to prevent and punish subordinates.[71] It was also pleaded that he knew or should have known of many of the crimes committed in Croatia and Bosnia.[72] Despite the clear and repeated notice of the type and scale of crimes committed by forces he created, supported, directed, and controlled, Milošević was alleged to have failed to take adequate, necessary, and reasonable measures to prevent or punish the perpetrators of the crimes and, in fact, personally promoted or oversaw the promotion of individuals who had committed these crimes.[73]

Finally, the joint criminal enterprise in Bosnia was alleged to have consisted of the forcible and permanent removal of the majority of non-Serbs, principally Bosnian Muslims and Bosnian Croats.[74] The prosecution case was that, in some municipalities, the campaign of persecution included or

[65] Ibid. para. 952. [66] Croatia indictment, para. 6. [67] Bosnia indictment, para. 6.
[68] Croatia and Bosnia pre-trial brief, above n. 26, para. 953. [69] Ibid. para. 977.
[70] Ibid. para. 984. [71] Ibid. para. 985. [72] Ibid. para. 986. [73] Ibid. para. 994.
[74] Ibid. para. 995.

escalated to include conduct committed with the intent to destroy in part the national, ethnical, racial, or religious groups of Bosnian Muslims as such.[75] Milošević was accused of being fully aware of these crimes[76] which, coupled with his participation in and (by his actions) furtherance of the plan, gave rise to an inference of his intent to destroy in part the Bosnian Muslim groups as such.[77] In any event, these genocidal acts were said to have been known to the accused and were foreseeable by him.[78] The prosecution sought initially to prove the crime of genocide only in relation to seven named municipalities, although further municipalities were identified as having been the site of genocidal crimes in the indictment.[79] Finally, the prosecution, in footnote 2076 of its Croatia and Bosnia pre-trial brief, noted that it would not seek to prove that genocide was committed in relation to Bosnian Croats.[80]

The prosecution case on 'Greater Serbia'

The prosecution case theory revolved around Milošević's espousal of and aspirations for a Greater Serbia. Because of the centrality given to this theory by the prosecution, and the number of senior Serbs said to be part of a joint criminal enterprise with this endeavour at the heart of their criminal plans, it is important to examine this aspect of the prosecution's case. The prosecution's failure to clearly plead and explain its case on this important issue demonstrates the difficulties it created for itself, the accused and the Trial Chamber in comprehending its case.

Discussion and clarification of the nature of the prosecution's case with respect to Greater Serbia developed out of the testimony of the defence witness Vojislav Šešelj. Šešelj asserted in evidence that the creation of a 'Greater Serbia' was never a policy of Milošević but rather that of himself and his Serbian Radical Party.[81] He testified that the historical meaning of the concept was the creation of an area consisting of all people speaking the Shtokavian dialect of the Serbian language and encompassing all of Bosnia and the majority of Croatia, except for the three districts of Zagreb, Križevci and Varaždin.[82] The definition offered by Šešelj raised

75 Ibid. para. 996. 76 Ibid. para. 1001. 77 Ibid. para. 1001. 78 Ibid. para. 1001.

79 Ibid. para. 997. According to footnote 2077, this reduced geographical focus was adopted both in the interests of judicial economy, in light of the Trial Chamber's oral ruling of 10 April 2002 as to the limitations on the time allocated to the Prosecution case, and in order to enable a concentration on the most egregious examples of genocidal crimes within Bosnia. 80 Kosovo pre-trial brief, above n. 14, para. 996, footnote 2076.

81 *Prosecution v. Milošević*, Hearing, 19 August 2005, Transcript, 42887; 24 August 2005, Transcript, 43201. 82 Ibid. Transcript 43320–1, 25 August 2005.

questions about the prosecution's case relating to the territorial aspirations and motives of Milošević. The prosecution position appeared inconsistent since, on the one hand, it argued that Milošević wanted to create a Greater Serbia and, on the other, that he never in fact advocated in favour of such a concept.

The prosecution's position with respect to Milošević's relationship with a Greater Serbia shifted over the different periods of the case. In the Croatia and Bosnia indictments, he was alleged to have been involved in a joint criminal enterprise with the creation of a Greater Serbia at its heart,[83] while the Kosovo indictment merely referred to the expulsion of a substantial portion of the Kosovo Albanian population from the territory of the province of Kosovo in an effort to ensure continued Serbian control over the province.[84] In applying for joinder of the three indictments before the commencement of the case, the prosecution asserted that the three indictments concerned 'the same transaction in the sense of a common scheme, strategy or plan, namely the accused Milošević's overall conduct in attempting to create a "Greater Serbia" – a centralised Serbian state encompassing the Serb populated areas of Croatia and Bosnia and Hercegovina, and all of Kosovo'.[85] In the prosecution's opening statement, it alleged that it was the search for power that motivated Milošević, so that his acts were not motivated by underlying ideology or a nationalist pretext.[86] In its response to the *amici curiae* motion for judgement of acquittal at the close of the prosecution case,[87] the prosecution referred to the 'planned Serbian state' several times[88] and an 'extended Serbia' relating to the territories in Bosnia and Herzegovina, which it argued Milošević wished to see incorporated into Serbia. Finally, the prosecution's case theory regarding Greater Serbia in relation to the accused manifested itself in a different approach in cross-examining defence witnesses.[89]

[83] See Bosnia indictment, paras. 6, 9, 22, 53, 65; Croatia indictment, paras. 6, 9, 22, 103.

[84] See Kosovo indictment, para. 16.

[85] *Prosecutor v. Milošević*, Case No. IT-99-37-PT, IT-01-50-PT, IT-01-51-I, Prosecution's Motion for Joinder, 27 November 2001 ('Prosecution joinder brief'), para. 13.

[86] *Prosecutor v. Milošević*, Hearing, 12 February 2002, Transcript, 9.

[87] *Prosecutor v. Milošević*, '*Amici curiae* Motion for Judgement of Acquittal Pursuant to Rule 98bis', Case No. IT-02-54-T, 3 March 2004 ('*Amici* Acquittal Motion').

[88] *Prosecutor v. Milošević*, 'Prosecution Response to *Amici curiae* Motion for Judgement of Acquittal Pursuant to Rule 98*bis*', Case No. IT-02-54-T, 3 May 2004 ('Prosecution Acquittal Response'), paras. 237, 337, 415,

[89] See, e.g., *Prosecutor v. Milošević*, Hearing, 15 December 2004, Čedomir Popov, Transcript 34587; Vojislav Šešelj, Transcript, 34587–8; 43218–19; 43224–5.

Becoming frustrated at the lack of clarity regarding this important aspect of the case, the Trial Chamber eventually pressed the prosecution to summarise its case on Milošević in relation to a Greater Serbia in two or three sentences, to which the prosecution responded as follows:

> [T]he ambitions of this accused at the material time and once the possibility for retaining the former Federal Republic of Yugoslavia were gone, his ambitions were to have an enlarged or he was party to the ambitions to have an enlarged Serbian state and that informed his actions.
>
> . . .
>
> [O]nce the decision had been made to let Slovenia go, Croatia was allowed to go or it was contemplated that Croatia could go on terms that it left but without the parts that were going to remain under Serbian control, and at that stage, again to pick up on His Honour Judge Bonomy's point, it wasn't the plan at that stage to include all of Bosnia except that. They faced the realities and restricted themselves to the parts as the accused himself says in various places dealing with it by percentages that it was realistic for them to retain.[90]

Ultimately, the prosecution succeeded in showing that it drew a distinction between the actions and intentions of Milošević with regard to the espousal of a Serb-controlled State from which non-Serbs were to be removed, and those of nationalists like Šešelj, who advocated a Greater Serbia based on an ideological and historical idea that encompassed broad swathes of territory of the former Yugoslavia. Unfortunately, it took well into the defence case, and after considerable questioning from the Trial Chamber, before this critical aspect of the prosecution case was clarified and understood. In the meantime, the unclear articulation of the idea of a Greater Serbia was relied upon to achieve joinder of the three indictments before the Appeals Chamber, and may have left Milošević as confused as the Trial Chamber about its application to the accused.

Pleading Practice and Problems with the Miloševič Indictments

The three *Milošević* indictments were defective in some material respects. This is apparent from an analysis of them in light of the developed Tribunal jurisprudence concerning the required 'form' (meaning its content and structure in relation to the case pleaded) of indictments. The content of an indictment is critical, as it is the accusatory instrument upon which the prosecution relies to bring its case. If it fails to plead material facts, one possible outcome is that an accused may be acquitted of crimes otherwise

[90] Ibid. 43265–6.

made out on the evidence because that accused was not sufficiently put on notice of the material allegations. Those pleading requirements familiar in most common law criminal systems can be recognised in the pleading practice of international criminal tribunals, except that significant relaxation of the requirements occur in respect of persons alleged to be responsible for crimes they did not themselves physically perpetrate. In the case of senior political figures alleged to have acted in concert with others, or to have had *de facto* control of military, paramilitary, and police structures, the subordinates of which are said to have physically committed the crimes, serious complexities arise. These complexities relate not only to the form the indictment should take and what is required of a prosecutor to put an accused on notice of the charges against them, but to the broader principle of the conduct for which a head of state or senior political official can be held criminally responsible, when the lines connecting the commission of a crime and the accused are very long and may be interrupted by multiple layers of culpable persons and entities.

Where the prosecution fails to plead its case in a clear manner, enabling accused to understand the case against them, there is a correlative threat to the fairness of the international criminal trial. Where the case pleaded is broad, this danger escalates because the inherent complexities multiply. The Milošević case exemplifies this problem. In this section, I will first review ICTY pleading practice (reflective of, or influential in, the approach generally taken in all the international criminal courts and tribunals), relating to the law on the form of indictments, which serves to protect important aspects of the normative structure of international criminal trials, in particular notice to accused of charges against them. Then I discuss the extent to which the Milošević indictments succeeded or failed to conform with this practice and the effect of this on the accused and the trial process.

The form of the indictment

The form of an indictment before the ICTY is governed primarily by Articles 18(4) and 21(4)(a) of the Statute and Rule 47(C) of the Rules.[91] Article 18(4) provides:

> Upon a determination that a *prima facie* case exists, the Prosecutor shall prepare an indictment containing a concise statement of the facts and the crime or crimes with which the accused is charged under the Statute.

[91] The Appeals Chamber has also held that the guarantees in Articles 21(2) and 21(4)(b) to 'a fair and public hearing' and 'adequate time and facilities for the preparation of his defence'

Article 21(4)(a) of the Statute provides:

> In the determination of any charge against the accused pursuant to the present Statute, the accused shall be entitled to the following minimum guarantees, in full equality: . . . to be informed promptly and in detail in a language which he understands of the nature and cause of the charge against him[.][92]

Rule 47(C) provides:

> The indictment shall set forth the name and particulars of the suspect, and a concise statement of the facts of the case and of the crime with which the suspect is charged.

The jurisprudence of the ICTY interpreting these provisions 'translates [them] into an obligation on the part of the prosecution to state the material facts [but not the evidence] underpinning the charges in the indictment'.[93] The pleadings in an indictment, though concise, must be detailed enough 'to inform an accused clearly of the nature and cause of the charges against him to enable him to prepare a defence effectively and efficiently'.[94] In general, material facts must be pleaded expressly,[95] although in certain limited circumstances, they need not be explicitly mentioned if those facts are 'necessarily implied in the indictment'.[96] The Appeals Chamber has furthermore noted that an indictment is 'the primary accusatory instrument'; if it does not plead with sufficient detail the essential aspects of the Prosecution case, it suffers from a material defect.[97]

These requirements are considered in detail in respect of the Milošević indictments below.

Footnote 91 *(cont.)*
are basic rights of the Accused that apply equally to the issue of notice of the crimes with which he is charged, and therefore are relevant to consideration of the form of the indictment. See *Prosecutor v. Kupreškić*, 'Appeal Judgement', Case No. IT-95-16-A, 23 October 2001 ('*Kupreškić* Appeal Judgment'), para. 88.

92 The Appeals Chamber has held that the guarantees under Article 21(4)(a) apply to the form of the indictment: *Kupreškić* Appeal Judgment, above n. 91, para. 88.

93 See *Prosecutor v. Halilović*, 'Decision on Prosecutor's Motion Seeking Leave to Amend the Indictment', Case No. IT-01-48-PT, 17 December 2004 ('*Halilović* Decision'), citing: *Kupreškić* Appeal Judgement, above n. 91, para. 88; *Prosecutor v. Krnojelac*, 'Decision on Preliminary Motion on Form of Amended Indictment', 11 February 2000, Case No. IT-97-25-PT, paras. 7, 12; *Prosecutor v. Krnojelac*, 'Decision on Preliminary Motion on the Form of Amended Indictment', Case No. IT-97-25-PT, 11 February 2000, paras. 17, 18; and, *Prosecutor v. Brđanin and Talić*, 'Decision on Objections by Momir Talić to the Form of the Amended Indictment', Case No. IT-99-36-PT, 20 February 2001 para.18.

94 *Halilović* Decision, above n. 93, para. 13. 95 Ibid.

96 Ibid. 97 Ibid. para. 13.

Review of indictments

Article 19 of the ICTY Statute provides:

> 1. The judge of the Trial Chamber to whom the indictment has been transmitted shall review it. If satisfied that a *prima facie* case has been established by the Prosecutor, he shall confirm the indictment. If not so satisfied, the indictment shall be dismissed.
> 2. Upon confirmation of an indictment, the judge may, at the request of the Prosecutor, issue such orders and warrants for the arrest, detention, surrender or transfer of persons, and any other orders as may be required for the conduct of the trial.

Rule 47(E) of the ICTY Rules provides:

> The reviewing Judge shall examine each of the counts in the indictment, and any supporting materials the Prosecutor may provide, to determine, applying the standard set forth in Article 19, paragraph 1, of the Statute, whether a case exists against the suspect.

The Tribunal has defined a prima facie case as 'a credible case which would (if not contradicted by the defence) be a sufficient basis to convict the accused on the charge'.[98] Review of an indictment to determine whether it establishes a prima facie case has two distinct components: (1) 'an assessment of whether, from the face of the indictment, it is alleged that the accused committed acts which, if proven beyond a reasonable doubt, are crimes as charged and are within the subject matter jurisdiction of the International Tribunal', and (2) an examination of the accompanying material to ensure that it supports the allegations in the indictment.[99]

Reviewing indictments has most often been referred to in the Tribunal jurisprudence as 'confirmation' of indictments. This nomenclature, although no doubt unintentional, has certainly betrayed the true approach taken, particularly in the early years of the Tribunal's practice. Indictments were almost invariably confirmed without significant critical attention by the reviewing judge. A cursory reading of many confirmed indictments reveals how inadequate many of the primary accusatory instruments before the ICTY are.

98 *Prosecutor v. Kordić, Blaškić, Čerkez, Šantić, Skopljak, and Aleksovski*, 'Decision on the Review of the Indictment', Case No. IT-95-14-I, 10 November 1995, 3.

99 Ibid. For a discussion of the review process, see sources referred to in above n. 1. For a discussion of the review process from a human rights perspective, see Salvatore Zappalà, *Human Rights in International Criminal Proceedings* (2003), 36–7.

A good example of this assertion is the *Kupreškić* case, in which the Appeals Chamber acquitted two accused convicted at trial on the basis that the indictment (as well as the pre-trial brief and evidence led) failed to put them on adequate notice of the case against them:

> By framing the charges against Zoran and Mirjan Kupreškić in such a general way, the Amended Indictment fails to fulfil the fundamental purpose of providing the accused with a description of the charges against him with sufficient particularity to enable him to mount his defence. Pursuant to Articles 18(4), 21(2), 21(4)(a) and 21(4)(a) and (b) of the Statute, the Prosecution should have articulated, to the best of its ability, the specific acts of the Defendants that went to the three different categories of conduct pleaded in the Amended Indictment.
>
> [T]he Appeals Chamber holds that the Amended Indictment failed to plead the material facts of the Prosecution case against Zoran and Mirjan Kupreškić with the requisite detail. By returning convictions on count 1 (persecution) on the basis of such material facts, the Trial Chamber erred in law. The Appeals Chamber is unable to conclude that Zoran and Mirjan Kupreškić were, through the disclosed evidence, the information conveyed in the Prosecution Pre-Trial Brief, and knowledge acquired during trial, sufficiently informed of the charges pertaining to [the relevant events].[100]

Inadequacies in pleading practices before the ICTY spread to the leadership cases as well. The outcome of the Trial Chamber's review of the indictment against Milošević's Belgrade colleagues in relation to Kosovo discussed below, as well as a review of all three indictments against Milošević himself, reveal material defects. This is critical to the analysis of the *Milošević* trial, to show how the prosecution proceeded on the basis of less than adequate accusatory instruments. In turn this will tend to show how critical it is, in a case of this size and complexity, that it proceed from the start in a well formulated and structured manner. It is fundamental to the process of achieving a fair trial, as well as to the prosecution's ability to secure a conviction, and it is also crucial to the ability of a court to manage such a complex trial.

Analysis of the Milošević indictments

The Kosovo indictment

The Kosovo indictment was the first against Milošević and included four other co-accused: Milutinović, Šainović, Ojdanić, and Stojilković (who

100 *Kupreškić* Appeal Judgement, above n. 91, para. 95.

was subsequently assassinated in Belgrade). Although Milošević was tried alone, and the Kosovo indictment was twice amended, it continued to carry the names of his co-accused, even when the three remaining co-accused finally surrendered to the custody of the Tribunal, signalling the start of pre-trial proceedings against them under that indictment in a separate case. A further indictment was subsequently issued against the Serb Generals Pavković, Lazarević, Đorđevic, and Lukić (the second Kosovo indictment). The indictment against Milutinović, Šainović, and Ojdanić was joined with the second Kosovo indictment, to form a seven-person indictment for all the Kosovo-related crimes during the 1999 period.[101]

(a) The first Lazarević Decision on the form of the indictment One decision emerging from a challenge to the second Kosovo indictment by Lazarević[102] is of great significance to consideration of the form of the *Milošević* Kosovo indictment. The virtual identity of the initial indictments in both cases, and the fact that they arose from the same set of events involving the same alleged joint criminal enterprise participants, provides a unique opportunity for comparison between the largely unrevised *Milošević* Kosovo indictment and the fully litigated and substantially amended second Kosovo indictment (and subsequently the joined Kosovo indictment).

Lazarević argued that the second Kosovo indictment was generally defective because it failed to plead, or plead sufficiently, the material facts as well as the type of connection between the material facts, the accused, his position, and his acts or omissions. The same Trial Chamber trying Milošević determined this motion, noting first that pleading practice in relation to an accused's *mens rea* had been developed by the Appeals Chamber in the *Blaškić* Judgement. It was noted in the *Lazarević* Decision that although the Appeals Chamber appeared to leave open the possibility of pleading an accused's *mens rea* simply by referring to his relevant state of mind, recent Appeals Chamber judgements have required that, where that state of mind is to be established by inference from other facts, particularly the acts and conduct of the accused, 'then the indictment may be

[101] Hereafter, the 'joined Kosovo indictment'. Đorđevic remains at large and is not being tried along with his co-accused on the joined Kosovo indictment.

[102] *Prosecutor v. Lazarević*, 'Decision, Decision on Vladimir Lazarevic's Preliminary Motion on Form of Indictment', Case No. IT-05-87-PT, 8 July 2005 (hereafter '*Lazarević* Decision'), para. 8. This Decision is important because it is a review of the form of the indictment of one of Milošević's Kosovo Generals, and the indictment against him is, in all material respects, the same as the Kosovo indictment against Milošević. This Decision will be dealt with in detail below.

defective if it does not include notice of these matters'.[103] For example, in the *Kordić* Appeal Judgement, a meeting Kordić was alleged to have attended – and which was critical to the prosecution case against him – was held to constitute a material fact that should have been pleaded in the indictment.[104] In the ICTR *Ntakirutimana* Appeal Judgement, several findings of fact by the Trial Chamber were quashed because the prosecution failed to plead specific crucial facts relating to the alleged acts and conduct of the accused. One such finding quashed related to murder, upon which the Trial Chamber had based its finding for the commission of genocide.[105]

In his challenge to the form of the indictment, Lazarević submitted that the indictment failed to inform him properly of the acts by which he was said to have concretely participated in planning, instigating or ordering each individual crime charged, whether directly or as part of a joint criminal enterprise, or aiding and abetting their planning, preparation or execution. The prosecution response was simply to confirm its intention to rely upon each form of responsibility charged for all counts of the indictment, without addressing the specific arguments raised.[106]

Two Appeals Chamber judgements, which post-dated confirmation of both the *Lazarević* and *Milošević* indictments, dealt directly with the obligation on the prosecution to plead material facts relevant to each form of responsibility alleged in an indictment. In the Blaškić indictment, the prosecution had, much like the second Kosovo indictment, merely repeated the wording of Article 7(1) of the ICTY Statute without providing further particulars of the alleged acts concerning the type of responsibility incurred. The Appeals Chamber held that '[t]his manner of pleading does not clearly inform the accused of the exact nature and cause of the specific allegations against him', and that the prosecution 'should have pleaded the particular forms of participation under Article 7(1) with respect to each incident under each count'.[107] With respect to 'instigation' in particular, the Appeals Chamber held that, as a distinct form of participation under Article 7(1), when pleaded, the instigating acts – and the instigated persons or groups of persons – must be described precisely.[108]

[103] *Lazarević* Decision, above n. 102, para. 9, citing *Prosecutor v. Blaškić*, 'Judgement', Case No. IT-95-14-A, 29 July 2004 ('*Blaškić* Appeal Judgement'), para. 219.

[104] *Prosecutor v. Kordić and Čerkez*, 'Judgement', Case No. IT-95-14/2-A, 17 December 2004 ('*Kordić* Appeal Judgement'), paras. 144, 177.

[105] *Prosecutor v. Ntakirutimana*, 'Judgement', Case No. ICTR-96-10 & ICTR-96-17-TA, 21 February 2003 (*Ntakirutimana* Appeal Judgement), paras. 86, 99, 555.

[106] See *Lazarević* Decision, above n. 102, para. 15.

[107] *Blaškić* Appeal Judgement, above n. 103, para. 226.

[108] Ibid. para. 226.

The *Kvočka* indictment similarly stated that the accused were individually responsible for the crimes charged in the indictment pursuant to Article 7(1), which was intended to incorporate any and all forms of individual criminal responsibility as set forth in Article 7(1). The Appeals Chamber in that case held that the prosecution 'failed to plead the material facts necessary to support each of these modes [of responsibility]. For example, despite pleading "ordering" as a mode of responsibility, the Indictment d[id] not include any material facts which allege[d] that any Accused ordered the commission of any particular crime on any occasion.'[109] The Appeals Chamber found that, 'in pleading modes of responsibility for which no corresponding material facts [were] pleaded, the Indictment [was] vague and therefore defective'.[110]

The *Lazarević* Decision noted that the only effort in this respect that the prosecution had made was to plead that by using the word 'committed', it did not intend to suggest that any of the accused physically perpetrated any of the crimes charged personally, but that they participated in a joint criminal enterprise as co-perpetrators.[111] Relying on appellate jurisprudence, the Trial Chamber held that the relevant pleadings in the indictment were vague and general, failing to plead 'the specific conduct that supports the bare averment that the Accused acted in each or any of the ways in which individual criminal responsibility may be attributable to him under Article 7(1) of the Statute'.[112] The Chamber held that, if the prosecution wished to infer that the accused acted in one or more of the ways set out in Article 7(1) of the Statute – and that he participated in a joint criminal enterprise – from the conduct of the forces over whom he exercised authority, his position in the military hierarchy and his relationship to others, in the military, police or political hierarchy, it had failed to explicitly plead this.[113] Furthermore, since the prosecution had not pleaded in the indictment the specific state of mind required for each form of responsibility under Article 7 (1) of the Statute, it was held that it should at least have pleaded the basis upon which this material fact was to be established.[114] The Chamber ordered the prosecution to identify either the specific conduct supporting the averment that the accused acted in each or any of the ways whereby individual criminal responsibility may be attributable to him under Article 7 (1) of the Statute; or, state that it was inviting the Chamber to infer that the Accused acted in one or more of the ways set out in that Article 'from

[109] *Prosecutor v. Kvočka et al.*, 'Judgement', Case No. IT-98-30/1-A, 28 February 2005, para. 41.
[110] Ibid. para. 41. [111] See *Lazarević* Decision, above n. 102, para. 17.
[112] Ibid. para. 19. [113] Ibid. [114] Ibid. para. 20.

the conduct of the forces over whom he exercised authority, his position in the military hierarchy and his relationship to others, in the military, police or political hierarchy'.[115] It furthermore ordered the prosecution to specify the state of mind required for each of the various forms of responsibility alleged pursuant to Article 7 (1) of the Statute and the facts by which this material fact was to be established.[116]

Another argument raised by the defence in that case, of considerable relevance also to the *Milošević* indictments, was the use by the prosecution of the phrase 'others known and unknown' with whom the accused was alleged to have participated in a joint criminal enterprise. The defence argued that the indictment failed to specify who were the 'others known' referred to, and that the use of the expression implied that the prosecution knew of names which had not been disclosed. In relation to those 'unknown', it argued that, if the prosecution was unable to provide names, it should 'at least approximately indicate the category to which such persons belong so that the accused can adequately organize his defence'. The prosecution responded that it fulfilled its obligation by specifying 'the identity of those engaged in the enterprise, including the names of some of the known persons participating in the enterprise and the category to which other participants belonged'.[117]

The Trial Chamber identified the use of the term as creating even graver concerns than that asserted by the defence. Because the prosecution pleaded specifically in reference to 'forces of the FRY and Serbia' as referring to personnel falling outside of the definition 'others known and unknown', the expression was said to be used 'in a confusing and misleading way throughout the Indictment'.[118] The Trial Chamber also held that use of the phrase 'others known' was a 'wholly inappropriate form of pleading':

> While it is submitted in the Prosecution response that it is impractical to name all known persons, no explanation has been given for saying so. The Trial Chamber does not accept the further Prosecution submission that to name those known 'goes beyond what is necessary to provide the Accused with a concise statement of the facts of the case'. In order to know the nature of the case he must meet, the accused must be informed by the indictment of the identity of those engaged in the enterprise, so far as their identity is known to the Prosecution. If the identity of other participants to the joint criminal enterprise is known to the Prosecution, as the use of the expression 'others known' suggests, the Trial Chamber is of the view that these identities constitute material facts to be pleaded in the Indictment.[119]

[115] Ibid. [116] Ibid. [117] Ibid. para. 22. [118] Ibid. para. 23. [119] Ibid. para. 24.

The Trial Chamber accordingly ordered the prosecution to clarify to whom the expression 'others known and unknown' refers and to state the identity of those participants in the joint criminal enterprise who are known. If the identity of participants was not known, the prosecution were required to plead the category to which they belonged.[120]

The defence argued that the indictment failed to specify any facts to support the prosecution's allegation that the crimes enumerated in counts 1 to 5 were 'within the object of' the joint criminal enterprise and that the accused and his co-perpetrators 'shared the joint criminal object'. The prosecution submitted that the manner in which it would establish that the members of the joint criminal enterprise shared the joint criminal object and related allegations was a matter for evidence.[121] However, the Trial Chamber held that the allegation of shared intent as pleaded in the indictment was confusing. Although the prosecution satisfactorily pleaded the mental element requirement for the extended form of joint criminal enterprise (relating to responsibility for acts which are the natural and foreseeable consequences of an agreed criminal enterprise), it failed to plead as a material fact the required mental element for participation in a joint criminal enterprise, there being 'no averment that the accused was aware of the existence of the joint criminal enterprise, nor . . . reference to material facts from which knowledge may be inferred'.[122] The prosecution was, therefore, ordered 'to identify the material facts upon which it intends to rely at trial to establish that the accused was aware of the existence of the joint criminal enterprise and possessed the requisite *mens rea*'.[123]

The final relevant challenge to the second Kosovo indictment concerned the alleged superior responsibility of the accused under Article 7(3) of the Statute. Where, as was pleaded in the *Milošević* indictments, the accused's individual criminal responsibility is alleged to arise under Article 7(3) of the Statute (superior responsibility), the minimum material facts that must appear in the indictment are as follows:

(a) (i) that the accused is the superior (ii) of subordinates, sufficiently identified, (iii) over whom he had effective control – in the sense of a material ability to prevent or punish criminal conduct – and (iv) for whose acts he is alleged to be responsible;
(b) the conduct of the accused by which he may be found to (i) have known or had reason to know that the crimes were about to be or had been committed by those others, and (ii) the related conduct of those others for whom he is alleged to be responsible. The facts relevant to

[120] Ibid. para. 26. [121] Ibid. para. 27. [122] Ibid. para. 29. [123] Ibid. para. 30.

the acts of those others will usually be stated with less precision, the reasons being that the detail of those acts (by whom and against whom they are done) is often unknown, and, more importantly, because the acts themselves often cannot be greatly in issue; and

(c) the conduct of the accused by which he may be found to have failed to take the necessary and reasonable measures to prevent such crimes or to punish the persons who committed them.[124]

The defence first submitted that the prosecution had failed to plead sufficient details about which subordinate structures and individuals in the accused's line of command perpetrated the crimes with which he was charged as a superior. It submitted that the prosecution should be required to plead the person or persons or, at least the category of persons, responsible for the commission of the crimes charged. The prosecution responded by stating that it had discharged its obligation for specificity by describing the subordinate units or formations for which the accused was said to be responsible. The Chamber held that at least the category of persons alleged to have committed the crimes charged should be pleaded and noted that, in spite of the massive crime-base covered in the indictment, the mere reference to 'forces of the FRY and Serbia' did not constitute a sufficient description of the categories of forces in question.[125]

The prosecution had included some description in the indictment of the corps, units, and groups that were allegedly subordinated to the accused, but had failed to explain why it would be impracticable to plead which of the units referred to in the indictment were involved in the events in each municipality. Furthermore, where specific forces were referred to, it was not clear whether the prosecution was pleading that only those forces and units were involved in the commission of the crimes charged. The Trial Chamber ordered the prosecution to specify the category of persons alleged to have committed the crimes charged 'by indicating which of the forces and units allegedly subordinated to the Accused were involved in the events in each municipality and specify whether it is the Prosecution's case that it is only those forces and units that were involved in the commission of the crimes charged'.[126]

The *Lazarević* defence also argued that the indictment failed to plead the relationship between the accused and the perpetrators of the crimes alleged to be his subordinates. The Trial Chamber agreed with the defence and held that the indictment did not specify (1) which units attached to

[124] See *Halilović* Decision, above n. 93. [125] Ibid. para. 32.
[126] Ibid. paras. 33–4 (footnotes omitted).

the VJ Priština Corps of the VJ 3rd Army (which Lazarević was alleged to have led) were commanded by the accused, or (2) the republic police units subordinated to, or operating in co-operation or co-ordination with, that corps or military-territorial units, civil defence units and other armed groups, over which it alleged that the accused exercised command authority or control. The Trial Chamber held that 'such particulars constitute material facts which the Prosecution should plead in the Indictment if . . . in a position to do so'.[127]

After joinder of the Kosovo case into one indictment against the seven remaining senior Belgrade officials,[128] excluding Milošević, the further challenges to the amended indictment eventuated in a final indictment in that case.[129] Of relevance to the *Milošević* indictment were final amendments required by the Chamber specifying the involvement of MUP and VJ units in the alleged crimes. The Chamber accepted that the phrase 'at least one VJ unit and at least one MUP unit participated in each of the charged crimes' adequately specified the physical perpetrators for the purposes of the indictment.[130] The decision also confirmed clarifications made concerning defects in the pleadings related to the alleged commission of crimes outside of the indictment period in 1998, accepting greater specification and detail provided in the amended indictment.[131]

These decisions are significant for consideration of the Kosovo indictment against Milošević, the sole accused for whom the initial defective Kosovo indictment remained in force for trial. The Trial Chamber stated at the conclusion of the *Lazarević* Decision that the prosecution 'should undertake a general review of the Indictment regarding all accused'.[132] Two more rounds of amendments were ordered before the Trial Chamber finally accepted the state of that indictment.[133] The prosecution in the *Milošević* case, despite seeking amendment to the Kosovo indictment twice, never sought to cure its material defects and the accused himself

127 Ibid. paras. 35–6.

128 See *Prosecutor v. Milutinović et al.*, 'Decision on Prosecution Motion for Joinder', Case No. IT-05-87-PT, 8 July 2005. One accused on the indictment, General Đorđević, remained at large.

129 See *Prosecutor v. Milutinović et al.*, 'Order Replacing Third Amended Joinder Indictment and Severing Vladimir Đorđević from the Trial', Case No. IT-05-87-PT, 26 June 2006; 'Redacted Third Amended Joinder Indictment'.

130 *Prosecutor v. Milutinović et al.*, 'Decision on Motion to Amend the Indictment', Case No. IT-05-87-PT, 11 May 2006 ('*Milutinović* Indictment Decision'), para. 6.

131 Ibid. para. 13. See also, *Prosecutor v. Milutinović et al.*, 'Decision on Defence Motions Alleging Defects in the Form of the Proposed Amended Joinder Indictment', Case No. IT-05-87-PT, 22 March 2006.

132 *Milutinović* Indictment Decision, above n. 130.

133 Ibid. para. 50.

never formally challenged it. Therefore, the *Milošević* Kosovo indictment was left in its defective form, the accused was left to prepare and conduct his defence on that basis and, had the case concluded, the Chamber would have had to render judgement on that indictment.

What would have been the effect of these defects on material aspects of the indictment relating to the accused's criminal responsibility? As can be seen from the appellate case law discussed above, one consequence might have been acquittals on certain charges or perhaps on the guilt of the accused overall.[134] And what of the Trial Chamber's role in this? One of the prosecution's general arguments against the *Lazarević* application was that an identical indictment was operative in the *Milošević* case, demonstrating that the *Lazarević* indictment conformed to the standards of specificity.[135] The Trial Chamber's response to this argument was to observe that the indictment was 'not challenged in the Milošević case'.[136] It has never been litigated in international criminal law, but it is possible that where an unrepresented accused fails to challenge the content of an indictment and the Chamber is aware of defects in it, consideration should be given by the Chamber to determining these issues *proprio motu*. It may be that, by the time the Chamber realised (from its work on the *Lazarević* Decision) that the *Milošević* indictment had material defects, the prosecution case had concluded and it would be difficult, or impossible, to amend the indictment without reopening the prosecution case or causing potential unfairness to one or both parties. However, I believe that a strong argument exists, particularly in a complex case involving a self-represented accused, for a court to pro-actively intervene where necessary to ensure that unfairness is not caused to an accused because of a failure to mount technical challenges.

Because the matter was never raised and the case never concluded, it will remain uncertain what the outcome of any material defects would have been, and whether fairness would have been considered compromised either by the Trial Chamber in judgement or the Appeals Chamber on appeal. However, in light of this analysis and the important issues it raises, I will examine the particular defects in the three *Milošević* indictments of relevance to his criminal responsibility.

(b) Defects in the form of the Milošević Kosovo indictment As already discussed, indictments listing verbatim all forms of responsibility under Article 7(1) must plead all the material facts relating to each form of

[134] See e.g., *Ntakirutimana* Appeal Judgement, above n. 105; *Kupreškić* Appeals Judgement, above n. 91. [135] *Lazarević* Decision, above n. 102, para. 12. [136] Ibid.

responsibility. The *Milošević* Kosovo indictment charged the accused with all forms of responsibility under Article 7(1). However, the Kosovo indictment did not include any material facts alleging that Milošević ordered the commission of any of the crimes charged. At best, such an order could be implied from the fact that Milošević was described as the highest-ranking superior in the country and that, for example, the campaign of terror and violence against the Kosovo Albanian civilians could not have been perpetrated without him ordering it.

Similarly, as with the *Blaškić* indictment alleging 'instigation' as a basis for Article 7(1) criminal responsibility, the Kosovo indictment contained no statement of facts concerning the instigating acts or instigated persons. Furthermore, the Kosovo indictment provided no specific information relating to Milošević planning any of the particular crimes charged. Neither is any specific mention made in the Kosovo indictment of any acts by the accused that would indicate he aided and abetted the physical perpetrators of the crimes in question. Again, the accused was left with nothing more than inference to suggest the manner in which it was alleged that he aided and abetted the commission of any crimes charged.

Milošević's responsibility pursuant to Article 7(1) of the ICTY Statute may of course be read in conjunction with the assertion in relation to each specific count that the forces of the FRY and Serbia were alleged to have been acting 'at the direction, with the encouragement, or with the support' of the accused. However, the Trial Chamber in the *Lazarević* Decision, facing identical drafting, held that these were all vague and general accusations made in relation to the accused without distinction, and did not discharge the prosecution's pleading responsibilities.[137]

In relation to the state of mind of an accused, the Kosovo indictment simply stated that the specific crimes enumerated there were executed by the forces of the FRY and Serbia 'acting at the direction, with the encouragement, or with the support of Slobodan Milošević'.[138] This statement appears to imply intent, as well as knowledge, possessed by the accused in relation to the crimes in question. However, other than Milošević's position of authority, no additional facts relating to his acts or conduct are pleaded from which an inference could be drawn about his state of mind. Despite the prosecution being required to cure the same defects in the *Lazarević* indictment, and the strong position taken by the Appeals Chamber in other cases (and leading to acquittals on appeal), the *Milošević* Kosovo indictment retained this unsatisfactory formulation.

[137] *Lazarević* Decision, above n. 102, paras. 18 and 19.

[138] Kosovo indictment, paras. 54, 63, 66, and 68.

The pleading requirements for responsibility as a member of a joint criminal enterprise have also been discussed in respect of the *Lazarević* Decision. The Kosovo indictment stated the purpose of the joint criminal enterprise and the period over which the enterprise was said to have existed.[139] As for the requirement that those engaged in the joint criminal enterprise be identified, a number of the accused's alleged co-conspirators were listed. However, the reference to 'others known and unknown',[140] as already discussed, was held by the Trial Chamber in the *Lazarević* Decision to constitute a material defect and the prosecution was ordered to amend it. The *Milošević* Kosovo indictment retained this phrase.

With respect to the requirement to plead the nature of the participation by the accused in the joint criminal enterprise, the Kosovo indictment referred simply to Milošević's 'significant contribution' to the enterprise, another vague and imprecise term. At best, it is possible that the various positions of authority held by Milošević and described in the Kosovo indictment are all facts and circumstances from which an inference could have been drawn as to the nature of his involvement in the joint criminal enterprise. However, it is unlikely that this satisfies the pleading requirements and seems an inappropriate way to plead an accused's responsibility for serious offences involving such a complex form of responsibility.

In respect of the *mens rea* requirements, the Kosovo indictment simply stated that the accused 'knowingly and wilfully participated in the joint criminal enterprise' and 'shared the intent and state of mind required for the commission of each of the crimes charged'.[141] As discussed above, the Trial Chamber in the *Lazarević* Decision, having looked at the identical pleading, held that the indictment was inadequate because it did not clarify the requisite mental element, namely, the intent to perpetrate the crimes enumerated in the indictment.

Given the reliance placed by the prosecution on joint criminal enterprise as a form of responsibility in cases involving high-level accused, defects relating to the form and content of that alleged enterprise are potentially egregious. Although the Milošević case never concluded, it seems possible that the Trial Chamber may have had difficulty finding that the accused had been put on sufficient notice of the form and content of that enterprise.

With regard to the superior responsibility of the accused, the Kosovo indictment again does not identify Milošević's subordinates in relation to

[139] Kosovo indictment, paras. 16 and 17.
[140] Kosovo indictment, para. 16.
[141] Kosovo indictment, para. 18.

specific crimes charged. The part of the indictment that deals with the crimes charged refers generally to the 'forces of the FRY and Serbia' and defines the term as including, *but not limited to*, the VJ, the MUP, military territorial units, civil defence units, *and other armed groups operating under authority, or with the knowledge of*, the accused.[142] This non-exhaustive list of subordinates, which also includes 'other armed groups', is vague. As held in the *Lazarević* Decision, it is unclear why the prosecution could not have named which particular units within the FRY and Serbia Forces participated in a particular crime in question.[143] Furthermore, with respect to the *mens rea* requirements that must be pleaded, there are no facts in the *Milošević* Kosovo indictment relating to his conduct by which he may be found to have known or had reason to know that the crimes were about to be committed or had been committed by his subordinates. The Kosovo indictment simply states that the campaign of terror and violence directed at Kosovo Albanian civilians was executed by the forces of the FRY and Serbia 'acting at the direction, with the encouragement, or with the support of Slobodan Milošević'. Again, there may be an inference of knowledge available on the basis that the accused's position of authority led to a conclusion that the crimes could not have been committed without, at least, his passive approval. However, as discussed in the analysis of the *Lazarević* Decision above, the Appeals Chamber has recently held that indictments are defective if they do not include express notice of matters establishing the state of mind of the accused by inference.

Defects in the form of the Croatia and Bosnia indictments

In contrast to the Kosovo indictment, the Bosnia indictment was clearer and less ambiguous. For example, the nature of Milošević's participation in the joint criminal enterprise was described in some detail.[144] The subordinates, over whom he was alleged to have exercised effective control, were clearly identified as the JNA/VJ, the MUP, and the Serbian State Security Service (DB), which directed and supported the actions of the special forces and Serb paramilitary groups operating in Bosnia.[145] In the parts of the Bosnia indictment that deal with specific counts, these forces were referred to and defined as belonging to 'Serb forces'; for each count the definition of 'Serb forces' was repeated and adjusted to include only those units that are alleged to have actually participated in the crime in question.

[142] Kosovo indictment, para. 27.

[143] Although it ultimately accepted an averment that at least one unit of the MUP and one unit of the VJ was involved in each offensive: *Milutinović* Indictment Decision, above n. 130.

[144] Bosnia indictment, para. 25.

[145] Bosnia indictment, paras. 30–2.

As for the *mens rea* of the accused in respect of participation in a joint criminal enterprise, the Bosnia indictment specified that Milošević knowingly and wilfully participated in the joint criminal enterprise while being aware of the foreseeable consequences of that enterprise, namely the crimes enumerated in the Bosnia indictment.[146] Finally, while all forms of responsibility under Article 7(1) of the ICTY Statute were pleaded, in this indictment the prosecution provided brief descriptions as to how the accused planned, ordered, instigated, and aided and abetted the crimes enumerated in the indictment.[147] The same problem remained, however, with respect to pleading the joint criminal enterprise by reference to 'other known and unknown participants'.[148] Furthermore, the prosecution did not plead the specific state of mind required for each of these forms of responsibility under Article 7(1).

Therefore, certain aspects of the pleadings in the Bosnia indictment did not conform to standards of sufficiency so as to inform Milošević of the nature of the crimes of which he is charged. The same is true of the Croatia Indictment which largely mirrored its Bosnian counterpart.

Conclusion on the defects in the three indictments

All three indictments suffered from defects, more or less material and significant. The Kosovo indictment raised particular concerns. However, it is possible that, had the Croatia and Bosnia indictments been litigated to the same extent, then further defects would have emerged beyond those I have identified. The effect of these defects or inadequacies on a final judgement will now remain undetermined. Differing outcomes are contemplated in the Tribunal's jurisprudence, the most extreme sanction being acquittal.

An accused before the ICTY has the right to a reasoned judgement under Article 23 of the Statute and Rule 98*ter* of the Rules. This means that 'all the constituent elements of a crime have to be discussed and supporting evidence has to [be] assessed by the Trial Chamber'.[149] More specifically, a chamber must address whether any fact that is 'material' – i.e. any fact necessary to establish an element of a crime or underlying offence – has been proved by the prosecution.[150]

Had the Trial Chamber in the *Milošević* case rendered judgement, it would have been required to address not only the 'material facts' pleaded in the indictment but also those regarding the number and identity of

146 Bosnia indictment, para. 26.
147 Bosnia indictment, para. 25.
148 Bosnia indictment, para. 7.
149 *Kordić* Appeals Judgement, above n. 104, para. 383.
150 Ibid. paras. 384–5.

victims contained in the indictments' schedules.[151] It is clearly possible that the Trial Chamber, in rendering judgement, could have entered acquittals on charges against the accused or even on forms of criminal responsibility. While this issue will now remain speculative, of relevance to consideration of this point is a statement by the Appeals Chamber in the *Kupreškić* case, which led to the acquittal of two accused convicted at trial:

> It is of course possible that an indictment may not plead the material facts with the requisite degree of specificity because the necessary information is not in the Prosecution's possession. However, in such a situation, doubt must arise as to whether it is fair to the accused for the trial to proceed. In this connection, the Appeals Chamber emphasises that the Prosecution is expected to know its case before it goes to trial. It is not acceptable for the Prosecution to omit the material aspects of its main allegations in the indictment with the aim of moulding the case against the accused in the course of the trial depending on how the evidence unfolds. There are, of course, instances in criminal trials where the evidence turns out differently than expected. Such a situation may require the indictment to be amended, an adjournment to be granted, or certain evidence to be excluded as not being within the scope of the indictment.[152]

Whatever the outcome of the trial in respect of the pleadings in the *Milošević* indictments would have been, there is a clear lesson to be learned, as can be seen from the ICTY and ICTR jurisprudence discussed above, in respect of complex international criminal law cases. Accuracy and clarity in pleadings is critical. In cases as broad and complex as leadership cases in international criminal law tend to be, the prosecution must know its case from the outset and put the defence on notice accordingly. No doubt considerable difficulties confront prosecutors trying cases of this nature. They are complex to construct and explain, being rooted in decades or centuries of history and being from a culture and language different to those prosecuting and determining the case. Witnesses are reluctant or afraid to come forward to testify against a head of state or

[151] See *Prosecutor v. Galić*, 'Decision on the Defence Motion for Indicating That the First and Second Schedule to the Indictment Dated 10th October 2001 Should be Considered as the Amended Indictment', Case No. IT-98-29-PT, para. 16 ('[S]chedules to an indictment form an integral part of the indictment.'); *Prosecutor v. Krstic*, 'Judgement', Case No. IT-98-33-T, 2 August 2001, para. 701 ('[T]he Trial Chamber must assess the seriousness of the crimes in the light of their individual circumstances. This presupposes taking into account quantitatively the number of victims. . . .'); *Prosecutor v. Deronjic*, 'Judgement', Case No. IT-02-61-S, 30 March 2004, para. 185 (considering that the 'large number of victims' was an 'aggravating circumstance' in the determination of sentence).

[152] *Kupreškić* Appeals Judgement, above n. 91, para. 92.

leader still with residual political influence – a point often made by the prosecution early in the Milošević case.[153] Evidence emerges over time and investigations continue – a point recently made by the chief prosecutor in the *Milošević* case, Geoffrey Nice QC.[154] However, neither the international community, nor a court, will sit patiently waiting for the perfect or optimal case to emerge – nor should they, when an accused awaits trial in custody.

Failure by the prosecution to resolve these complexities in the process of investigation and execution of indictments will threaten the fair and expeditious trial framework of international criminal trials. In this respect, there are aspects of the process that can better achieve a more succinct and focused prosecution, which the *Milošević* trial would clearly have benefited from.

The scope of the prosecution case should be addressed at the earliest possible time in a rational and balanced manner. It is possible that the greatest flaw in the prosecution approach to the *Milošević* case was trying to prove too much. The construction and pursuit of the broadest possible case made the trial an almost unmanageable process, threatening the fairness of the trial and certainly its expedition. This is because the prosecution could not, and perhaps could not reasonably have been expected to, conduct efficiently such an enormous case. The prosecution, by applying for joinder of the three indictments, and the Appeals Chamber in granting the application, created significant case management problems later faced by the Trial Chamber and the parties. The Appeals Chamber recognised the scope and complexity of such a grand case and gravely warned the prosecution of the risks,[155] but nonetheless allowed the joinder of the indictments to proceed. But it is the prosecution that must take responsibility for the scope of its case, having prepared and presented such a case and pressed joinder on appeal. It then aggressively resisted endeavours by the Trial Chamber to consider severance at various points in the trial process in an attempt to achieve a manageable trial outcome.[156]

[153] See, e.g., *Prosecutor v. Milošević*, 'Decision on Prosecution Motion for Protective Measures for Sensitive Source Witnesses Testifying During the Croatia Phase of the Trial', Case No. IT-02-54-T, 17 September 2002.

[154] Third interview of Geoffrey Nice, 'Sense Tribunal' <http://www.sense-agency.com/en/stream.php?sta=3&pid=7997&kat=3> at 5 October 2006; Joshua Rozenburg, 'Trying Milošević: What Went Wrong', Telegraph.co.uk, <http://www.telegraph.co.uk/news/main.jhtml?xml=/news/2006/09/14/nlaw14.xml> at 5 October 2006.

[155] See Appeal Joinder Decision', above n. 2, paras. 26–7.

[156] Joinder will be discussed in detail later in this chapter; severance is discussed in detail in chapter three of this book.

The prosecution has persistently stated its responsibility to all the victims of the conflicts in the three indictments,[157] a clearly legitimate concern and one echoed by human rights groups.[158] However, it is difficult to imagine that it is possible to satisfy the legitimate needs and interests of all the victims of three conflicts over eight years, particularly in the context of a single criminal trial. The ICTY Statute and Rules provide no substantive rights for victims to participate in the proceedings or obtain reparations.[159] Although the Tribunal gave consideration to setting up a commission to deal with these issues, problems related to its functioning in the context of an international criminal tribunal (including questions relating to retroactivity of its operation, funding and constitutional authority) meant that it never evolved into a serious possibility.[160] Ultimately, the prosecution

[157] See e.g., *Prosecutor v. Milošević*, 'Prosecution Submission in Response to the Trial Chamber's 22 November 2005 "Scheduling Order for a Hearing" on Severing the Kosovo Indictment', Case No. IT-02-54-T, 29 November 2005, para. 49: 'The individuals who are victims of the wars have a right to a public resolution of the conflicts they experienced. Some are elderly or ill and might not live to see another trial; those who would survive deserve to have a timely public and just resolution of the crimes committed against them or their families and friends.' See also, reference of the Prosecutor to 'the thousands of victims who are demanding justice': *Prosecutor v. Milošević*, Hearing, Case No. IT-01-50-PT & IT-01-51-I & IT-99-37-PT, 11 December 2001, Transcript, 69, 91; *Prosecutor v. Milošević*, Hearing, 12 February 2002, Transcript, 10–11.

[158] See, e.g., comments by Richard Dicker, head of the International Justice Programme at Human Rights Watch, criticising the ICC Prosecutor for not indicting Thomas Lubanga for a broader range of crimes: Institute for War and Peace Reporting ('IWPR'), 'ICC Prosecution Defends its Tactics', http://www.iwpr.net/?=f&p=tri&o=a6e19c2fec1d248789222860dd21c84c&1=EN 1 August 2006, 2.

[159] ICTY Rules 105 and 106 provide procedures for restitution of property and compensation but neither provision has been utilised. See David Tolbert and Frederick Swinnen, 'The Protection of, and Assistance to, Witnesses at the ICTY' in Hirad Abtahi and Gideon Boas (eds), *The Dynamics of International Criminal Justice: Essays in Honour of Sir Richard May* (2006), 193; Pascale Chifflet, 'The Role and Status of the Victim', in Gideon Boas and William A. Schabas (eds), *International Criminal Law Developments in the Case Law of the ICTY* (2003), 102–103.

[160] See David Tolbert and Frederick Swinnen, above n. 159, 195; 'Report attached to a letter dated 12 October 2000 from the President of the International Tribunal for the former Yugoslavia addressed to the Secretary-General', U.N. Doc. S/2000/1063, annex. Provisions relating to victim rights and representation are entrenched in the ICC Statute, although no practice exists at this stage concerning how this process will operate: see Pascale Chifflet, above n. 159, 104–109; Sam Garkawe, 'The Victim-Related Provisions of the Statute of the International Criminal Court: A Victimology Analysis' (2001) 8 *International Review of Victimology* 284; Theo van Boven, 'The Position of the Victim in the Statute of the International Criminal Court', in Herman von Hebel, Johan G. Lammers & Jolien Schukking (eds), *Reflections on the International Criminal Court: Essays in Honour of Adriaan Bos* (1999) 81–2. Efforts were also made to establish a Truth and Reconciliation Commission concerning events in the former Yugoslavia, although this never eventuated: see Pascale Chifflet above n. 159, 109.

would do little justice to victims by presenting a massive case in which it was unable to lead sufficient evidence to explain, let alone establish many of the alleged offences. In this respect, the choices made by prosecutors of Saddam Hussein to initially indict him for the Dujail incident, and the ICC Prosecutor to indict Thomas Lubanga only for conscripting child soldiers, seem a rational and practical approach, and – in the latter case at least – was a direct reaction to the *Milošević* trial.[161]

Other considerations that the prosecution has stated led to such a broad case being pursued included the importance of telling the truth about what happened in the conflicts and the historical record that the trial will leave. In December 2001, the ICTY Prosecutor, Carla Del Ponte argued that joinder of the three indictments into a single trial 'would finally make it possible to know the truth as to the real responsibilities of the accused Milošević'.[162] Del Ponte also argued that a single trial against Milošević was an important element of reconciliation and peace in the former Yugoslavia, referring to UN Security Council Resolution 1329.[163] At the opening of the trial, Del Ponte also referred to the historical context in which this trial was to occur and the importance of this to the prosecution: 'I recognise that this trial will make history, and we would do well to approach our task in the light of history'.[164] Finally, it has unsurprisingly been asserted that politics dictated the Prosecutor's actions in charging Milošević with such a broad array of crimes resulting in 'a whale of a trial'.[165]

These considerations were the apparent motivating factor for the prosecution to lead such a broad case. As early as the close of the prosecution case it was apparent that this was a case the breadth of which it could not prove. In a judgement of acquittal ruling by the Chamber after the close of the prosecution case, by not leading evidence (or leading insufficient evidence) on a large number of crime base incidents pleaded, the prosecution case was in fact reduced.[166]

161 See IWPR, 'ICC Prosecution Defends its Tactics', above n. 158.

162 *Prosecutor v. Milošević*, Hearing, Case No. IT-01-50-PT & IT-01-51-I & IT-99-37-PT, 11 December 2001, Transcript, 69.

163 Ibid.

164 *Prosecutor v. Milošević*, Hearing, 12 February 2002, Transcript, 8. See also, *Prosecutor v. Milošević*, Hearing, 10 April 2002, Transcript, 2755.

165 See Chris Stephen, 'Pressures on Hague court undermining its work', <http://www.ireland.com/newspaper/ireland/2005/1121> at 1 August 2006.

166 After receiving full written submissions, the Trial Chamber issued the following decision: *Prosecutor v Milošević*, 'Decision on Motion for Judgement of Acquittal', Case No. IT-02-54-T, 16 June 2004 ('Trial Chamber Acquittal Decision'). See discussion below in Section IV of this chapter.

It would have been preferable for the prosecution to have constructed a narrower case from the start so that the accused and the Trial Chamber would have been in a better position to understand and deal with the case against Milošević, and so that the legitimate extra-legal considerations raised by the prosecution could have been more adequately reflected in the limited framework of the international criminal trial – a forensic process dedicated primarily to the establishment of guilt or innocence of an individual. Furthermore, earlier preparation and issuance of its indictments, particularly for Croatia and Bosnia, would have given the accused and the Chamber greater opportunity to prepare for the trial.

There is reluctance on the part of the ICTY Office of the Prosecutor (shared in other international criminal courts and tribunals) to amend its indictments, even in the face of apparent deficiencies. The reason for this may be an understandable defensiveness about the prosecutorial pleading instrument and a concern that acknowledging defects in the instrument, which was initially confirmed by a judge and on which basis an accused has often been arrested and detained, might weaken its adversarial position.

Failure to construct satisfactory accusatory instruments in the first place is probably related to several factors. First, the Office of the Prosecutor at the ICTY was for many years 'investigations-driven', meaning that investigators went into the field and collected all evidence of possible relevance and thereafter lawyers constructed indictments and sought to fashion a case out of the growing quantity of available material. There is a folklore anecdote at the ICTY that in the first months of the Tribunal's existence Graham Blewitt (former Deputy Prosecutor) kept all the prosecution evidence in two binders in his filing cabinet. This quickly swelled to become millions of pages of documents and other material. This investigations-up approach no doubt caused difficulties in defining and constructing prosecution cases of such magnitude. Second, the sheer size of these cases makes them extremely difficult to construct and conduct. When a case consists of hundreds of witnesses or, as in the *Milošević* case, a proposed list of over 1,000 witnesses, traversing vast areas of crime base and all possible forms of criminal responsibility, it will invariably be profoundly complex and difficult to frame. These problems, if unresolved, will inevitably be reflected in flawed accusatory instruments, particularly where – as was apparent in the *Milošević* case – investigations were ongoing and the prosecution theory was incomplete or uncertain at the start of the case. Finally, the adversarial mindset of the prosecution, largely staffed by American trial attorneys (as well as common lawyers from other countries), and no doubt reinforced by the typically uncooperative approach taken by defence counsel, may tend to prevent an open acknowledgement of the difficulties and deficiencies that warrant attention.

Finally, an assessment of the *Milošević* indictments, in light of the law relating to review of indictments generally before the ICTY, raises questions which are broader than prosecutorial responsibility. As already suggested, the Trial Chamber should itself have intervened *proprio motu* to address apparent material defects in the indictments. It may be that a reluctance to do so is fed by the ostensibly adversarial nature of the proceedings before the ICTY, and – to a similar effect – in all international criminal courts and tribunals. However, the nature of these complex trials and the fact that a judge is required to confirm an indictment before a case can proceed, suggests that judicial intervention is a contemplated part of the process. Furthermore, it is apparent that the state of many indictments before the ICTY, particularly those issued early in the Tribunal's existence, suggests that reviewing judges tended to confirm indictments even when materially defective. This may in part be due to the unilateral nature of the reviewing process, which takes place between the prosecution and the judge, obviously without any input from the defence.

One way to test the indictment early enough to impact materially on pre-trial preparation would be to create another (this time adversarial *inter partes*) opportunity for review of the indictment. Once the supporting material to the indictment has been disclosed to the accused and their counsel (within thirty days of initial appearance),[167] a procedure could be created to conduct a further review of the prosecution indictment, this time before a full trial chamber and with a represented accused, to challenge the sufficiency of the supporting material in relation to each count in the indictment. This would force the prosecution to justify its case in relation to all allegations made and eventuate in deletions, amendments or clarifications of the charges in the indictment. The further process concerning the form of indictments already provided for in Rule 72 of the ICTY Rules could then proceed, which would deal with the sufficiency of the pleading process. Alternatively, both the *inter partes* review process and challenges to the form of the indictment could be dealt with simultaneously. By the time this process was concluded, a thorough review of the form and content of the indictment would have taken place, putting the parties and the Chamber in a far better position to proceed to trial with a

[167] Rule 66(A)(i) of the ICTY Rules.

clear understanding of the nature and scope of the prosecution case. It would also set the Trial Chamber up for some important case management activity prior to trial.

It is clear from the evident lack of prosecutorial restraint that the court must exercise coercive control over the prosecution in the scope and presentation of cases in international criminal law. Provision for such intervention is essential to enable a court to fulfil its duty to ensure that a fair trial is given. This will serve the interests of international criminal justice and the earlier it is provided for in the proceedings the less likely it is that courts will be placed in the more questionable position of intervening in the accusatory instrument later in the case.

Joinder of the Miloševič Indictments

Another issue of considerable importance to the scope and conduct of the *Milošević* case was the joinder of the three indictments.

The *Milošević* indictments were filed and confirmed as three separate indictments constituting three distinct cases against a single accused. It is unclear whether the prosecution always intended to join these three cases into one case spanning three conflicts over eight years or whether that decision was taken subsequent to the issuance of the Kosovo indictment.

Joinder application before the Trial Chamber

On 27 November 2001, shortly after the confirmation by Judge May of the initial Bosnia indictment, the prosecution filed a motion pursuant to Rule 49 of the ICTY Rules in which it sought to join the three indictments against the accused into one.[168] Rule 49 provides that, '[t]wo or more crimes may be joined in one indictment if the series of acts committed together form the same transaction, and the said crimes were committed by the same Accused'. A 'transaction' for these purposes is defined in Rule 2 of the Rules as '[a] number of acts or omissions, whether occurring as one event or a number of events, at the same or different locations and being part of a common scheme, strategy or plan'.

Based on a reading of these Rules, the prosecution argued that the three indictments concerned the same transaction in the context of a common scheme, strategy, or plan, 'namely the accused Milošević's overall conduct

[168] *Prosecutor v. Milošević*, 'Prosecution's Motion for Joinder, filed 27 November 2001 and Prosecution's Corrigendum to Motion for Joinder Filed 27 November 2001', Case Nos. IT-99-37-PT; IT-01-50-PT; and IT-01-51-PT, 10 December 2001 ('Motion for Joinder').

in attempting to create a "Greater Serbia." '[169] In support of this view, it pointed to paragraph 6 of the Croatia and Bosnia indictments, and paragraph 16 of the Kosovo indictment, all of which essentially alleged the forcible removal of non-Serbs from the respective territories through the commission of crimes sanctioned under the ICTY Statute.

The prosecution also argued that joinder of the indictments would lead to a more fair and expeditious trial for the accused. A single trial would, it was argued, be shorter and would provide a more consolidated trial timetable. Without joinder, the accused could face a trial at the same time as confronting two other pre-trial phases. More than one trial would require repeated testimony and the consideration by other Trial Chambers of the degree to which evidence or findings from one trial should be incorporated into another. In a single trial, it was said that the aggravating and mitigating factors – probably common to all three indictments – could be determined together.[170] The prosecution also argued that a single trial would promote judicial economy. The number of witnesses called may be less in that some witnesses, such as those testifying on history or policy, would not have to testify three times, and the provision of exculpatory evidence would also be better facilitated with one trial.[171]

It was argued that the trauma to victims would be lessened if they only needed to testify once. In addition, security concerns would be lessened if the witnesses only had to travel to The Hague to testify once.[172] Finally, it was submitted that a single trial would ensure that judgements were not conflicting, since the same Chamber would decide issues of credibility and evaluate all the evidence. A single trial would also obviate concern about the appeal of one while the second or third trial was still ongoing.[173]

On 13 December 2001, the Trial Chamber allowed the prosecution motion to the extent that the Croatia and Bosnia indictments would be joined, but denied joinder of the Kosovo indictment.[174] The principal issue in dispute was whether the events to which all three indictments related formed part of the same transaction, that is, part of a common scheme, strategy or plan. The Trial Chamber reasoned that the reference to a 'series' and the use of the phrase 'committed together' in Rule 49 indicated that the acts in question must be connected and that there is no power to join unconnected acts on the ground that they form part of the same plan. This plan must be such that the counts represent interrelated

[169] Ibid. 5. [170] Ibid. 14–15. [171] Ibid. 15–17. [172] Ibid. 18. [173] Ibid. 18–19.

[174] *Prosecutor v. Milošević*, 'Decision on Prosecution's Motion for Joinder', Case Nos. IT-99-37-PT; IT-01-50-PT; and IT-01-51-PT, 13 December 2001 ('Trial Chamber Joinder Decision'), para. 3.

parts of a particular criminal episode. The Chamber also stated that in case of dissimilarity in time and place, the conclusion that the counts represent interrelated parts of a particular criminal episode would be more difficult to draw.[175]

The Chamber went on to hold that Rule 49 must be interpreted in the light of the entitlement of the accused to a fair hearing, pursuant to Article 21(2) of the Statute, so that joinder would not be permitted where it would prejudice the accused's right to a fair hearing. Furthermore, joinder should not be granted where the interests of justice would be prejudiced. Finally, the Chamber held that factors such as judicial economy, especially the avoidance of duplication of evidence and the avoidance of hardship to witnesses, should be taken into account.[176]

The Trial Chamber ultimately held that, because of the geographic and temporal differences between the Kosovo indictment and the other two indictments, as well as the distinction in the way the accused was alleged to have acted as pleaded in the three indictments, it could not be said to form part of a series of acts committed together in the sense of 'the same transaction' as far as the Kosovo indictment was concerned. This conclusion was reached on the basis of several considerations. First, there was a gap of more than three years between the last events in Bosnia and the first events in Kosovo.[177] Second, while the conflicts in Croatia and Bosnia took place in neighbouring states to the FRY, those in Kosovo took place in the FRY itself.[178] Third, the accused was alleged to have acted 'indirectly' in relation to Croatia and Bosnia, but 'directly' (as the Supreme Commander of the Armed Forces of the FRY) in relation to Kosovo.[179] Finally, and most significantly for the purposes of this analysis, there was no reference to a 'Greater Serbia' plan in the Kosovo indictment.[180] The Trial Chamber concluded that the nexus would be too nebulous to point to the existence of a 'common scheme, strategy or plan' required for the 'same transaction' under Rule 49.[181] The Chamber also reasoned that the expectation that only twenty witnesses would have to repeat their evidence in separate trials would not be of great significance given the overall numbers of witnesses proposed.[182] The Trial Chamber felt that it would not be unduly influenced by prejudicial evidence in one trial affecting another. In case of such risk the evidence would have to be excluded.[183]

Finally, two points which have become of great significance in hindsight were made by the Trial Chamber: (1) it felt that a single trial of the

[175] Ibid. para. 36. [176] Ibid. para. 38. [177] Ibid. para. 42. [178] Ibid. para. 43.
[179] Ibid. para. 44. [180] Ibid. para. 45. [181] Ibid. [182] Ibid. para. 48.
[183] Ibid. para. 50.

expected length would be far too long and that two trials would enable the Trial Chamber to manage the cases more easily;[184] and (2) if the accused had to defend himself on the content of three indictments together this would be onerous and prejudicial, particularly in the case of the Kosovo indictment and its different circumstances.

Joinder application on appeal

On 15 January 2002, the prosecution filed an interlocutory appeal against the Trial Chamber's decision.[185] The Appeals Chamber allowed the prosecution's appeal and ordered that the three indictments would be tried together as one trial.[186] This was to be the first of a number of poorly reasoned rulings by the Appeals Chamber in respect of the *Milošević* trial. The decision set in train a trial that was to prove unmanageable (because of the Appeals Chamber's ruling) and one that would never conclude, and it therefore requires detailed consideration.

The Appeals Chamber held that the Trial Chamber had misdirected itself as to the correct interpretation of Rule 49; this error of law invalidated the decision and vitiated the exercise by the Trial Chamber of its discretion. In the exercise of its own discretion, the Appeals Chamber held that upon a correct interpretation of Rule 49, the acts alleged in the Croatia, Bosnia, and Kosovo indictments formed the same transaction.[187] After reasoning that Rule 49, dealing with joinder of crimes, must be considered in conjunction with Rule 48, dealing with joinder of accused – as each is based upon events which must form 'the same transaction'[188] – the Appeals Chamber held that Rule 49 does not require the events in Kosovo to have been 'committed together' with the events in Croatia and Bosnia. It gave several reasons for this. First, an interpretation requiring the prosecution to establish that all the offences to be joined were committed together 'creates an unnecessary dichotomy between the test for the joinder of offences (which would require the indictment to show that they were committed together for the purposes of Rule 49) and the test for the joinder of accused (where Rule 48 has no such requirement)'.[189] Furthermore, the definition of the term 'transaction' in Rule 2 contemplates a much less restrictive approach by permitting the common scheme, strategy or plan to

[184] Ibid. para. 47.

[185] The prosecution had filed, on 20 December 2001, an 'Application for Leave to File an Interlocutory Appeal', which the Appeals Chamber granted on 9 January 2002.

[186] Appeal Joinder Ruling, above n. 2.

[187] Ibid.

[188] Appeal Joinder Decision, above n. 2, para. 13.

[189] Ibid. para. 14.

include an event at the same or different locations. Thus, the Appeals Chamber concluded that there 'is no logical explanation immediately apparent for a distinction to be drawn between allowing different locations but not allowing different events at different times'.[190]

Second, the Appeals Chamber focused on the fact that an interpretation of Rule 49 requiring the offences to have been committed together does not exist in the French version of the Rule, where it states in respect of the words 'if the series of acts committed together form the same transaction', '*si les actes incriminés ont été commis à l'occasion de la même opération*'.[191] The Appeals Chamber referred to Rule 7 of the ICTY Rules, which states that in case of discrepancy between the English and French texts of the Rules, the version which is 'more consonant with the spirit of the Statute and the Rules' shall prevail. According to the Appeals Chamber the apparent discrepancy was not intractable.[192] It also reasoned that its textual interpretation was in accordance with Article 33 of the 1969 Vienna Convention on the Law of the Treaties, dealing with interpretation of treaties authenticated in two or more languages.[193] It concluded by interpreting the English version of Rule 49 as follows: 'if the series of acts committed (by the accused) together (in the sense of "considered together as a whole") form the same transaction. . .'.[194] On the basis of this interpretation, the Appeals Chamber held that the acts alleged in all three indictments formed part of the same transaction. Referring to the reasoning of the Trial Chamber which led it to reject a Kosovo joinder, the Appeals Chamber held that each of the matters articulated were relevant considerations, but none was decisive.[195]

The ruling is questionable for two reasons. First, in respect of the same transaction definition, in spite of its importance, the Appeals Chamber adopted and implemented in a wholesale manner the submissions of the prosecution on appeal, without material extrapolation of the issue. Second, the approach to this issue stretched the boundaries of logic. The Chamber held that the delay of three years between the last events in Bosnia and the first events in Kosovo were consistent with the definition of a 'common scheme, strategy or plan' because the transaction did not

[190] Ibid. [191] Appeal Joinder Decision, above n. 2, para. 15. [192] Ibid.

[193] Ibid. para. 16. In this context the Appeals Chamber referred to a Commentary upon Article 75 of the Draft Convention (not relevantly differing from Article 33) in which the International Law Commission stressed that 'in law there is only one treaty – one set of terms (. . .) and one common intention with respect to those terms – even when two authentic texts appear to diverge' and 'every effort should be made to find a common meaning for the texts before preferring one to another'.

[194] Ibid. para. 17. [195] Ibid. para. 20.

have to maintain exactly the same parameters at all times but may include the achievement of a long-term aim. Here, that alleged long-term aim was to establish or maintain control by the Serb authorities over particular areas which were or were once part of the former Yugoslavia.[196] The Appeals Chamber reasoned that, even though the indictments did not explicitly bring out the overall nature of the prosecution case, they made it sufficiently clear that the common purpose behind all the alleged events was the forcible removal of the majority of the non-Serb civilian population from areas which the Serb authorities wished to establish or to maintain as Serbian-controlled areas by the commission of the crimes charged.[197] The fact that some events occurred within a province of Serbia and others within neighbouring states was held to be consistent with this interpretation.[198] However, by the time of the commission of alleged crimes in Kosovo, the accused was the head of the state in which the alleged crimes were committed. Therefore, it could not be said that the accused was seeking territorial expansion, as alleged in respect of Croatia and Bosnia. Rather, the allegation must have been that he was seeking the expulsion or displacement of a large portion of his own population. The fact, however, that the accused was alleged to have acted directly in the province but indirectly in the neighbouring states merely reflected, according to the Appeals Chamber, the available means by which the accused is alleged to have sought to achieve the same result.[199]

Interestingly, in a much later decision on an application to join three cases which were geographically and temporally very different, a special Trial Chamber composed of the presiding judges of all three Trial Chambers stated:

> The very wide interpretation of the notion of 'same transaction' adopted by the Appeals Chamber in the *Milošević* case leads the Trial Chamber to the conclusion that the requirement of 'same transaction' has been met in this case as well. Indeed, the Appeals Chamber decision makes it very difficult for any Trial Chamber seized of a joinder request alleging that the accused had a 'common purpose' to conclude that such a requirement has not been met, even if the common purpose is a very broad and long-term one.[200]

[196] Ibid. para. 21. [197] Ibid. para. 20. [198] Ibid.

[199] Appeal Joinder Decision, above n. 2, para. 20.

[200] *Prosecutor v. Martić; Prosecutor v. Stanišić and Simatović; Prosecutor v. Šešelj*, 'Decision on Prosecution Motion for Joinder', Case Nos. IT-95-11-PT, IT-03-69-PT, IT-03-67-PT, 10 November 2005.

Under the Appeals Chamber's extremely broad approach, it would be possible to try together most, if not all, Serb accused across the entirety of Croatia, Bosnia and Kosovo for all events, so long as an aspect of the case against them was participation in a plan to ethnically cleanse a geographical region of non-Serbs – ostensibly encompassing all indictments against Serbs before the ICTY.

A final aspect of the decision to join these three indictments into one trial was acceptance by the Appeals Chamber that the same transaction tying these indictments together was a loosely described and defined Greater Serbia espoused by the accused. It was the idea of a Greater Serbia that appears to have been the forensic basis prompting the Appeals Chamber to its decision. As discussed above, the prosecution's case on this crucial issue seemed to shift, remaining unclear until, when pressed by the Trial Chamber three and a half years later during the cross-examination of a defence witness, it explained more clearly what was meant by a Greater Serbia and the role ascribed to Milošević as a proponent of it.[201]

The Appeals Chamber decision on joinder was one of the most significant decisions rendered in the case. Its legal and practical consequences were profound, and the untimely and unsatisfactory conclusion of the trial can be tied four years back to this ruling. In the framework of international criminal trials, this ruling stands as a warning to the overextension of same transaction theories and the underestimation of the importance of practical case management issues in the exercise of a court's discretion to join events or indictments into large complex cases.

Rule 98*bis* (Judgement of Acquittal) Decision

At the close of the prosecution case, pursuant to Rule 98*bis*, an accused may file a motion for judgement of acquittal. Although subsequently amended to streamline this process, at the time the *Milošević* Decision was rendered Rule 98*bis* read as follows:

(A) An accused may file a motion for the entry of judgement of acquittal on one or more offences charged in the indictment within seven days after the close of the Prosecutor's case and, in any event, prior to the presentation of evidence by the defence pursuant to Rule 85 (A)(ii).

(B) The Trial Chamber shall order the entry of judgement of acquittal on motion of accused or *proprio motu* if it finds that the evidence is insufficient to sustain a conviction on that or those charges.

[201] See detailed analysis of the prosecution case regarding 'Greater Serbia' earlier in this chapter.

Although the accused did not file a motion for judgement of acquittal, the Trial Chamber had already authorised the *amici curiae* to file such a motion on his behalf,[202] which they did on 3 March 2004.[203] The prosecution case closed on 25 February 2004.[204] After receiving written submissions, the Trial Chamber rendered its 'Decision on Motion for Judgement of Acquittal' on 16 June 2004.

The judgement of acquittal procedure is a concept of the common law, where it is sometimes known as a submission that there is 'no case to answer'. It calls for a determination of the issue after the close of the prosecution case, but before the defence presents its case. The Rule is crafted as a procedural safeguard to ensure that in circumstances where 'even on its own evidence the prosecution has failed to prove its case', the proceedings against an accused can be terminated.[205] The test for determining whether the evidence is insufficient to sustain a conviction is 'whether there is evidence (if accepted) upon which a tribunal of fact *could* be satisfied beyond reasonable doubt of the guilt of the accused on the particular charge in question'; therefore, 'the test is not whether the trier of fact would in fact arrive at a conviction beyond reasonable doubt on the Prosecution evidence if accepted, but whether it could'.[206]

The Trial Chamber Acquittal Decision took some months to produce and is over 140 pages in length. Why did the Chamber give so much attention to the applicable test and why was the judgement so extensive? Many of the Trial Chamber judgements of acquittal before the Tribunal, with the notable exception of *Jelisić*, who was acquitted of genocide on a *proprio motu* exercise of Rule 98*bis* by the Chamber, were brief rejections without much reasoning or analysis. The reason for such an extensive judgement in *Milošević* probably lay in the fact that there were a large

[202] On 7 April 2003, the *amici curiae* filed a motion seeking directions on their future role, including the question as to whether they should file a motion pursuant to Rule 98*bis* of the Rules of Procedure and Evidence ('Rules') at the close of the Prosecution case: '*Amici curiae* Request for Directions Upon the Manner of Their Future Engagement in the Trial and Procedural Directions Under Rule 98 *bis* (A)', 7 April 2003. On 27 June 2003, the Trial Chamber issued an order stating, *inter alia*, that 'the *amici curiae* may submit a Motion pursuant to Rule 98*bis* within seven days of the close of the Prosecution case': 'Order on *Amici curiae* Request Concerning the Manner of Their Future Engagement and Procedural Directions under Rule 98*bis*', 27 June 2003.

[203] *Amici* Acquittal Motion, above n. 87.

[204] See 'Decision on Notification of the Completion of Prosecution Case and Motion for the Admission of Evidence in Written Form', 25 February 2004.

[205] Richard May and Marieke Wierda, *International Criminal Evidence* (2002), 126.

[206] *Prosecutor v. Jelisić*, 'Judgement', Case No.: IT-95-10-A, 5 July 2001 ('*Jelisić* Appeal Judgement'), para. 37.

number of 'crime base' allegations in the Croatia and – particularly – Bosnia indictments for which acquittals were entered. There were important legal questions raised concerning the existence of an armed conflict in Kosovo, the legal tests for deportation and forcible transfer and the existence of Statehood for Croatia, which impacted on the internationality of the armed conflict and therefore the application of grave breaches of the Geneva Conventions to crimes charged against Milošević in the Croatia indictment.

Did Milošević intend to commit genocide?

The Decision contained an important close call on the crown jewel of the prosecution case on Bosnia: the assertion that Milošević possessed the special intent required for genocide. The Bosnia indictment charged him with participation in a joint criminal enterprise, the purpose of which was the 'forcible and permanent removal of the majority of non-Serbs, principally Bosnian Muslims and Bosnian Croats, from large areas of the Republic of Bosnia and Herzegovina.'[207] It alleged that thousands of Bosnian Muslims and Bosnian Croats were killed, and included the Srebrenica massacre in July 1995.[208]

In its Motion for judgement of acquittal, the *amici curiae* argued that the prosecution did not adduce any or sufficient evidence that the accused planned, instigated, ordered, committed, or otherwise aided and abetted in the planning, preparation, or execution of a genocide, any genocidal acts, or that he was complicit in such, and that the *mens rea* requirement for establishing the crime of genocide is incompatible with the *mens rea* requirement for the third category of a joint criminal enterprise (concerning acts that were a natural and foreseeable outcome of an agreed criminal enterprise) and command responsibility.[209]

The Trial Chamber had noted in the Judgement of Acquittal Decision that the prosecution conceded 'there is little direct evidence to that precise effect, such as a specific order to commit genocide signed by the accused or a confession by him'.[210] It argued that the Trial Chamber must instead look at all the facts and circumstances proved in the prosecution case and that 'if a sufficient number of circumstances can be objectively identified that together demonstrate a coherent series of actions on the part of the accused, a reasonable tribunal of fact would be entitled to

[207] Bosnia indictment, para. 6. [208] Ibid. para. 32 (a).

[209] *Amici* Acquittal Motion, above n. 87, paras. 161–2.

[210] Trial Chamber Acquittal Decision, above n. 166, para. 121; Acquittal Response, above n. 88, para. 249.

draw the necessary inference that the accused did intend the destruction of part of the Bosnian Muslim group'.[211] The establishment of the specific intent required for genocide is most usually inferred from the evidence. As the Appeals Chamber in the *Jelisić* case held, in the absence of direct evidence, proof of the accused's specific intent may be inferred from

> a number of facts and circumstances, such as the general context, the perpetration of other culpable acts systematically directed against the same group, the scale of atrocities committed, the systematic targeting of victims on account of their membership of a particular group, or the repetition of destructive and discriminatory acts.[212]

The prosecution argued that inferences could be drawn from the crime-base evidence, together with evidence of the acts and the role of the accused himself.[213]

The Chamber embarked on a lengthy analysis of the crime base evidence in all the municipalities relied on by the prosecution. The territorial scope, as well as the relevant target groups, of the prosecution case in respect of genocide was plagued by confusion and inconsistencies. The Bosnia indictment initially pleaded that Milošević was responsible for a campaign of genocide in Bosnia and Herzegovina against the Bosnian Muslim and Bosnian Croat population. However, in its pre-trial brief, the prosecution indicated, in a footnote, that it would not seek to prove that genocide was committed against the Bosnian Croats and that it intended to proceed to prove the crime of genocide only in respect of seven municipalities (instead of the fourteen pleaded in the indictment).[214] To make matters more confusing, after reducing to seven the municipalities in respect of which the prosecution would seek to prove genocide, it then expressly deleted, in the amended Bosnia indictment of 22 November 2002, the territories of Zvornik and Bratunac; and, in its Response to the Motion for Judgement of Acquittal it submitted that it had led evidence on four municipalities: Brčko, Sanski Most, Prijedor, and Srebrenica.[215] The specific areas to be considered for the crime of genocide were therefore

[211] Ibid.

[212] *Jelisić* Appeal Judgement, above n. 206, para. 47; Trial Chamber Acquittal Decision, above n. 166, para. 120.

[213] Acquittal Response, above n. 88, para. 246.

[214] Croatia and Bosnia pre-trial brief, above n. 26, 31 May 2002, para. 997, footnote 2077 states that this reduced geographical focus was adopted both in the interests of judicial economy in light of the Trial Chamber's oral ruling of 10 April 2002 as to the limitations on the time allocated to the Prosecution case and in order to enable a concentration on the most egregious examples of genocidal crimes within Bosnia and Herzegovina. The municipalities are: Bosanski Novi, Brčko, Ključ, Kotor Varoš, Prijedor, Sanski Most, and Srebrenica.

[215] Acquittal Response, above n. 88, para. 376.

further limited. However, the prosecution submitted, in a footnote, that there is also 'limited evidence' in relation to Kotor Varoš, Ključ, and Bosanski Novi,[216] and then went on to assert that genocidal acts were perpetrated in other unnamed municipalities, 'in fact wherever required to implement the strategic objective of the SDS leadership',[217] and that there is sufficient evidence of crimes within the meaning of Article 4(2) of the Statute in municipalities other than the identified four, including Zvornik and Bratunac (which it had deleted in the amended Bosnia indictment).[218] The prosecution went on to refer to other evidence (for example, in relation to Bijeljina and Teslić)[219] that it claimed supported its case that genocide was committed in a number of other municipalities. However, as the Chamber noted, Teslić was not referred to either in the initial or amended indictments or in the Pre-Trial Brief as a territory on which the prosecution relied to establish genocide.

Somehow, the Trial Chamber managed to untangle the mess, and in doing so gave the prosecution the benefit of considerable doubt, to determine that genocide was pleaded in respect of the following territories in Bosnia and Herzegovina: Brčko, Prijedor, Sanski Most, Srebrenica, Bijeljina, Kotor Varoš, Ključ, and Bosanski Novi.[220] It therefore ruled out consideration of genocide in the two deleted municipalities (Zvornik and Bratunac) and the municipality never before mentioned (Teslić). The Trial Chamber, after surveying the prosecution evidence, found that a reasonable Trial Chamber *could* find beyond reasonable doubt that there existed a joint criminal enterprise, which included members of the Bosnian Serb leadership, the aim and intention of which was to destroy a part of the Bosnian Muslims as a group, and that its participants committed genocide in Brčko, Prijedor, Sanski Most, Srebrenica, Bijeljina, Ključ, and Bosanski Novi, but found there was no evidence in respect of Kotor Varoš.[221] The Chamber also held, after reviewing evidence concerning the leadership role of the accused and his relationship with the top Bosnian Serb political and military authorities, that it could find that the accused was a participant in that joint criminal enterprise.[222]

Beyond its obvious importance for the prosecution's case, this finding is important for another crucial reason: Judge Kwon dissented. The majority concluded that sufficient evidence existed only to the required sufficiency to avoid a judgement of acquittal – that a reasonable Trial Chamber *could*

[216] Ibid. para. 152, note 746. [217] Ibid. para. 376. [218] Ibid. para. 377.
[219] Ibid. 153, note 748. [220] Trial Chamber Acquittal Decision, above n. 166, para. 138.
[221] Ibid. para. 323(1).
[222] Ibid. para. 288. The Chamber set out in detail the evidentiary basis for this conclusion.

ultimately find on the evidence beyond reasonable doubt. Judge Kwon agreed that there was sufficient evidence upon which a Trial Chamber could convict the accused of (i) genocide under the third category of joint criminal enterprise, (ii) aiding and abetting or complicity in genocide, or (iii) genocide as a superior.[223] However, he went on to reason that, taking the evidence from the prosecution's case at its highest, 'the furthest that a Trial Chamber could infer in relation to the *mens rea* requirement is the knowledge of [Milošević] that genocide was being committed in the specified municipalities in Bosnia and Herzegovina, but not the genocidal intent of the Accused himself'. He stated that the latter conclusion could not be automatically inferred from the finding that the accused knew that the principal perpetrators were committing genocide, or that it was reasonably foreseeable to him that genocide could be committed as a consequence of the commission of other crimes. 'And, with the evidence presented, finding of the genocidal intent of the Accused is too tenuous.'[224] In light of this, a considerable question mark was left hanging over this crucial and emotive aspect of the prosecution's case in respect of Bosnia – that Milošević had the specific intent to commit genocide in Srebrenica and elsewhere.

Dismissal of numerous allegations in Croatia and Bosnia indictments

The *amici curiae* argued that the prosecution did not adduce any or sufficient evidence in relation to 185 separate allegations contained in the three Indictments.[225] The prosecution conceded, in respect of some of the challenged allegations in the three indictments, that there was no or insufficient evidence to meet the legal standard required under Rule 98*bis*, but that many of the challenges to the indictments were supported by the evidence adduced during the prosecution case-in-chief.[226] The Trial Chamber granted the Motion in relation to 183 allegations – all but two allegations involving sniping and shelling incidents in and around Sarajevo.[227] Over forty separate allegations in the schedules of the Bosnia indictment and about five allegations in the Croatia indictment were dismissed on a finding by the Trial Chamber that there was sufficient evidence to support the allegations. As aptly summed up by one commentator:

223 Trial Chamber Acquittal Decision, 'Dissenting Opinion of Judge Kwon', above n. 166, para. 2. 224 Ibid. para. 3.

225 *Amici* Acquittal Motion, above n. 87, sections III.E, IVD, and VC.

226 Acquittal Response, above n. 88, 25 (Kosovo), 61 (Croatia), 174 (Bosnia).

227 Ibid. paras. 311–12, 314–15.

> [A]t the end of a lengthy and detailed ruling (142 pages), the Trial Chamber opens its disposition as follows: 'the effect of the Trial Chamber's determination is that it has found sufficient evidence to support each count challenged in the three Indictments'. The reason for this overall 'zero effect' intimately relates to the purpose of the exercise at the stage of a Rule 98*bis* motion which, quite simply, involves in inquiry as to whether, taking the Prosecution's case at its highest, a Trial Chamber could be persuaded beyond reasonable doubt to convict the accused. Indeed, 'rarely, a case will arise where the only evidence in support of a conviction is so inherently incredible that no Trial Chamber could accept its truth.' [228]

Conclusion

This 'zero effect' in terms of the 66 counts in the three indictments does not adequately explain the significance of the Acquittal Decision. It is really a piece in the jigsaw puzzle of analysing the prosecution case. What is clear is that the prosecution itself was unable to lead evidence on all of the charges against the accused. There is an important distinction between a 'charge' and a 'count' in an indictment. A count will often consist of many, sometimes hundreds or thousands of, different charges that describe alleged criminal conduct in respect of a particular area or series of transactions. Hundreds of charges contained in a count could be dismissed without the count actually falling – so long as at least one charge is left. Indeed, this is exactly what happened in respect of the prosecution case against Milošević concerning alleged sniping and shelling in Sarajevo. Despite the very low evidentiary threshold to establish a charge at the judgement of acquittal stage, the strain of the breadth and scope of the prosecution case could clearly be seen, with acquittals being entered in respect of over one thousand charges across the Croatia and Bosnia indictments.

An interesting aspect of the *amici curiae* Motion is that, except in some limited respects, they did not seek to challenge the heart of the indictments against the accused – that is, his criminal responsibility for the offences charged. In their Motion the *amici* expressly stated that they did not challenge the prosecution case in respect of the criminal responsibility of the accused. This reticence is curious, given the relative success achieved in respect of the crime base evidence challenged and the dissent of Judge Kwon in respect of the accused's lack of genocidal intent. Perhaps the *amici curiae* were concerned that unsuccessful challenges on the

[228] Idi Gaparayi, 'The Milošević Trial at the Half Way Stage: Judgement on the Motion for Acquittal' (2004) 17 *Leiden Journal of International Law* 737, 766.

accused's actual responsibility might create an undesirable expectation or impression. Perhaps the prosecution can consider itself fortunate this avenue was not pursued further.

Conclusion

The preparation and conduct of the prosecution case is one of the most important aspects of a trial, and in a complex international criminal trial of a former head of state or senior official it is critical. In an ostensibly adversarial system, such as that which operates in international criminal law, the prosecution has a particular duty in the investigation process and in shaping and presenting a well-conceived and manageable case. Where the range of crimes available to prosecute someone in a position of authority covers a broad temporal and geographical scope, the prosecution has competing responsibilities to consider. In the *Milošević* case, it chose to plead an expansive case, apparently out of a sense of the political and historical significance of the trial and in an effort to do justice to the victims over three conflicts. However, a different and preferable approach is possible; one which focuses on the core criminal conduct of the accused and selects representational crimes to establish the case. This was the first and most profound error made by the prosecution. It should have focused its case on a sufficiently discrete series of criminal acts to explain the accused's role while remaining within the boundaries of a manageable case. The prosecution of Milošević is not the only example of such an approach and this is an aspect of complex international criminal trials that will have to be addressed, either by self-imposed prosecutorial restraint or by the court intervening with coercive measures.

The indictments in the *Milošević* case have been shown to be materially defective. Perhaps these defects would have been considered by the Trial Chamber as sufficiently cured by the evidence led, avoiding acquittals on the basis of the flawed pleadings. As discussed, the Trial Chamber also had a role in the failings of the indictments by not requiring their amendment *proprio motu*. This point, although never tested, is particularly apposite in light of the self-representation by the accused in this trial. Whatever the position of a court in this respect, the prosecution has a primary obligation to ensure its indictments are clear and adequately pleaded. Although seeking amendment to all three indictments on more than one occasion, the prosecution never sought to cure apparent material defects therein. Even if sought late in the case, and even if rejected as being unfairly prejudicial to the accused, the prosecution could have endeavoured to do so and thereby put the accused and the Chamber on notice. This was another error in the prosecution's handling of the *Milošević* case, as in others.

In this chapter I have also examined the joinder of the three indictments against Milošević. Based upon the shifting idea of a Greater Serbia and on the belief that a case of this magnitude was possible, the prosecution argued, and the Appeals Chamber ordered, that the case be joined into one enormous trial. Interestingly, the Appeals Chamber clearly had some apprehension about the scope of the case, as evidenced by paragraph 26 of its Decision on joinder. This paragraph evinced a concern about the potential scope of a joined case and its manageability, and appeared to leave open the possibility, however unrealistic, for the Trial Chamber to later sever one or more of the indictments.[229] However, despite the preferable interpretive approach of the Trial Chamber to the question of joinder and its conclusion on the impact of joinder on case management, the case proceeded covering three conflicts over eight years, containing 66 counts with over 7,000 allegations. It is difficult to see, particularly in light of the trial's conclusion, how this served the interests of the prosecution, the accused, the victims or the international community. Seeking joinder was another grave error on the part of the prosecution. The point is intimately connected to the assertion that the prosecution must reduce the breadth of indictments and make them manageable. Running a trial on any one of the *Milošević* indictments would have tested the boundaries of manageability; the three indictments joined into one case was clearly not conducive to best practice in the conduct of complex international criminal trials.

The discussion in this chapter is in no way intended to suggest that the prosecution had not made out its case on some or all of the counts charged in the indictments, other than those dismissed in its judgement of acquittal. Nor is it intended to suggest everything the prosecution did was flawed or strategically wrong. On the contrary, much of its case was well run, clever and constructive of an overall picture of events and the role of Milošević in them. The title of the chapter and its content is critical of the prosecution because it pursued a flawed strategic approach to its case, causing it to be overly broad, complex and unmanageable. In this sense, the fair and expeditious conduct of the trial was threatened.

The range of issues discussed in this chapter give an anatomical understanding of the *Milošević* case and a foundation for understanding the sorts of issues that arise in the context of complex international criminal

[229] Appeal Joinder Decision, above n. 2, para. 26.

trials. This chapter sets the framework for the analysis of the book, showing how this trial and trials like it manifest particular problems that require careful consideration so that future trials, and future courts and tribunals wrestling with such cases, can develop practices and procedures that achieve fair and expeditious trials. The following two chapters analyse the range of issues that arise in complex international criminal trials, particularly those relating to senior political leaders.

3

Case Management Challenges in the Milošević Trial

The Trial Chamber used a heavy hand in the management of the *Milošević* trial – far more so than in most international criminal trials before it. The accused himself was, especially early on in the trial, obstructive in a number of ways. In opening arguments, the cross-examination of prosecution witnesses and in the presentation of his defence, he mounted a highly politicised case, often straying from the forensic into long speeches or vitriol. He refused to recognise the legitimacy of the Tribunal from the start, although he ultimately cooperated in many respects with the trial process. He was found to have manipulated his own health for strategic gain and was in other ways highly disruptive. This was also one of the largest cases imaginable. Milošević represented himself throughout the trial, except for a brief period between the decision of the Trial Chamber imposing defence counsel on him, and the effective reversal by the Appeals Chamber of that decision two months later.

At the same time, there should be no illusion or mystique about why this case took so long and why it was so complicated. The prosecution embarked on an extraordinarily broad and complex case. For the myriad of problems associated with the particularities of this accused and his conduct throughout the trial, it was the prosecution that authored the course of this trial – as is normally the case in an adversarial criminal trial process.

This chapter will first analyse the prosecution and defence cases in the *Milošević* trial, considering the way in which the Trial Chamber sought to manage the proceedings. In case management terms, the *Milošević* trial presented profound complexities and conundrums, and the Chamber struggled in these circumstances to render the trial fair and reasonably expeditious. The case management approaches employed to achieve this end were, in many respects, pioneering, and provide important precedents for the management of complex international criminal and other trials in future.

However, while the scale and context of the case management issues considered by the Chamber were extraordinary and unique, the fundamental case management concerns underpinning the trial process were not. Domestic legal systems have struggled for some time with how to cope with the scale, complexity and length of individual cases, as well as how to manage the large volume of cases in their courts. The second substantive section of this chapter will consider case management principles applied in national legal systems, particularly the common law systems where courts appear to be straining for solutions in the context of the adversarial trial process, as well as its developing application in international criminal law. This insight will assist in a meaningful consideration of the impact of the *Milošević* trial on regulatory and jurisprudential developments in this area, both in positive and negative response to that case. From the sum of this analysis, I will consider how case management of future complex international criminal trials might develop, and appropriate reforms that will help achieve best practice in the conduct of these trials.

Before turning to the *Milošević* trial, it is necessary to clarify some issues and nomenclature. As will become apparent from section two of this chapter, consideration of the approaches of the two major legal systems of the world, the common law and civil law systems, impact on the questions under consideration in the international criminal law context. In case management terms, the civil law system contains more innate procedures that flow from its court-driven structure. The common law, on the other hand, with a greater party-driven adversarial structure, has had to develop principles and practices to contain the scope and nature of individual cases, as well as their volume. In this sense, international criminal law can learn from the civil law system as well as the regulatory activity of common law systems seeking to deal with similar case management problems.

There are two important preliminary issues. First, while two basic forms of case management have developed – individual case management (controlling the scope and conduct of an individual case) and case flow management (managing the volume of cases) – only the former is of significance to international criminal law where there are relatively few cases of a very large and complex nature. Secondly, within the individual case management paradigm, I consider there to be two different approaches, which I describe as 'micro' and 'macro' case management. Micro case management deals with the detailed intervention by a court in the structure and scope of a party's case, whereas macro case management refers to more global forms of intervention available to a chamber to control the scope of a party's case, such as limits on the overall time a party has to lead its case.

These two issues will be analysed in more detail in section two of this chapter, giving broader context to and leading into conclusions about the future development of case management for complex international criminal trials.

Managing the Miloševič case

The prosecution case

The scope of the prosecution case

The obvious, and often stated, reason for the size and scope of the prosecution case was a desire to hold accountable the (or, at least, *an*) alleged 'mastermind' of the conflicts, and to do justice to the countless victims across the former Yugoslavia.[1] However, even the prosecution acknowledged early on the enormity and complexity of the task it had set itself. At a status conference soon after Milošević had been arraigned, the prosecution stated that it was intending to issue indictments against the accused for Croatia and Bosnia and seek joinder,[2] in circumstances where it could not even contemplate the structure of its case against him for Kosovo. The Trial Chamber, having sought from the prosecution details concerning 'the state of readiness for the trial, the number of prosecution witnesses and a time estimate, and any matters relating to disclosure',[3] received the response: 'There are just too many variables.'[4] Interestingly, this comment having been made by a senior trial attorney, the Prosecutor herself stated to the Chamber at the same hearing: 'I must confirm that we are trial ready for this indictment, but obviously our work is not finished and so that is what caused our problems. But for this indictment, we are trial ready.'[5] As was to become clear early in the trial, this was not the case. However, the Trial Chamber set deadlines for the production of material and the commencement of the trial,[6] and the trial did start on 12 February 2002.

Another enlightening prosecution submission came two months after the trial commenced. On 5 April 2002, it filed an unusual document, in which it sought to inform the Trial Chamber of 'its position on various

1 See e.g., *Prosecutor v. Milošević*, 'Prosecution Submission in Response to the Trial Chamber's 22 November 2005 "Scheduling Order for a Hearing" on Severing the Kosovo Indictment', Case No. IT-02-54-T, 29 November 2005, para. 49: 'The individuals who are victims of the wars have a right to a public resolution of the conflicts they experienced. Some are elderly or ill and might not live to see another trial; those who would survive deserve to have a timely public and just resolution of the crimes committed against them or their families and friends.'

2 *Prosecutor v. Milošević*, Hearing, 3 July 2001, Transcript, 12. 3 Ibid. 8. 4 Ibid. 12.

5 Ibid. 14. 6 Ibid. 13–14.

procedural/evidentiary issues that will arise in the course of the trial', and suggested that the Chamber consider 'possible creative solutions' to problems it had identified.[7] In describing the context for certain recommendations made, the prosecution revealed that the number of witnesses it proposed to call to deal with the Kosovo indictment was 'in all cases premised on the possibility that the accused would take little or no part in the trial process (given his often-stated refusal to recognise the court)', and that the 'estimates given as to the time to be taken were based on the possibility of there being no cross examination by the accused'.[8] The prosecution complained that Milošević's 'attitude to the trial process, in which he is now fully engaged', including opposition to the admission of written testimony in lieu of oral testimony (pursuant to Rule 92*bis* of the Rules) and his 'substantial challenge' in cross-examination to crime base evidence,[9] made it extremely difficult for the prosecution to lead a full case in the time available to it without using proposed forms of summarising and written evidence, which would enable it to lead more evidence in less time.

The prosecution's Trial Proceedings Motion is a fascinating document, not the least because it suggests that the prosecution had based its trial strategy on a defiantly mute accused, who would silently watch a mountain of prosecution evidence be led against him, at the end of which presumably the Trial Chamber would render its judgement. Having sought and obtained (from the Appeals Chamber) joinder of the three indictments into one enormous case against the accused, and having realised the full scope of Milošević's aggressive adversarial engagement in the case, the prosecution found itself in something of a quandary.

At this stage of the trial, the Kosovo part of the case was in full swing, but the Croatia and Bosnia parts of the case were in a quasi pre-trial stage with the pre-trial disclosure, witness and exhibit lists and other trial readiness activities ongoing in the other two parts of the case.

Before proceeding further into a discussion of the prosecution case and its strategy, it is important to review the proposed scope of the case and how the prosecution intended to present it. In its pre-trial witness list, the prosecution identified 231 witnesses which it intended to call for the Kosovo part of the case.[10] At the pre-trial conference for the Kosovo part of

[7] *Prosecutor v. Milošević*, 'Prosecution's Position in Relation to Management of Trial Proceedings and the Regime for Presentation and Admission of Evidence With Comments on Issues Concerning the Accused's Health', Case No. IT-02-54-T, 5 April 2002 ('Trial Proceedings Motion'), para. 2. [8] Ibid. paras. 7(c) and 7(d). [9] Ibid. para. 4.

[10] *Prosecutor v. Milošević*, 'Prosecution's Pre-Trial Brief Pursuant to Rule 65*ter*(E)(i)', Case No. IT-99-37, 26 November 2001.

the case on 9 January 2002, the Prosecution submitted that 110 of those 231 witnesses would be called *viva voce*, leaving the testimony of the remainder to be presented in writing pursuant to Rule 92*bis*.[11] The Rule 92*bis* group of witnesses would fall into the 'crime base' category, meaning that they would testify to crimes committed, as opposed to any responsibility of the accused for them. The anatomy of the remainder of the witness list was broken down by the prosecution as follows: 48 crime base witnesses and investigators to cover the crime base allegations; 25 policy witnesses; 11 experts; 25 to 30 insiders; up to 20 international witnesses, and six 'miscellaneous' witnesses, 'for a total of 110'.[12]

The exchange between the prosecution and the Trial Chamber at the pre-trial conference showed how difficult it was to lead sufficient evidence on the range of underlying offences pleaded in the indictment, while keeping the case within reasonable limits. The prosecution initially estimated that, optimistically, it might conclude its case on Kosovo by the end of July 2002 – or, taking into consideration the August court recess, perhaps the end of September 2002.[13] The Chamber found that unacceptably long, and cautioned the prosecution that it should seek to lead one witness per incident and not to bring repetitive crime base evidence, and not to seek corroboration for matters that did not appear to be the subject of serious dispute.[14] This was a classic example of micro case management of the prosecution case, but which carries with it risks related to the extent of the court's intervention in the prosecution's case. Even leading crime base evidence, it is difficult to conceive how one witness per incident is ever going to be sufficient to establish the detail of events (remembering that an 'incident' in such indictments invariably includes multiple offences often in several proximate but distinct locations), the scope of the alleged attack and other related requirements for the establishment of the offices charged. Because the judgement was never rendered and also because the prosecution effectively ignored this order, no measurable consequence flowed from the Chamber's direct interference in the presentation of the prosecution case. However, the copious acquittal of individual allegations in the Chamber's judgement of acquittal decision in areas of the case against the accused suggests that some risk may have attached to the Chamber's ruling in this respect. The Chamber ultimately ruled, in respect of the scope of the Kosovo case, as follows:

> [W]e consider that a total of 90 witnesses should be sufficient, having regard to the size and complexity of the case, but that will not prevent you

[11] *Prosecutor v. Milošević*, Hearing, 9 January 2002, Transcript, 235. [12] Ibid. 236.
[13] Ibid. 239. [14] Ibid. 240–2.

> making the application during the trial for additional witnesses on good cause for challenge if the witnesses come forward. But you should work on the basis of 90 as being sufficient and see if you cannot cut down some of the other witnesses in that regard. And if you go above that number, then you'll have to justify it.[15]

The Trial Chamber also ordered that the prosecution should conclude its case on Kosovo by early August 2002, giving it over five months.[16]

The Prosecution made numerous submissions during the course of its case on Kosovo to expand its witness list and lead more evidence, some of which the Trial Chamber granted and some of which it did not.[17] The Prosecution case on Kosovo largely concluded on 11 September 2002, although it led witnesses throughout its case dealing with all three indictments (so-called 'crossover witnesses').

The Trial Chamber had ordered, on 4 February 2002, that the trial in relation to Kosovo would commence on 12 February 2002,[18] which it did. In the same ruling, the Chamber made case preparation orders in respect of the Croatia and Bosnia parts of the case. It ordered the prosecution to be trial-ready on those charges by 1 July 2002; to make proper pre-trial disclosure; and to produce its Rule 65*ter* witness and exhibit lists, and its pre-trial brief, by 2 April 2002.[19] After several extensions of time, the prosecution filed its pre-trial material for the Croatia and Bosnia part of the case on 31 May 2002.[20] If the scope of the prosecution case with respect to Kosovo seemed daunting, the case pleaded in respect of Croatia and Bosnia was more so. The prosecution proposed to lead some 600 witnesses in relation to these two indictments, including 275 who would testify *viva voce*. This was itself a reduction from early indications by the prosecution that it would lead over 1,000 witnesses in respect of the Croatia and Bosnia parts of the case.[21] An interesting aspect of this was the breakdown in numbers of witnesses into categories

15 Ibid. 246. 16 Ibid. 246–7.

17 See e.g., *Prosecutor v. Milošević*, 'Decision on Prosecution Motion to Call Additional Witnesses and for Orders for Protective Measures', Case No. IT-02-54-T, 5 July 2002; 'Decision on Prosecution's Motion for Leave to Call a Witness', Case No. IT-02-54-T, 9 July 2002; 'Decision on Prosecution Motion for Leave to Call a Witness', Case No. IT-02-54-T, 30 August 2002.

18 *Prosecutor v. Milošević*, 'Order for Commencement of Trial', Case No. IT-02-54-PT, 4 February 2002. 19 Ibid.

20 *Prosecutor v. Milošević*, 'Prosecution's Submission Pursuant to Rule 65ter (E)(ii)', Case No. IT-02-54-PT, 31 May 2002; 'Prosecution's Submission Pursuant to Rule 65ter (E)(ii) List of Witnesses the Prosecution Intends to Call', Case No. IT-02-54-PT, 31 May 2002.

21 *Prosecutor v. Milošević*, Hearing, 10 April 2002, Transcript, 2780.

relating to establishing the commission of underlying crimes and those relating to the responsibility of, or linkage to, the accused. For the establishment of underlying offences in which it was never suggested Milošević had any direct involvement (so-called 'crime base' evidence), the prosecution intended to bring 422 witnesses. Other groups of experts and 'in house' witnesses (meaning investigators and others who can present documented investigations on particular aspects of the indictments) amounted to 41 witnesses. An important group called 'insiders' amounted to 110 witnesses. These witnesses were supposed to establish the workings of the government, army, police, paramilitary units, and other relevant institutions or groups, and to tie the long line between the crimes alleged and the accused. Finally, a group of 32 witnesses were proposed to testify to the acts and conduct of Milošević himself, the crux of the prosecution case.[22]

The proposed scope of the prosecution case, when broken out into witness groups and the time it was proposed it would take to lead the case, shows something of the anatomy of a trial of this nature against a former head of state or other senior official. So much of the prosecution's case, time and energy are focused on the underlying offences with no immediate link to the accused, that questions must be raised as to the very nature and viability of these cases as pleaded. Of course, the whole fabric of the case rests on these crimes having been committed, and committed by someone linked in a material legal sense to the accused. Eighty percent of the intended prosecution case as proposed dealt with the commission of offences, not the personal responsibility of Milošević himself. This fact must raise questions about the methodology employed in the construction and presentation of such cases, and again returns the analysis to the question of whether prosecution of such a case should seek to cover such a large crime base. One alternative approach is a case focusing on a limited series of crimes *representative of* the accused's alleged role. For example, instead of leading evidence on crimes committed in forty-seven different municipalities in Bosnia, as the prosecution pleaded in its *Milošević* Bosnia indictment, it could select a dozen or so municipalities for which it has strong evidence, which it believes will sufficiently establish the widespread or systematic nature of the attack and satisfy all of the other jurisdictional or contextual elements for offences to which it seeks to link the Accused. This is similar to an approach canvassed by Judge Robinson early in the *Milošević* trial. He stated that a measure

[22] Ibid. See also *Prosecutor v. Milošević*, Hearing, 25 July 2002.

available to the prosecution would be 'just simply to reduce the size of the Prosecution case':

> [I]n the three years and three months I've been here, it's become quite clear to me that the prosecution of the most serious breaches of international humanitarian law cannot take place if there is brought to court and if there is sought to be presented in court evidence from every municipality or every crime site or every incident that is mentioned in the indictment. You may indict it, but I think serious consideration will have to be given by this Tribunal as to what is to be presented in court as evidence. If you have 47 municipalities, the question is: Why do you need to present evidence from the 47? Why can't you present evidence from a half of that or a third of that? And if you started in that way, instead of six seventy-eight [*sic*] witnesses for Bosnia and you were to take a third of the municipalities, you will probably have - I don't know - a third of that number. But that is really the problem that we have to grapple with. And until we can grapple with it, I think the Tribunal will always be facing a very serious problem. And under the international scrutiny as it is, I think it is going to be increasingly difficult for the Tribunal to devise strategies that will bring its work to an end. And I raise this as a matter for consideration, and perhaps it may have to be taken up at a different level, on an institutional basis, that the size of the Prosecution case, for the purposes of presentation of evidence, should be different, should be less than what is indicted.[23]

The Trial Chamber, at the pre-trial conference for Croatia and Bosnia, indicated its intention to reduce the number of municipalities in the Bosnia case. By that stage, the prosecution had indicated its intention to 'lead comprehensive evidence on 14 of the 47 and not to call evidence on a further nine'.[24] The Chamber expressed the view that this should be reduced further: 'We recognise the complexity and the seriousness of what happened, but this is a criminal trial, and the evidence must be brought within a manageable scope.'[25] However, the Chamber did not insist on this reduction and concluded that 'there may be reasons for additional evidence, but that's what broadly we have in mind'.[26]

In respect of the scope of the Bosnia indictment, in particular, the prosecution took little notice of the Trial Chamber's comment concerning reduction in the scope of its case. As has been discussed in chapter 2, the prosecution never sought to amend its indictments or clearly stipulate reductions on the terms requested by the Trial Chamber. The reticence

23 *Prosecutor v. Milošević*, Hearing, 10 April 2002, Transcript, 2775–6.
24 *Prosecutor v. Milošević*, Hearing, 25 July 2002, Transcript, 8610. 25 Ibid.
26 Ibid.

shown by the Trial Chamber to order the prosecution to reduce the crime base scope of the Bosnia indictment is undoubtedly in part related to the dangers involved in this form of micro case management.[27] Reduction in the number of witnesses and the time available to a party to lead its case is a measure more consistent with the adversarial model of the criminal trial, although it is still used relatively sparsely in common law systems. However, actually disposing of whole portions of the prosecution case, where the indictment is lawfully issued and confirmed, is anathema to the adversarial criminal law system. Yet, if managed properly and at the correct stage of the pre-trial process, this may indeed be an important aspect of the future of international criminal trial case management. It is not entirely clear from his in-court comments whether Judge Robinson proposed a reduction in the scope of a prosecution indictment during the conduct of a case or during the pre-trial process. However, it is really a tool that should be exercised at the pre-trial stage, when there is time for consideration by the prosecution of the legal and policy effects of a reduction in an indictment. Although amendments to Rule 73*bis*(D) and a new Rule 73*bis*(E) suggest a reduction in counts in an indictment could take place during the trial, this is unrealistic and impractical and may also be inherently unfair. As discussed in chapter 2, an apparently significant reason for the prosecution pleading such a broad case against the accused, and that all aspects of the case be joined, is the sense of responsibility to the victims, history and to peace and reconciliation in the region of the former Yugoslavia. If these considerations are to be prevalent in prosecutorial decision-making in international criminal law (a perspective with which I disagree) then the prosecution needs time to assimilate the effects of a reduced case on these issues, particularly where it is done by coercive means. Furthermore, and more importantly than extra-legal policy considerations, the defence must know what case it is to prepare for and have the time to adjust its case strategy and preparations accordingly. Indeed, it appears that Judge Robinson was contemplating a pre-trial rationalisation of a prosecution indictment and in July 2003, well after his in-court comments were made, Rule 73*bis* was amended to reflect the proposition that at the pre-trial conference the Chamber could interfere in the scope of the prosecution case.

This is a radical case management power and envisages an approach that has the potential to substantially reduce the scope and time of complex international criminal law cases. Of course, as discussed already,

[27] See discussion in section II of this chapter.

it has certain risks attached to it, again relating to the interference by a court in an adversarial structure. However, in circumstances where a prosecutor in such cases fails to exercise reasonable restraint, this is a methodology that may come closer to facilitating a workable balance between fairness and expedition in the conduct of such trials. Furthermore, as the influence of the civil law spreads into the infrastructure of international criminal law, invasive judicial intervention not just on the perimeters of the prosecution case but also at the heart of its scope and content will seem more acceptable and appropriate, and risk less ardent criticism from the international community it serves. Whether these developments occur in a more cooperative or collaborative environment between the court and the parties or whether the court finds itself having to force the parties into such an approach remains to be seen.

The consequence of the prosecution not adopting the Chamber's recommendations in the *Milošević* trial to reduce the scope of its indictments was an unmanageably long case. The prosecution ultimately led 352 witnesses across the three indictments, broken down as follows:

Total number of Prosecution witnesses: **352**
Total number of *viva voce* witnesses: **114 (32.4%)**
Total number of Rule 92*bis* witnesses [testimony in written form]: **189 (53.7%)**
With Cross examination: **135 (38.4%)**
Without Cross-examination: **54 (15.3%)**
Total number of Rule 94*bis* witnesses [experts]: **20 (5.7%)**
Total number of Rule 89(F) witnesses [examination-in-chief in written form]: **26 (7.4%)**
Total number of Rules 92*bis*/89(F) witnesses: **3 (0.9%)**[28]

Although the prosecution never sought to amend its indictments to significantly reduce the scope of the case, it was clear that it either did not seek to lead evidence on some crimes charged[29] or led insufficient evidence on others to pass a review on judgement of acquittal. A detailed review of the 'red-lined' indictments, following the judgement of acquittal decision of the Chamber, reveals a reduction in the number of crimes

[28] *Prosecutor v. Milošević*, 'Decision in Relation to Severance, Extension of Time and Rest', Case No. IT-02-54-T, 12 December 2005 ('*Milošević* Severance and Time Decision'), para. 21.

[29] See *Prosecutor v. Milošević*, 'Prosecution Response to Amici Curiae Motion for Judgement of Acquittal Pursuant to Rule 98 *bis*', Case No. IT-02-54-T, 23 March 2004, 25, 61, 174.

alleged from 7,604 to 6,547.[30] This calculation does not deal with findings on numerous charges that were not challenged at the judgement of acquittal stage, or those which had passed the lower standard required at this stage, but on which the Trial Chamber would have had to rule beyond reasonable doubt in its final judgement.

Again, a comparison can be made with the prosecution of Saddam Hussein. He was initially charged for the limited Dujail incident, by which presumably the prosecution sought to characterise his broader conduct. Had the prosecution in that case sought to indict and try Hussein for the full range of his possible criminal conduct under the jurisdiction of the Iraqi Tribunal, the case would look something like the *Milošević* trial.[31] The prosecution in the *Milošević* trial, in its Trial Proceedings Motion, sought to persuade the Trial Chamber to introduce large amounts of evidence concerning crime base events in a flexible manner not typically accepted in adversarial criminal law systems. It expressed its concern that not acceding to these requests would deprive 'the Chamber of valuable material required for the purposes of establishing the truth'.[32] The tone of this prosecution submission gives a clear indication of the extraordinary dilemma it faced, having led such an expansive case and the Accused now clearly aggressively challenging that case. The solutions proposed[33] reflect the difficulty of leading sufficient evidence on

30 This assessment is based on a review of the indictments submitted by the Prosecution in *Prosecutor v. Milošević*, 'Submission of Red-Lined Versions of Indictments Pursuant to Trial Chamber "Order to Prosecution on Indictments Following Rule 98 *bis* Decision", filed 20 July 2004', Case No. IT-02-54-T, 11 August 2004.

31 Of course, Hussein was subsequently charged for genocide of the Kurds in Anfal in northern Iraq during the 1988 campaign and his second trial for those charges commenced on 21 August 2006, and was halted upon the execution of Hussein for the Dujail conviction. This narrow point is not made to suggest that the SICT has conducted a fair or proper trial against Hussein. Indeed, opinion is strongly against such a view: see, e.g., Diane Marie Amann, '"The Only Thing Left is Justice": Cherif Bassiouni, Saddam Hussein, and the Quest for Impartiality in International Criminal Law' in David E. Guinn (ed.), *Coming of Age in International Criminal Law: An Intellectual Reflection on the Work of M. Cherif Bassiouni* (forthcoming); report by Human Rights Watch on the removal of Judge Abdullah al-Amiri, the presiding judge of the Hussein trial, by a decision of the Prime Minister and Cabinet because, according to a Government spokesman, 'he ha[d] lost his neutrality after he made comments saying Saddam is not a dictator': 'Removal of Judge a Grave Threat to Independence of Genocide Court', Human Rights Watch, 19 September 2006 <http://hrw.org/english/docs/2006/09/19/iraq14229.htm> at 4 October 2006.

32 Trial Proceedings Motion, above n. 7, para. 14.

33 For a candid discussion of these proposals by the Principal prosecutor see, Geoffrey Nice and Philippe Vallières-Roland, 'Procedural Innovations in War Crimes Trials' in Hirad Abtahi and Gideon Boas (eds.), *The Dynamics of International Criminal Justice: Essays in Honour of Sir Richard May* (2005), 141.

such a broad range of charges within a limited (reasonable) time. The prosecution may have contemplated at times that it had simply bitten off more than it could chew, but it did not seek to address this issue by reducing the scope of its case. The effect of not doing so reflects one of the key challenges in managing complex international criminal trials.

It is in the context of these observations that I now turn to a review of the Trial Chamber's management of the Prosecution case in *Milošević*.

Trial Chamber's management of the prosecution case

The Trial Chamber initially endeavoured to control the case by using Rule 73*bis* of the ICTY Rules to reduce the number of witnesses and scope of overall evidence, employing macro and micro case management approaches. In the Kosovo part of the case, the Chamber had ordered the prosecution to lead no more than 90 witnesses, although it allowed the prosecution to apply to add witnesses on good cause being shown.[34] Good cause was shown by the prosecution in respect of 43 additional witnesses, because it ultimately led 133 witnesses for the Kosovo part of the trial.[35] The Trial Chamber's attempt to control the prosecution case, by limiting the number of witnesses and containing the presentation of cumulative or repetitive evidence, can be seen in its first substantive decision on the admission of testamentary evidence pursuant to Rule 92*bis* of the ICTY Rules. This Rule was designed to provide a regime whereby a Trial Chamber can admit into evidence written statements containing evidence which would otherwise be led in a testimonial form.[36]

The prosecution first disclosed witness statements it intended to lead by way of Rule 92*bis* in the period of January and February 2002.[37] In its

[34] *Prosecutor v. Milošević*, Hearing, 9 January 2002, Transcript, 246.

[35] See ICTY official website http://www.un.org/icty/cases-e/index-e.htm 15 October 2006.

[36] See discussion of the right to confront witnesses in chapter 1.

[37] On 25 January 2002, the Prosecution disclosed to the *amici curiae* three witness statements which it intended to apply to have introduced under Rule 92*bis* of the Rules. The Prosecution informed the Trial Chamber that it would seek to tender evidence of a number of witnesses in the form of Rule 92*bis* statements in relation to the Kosovo indictment and disclosed the statements of the first 23 witnesses which it sought to have admitted. The *amici curiae* submitted an '*Amici Curiae* Brief on Rule 92*bis* Procedure' on 20 February 2002 to which the Prosecution responded in 'Prosecution's Response to "*Amici Curiae* Brief on Rule 92*bis* Procedure" and Motion for Admission of Statements Pursuant to Rule 92*bis*' on 26 February 2000, and in 'Prosecution's Additional Response to "*Amici Curiae* Brief on Rule 92*bis* Procedure" and Motion for Admission of Statements Pursuant to Rule 92*bis*' on 11 March 2002. A hearing on the matter was held on 11 March 2002, and the Trial Chamber gave its oral decision on the day after the hearing: *Prosecutor v. Milošević*, 'Decision on Prosecution's Request to Have Written Statements Admitted Under Rule 92*bis*', Case No. IT-02-54-T, 21 March 2002, paras. 1–3.

oral ruling on the Prosecution application, the Trial Chamber admitted 23 statements under the Rule, but subject to two conditions:

> The first is this: Because of the cumulative nature of the evidence and the fact that it will increase the already very extensive number of witnesses proposed to be called by the Prosecution in this case, and bearing in mind the need for an expeditious trial, the Prosecution will be limited to four witnesses per municipality, including the viva voce witnesses already called. The Prosecution is to select which of the Rule 92 bis statements it wishes to have admitted for those municipalities where at the moment it is proposed more than four witnesses. . .
>
> The second condition is this: Because, in the view of the Trial Chamber, the evidence proposed to be given is the subject of an important issue in this case, those witnesses whose statements are admitted will be required to attend for cross-examination, the Prosecution being allowed in each case to ask some introductory questions.[38]

A crucial aspect of this Decision was the clear importance given to the expedition of the trial process. The Chamber stated that the limitation of four witnesses for each municipality was based on the requirement that the trial be expeditious, but also on the 'cumulative nature of the evidence'. This is an example of micro management of the prosecution case and is a technique unavailable or rarely utilised in an adversarial criminal law system. As discussed earlier, the difficulty that arises in limiting numbers of witnesses, particularly on the basis that the proposed testimony is cumulative, is that it is extremely difficult to ascertain the scope and effectiveness of a party's evidence until all the evidence has been led in a case. If acquittals are entered in respect of crimes alleged in those places because of insufficient or inadequate evidence, the question arises as to whether the Chamber's intervention at that level of the case adversely affected the prosecution's ability to establish crimes charged in the indictment. The problem is unique to the adversarial system of criminal justice, which applies in international criminal law. It is the prosecution, a party to the proceedings, that brings the charges and seeks to establish them, and the court is there to ensure fairness and determine the case. It is unlike civil law systems, where it is more often a judicial function to oversee the investigation of and prepare the case, the trial court working from a dossier prepared by an independent judge. Given that at this point in the development of international criminal law, the structure of the system is profoundly adversarial in nature, a safer and relatively

[38] *Prosecutor v. Milošević*, Hearing, 12 March 2002, Transcript, 1974–5.

effective case management approach is that ultimately adopted by the Trial Chamber in the *Milošević* trial (and followed broadly in the ICTY at least) of limiting the time available to the parties and allowing them to choose how best to use it. This may not be the case in future if there is a shift in the adversarial emphasis changes.

Interestingly, even utilising micro management techniques to order the limitation in numbers of witnesses per municipality for the Kosovo part of the *Milošević* case, the prosecution ignored the order and led expansive numbers of witnesses in some areas. For the Orahovac municipality the Prosecution led eleven witnesses, seven for Srbica, eight for Suva Reka, eleven for Đakovica, nine for the relatively limited case concerning Istok and fourteen for the Štimlje municipality (which included the notorious events in Račak village).

In fact, a curious feature of the *Milošević* case is the extent to which orders made by the Trial Chamber were not complied with. This example is joined by that referred to above concerning a limitation on the prosecution of one witness to be led per incident. Milošević himself persistently ignored orders to disclose or produce witness and exhibit lists in the time allocated. Different time limitations were persistently ignored or not complied with and even defence witnesses at times refused to cooperate with court orders – in one instance leading to contempt proceedings.[39] Perhaps it was a consequence of the enormity of the case, the difficulty in managing and constraining an accused like Milošević and the desire of the Chamber to balance compliance with its orders and some smoothness in the maintenance of the proceedings. This is a lesson to be drawn that in future complex international criminal trials the court should ensure compliance and proper respect for the court and its orders. As discussed, compliance with the particular decisions regarding limitations on witness numbers for particular municipalities or incidents would have raised potentially serious problems at the point of weighing the evidence and making final determinations. However, failure by a court to implement its orders has the impact of creating an atmosphere of (at least, procedural) impunity in the trial proceedings. For sophisticated and manipulative accused, such as Milošević, particularly when self-represented, it becomes extremely important that a court consider its orders to ensure their enforceability and, when breached, issue strict sanctions. The *Milošević* case stands as an example of a trial in which the

[39] See *Prosecutor v. Milošević*, 'Decision on Interlocutory Appeal on Kosta Bulatović Contempt Proceedings', Case No. IT-02-54-A-R77.4, 29 August 2005.

accused was seen to be able to exercise a significant degree of control over the proceedings – at times the Chamber indeed looked powerless – which led some to claim that it was the accused himself that was dictating the course of the trial.[40] The problem with this is that trials of such accused are, at any rate, difficult to control. Where a court is trying a person used to considerable power and control, and able to manipulate legal proceedings structured to accord an accused considerable fair trial rights, such accused are in a position to make mischief of the trial process. *Milošević* was able to do this to the detriment of the trial. As is discussed in detail elsewhere in this book, in areas of self-representation, manipulation of his health, non-compliance with procedural orders and courtroom decorum, and in leading evidence or cross-examining on areas irrelevant to the forensic case, Milošević was able to exploit the Tribunal's hesitation or failure to enforce its orders in such a way that compromised its authority and gave the perception that it was not in control of its own proceedings.

Even though by the time of the pre-trial conference for the Croatia and Bosnia phase of the *Milošević* case, the Trial Chamber had determined the case management strategy as one relating primarily to the limitation of time, it did make an initial attempt at limiting the number of witnesses proposed by the prosecution for this part of the case. Furthermore, it attempted to curtail the scope of the case by suggesting a narrowing of the crime base in the Bosnia indictment. On 25 July 2002, having received the Prosecution's Rule 65*ter* pre-trial brief and material for the Croatia and Bosnia parts of the case, the Trial Chamber held a pre-trial conference to establish the manner in which this part of the case would proceed. In relation to the number of witnesses proposed to cover the two indictments, the Trial Chamber ordered the prosecution to reduce the number of witnesses it intended to call, noting that on the basis of the over 560 proposed witnesses, 'we would be looking at a prosecution case of something in the order of two to two and a half years from now, and we have to say that we regard that as an unmanageable length and not consistent with a fair and manageable trial'.[41]

40 See e.g., *Prosecutor v. Milošević*, Hearing, Transcript, 32322–3 (Geoffrey Nice on Milošević's obstructionism as justifying imposition of counsel); First interview of Geoffrey Nice, 'Sense Tribunal' http://www.sense-agency.com/en/stream.php? sta5h3&pid5h7979&kat5h3> at 30 August 2006; Third interview of Geoffrey Nice, 'Sense Tribunal' <http://www.sense-agency.com/en/stream.php?sta5h3&pid5h7997&kat5h3> at 30 August 2006; Michael Scharf, 'Self-Representation versus Assignment of Defence Counsel before International Criminal Tribunals' (2006) 4 *Journal of International Criminal Justice* 31.

41 *Prosecutor v. Milošević*, Hearing, 25 July 2002, Transcript, 8610–1.

The clear indication from the Trial Chamber was for a reduction in the amount of *viva voce* evidence, as well as areas of expertise which were either duplicative or of questionable relevance. This desire to limit both the overall time and the number of witnesses was probably premised on an understandable apprehensiveness that the prosecution would seek to lead an expansive case and that it might be difficult to keep it to the time limitation ordered. It appears to be important in the process of case managing a trial of this kind, that the chamber convey to the parties a profound understanding of the nature of the proposed case. It is practical psychology to deduce that the clearer it is to a party that the chamber knows the case, the more effective its rulings will be on the affected party. Difficulties arise in this respect in cases like this, where it is hard to ascertain the full depth and nature of a case – indeed it appears difficult for the parties themselves to be in such a position before leading their evidence. Reference has already been made to the prosecution's own early statistics on the scope of its case on Croatia and Bosnia, in which it intended to call over 1,000 witnesses.[42] The Chamber had stated as far back as April 2002, again in reference to the size of the proposed Prosecution case: '[T]his is why we have in mind the time limit . . . No trial can take place in those circumstances.'[43] The statement later made, that a Prosecution case lasting two to two and a half years was unmanageable and unacceptable to the Chamber, was not so far off what actually occurred, although this also had much to do with interruptions caused by the ill health of the accused and a reduced sitting schedule for the same reason.

The prosecution in response requested the Chamber at that stage not to reduce the numbers of witnesses because that would be 'unlikely in itself to achieve anything except probably unwarranted anxiety on the part of the Prosecution trying to budget when it's going to be reducing witness numbers and time taken in any event'.[44] The prosecution stated that it believed by treating the Croatia and Bosnia cases as a whole, the overall length of the case would be reduced.

Ultimately, after hearing submissions from the parties, the Trial Chamber ordered that there should be a total of no more than 106 live witnesses in relation to the Bosnia indictment and 71 in relation to the Croatian indictment, or a total of 177 live witnesses.[45] The Chamber also ordered that, 'given the time which is available and the rate at which the case has been going . . . this evidence should be heard by the 16th of

[42] *Prosecutor v. Milošević*, Hearing, 10 April 2002, Transcript, 2780. [43] Ibid.
[44] Ibid. 8617. [45] Ibid. 8641.

May, 2003'.[46] The Chamber acknowledged at the time that there would be the opportunity to put forward witnesses under Rule 92*bis* and that, 'if the circumstances alter during the trial, the Prosecution may apply under the Rule for variation of this order. However, such variation will only be made for good cause.'[47]

The prosecution ultimately led 195 witnesses as *viva voce* testimony for the Croatia and Bosnia part of the trial, and the evidence-in-chief of a considerable number of these witnesses was introduced through Rule 92*bis* or Rule 89(F).

As stated, the Trial Chamber ultimately sought to manage the *Milošević* trial by limiting the time available to the Prosecution to lead its case. On 10 April 2002, the Trial Chamber ordered that the Prosecution would have to conclude its case by 10 April 2003:

> [W]e have decided that the Prosecution should have one year from today to conclude their case. That will give them a total of 14 months in which to finish the case . . . In the view of the Trial Chamber, no Prosecution case should continue for a period longer than that.[48]

This ruling led the prosecution to appeal and, on 16 May 2002, the Appeals Chamber rendered its decision upholding the Trial Chamber's order.[49] The Appeals Chamber upheld the power of the Trial Chamber to control the conduct of the proceedings by imposing limits on the length of the prosecution case. This power, although reflected in (then) Rule 73*bis*(E) of the ICTY Rules, dealing with pre-trial case management, was an inherent power possessed by 'every court' and which could be exercised before or during proceedings.[50] The prosecution had already showed, in its Trial Proceedings Motion of 5 April 2002, that it could at times lack perspective in pursuing the extraordinary task it had set for itself. A further example of this lack of perspective appeared in an argument on this issue before the Appeals Chamber. It had submitted that the power of the Trial Chamber to control the proceedings was not intended 'to provide a vehicle for a Trial Chamber to unduly interfere with the presentation of the prosecution case' and that it had 'invad[ed] the sphere of prosecutorial autonomy', and thus violated Article 16(2) of the ICTY

[46] Ibid. [47] Ibid.

[48] *Prosecutor v. Milošević*, Hearing, 10 April 2002, Transcript, 2782–4. Five days later the Prosecution sought clarification of what was meant by the use of the word 'should' in the ruling, and the Chamber clarified that 'is a mandatory order' (*Prosecutor v. Milošević*, Hearing, 15 April 2002, Transcript, 3029).

[49] *Prosecutor v. Milošević*, 'Reasons for Refusal of Leave to Appeal From Decision to impose Time Limit', Case No. IT-02-54-T, 16 May 2002. [50] Ibid. para. 10.

Statute.[51] This provision states that the prosecutor 'shall act independently as a separate organ of the International Tribunal. He or she shall not seek or receive instructions from any Government or from any other source'. The prosecution went on to argue that the Trial Chamber's decision limiting the time in which it could lead its case interfered with the prosecutor's right to a fair trial under Article 20.[52] The Appeals Chamber found that the claim that the order made by the Trial Chamber had interfered with the independence of the prosecutor was misconceived.[53] Although the Statute, and the 'largely adversarial' nature of the proceedings before the Tribunal, gives the prosecutor complete discretion in the investigation of serious violations of international humanitarian law:

> once the indictment has been confirmed by a judge, and once the indictment has been filed, the Prosecutor becomes a party before the Tribunal, and thus subject to the power of a Chamber to manage the proceedings, in the same way as any other party before the Tribunal. It is erroneous to suggest that the Prosecutor has independence in relation to the way in which her case is to be presented before a Trial Chamber which the accused person does not have. The Tribunal's Statute itself provides to the contrary. Article 21 is stated in uncompromising terms: 'All persons shall be equal before the International Tribunal.' That equality is fundamental to the fairness of the trials which are conducted before the Trial Chambers. It has not been infringed in the present case.[54]

The prosecution's assertion that it somehow possessed an independent right to a fair trial, let alone that such a right had been violated by the Trial Chamber exercising control over the conduct of the proceedings, shows a strained logic. The only real question to be posed was whether the exercise of the Trial Chamber's discretion was lawful. As the Appeals Chamber put it, the issue in an appeal from such a decision is 'not whether the decision was correct, in the sense that the Appeals Chamber agrees with that decision, but rather whether the Trial Chamber has correctly exercised its discretion in reaching that decision'. Provided that the Trial Chamber has properly exercised its discretion, its decision will not be disturbed.[55] The Appeals Chamber had considered a similar issue in the *Galić* case, stating there:

> [The power to impose time limits] is a powerful tool for preventing excessive and unnecessary time being taken by the prosecution, and it is intended

[51] *Prosecutor v. Milošević*, 'Prosecution's Application for Leave to File an Interlocutory Appeal', Case No. IT-02-54-T, 16 April 2002, para. 7. [52] Ibid. 11. [53] Ibid. 12.
[54] Ibid. 13. [55] Ibid. 14.

> to ensure that the prosecution litigates only those issues which are really in dispute and which are necessary to determine for the purposes of its case. Its introduction followed serious excesses by prosecution teams in the past . . . [It] requires the Trial Chamber to consider with care whether the issues really in dispute have been clearly identified so that a proper assessment of the time needed for the prosecution can be made.[56]

In the *Milošević* case, the Appeals Chamber found no misapplication of its discretion and no inconsistency with the terms of the *Galić* Decision. It is noteworthy that the *Galić* Decision, in December 2001, was concluding that the powerful case management tool of limiting the time in which a party may lead its case, Rule 73*bis* of the ICTY Rules, was created in response to the 'serious excesses by prosecution teams in the past'. The statement is important because its source can only have been the plenary discussions, which is the forum at which rules of procedure and evidence are adopted. All the permanent Judges of the ICTY, acting as quasi-legislators under Article 15 of the ICTY Statute, 'adopt rules of procedure and evidence for the conduct of the pre-trial phase of the proceedings, trials and appeals, the admission of evidence, the protection of victims and witnesses and other appropriate matters'. Rule 6 of the Rules of the ICTY regulate the amendment process, requiring a majority of ten of the current sixteen permanent Judges for an amendment to the Rules to be approved. As a result, the Judges acting in plenary must have discussed and determined that the prosecution had been acting excessively in the scope of cases led to that point. The content of the plenary sessions is confidential and the Appeals Chamber gives no detail of what led the plenary to adopt this Rule, but it must have been significant for the Judges to take such strong and clear action. It is clear that, prior to 2001, *Blaškić* and *Kordić* were ICTY cases that had been very broad (the latter saw 241 witnesses testify over 240 days, and 4,665 exhibits were admitted).[57] Even so, these cases had been limited to the conflict in the Lašva Valley in Central Bosnia. The *Milošević* case was many times larger than either of these cases and it is clear that the sentiment behind Rule 73*bis*, as expressed by the Appeals Chamber, would be applicable to that case.

The Trial Chamber had considered it necessary that the anticipated length of the prosecution case be reduced so as to make the trial manageable. This was not the case in which it was appropriate to establish every

[56] *Prosecutor v. Galić*, 'Decision on Application by Prosecution for Leave to Appeal', Case No. IT-98-29-AR73, 14 December 2001, para. 7.

[57] See *Prosecutor v. Kordić and Čerkez*, 'Judgement', Case No. IT-95-14/2-T, 26 February 2001, para. 3.

serious violation for which evidence was available; the prosecution would have fourteen months in which to present its case and, as a consequence, would have to reduce the number of incidents to be proved to those which it could prove within that period. The Trial Chamber also stated that it would review its decision in the light of unforeseen circumstances.[58] The Appeals Chamber held that '[i]n the circumstances of this case, which were exceptional, the Trial Chamber was entitled to take such a course, and error in the exercise of its discretion has not been established'.[59]

The Trial Chamber did subsequently extend the time available to the Prosecution to lead its case-in-chief. At the pre-trial conference concerning the Croatia and Bosnia case on 25 July 2002, it ordered an extension of that time to 16 May 2003.[60] After numerous interferences with the sitting schedule, the prosecution case finally closed a considerable time thereafter, on 25 February 2004.[61]

The prosecution later expressed its view that the case it led in the *Milošević* trial was very contained and focused, and presented itself as having led a very succinct case.[62] This assertion of the prosecution was never dealt with directly by the Trial Chamber. However, the Chamber clearly believed that the case was overly long. The prosecution case strategy and the breadth caused an enormous amount of time to be taken in procedural and administrative matters, contested issues and is, in part, the reason for the amount of time taken in cross-examination of prosecution witnesses. However, in one sense the prosecution's claim to brevity is not entirely misplaced. Given the scope of the case it sought to lead, one might conclude that the time taken to lead such a case was not excessive. The crucial discussion concerns the scope of the case in the first place, how it was to be managed by the accused and, indeed, the Trial Chamber. Although the case was never to conclude, it was clear that the accused's task of leading evidence to meet the prosecution case against him was virtually impossible (in significant part due to his own attitude to the conduct of his case) and the Chamber's task of synthesising the evidence and determining all the issues in it was an enormous challenge. At the same hearing in which the Prosecution congratulated itself on leading a manageable case, counsel assigned to the accused produced some disturbing figures revealing the

[58] *Prosecutor v. Milošević*, 'Reasons for Refusal of Leave to Appeal From Decision to impose Time Limit', Case No. IT-02-54-T, 16 May 2002, para. 16.

[59] Ibid. [60] *Prosecutor v. Milošević*, Hearing, Transcript, 25 July 2002, 8641.

[61] See *Prosecutor v. Milošević*, 'Decision on Notification of the Completion of Prosecution Case and Motion for the Admission of Evidence in Written Form', Case No. IT-02-54-T, 25 February 2004.

[62] *Prosecutor v. Milošević*, Hearing, Transcript, 29 November 2005, 46643.

scope of the case. As at 24 November 2005, there had been 46,639 pages of transcript and 2,256 separate written filings amounting to 63,775 pages.[63] The prosecution had introduced 930 exhibits, amounting to 85,526 pages (excluding the content of DVDs and CD-ROMs containing further material), as well as 117 videos.[64] The most extraordinary statistic, however, concerns the scale of material disclosed to Milošević. The combination of Rule 66(A)(ii),[65] Rule 66(B),[66] and Rule 68[67] material disclosed amounted to over 1.2 million pages of documentation.[68]

The Accused, as far back as the pre-trial conference for Croatia and Bosnia in July 2002, had referred to the effect of the Prosecution's massive case:

> In connection with what you are considering and deliberating about, I believe it would be logical for you also to review the answer to the question: What is the purpose of providing material that nobody has time to read? What occurs to me also is something that Mr. Kay said at one point when we had a discussion about the scheduling length and joinder of these various cases. Namely, he said that there was no human being able of handling such a trial. Perhaps that is precisely what the Prosecutor is guided by.[69]

Again, in November 2005, Milošević articulated his position on what was the effect of the amount of material disclosed:

> [I]t's an enormous amount of material. And that every participant in this trial had to read 500 to 1,000 pages per day every day over the space of

63 Ibid. 46701. 64 Ibid.

65 '(A) Subject to the provisions of Rules 53 and 69, the Prosecutor shall make available to the defence in a language which the accused understands within the time-limit prescribed by the Trial Chamber or by the pre-trial Judge appointed pursuant to Rule 65 *ter*. . . (ii) copies of the statements of all witnesses whom the Prosecutor intends to call to testify at trial, and copies of all written statements taken in accordance with Rule 92 *bis*; copies of the statements of additional prosecution witnesses shall be made available to the defence when a decision is made to call those witnesses.'

66 'The Prosecutor shall, on request, permit the defence to inspect any books, documents, photographs and tangible objects in the Prosecutor's custody or control, which are material to the preparation of the defence, or are intended for use by the Prosecutor as evidence at trial or were obtained from or belonged to the accused.'

67 'Subject to the provisions of Rule 70, (i) the Prosecutor shall, as soon as practicable, disclose to the Defence any material which in the actual knowledge of the Prosecutor may suggest the innocence or mitigate the guilt of the accused or affect the credibility of Prosecution evidence; (ii) without prejudice to paragraph (i), the Prosecutor shall make available to the defence, in electronic form, collections of relevant material held by the Prosecutor, together with appropriate computer software with which the defence can search such collections electronically. . .'.

68 *Prosecutor v. Milošević*, Hearing, Transcript, 29 November 2005, 46701.

69 *Prosecutor v. Milošević*, Hearing, Transcript, 25 July 2002, 8639.

> three and a half years, without exception and without all their other obligations.
>
> And a normal human being is quite certainly not able to read even a small portion of that. And as I believe that nobody could claim to be a superpowerful human in any sense here, then we come to the conclusion that the situation is quite unrealistic and in this hall for three and a half years we have had a group of people taking part in something that we can call or is called a trial, whereas none of the participants in the proceedings knows what it says in the files on the basis of which the discussions are being held here.[70]

I referred, in chapter 1 above, to a prosecution report concerning the extraordinary resources it had poured into the identification and production of Rule 68 material (exculpatory or mitigatory in nature) to the Accused, a process that was said to have required 'the equivalent of twenty-six "person years" of labour and cost nearly 1.5 million U.S. dollars'.[71] Of course, an argument to meet the obvious resource imbalance this evidences might be that these cited resources contributed to producing material which 'may suggest innocence or mitigate the guilt of the accused or affect the credibility of Prosecution evidence'.[72] Therefore, it might be said that the resources employed by the prosecution to determine the existence and disclosure of this material was in fact of benefit to the accused. However, it raises questions both about the scope of the case and whether the principle of equality of arms is met. The importance of the relative equality of resources between the parties is a matter discussed in chapter 1 of this book, and its particular import in the case is one to which I will return in chapter 4 and when considering the future conduct of complex international criminal trials in my conclusions. However, the point raised by Milošević above is an important one in case management terms, because it impacts on the capacity of an accused to prepare for and conduct his case and therefore on the ability of the court to ensure that he receives a fair trial. The issue is one which is raised persistently in international criminal trials, even where accused are represented by sophisticated legal counsel.[73] In a complex trial of a self-represented accused, it becomes increasingly important to ensure that the accused is not buried in paper and rendered incapable of effectively preparing and conducting his defence. This would render the case unmanageable and compromise its fairness.

70 *Prosecutor v. Milošević*, Hearing, Transcript, 29 November 2005, 46687.

71 *Prosecutor v. Milošević*, 'Prosecution's Comprehensive Report Concerning Its Compliance to Date with Rule 68', Case No. IT-02-54-T, 20 February 2004, para. 2.

72 Rule 68(A).

73 See e.g., *Prosecutor v. Milutinović et al.*, 'Second Decision on Motions to Delay Proposed Date for Start of Trial', Case No. IT-05-87-PT, 28 April 2006.

The defence case

Conduct of the defence case

The length of the prosecution case literally set the basis for the defence case. However, the process of preparing for and managing the conduct of a defence case, in circumstances where the accused was at the time self-represented and, in some material respects, uncooperative, posed a significant challenge to the Trial Chamber to ensure a fair trial and one that would also be acceptably expeditious. How was the accused to investigate, proof witnesses, collect and prepare considerable documentation, have privileged access to lawyers, witnesses, investigators and others, all from the confines of the United Nations Detention Unit in the Hague? And once all the facilities were provided and practical arrangements made, how was Milošević to be sufficiently informed of, and forced to comply with, the myriad of rules relating to disclosure, notice, the leading of witnesses and other matters? Early in the case, and following complaints by Milošević, and submissions made by the *amici curiae*, about the facilities available to him, the Trial Chamber issued rulings on the facilities to be provided to the accused for his defence.[74]

The Chamber grappled with problems of non-compliance, seeking to ensure compliance by the accused with the disclosure rules and adjusting in what appeared to be a pragmatic way to non-fulfilment or inadequate compliance with Trial Chamber orders. On 17 September 2003, while still in the prosecution case-in-chief, the Trial Chamber issued a ruling dealing with the preparation and presentation of the defence case.[75] This was the first significant step the Chamber took in the management of the defence case. The order required Milošević, within six weeks of the close of the prosecution case, to file the list of witnesses he intended to call, to file the list of exhibits he intended to offer in his case and to serve on the prosecutor copies of these exhibits. The Chamber stated that it might refuse to hear a witness whose name did not appear on Milošević's list of witnesses and that if he wished to add any witnesses or exhibits after the pre-defence conference, he would have to show good cause for doing so. Milošević was warned to bear in mind that during his examination of witnesses, the Chamber would exercise control over the mode and order of interrogation and presentation of evidence so as to

[74] For a detailed discussion of resources made available to the accused in this trial, see chapter 4.

[75] *Prosecutor v. Milošević*, 'Order Concerning the Preparation and Presentation of the Defence Case', Case No. IT-02-54-T, 17 September 2003.

ensure it was effective for the ascertainment of truth and to avoid the needless consumption of time, and was reminded that his time would be limited and he should focus on relevant areas of evidence. Finally, Milošević was encouraged to avail himself of the provisions under Rule 92*bis* with respect to the admission of evidence in written form.[76] As will be seen, the Chamber did persistently caution the accused on irrelevant and cumulative questioning of his witnesses and occasionally cut short the evidence he led.[77] However, given that by the time Milošević died in his prison bed (some 80 per cent of the way through the time allocated to conduct his case) he had still not touched on most of the Croatia and Bosnia charges in the indictment and had not tendered a single written statement, it is apparent that this form of *ad hoc* micro case management had little positive impact on expediting the defence case or forcing the presentation of a representative range of defence evidence to meet the prosecution case.

Milošević initially submitted a list of 1,631 witnesses.[78] He later told the Chamber that this number had been substantially culled from a list of over 5,000 potential witnesses.[79] A pre-defence conference was held by the Trial Chamber on 17 June 2004, following which the Chamber issued a series of orders to Milošević on how he was to conduct his case and the manner in which disclosure was to be made, including: that he was to produce a weekly list of witnesses to be called at the following week's trial; disclose to the prosecution copies of all exhibits on his Rule 65*ter* list within seven days (which, like witness identity disclosure and applications for protective measures, he had failed to do under order previously);[80] to make

76 Ibid.

77 See, e.g., *Prosecutor v. Milošević*, Hearing, 1 March 2006, Transcript, 49141, 49143–4, 49147–9 (witness Alice Mahon); 6 February 2006, Transcript, 48083–5, 48087–8 (witness Branko Kostić); 20 September 2005, Transcript, 44361, 44364-7 (witness Vojislav Šešelj); 15 June 2005, Transcript, 40744-9 (witness Obrad Stevanović).

78 See reference in *Prosecutor v. Milošević*, 'Order to the Accused on Protective Measures for Defence Witnesses', Case No. IT-02-54-T, 27 May 2004.

79 See e.g., *Prosecutor v. Milošević*, Pre-Defence Conference, 17 June 2004.

80 In respect of Milošević's non-compliance, see *Prosecutor v. Milošević*, 'Order to the Accused on Protective Measures for Defence Witnesses', Case No. IT-02-54-T, 27 May 2004; *Prosecutor v. Milošević*, 'Omnibus Order on Matters Dealt with at the Pre-Defence Conference', Case No. IT-02-54-T, 17 June 2004; *Prosecutor v. Milošević*, 'Order to the Accused on Compliance with Disclosure Obligations', Case No. IT-02-54-T, 6 July 2004; *Prosecutor v. Milošević*, 'Order on *Amici Curiae* Motion In Relation to Accused's Disclosure Obligations and Request for Additional Time', Case No. IT-02-54-T, 6 July 2004; *Prosecutor v. Milošević*, 'Order on Application by the Accused to Add Four Witnesses to his Witness List', Case No. IT-02-54-T, 3 December 2004; *Prosecutor v. Milošević*, 'Order to Accused to Produce a List of his Next 50 Witnesses and Finalise Compliance with Rule

written filings when ordered by the Trial Chamber to do so, in particular as to the production of documents or other information from states (again, something he had previously refused to do); to make an opening statement of not more than four hours, to which the prosecutor was not allowed to respond; and, to make a separate written application for each witness whom he would seek to subpoena.[81]

The presentation by Milošević of his case was interrupted early on by a series of absences related to his cardiovascular condition, apparently at least in part caused by non-compliance with his prescribed medication regime.[82] By the end of 2005, more than 75 per cent through the time allocated to Milošević to present his defence, he had led just over forty witnesses; tendered 328 exhibits at 9,000 pages; and introduced 50 video tapes, stills or excerpts.[83] But most significantly, as noted by counsel assigned to him, only about 15 per cent of the time taken by the defence case had covered issues relating to Croatia and Bosnia. Effectively Milošević had dealt almost exclusively with the Kosovo indictment.[84]

Trial Chamber's management of the defence case

The Trial Chamber made extraordinary practical arrangements for Milošević to be able to prepare for his defence, and sought to ensure compliance with disclosure and notice rules within the context that he was a detained accused representing himself, although in some significant respects it failed to enforce its orders.

The Trial Chamber determined early on that it would accord Milošević the same amount of time the prosecution used in leading its case. The formula the Chamber used to determine this was to calculate the time used by the prosecution to lead its case-in-chief (time taken in examination-in-chief and re-examination of witnesses), exclusive of general administrative time and cross-examination.[85] This approach was at the time novel and innovative (although it is now becoming more common in the conduct of

65*ter*,Obligations Regarding Exhibits', Case No. IT-02-54-T, 7 December 2004; *Prosecutor v. Milošević*, 'Omnibus Order on Matters Arising Out of Status Conference on the Defence Case', Case No. IT-02-54-T, 22 April 2005; *Prosecutor v. Milošević*, 'Order to the Accused to Produce the List of Witnesses He Intends to Call for the Remainder of His Case', Case No. IT-02-54-T, 5 October 2005.

81 *Prosecutor v. Milošević*, 'Omnibus Order on Matters Dealt with at the Pre-Defence Conference', Case No. IT-02-54-T, 17 June 2004.

82 See *Prosecutor v. Milošević*, 'Reasons for Decision on Assignment of Defence Counsel', Case No. IT-02-54-T, 22 September 2004, para. 67.

83 *Prosecutor v. Milošević*, Hearing, Transcript, 29 November 2005, 46701.

84 Ibid. 46700.

85 *Prosecutor v. Milošević*, Hearing, Transcript, 2 September 2003, 25947–8.

international criminal trials[86]) and is distinguishable from the approach taken by the Trial Chamber in the *Orić* case, where the Chamber imposed time and witness limitations on the accused which it had not imposed on the prosecution.[87] Interestingly, in the earliest reference to these matters in September 2003, the Chamber still sought to limit, although in only the most general terms, the number of witnesses Milošević could lead, although the main focus of the case management approach even at the start of the defence case concerned the limitation of the time available. The Chamber, in a hearing on the matter, informed Milošević that the number of witnesses he could call would be based upon the number of the witnesses that the prosecution called.[88] It stated that allowance would be made for prosecution witnesses whose evidence was admitted by way of transcript or written statement and who did not appear for cross-examination. In respect of the time to be available to the accused, the Chamber held that this was to be 'based upon the time which the Prosecution have had to present their case, the time spent on examination-in-chief, and re-examination in the case of the witnesses. That will be calculated on the basis of the log being kept by the Registry.'[89] The Chamber left the specific calculations to be made 'in due course'.[90]

On 25 February 2004, the day after the prosecution case formally closed, the Trial Chamber issued an Order that 'the Accused should have the same time as the prosecution had to present his (the Accused'[s]) case-in-chief', and set out the following calculation of time available to him:

(1) The Prosecution had spent approximately 360 hours presenting its case in chief, or approximately 90 sitting days, which would be the amount of time for the accused to present his case-in-chief;
(2) However, to that was added two-thirds of that time for cross-examination of defence witnesses and administrative matters, which amounts to approximately 240 hours, or 60 sitting days; and
(3) Therefore, the Accused should have 150 sitting days in which to present his case, which should be subject to adjustment depending on the time taken in cross-examination and administrative matters[.][91]

At the pre-defence conference on 17 June 2004, the Chamber explicitly reaffirmed its management of the defence case on the limitation of time,

[86] See, e.g., *Prosecutor v. Prlić et al.*, 'Revised Version of the Decision Adopting Guidelines on Conduct of Trial Proceedings', Case No. IT-04-74-PT, 28 April 2006 ('*Prlić* Order').

[87] See above n. 105. [88] Ibid. 25947. [89] Ibid. 25948. [90] Ibid.

[91] *Prosecutor v. Milošević*, 'Order Re-Scheduling and Setting the Time Available to Present the Defence Case', Case No. IT-02-54-T, 25 February 2004.

signifying its abandonment of any micro management approach in favour of a global approach to the length of Milošević's case:

> The Trial Chamber adheres to its order limiting the Accused to 150 sitting days in the presentation of his case. The Trial Chamber notes that it does not seek to limit the number of witnesses the Accused may call, but encourages him to make use of the procedures available under Rules 92 *bis* and 89(F), and whilst placing no limit on the specific number of witnesses the Accused may call, the evidence led must be relevant and not overly cumulative.[92]

On 19 May 2005, the Trial Chamber ordered some modifications in the use of time in the defence case. The prosecution's allocation of time for cross-examination was revised to 216 hours or 54 sitting days, being 60 per cent of the time allotted to the accused. It was also determined that a separate record of time spent on administrative matters should be kept, but that it would not be counted against the time allotted to the accused. The Trial Chamber further clarified that administrative matters are those which do not fall into the category of procedural issues arising from examination of witnesses, including discussion of the admissibility of exhibits and other matters as determined by the Trial Chamber.[93]

It was the use, or misuse, of time that preoccupied much of the Chamber's management of Milošević in the presentation of his case. The Trial Chamber repeatedly emphasised the time which was allocated to him to present and conclude his case, regularly issued details of the use by the parties of the time allocated, and provided for them to challenge the Chamber's calculation.[94] In a Decision on 12 December 2005, the Trial Chamber noted that it had repeatedly had cause to warn Milošević not to waste time and that he needed to use the time available to lead evidence in relation to all three indictments against him,[95] as well as counselling and warning him that he should make use of the facility of written testimony,

92 *Prosecutor v. Milošević*, 'Omnibus Order on Matters Dealt with at the Pre-Defence Conference', Case No. IT-02-54-T, 17 June 2004, Order (1).

93 *Prosecutor v. Milošević*, 'Third Order on the Use of Time in the Defence Case and Decision on Prosecution's Further Submissions on the Recording and Use of Time During the Defence Case', Case No. IT-02-54-T, 19 May 2005.

94 After several periodic orders from the Trial Chamber, the Chamber Senior Legal Officer was ordered to publish the time used on a monthly basis. Toward the end of the defence case, it was published on a weekly basis.

95 *Milošević* Severance and Time Decision, above n. 28, para. 16, footnote 40, making reference to over sixty such documented occasions between 17 September 2003 and 6 December 2005.

pursuant to Rules 89(F) and 92*bis*, to enable him to lead a reasonable amount of evidence in the time allotted to him.[96]

However, the Trial Chamber did not focus solely on the misuse of time. It also expressed grave concern over the imbalance in the coverage Milošević was giving the case against him. As already noted, assigned counsel had identified that after 75 per cent of the accused's case, he had only spent some 15 per cent of that time on Croatia- and Bosnia-related matters. The Chamber also expressed concern at the limited number of witnesses Milošević had been able to bring in the time available, and how he was going to lead sufficient evidence to answer the case against him. On 5 October 2005, the Trial Chamber decided that, because by that stage Milošević had exceeded two-thirds of his allotted 360 hours for the presentation of his defence case-in-chief, it was appropriate for him to provide certain specific information about his case, including (1) the witnesses he intended to call during the remainder of his allotted time; (2) which remaining witnesses he intended to introduce by way of written evidence, whether by way of Rule 92*bis* or Rule 89(F); and (3) the time he estimated each witness will take.[97]

On 17 October 2005, the accused produced a list of 199 witnesses, additional to the thirty-nine witnesses he had already called by that time, which amounted to over 450 hours of estimated evidence-in-chief. None of the witnesses listed were presented in written form.[98] On 8 December 2005, there was an oral hearing on the question of an extension of time for the presentation of the defence case,[99] at which Milošević made an application for an additional 380 hours of time for questioning witnesses.[100] In doing so, he stated that this contemplated an average of two hours per witness for his proposed remaining 190 witnesses.[101] Counsel assigned to

[96] *Prosecutor v. Milošević*, 'Decision in Relation to Severance, Extension of Time and Rest', Case No. IT-02-54-T, 12 December 2005 ('*Milošević* Severance and Time Decision'), para. 16, footnote 41, making reference to over a dozen occasions between 17 September 2003 and 6 December 2005.

[97] *Prosecutor v. Milošević*, 'Order to the Accused to Produce the List of Witnesses He Intends to Call for the Remainder of His Case', Case No. IT-02-54-T, 5 October 2005.

[98] *Milošević* Severance and Time Decision, above n. 28, footnote 28 of which reads as follows: 'The list was produced as an *ex parte* and confidential list, a redacted version of which was later provided to the prosecution and assigned counsel. At a hearing on 18 October 2005, the accused asserted that the estimated evidence-in-chief amounted to only 422 hours [Transcript, 45315]. The Trial Chamber notes this is inaccurate and that the estimate does not include time for named "hostile witnesses" on the list.'

[99] This followed considerable argument from the Accused, Prosecution and Assigned Counsel during the 29 November 2005 hearing on severance, which will be discussed further below.

[100] *Prosecutor v. Milošević*, Hearing, 8 December 2005, Transcript, 47223.

[101] Ibid.

Milošević supported the application by submitting that there was an 'inequality in strength' between the prosecution and accused, and that this inequality had to be taken into account in determining the question of time allocated to the accused to present his case.[102] This argument raised once again the issue in the trial concerning equality of arms. The prosecution argued that no extension of time should be granted unless the Trial Chamber concluded that the accused was 'disabled . . . because he *cannot* apply his intelligence and reason to the forensic situation in which he finds himself'.[103] It submitted that the accused's estimate of two hours per witness was inconsistent with the reality of Defence witnesses to date, which had averaged around six hours. The prosecution also reiterated prior arguments that Milošević had been on considerable notice of the time limitations imposed, and he should bring his evidence within that time and to use the facilities and resources available to him to achieve this.[104] The Trial Chamber noted in its decision 'that 380 hours is 20 more than the 360 hours already allotted him to present his case. Taking into account time for examination, cross-examination and re-examination, as well as administrative matters, this would amount to an addition of a period approaching 18 months.'[105]

Milošević had, throughout the course of his defence case, challenged the allocation of time he had been given, claiming that the prosecution had been given twice as long, although he never articulated clearly on what basis this was asserted. The Trial Chamber, at a hearing on 20 October 2005, warned Milošević that his mischaracterisation of the differentiation in time between himself and the Prosecution was 'mischievous if not malicious'.[106] The Chamber ordered the registry to provide Milošević with the same calculations upon which the Chamber based its determination that he would have 360 hours to present his case.[107] It was in fact the case that the prosecution case ran over a longer period and more sitting days than the accused's case, although the Trial Chamber explained why that was:

> The Chamber has repeatedly explained to the Accused the methodology for calculating the allocation and use of time. The reasons for there being a greater number of witnesses led by the Prosecution and a greater number

[102] Ibid. 47230.
[103] Ibid. 47231-2. See *Milošević* Severance and Time Decision, above n. 28, para. 13.
[104] See *Prosecutor v. Milošević*, 'Prosecution Submission in Response to the Trial Chamber's 22 November 2005 "Scheduling Order for a Hearing" on Severing the Kosovo Indictment', Case No. IT-02-54-T, 29 November 2005.
[105] *Milošević* Severance and Time Decision, above n. 28, para. 14.
[106] *Prosecutor v. Milošević*, Hearing, 20 October 2005, Transcript, 45536.
[107] Ibid. 45529.

> of actual court days being used during the Prosecution case, while the amount of time taken in evidence-in-chief remains the same, are that: (1) the Prosecution led a significant quantity of its evidence in writing; and, (2) the Accused and *Amici* used up approximately 55% of the overall time in cross-examination of Prosecution witnesses, whereas the Prosecution is allocated 37.5% of the overall time to cross-examine Defence witnesses.[108]

At this late stage of the case, the Trial Chamber finally confronted the critical question relating to the fairness of restricting an accused to the time the prosecution was given to present its case, a crucial question of principle in the use of this case management technique in any trial. Assigned counsel had submitted that '[t]he question of the fairness of the time allocated to [the Accused] . . . should be to enable him to present an effective defence'.[109] The Chamber considered this question and determined as follows:

> Equality of time is one basis on which fair and equal treatment of parties in the presentation of their respective cases can be achieved. Had the Accused made a genuine effort to present his defence in the time allotted to him, by using the resources available and the means of presenting evidence available within the Rules, he might be able to demonstrate that equality of time does not in this instance achieve fairness. However, he has presented no basis on which the Trial Chamber could conclude that this is unfair or that some other allocation of time or other arrangement for the presentation of the Defence case is necessary to achieve fairness. The Trial Chamber is satisfied, on its experience of the Accused in this case, that he has deliberately used the time available to him so that at the end of that time he would have led little or virtually no evidence on the Croatia and Bosnia parts of the case, thus seeking to provide a foundation for a request for additional time.
>
> The proper test must be whether the Accused has been given a reasonable and adequate opportunity to present his case. The Trial Chamber considers, for all the reasons set out above, that the Accused has failed to take a reasonable approach to the presentation of his case. The Chamber considered equality of time to be an appropriate measure of fairness when it allocated the time and continually reviewed the time used and counselled the Accused accordingly. On the basis of the present circumstances, that remains the position. On 12 February 2006, this trial will have been running for four years. The conclusion of the Accused's allotted time will take the trial well into March 2006. Once rebuttal and rejoinder cases are heard and concluding arguments made, it is likely the trial hearings would

[108] *Milošević* Severance and Time Decision, above n. 28, para. 19.
[109] *Prosecutor v. Milošević*, Hearing, 8 December 2005, Transcript, 47230.

> still not conclude until the middle of 2006. Judgement drafting will occupy a further substantial period. The Trial Chamber's fundamental obligation is to bring this trial to a fair and expeditious conclusion.[110]

The issue goes back to the principle of the equality of arms, which the *Tadić* Appeals Chamber noted 'obligates a judicial body to ensure that neither party is put at a disadvantage when presenting its case' but that this did not mean that an accused 'is necessarily entitled to precisely the same amount of time or the same number of witnesses as the prosecution': 'a principle of proportionality, rather than a strict mathematical equality, governs the relationship between the time and witnesses allocated to the two sides'.[111]

It is important to an understanding of the applicability of this case management measure to other international criminal trials, to note that the Chamber applied its reasoning to the particular facts of this case. As has been discussed earlier in this chapter particularly in respect of case management approaches in complex international criminal trials, the facts of each case are particular and case management strategies have to be tailored to the individual case. What is applicable and consistent with the principles of fairness and expedition in one such case may not be appropriate in another. The Trial Chamber here considered the *bona fides* of Milošević and the requirement for expedition as critical factors in its assessment. The decision is ostensibly underscored by the fact that the Chamber had endeavoured laboriously to get Milošević to use his time efficiently and appropriately, to use available methods for the admission of testamentary evidence in writing,[112] and to focus his case, but had been persistently frustrated by the accused's intransigence. The Chamber used its Decision to urge Milošević to use his remaining time well and even left the door ajar for Milošević to return to the Chamber on the question of an

110 Ibid. paras. 24–5.

111 *Prosecutor, v. Tadić*, Case No. IT-94-I-A, Judgement, 15 July 1999 ('*Tadić* Appeal Judgement'), paras. 44, 48, 50. See also *Prosecutor v. Orić*, 'Interlocutory Decision on Length of Defence Case', Case No. IT-03-68-AR73.2, 20 July 2005 ('*Orić* Appeals Decision'), para. 8; *Prosecutor v. Martić*, 'Decision Revising the Time Available to the Defence for Presenting Evidence and Incorporating Scheduling Order', Case No. IT-95-11-T, 7 September 2006, 2.

112 The Chamber gave much emphasis to this within its Decision, stating: 'It is apparent that the Accused has sufficient resources to make use of written testimony. The fact is that he has made no effort to do so. His submissions are not that he would like to present evidence in writing but has experienced the difficulties alluded to by Assigned Counsel. On the contrary, he relies on the misguided view of what is required for a trial to be public. Evidence presented in writing, subject to public scrutiny, is no less public than *viva voce* evidence.' (*Milošević* Severance and Time Decision, above n. 28, para. 22).

extension of time, if there were 'a clear indication in the future that he makes proper and efficient use of time'.[113] It held that it would not in the circumstances allow the Accused additional time and 'strenuously urged [him] to move on to deal with his case on the Croatia and Bosnia indictments'.[114]

As it turned out, Milošević died before the conclusion of his defence case. By that time, he had still led little evidence related to Croatia and Bosnia and had led no evidence in written form. By late 2005 the Chamber's approach to the case had crystallised into a clear macro case management approach. While it had endeavoured during the prosecution case, and early in the defence case, to micromanage witness numbers and control the presentation of cumulative or irrelevant evidence, by late in the trial the Chamber had determined that a global approach to limiting the time available, coupled with counselling parties on the consequences of non-compliance, emerged as the preferred methodology.

For trials of this nature, with high-ranking and difficult accused, this appears to be an effective and relatively safe approach to case management. Other endeavours attempted by the Chamber, including limiting overall witness numbers and confining the amount of evidence that could be led on particular areas of the prosecution case, were less successful, mainly because the parties ignored them and the Chamber was either unable or unwilling to enforce the approach. Generally speaking, the evaluation of case management decisions and approaches largely depends on the ends that case management practices are designed to achieve. The stated goal of the Trial Chamber in *Milošević*, like those of other international criminal trials, is to achieve a fair and expeditious trial. In the context of the *Milošević* case, forms of micro management attempted failed to yield results. The accused was able to circumvent binding orders on him and to use his health and self-represented status to advantage in controlling the trial process. The one methodology that appeared to be manageable and enforceable was to impose strict time limits. In this sense, case management techniques may be said to be successful when they are enforceable and enforced, and yet still respect the principles of fairness and expedition under which international criminal trials operate. What will work may vary from trial to trial, based on the particularities of each case, but in the practice of the ICTY (since *Milošević* pioneered the technique) limitations on time appear to be growing as a preferred form of macro case management.[115] Where specific orders about time to be used in

[113] Ibid. para. 26. [114] Ibid. [115] See, e.g., *Prlić Order*, above n. 86.

examination, cross-examination, and re-examination; administrative time; procedural issues; questions from the Bench, etc., and a clear record of specific time used is kept, the experience of the *Milošević* case appears to suggest that this will be effective. Of course, the Trial Chamber in that case never faced the ultimate test of foreclosing on the accused his case (in the face of an application for a substantial extension, where he had led little evidence on large aspects of the case against him), but the developed principle is sound.

Consideration by the Trial Chamber of more radical case management approaches

Numerous issues plagued the management of the *Milošević* case and led the Trial Chamber to take sometimes radical action, including the scope of the case; the effect on the proceedings of the accused's conduct and attitude; the fact that this accused was self-represented and the profusion of consequences that flowed from this; and, Milošević's ill health – one of the most prevalent problems in the trial (indeed, one that led to the death of the accused and the trial's untimely end).

The issues that plagued the conduct of the *Milošević* case caused the Trial Chamber to consider more radical case management approaches in an endeavour to conclude the trial somehow. The imposition of assigned counsel, the provision of extensive and extraordinary resources to the accused, the plethora of alternative forms of representation and support, were all measures employed in an endeavour to achieve a fair and expeditious trial.

However, one further and more radical approach was contemplated publicly on two occasions by the Trial Chamber, and warrants some attention.

Severance of one or more indictments

As discussed in chapter 2, the Appeals Chamber had granted the prosecution application to join the three indictments against Milošević into one case. However, in its ruling on joinder, the Appeals Chamber left open the possibility of severance:

> Finally, if with the benefit of hindsight it becomes apparent to the Trial Chamber that the trial has developed in such a way as to become unmanageable – especially if, for example, the prosecution is either incapable or unwilling to exercise the responsibility which it bears to exercise restraint in relation to the evidence it produces – it will still be open to the Trial Chamber at that stage to order a severance of the charges arising out of one

> or more of the three areas of the former Yugoslavia. Nothing in the present Decision or in these reasons will prevent it from doing so.[116]

This passage became an important one in the contemplation by the Trial Chamber of how to manage a case that appeared at times to be derailing. The Trial Chamber twice raised the prospect of activating this passage of the Appeals Chamber ruling. First, in the context of the persistent ill-health of the accused and as part of its overall consideration of the future conduct of the case, the Trial Chamber, in July 2004, invited written submissions to consider ways to conclude the trial in a fair and expeditious manner, including the possibility of severing one or more of the indictments.[117]

At the time of filing its written submission on this issue, the prosecution was vigorously arguing for the imposition of defence counsel as a solution to the consistent problems that arose in the conduct of the trial.[118] It raised a number of arguments against severance.[119] It submitted that each indictment was equally meritorious and should be tried to conclusion as part of a single trial; that the issue of severance arises mainly because of the accused's own conduct in defending himself and a rational decision to get assistance from counsel would have rendered the trial manageable, including the maintenance of his health and the effect it had on the trial. The prosecution also stated that there was nothing about the accused's health that indicated his condition could not be stabilised in order to permit him to stand trial with assistance of counsel, and there was nothing about his health that indicated he could stand trial for one or two indictments, but not three. Justice, it was said, should be delivered on all three indictments to the world at large as well as to the victims of crimes in all three wars concerned. The prosecution here argued that the severance would 'inevitably lead to the other indictment(s) not being tried'.[120] Taking the seeming advantage of bringing an early resolution on one part of the trial would, it was argued, 'undermine the interest of having the fullest possible inquiry into 10 years of alleged criminal impunity engaged in by this Accused (in association with politicians, mil-

[116] *Prosecutor v. Milošević*, 'Reasons for Decision on Prosecution Interlocutory Appeal from Refusal to Order Joinder', Case No. IT-02-54-AR73, 18 April 2002, para. 26.

[117] *Prosecutor v. Milošević*, 'Further Order on Future Conduct of the Trial Relating to Severance of One or More Indictments', Case No. IT-02-54, 21 July 2004.

[118] See *Prosecutor v. Milošević*, 'Prosecution's Submissions in Response to the Trial Chamber's 19 July 2004 Further Order on Future Conduct of the Trial', Case No. IT-02-54, 26 July 2004.

[119] *Prosecutor v. Milošević*, 'Prosecution's Submission in Response to the Trial Chamber's 21 July 2004 Further Order on Future Conduct of the Trial Relating to Severance of One or More Indictments', Case No. IT-02-54, 27 July 2004.

[120] Ibid. para. 23.

itary men and others)'.[121] It was submitted that 'the joint trial was and is manageable'.[122] The Prosecution also argued that, at that time, it was premature to consider the possibility that all three indictments may not reach a final conclusion[123] and questioned whether there would be any practical benefit in severing the indictments.[124]

The *amici curiae* filed a response, stating that they had 'received communications from one of the legal associates to the accused that Milošević objects to severance at this stage in the proceedings'.[125] They characterised concerns which the accused might have to the proposal. It was argued that the prosecution had presented its evidence as a 'single case' by focusing on the continuity of actions by the accused within a common plan to create a 'Greater Serbia'. The accused should therefore be given the opportunity to contradict directly the prosecution's case as it was submitted. It was also argued that severance would restrict Milošević's opportunity to answer the prosecution evidence and case theory and '[e]ffectively, the Accused would be denied the opportunity to confront the full thrust of the case alleged'. Like the prosecution, they submitted that the accused prepared his defence in the context of a single case and severance would require substantial reorganisation. There were a large number of 'cross-over' witnesses (dealing with evidence over two or three of the indictments) and it was argued that it would contravene the notion of judicial economy if witnesses were required to testify on more than one occasion. Finally, it was somewhat obscurely argued that, in light of the substantial defence preparation already undertaken, it would be significantly more onerous and detrimental to the accused's health if the case was severed.[126]

On the issue of interpreting paragraph 26 of the Appeals Chamber's joinder ruling, the prosecution submitted that severance of the kind contemplated by the Trial Chamber was provided for at the stage of preliminary motions (during the pre-trial stage), and not later. However, it did acknowledge that the Appeals Chamber had left open the possibility for severance to occur during trial although it was unclear how that would work.[127] The *amici curiae* argued that the Appeals Chamber had left open the possibility of severance at a later stage in the proceedings and that Rule

121 Ibid. para. 22. 122 Ibid. 123 Ibid. paras. 14–16. 124 Ibid. paras. 17–21.

125 *Prosecutor v. Milošević*, 'Amici Curiae Submissions on the Trial Chamber's Further Order on Future Conduct of the Trial Relating to Severance of One or More Indictments Dated 21 July 2004', Case No. IT-02-54-T, 27 July 2004. 126 Ibid. para. 16.

127 *Prosecutor v. Milošević*, 'Prosecution's Submission in Response to the Trial Chamber's 21 July 2004 Further Order on Future Conduct of the Trial Relating to Severance of One or More Indictments', Case No. IT-02-54, 27 July 2004, para. 11.

54 of the ICTY Rules gave the Chamber power to make such orders as may be necessary for the conduct of the trial.[128]

The Trial Chamber considered these arguments and decided not to sever. It gave no reasoning at the time, simply stating that, while it had considered all the submissions on the issue[129] and severance of one or more of the indictments remained an option, it would 'not give further consideration to it at this time'.[130] However, it is apparent that the Chamber by this stage was focusing its case management activity on assigning defence counsel to the accused, and this may be why it so briskly dismissed the possibility of severance.[131]

In November 2005, 75 per cent of the way through the defence case, the Trial Chamber once again raised the possibility of severance. On 22 November of that year, the Trial Chamber ordered the parties to make submissions on severing the Kosovo Indictment and concluding that part of the trial'.[132] Oral argument was heard on 29 November 2005. The prosecution also submitted a 50-page filing on the day of the hearing[133] and made lengthy oral submissions. Its position, which incorporated many of the arguments raised in its 2004 submissions, was summarised by the Chamber as 'complete opposition to severance of the Kosovo indictment'. Milošević also expressed his profound opposition to severing the Kosovo indictment,[134] a position consistent with his approach to the trial and

128 Ibid. para. 15.

129 *Prosecutor v. Milošević*, Case No. IT-02-54: 'Prosecution Submission in Response to the Trial Chamber's 21 July 2004 "Further Order on Future Conduct of the Trial Relating to Severance of One or More Indictments" ', 27 July 2004; 'Amici Curiae Submissions on the Trial Chamber's Further Order on Future Conduct of the Trial Relating to Severance of One or More Indictments dated 21 July 2004', 27 July 2004; 'Addendum to "Prosecution Submission in Response to the Trial Chamber's 19 July 2004 Further Order on Future Conduct of the Trial" and also to "Prosecution Submission in Response to the Trial Chamber's 21 July 2004 Further Order on Future Conduct of the Trial Relating to Severance of One or more Indictments" ', 6 August 2004.

130 *Prosecutor v. Milošević*, 'Scheduling Order Concerning Recommencement of the Trial', Case No. IT-02-54-T, 25 August 2004.

131 This is apparent from the brief discussion of severance in the Chamber's decision assigning counsel, as well as a subsequent decision on the issue: *Prosecutor v. Milošević*, 'Reasons for Decision on Assignment of Counsel', 22 September 2004, Case No. IT-02-54-T, para. 17; *Milošević* Severance and Time Decision, above n. 28, para. 7.

132 *Prosecutor v. Milošević*, 'Scheduling Order for a Hearing', Case No. IT-02-54-T, 22 November 2005, 4.

133 *Prosecutor v. Milošević*, 'Prosecution Submission in Response to the Trial Chamber's 22 November 2005 "Scheduling Order for a Hearing" on Severing the Kosovo Indictment', Case No. IT-02-54-T, 29 November 2005.

134 *Milošević* Severance and Time Decision, above n. 28, para. 7; Hearing, 29 November 2005, Transcript, 46696.

conduct that left all those involved with a sense that he had every intention of dragging it out as long as possible. The assigned counsel rebutted some of the prosecution arguments and focused on the unmanageability of the trial as caused by the presentation of the prosecution case.[135] Interestingly, the assigned counsel did not expressly object to severance of the Kosovo indictment. They trod a careful path in oral argument, focusing on the unmanageability of the case the prosecution had presented. Read closely, this submission could easily have been taken as support for severance, a position not consonant with that expressed by the accused (and probably the reason why the submissions were not more explicit).

It was left to the *amicus curiae*, Professor McCormack, to make strong submissions in favour of severing the Kosovo indictment. He submitted that severance was an appropriate mechanism for the Trial Chamber to bring an important aspect of the case to an expeditious conclusion.[136] He argued that 'the single most compelling argument in favour of severance of the Kosovo indictment is the length of time of the trial to date'.[137] He suggested that the Chamber, in balancing the rights of the accused, including that of self-representation and the opportunity to present a defence, must pay due regard to the 'also important objective of a reasonably expeditious resolution of the case'.[138] The *amicus* argued that what the Appeals Chamber had anticipated in paragraph 26 of its joinder decision was that if the trial were to become unmanageable, the option of severance existed. He concluded that, by November 2005, it was arguable that the trial had become unmanageable in terms of an expeditious resolution of the trial:

> I'm not suggesting that the trial can't be managed. Clearly it is being managed. But I think in terms of the objective that has been recognised a number of times throughout the trial, the importance of expeditious resolution, there is a serious question about whether, in fact, the trial, as currently constituted, with the joinder of all three indictments, really is manageable.[139]

The Trial Chamber, in its decision, found that the question of severance was 'closely related to the time that is likely to be necessary for the conclusion of the whole trial' and decided to consider whether an extension of time would be granted to the accused, as well as any rest period, together with severance.[140] Having ruled that Milošević would be given a period to

135 *Prosecutor v. Milošević*, Hearing, 29 November 2005, 46697-711.
136 *Prosecutor v. Milošević*, Hearing, 29 November 2005, 46714-15.
137 Ibid. 46711. 138 Ibid. 46712. 139 Ibid. 46714-15.
140 *Milošević* Severance and Time Decision, above n. 28, para. 9.

rest, but would not be granted an extension of time allotted him to conclude his case, the Chamber ruled that this 'should lead to the conclusion of the trial within the anticipated time scale' and, in these circumstances, the Trial Chamber did not consider it appropriate to sever the Kosovo indictment.[141]

Given the overall course and length of the trial, and not the least its untimely end, it is difficult to resist the conclusion that the Chamber had missed an opportunity to close off a part of the case and render judgement. This would at least have given an outcome to an aspect of the case. Indeed, in light of Milošević's medical history and the course of the trial, it may be that severance of the Kosovo indictment would better have been affected in September 2002, at the conclusion of the prosecution case on Kosovo and when it became clear that the accused was suffering from a grave medical condition which was likely to cause significant disruption to the trial – a trial which was always going to be extensive. As in July 2004, the Chamber – in its December 2005 Decision – declined to give detailed reasons for its decision not to sever. It may have been influenced by the vehement opposition of the prosecution and accused. However, the arguments of the latter, like those of assigned counsel, really related to the expansiveness of the prosecution case and the unmanageability of the volume of disclosed material and breadth of the indictments. Milošević explicitly rejected severance as an option, but – like those of assigned counsel – many of his arguments could be used to support a decision to sever. Interestingly, the prosecution revived its previous argument that if Kosovo was severed and tried first, it would be 'necessary either – and entirely artificially – to attempt to exclude all consideration of [Milošević's] earlier activity and of all the documents that demonstrate his mental state and actions during the Croatian and Bosnian war or to require him to lead all his evidence on those topics (effectively all the evidence that would be led in a single joined trial)'.[142] However, at that stage of the proceedings, this argument seems unpersuasive, for several reasons. First, the Trial Chamber had in its initial joinder decision held that while a single transaction could be said to exist between the Croatia and Bosnia indictments, the same was not true for Kosovo. The evidence led in the prosecution case showed a clear distinction between the nature and extent of the accused's involvement in events between Croatia and Bosnia on the

[141] Ibid. para. 27.

[142] *Prosecutor v. Milošević*, 'Prosecution Submission in Response to the Trial Chamber's 22 November 2005 "Scheduling Order for a Hearing" on Severing the Kosovo Indictment', Case No. IT-02-54-T, 29 November 2005, para. 52.

one hand (as a *de facto* political figure of power and influence), and Kosovo on the other (as a head of state with *de jure* powers and responsibilities). Finally, the prosecution's clarification of its position in respect of the accused's 'Greater Serbia' aspirations ascribed to him a desire to unite all Serbs in one state. However, the three indictments dealt differently with this characterisation of 'Greater Serbia'. While for Croatia and Bosnia, the idea entailed re-engineering borders and boundaries, as well as expelling non-Serbs from certain areas (in a collapsing State environment in which the Accused had little relevant *de jure* powers), for Kosovo it is pleaded as a removal of a portion of the Kosovo Albanian population from the territory of Kosovo (a part of Serbia, over which the Accused was head of State) to ensure continued Serbian control.

The prosecution also expressed a concern in its submissions in July 2004, and again in 2005, that to sever one indictment would leave the others untried. Presumably, if Kosovo had been severed, and the accused were to be convicted and harshly sentenced, it would ultimately have been for the Prosecutor to insist on concluding the remainder of the trial – although she may have felt less inclined in such circumstances. If Milošević had been acquitted, there would have been an obvious argument for the continuation of the trial. This, however, would inevitably be for the Prosecutor herself, and not the Trial Chamber, to decide. There does not appear to be any provision or principle supporting the proposition that a Chamber may, once an indictment is brought and a case commenced, simply refuse to hear and determine the remainder of the criminal charges against an accused, regardless of the outcome of other charges against the same accused. No doubt the Prosecutor would prefer it were the Chamber – and not she – who would be attributed responsibility for the political consequences of severance.

The Trial Chamber did not seize the opportunity to sever and conclude the Kosovo part of the case. In one respect, this is hardly surprising. Such a radical case management approach is unprecedented in international criminal trials[143] and, in circumstances where the parties themselves are equally vehemently opposed, the Chamber might rightly feel timidity in such a course of action. On the other hand, a trial that had lasted four years already, and in circumstances in which the accused had led almost entirely evidence relating to only one indictment (Kosovo), one solution

[143] Although it is a possibility provided for in the *Indictments Act 1915* of England and Wales: see P. J. Richardson *et al.* (eds.), *Archbold: Criminal Pleading, Evidence and Practice*, (2003) ('Archbold'), 1–166.

was presented which might improve on the lack of expedition of the trial and enable some closure of an important trial. Also importantly, it might have accorded greater fairness to the accused in the sense that a judgement would be issued on the presentation of considerable evidence by both sides on a single indictment. This outcome would be less likely where judgement would have been issued on three indictments on which the accused had led little evidence in challenge to two of them, even where the reason for this is the wilfully poor management by the accused of the evidence led in his case. The latter point is really related to the overall management of the case. The Chamber determining that the *Milošević* case was to be limited in time, meant that he would have led very little evidence on the enormous Croatia and Bosnia parts of the case, having focused over 80 per cent of his entire time on Kosovo. The perception of some would undoubtedly have been that Milošević had been unfairly treated. Severance of the Kosovo indictment would have cured this and many other ills in the fair and expeditious trial paradigm. Ultimately, it is clearly regrettable that the Chamber did not follow the submissions of the *amicus* to 'steer a course . . . [toward the] . . . expeditious resolution of the case'.[144]

Case management principles in national and international criminal law

As stated at the beginning of this chapter, the nature and circumstances of the *Milošević* case were unique but the fundamental case management issues with which it struggled were not. Procedural mechanisms for the conduct of criminal and civil proceedings have been under scrutiny in some common law jurisdictions for decades and provide a context for the kinds of issues that arose in the *Milošević* case and which must be addressed in future complex international criminal trials. This section first considers the broader context of case management in national law practice. It then examines these issues in the developing regulatory structure of international criminal law and some of the international criminal trials. This will lead to an analysis of the framework for consideration of the lessons to be learnt from the *Milošević* case and the development of reforms for the future conduct of these trials. Its focus is on the ICTY, where most of the grappling with and development of case management reforms in international criminal law have thus far occurred.

[144] *Prosecutor v. Milošević*, Hearing, 29 November 2005, 46712.

Case management in common law systems

The idea of case management has largely been discussed in the context of common law jurisdictions, where judges and courts have retreated from a strict adversarial approach and have been prepared to play a more interventionist role in structuring, supervising and controlling trial proceedings. In an effort to reduce the length of proceedings and prevent delay, judges have increasingly taken on the role of managers in an attempt to ensure that justice is delivered in a timely and efficient manner. It is in the United States that case management appears to be most developed, with court rules and guidelines,[145] special judicial training sessions addressing case flow and management issues,[146] and a body of academic literature tracking these developments.[147] In recent years, there have also been similar developments in Canada,[148] Australia[149] and the United Kingdom.[150]

Common law jurisdictions traditionally adhered to an adversarial framework, where the parties themselves have primary responsibility for the running of litigation.[151] In this system the judge assumes a relatively passive role, acting as an umpire between the parties, who have control

145 See, e.g., American Bar Association, 'Criminal Justice Section Standards – Speedy Trial', approved by the American Bar Association's House of Delegates in August 2004 http://www.abanet.org/crimjust/standards/speedytrial_toc.html at 1 October 2006 ('ABA Report'); Michigan State Court Administrative Office, 'Caseflow Management Guide' (2004) http://www.courts.michigan.gov/scao/resources/publications/manuals/cfmg.pdf at 1 October 2006 ('Michigan State Court Report').

146 Roger A. Hanson and David B. Rottman, 'United States: So Many States, So Many Reforms' (1999) 20 *Justice System Journal* 121, 124–5; 127–9.

147 See, e.g., Holly Bakke and Maureen Solomon, 'Case Differentiation: An Approach to Individualized Case Management' (1989) 73 *Judicature*,17; Robert F. Peckham, 'A Judicial Response to the Cost of Litigation: Case Management, Two-Stage Discovery Planning and Alternative Dispute Resolution' (1985) 37 *Rutgers Law Review* 253; Norma Shapiro *et al.*, 'Pretrial Case Management in the Federal System – "Keeping the Cost of Justice Reasonable"' (1984) 14 *Golden Gate University Law Review*, 611.

148 See, e.g., Doris I. Wilson, 'Managing Litigation in Canada' (2002) 5 *Canadian Forum on Civil Justice*, http://www.cfcj.fcjc.org/issue_5/n5-dwilson.htm at 1 October 2006.

149 See, e.g., Australian Law Reform Commission, *Managing Justice: A Review of the Federal Civil Justice System*, Report No 89 (1999) ('ALRC Report'); Kenneth Hayne, 'Judicial Case Management and the Duties of Counsel', address to the Readers of the Bar Practice Course, Brisbane, 24 Wednesday February 1999 http://www.hcourt.gov.au/speeches/haynej/haynej_bris.htm at 1 October 2006.

150 See, e.g., Jenny McEwan, 'Co-operative Justice and the Adversarial Criminal Trial: Lessons from the Wolf Report' in Sean Doran and John D. Jackson (eds.), *The Judicial Role in Criminal Proceedings* (2000), 171.

151 ALRC Report, above n. 149, para. 6.3. See also A. T. H. Smith, in Christine van den Wyngaert (ed.), *Criminal Procedure Systems in the European Community* (1993).

over the collection, presentation, and testing of evidence.[152] In recent decades, courts in common law jurisdictions have assumed an increasingly prominent role in terms of managing cases. This has stemmed largely from increasing caseloads that, absent judicial intervention, would cause unacceptable delay.[153]

There is often a distinction drawn in the literature between 'case management' and 'caseflow management'. In the Canadian context, the former has been defined as meaning the management of a case by an individual judge, whereas the latter refers to systematic court management processes (such as the organisation of different types of cases into different 'tracks').[154] However, the boundaries between these forms of management of proceedings are not fixed and there is considerable overlap in common law jurisdictions between them.[155] Indeed, they are increasingly seen as important co-related forms of management. The reason for a two-tiered approach to case management in common law systems appears to be a recognition that the problem of delay stems both from the court system and the handling of individual cases within that system. As such, concerns of delay and efficiency cannot be addressed without addressing both elements of the problem. The allocation and differential treatment of cases represents a broader solution that aims to improve the efficiency and functioning of a particular court system as a whole. Yet, without a concurrent focus on individual case management issues, any system-wide or overarching solution appears likely to be ineffective. The individual case management approach ensures that each case, once allocated to a particular judge, moves through the court system efficiently.

Caseflow management or differential case management

One aspect, or extension of, caseflow management is the concept of 'differential case management', essentially a system for assigning particular cases to different 'tracks' with different timelines and management procedures.[156] Underpinning the concept of differential case management is the idea that different types of cases require different treatment, and not all cases are suitable for the same type of resolution. The US-based National Center for State Courts has commented that because all cases are

[152] Ibid.

[153] Dinah Shelton, 'Ensuring Justice with Deliberate Speed: Case Management in the European Court of Human Rights and the United States Courts of Appeals' (2000), 21 *Human Rights Law Journal* 337, 338.

[154] Doris I. Wilson, above n. 148.

[155] Ibid.

[156] Ibid. This is also referred to in some of the literature as 'differentiated case management', although they appear to be interchangeable terms.

not alike, they should not be treated alike. Because 'most litigation is "ordinary", and traditional steps in the legal process are designed for complicated, high-stakes, and hotly contested cases, procedures need to be redesigned to fit the bulk of litigation'.[157]

Differential case management is a system for dividing cases into categories, so that different procedural approaches can be adopted (such as time-limits for discovery and different deadlines for submissions).[158] Various models of differential case management have been tested, with individual courts and jurisdictions tending to develop particular models to suit their individual needs. Essentially, a system of differential case management requires all cases to be initially screened so that they can be assigned to a particular track. Assignment of cases will depend on particular characteristics that are identified, such as the nature or complexity of the case or its subject-matter.[159] As well as considering the characteristics of the case, the assignment to a particular track may include a discussion of the time actually required to prepare and conduct the case.[160] While the categories or tracks of cases will vary between jurisdictions, it is common for such case management systems to have at least three tracks: complex, simple and standard.[161] For each track there will be different timelines imposed for the completion of certain events.[162]

According to Holly Bakke and Maureen Solomon,

> [Differential case management] is an attempt to define case-specific features which distinguish among cases as to the level of case management required. Thus, the essence of differential case management is reorganization of the caseflow system to recognize explicitly that the speed and method of case disposition should depend on cases' actual resource and management requirements (both court and attorney) *not* on the order in which they have been filed.[163]

The authors suggest that differential treatment of different cases is not completely novel, and that precursors can be found in the procedural and managerial differentiation between civil and criminal cases which is common in most courts.[164]

157 National Center for State Courts, 'Frequently Asked Questions: Differentiated Case Management', http://www.ncsconline.org/WC/FAQs/DiffCMFAQ.htm 1 October 2006.

158 Ibid.

159 Ibid. Michigan State Court Administrative Office, *Caseflow Management Guide* (2004), 20, http://www.courts.michigan.gov/scao/resources/publications/manuals/cfmg.pdf 1 October 2006.

160 Holly Bakke and Maureen Solomon, above n. 147, 18.

161 Doris I. Wilson, above n. 148.

162 Holly Bakke and Maureen Solomon, above n. 147, 20.

163 Ibid. 18.

164 Ibid.

This differential, or system-centred, approach to case management is reflected in the American Bar Association's Standards relating to Speedy Trial and Timely Resolution of Criminal Cases. For instance, Standard 12-1.5 provides that jurisdictions should devise caseflow systems that 'enable an early assessment of the complexity and prospect for non-trial resolution of cases', and Standard 12-1.3 provides that in differentiating between types of cases, jurisdictions should take account of the relative seriousness and complexity of different types of cases, and distinguish between defendants in detention and defendants on pre-trial release. The Standards also contain provisions relating to implementing and enforcing time-limits for various stages of the proceedings.[165]

Individual case management

Combined with these court-wide, systems-based approaches to case management, the problem of delay has also been addressed by focusing on how individual cases are handled. This individual system of case management has been described by one commentator as

> the managerial intervention by a judicial officer soon after a case has been filed. The purpose of this intervention is to reduce dilatory and inefficient litigation practices and to promote fair, speedy, and inexpensive resolution of disputes. It often involves early identification of disputed issues of fact and law, establishment of a procedural calendar for the case, and exploration of consensual mechanisms of resolution of the case other than through a court trial.[166]

Individual case management measures may include pre-trial conferences, the cutting short of long or irrelevant cross-examination, permitting the adjournment or vacation of trial dates only for compelling reasons, deadlines for the exchange of documents, time limits for other events, and status reviews.[167]

This type of case management focuses on the disposition of individual cases by a judge, and is sometimes referred to as 'judicial monitoring', 'individual list', 'single judge', 'single docket' or 'individual docket'.[168] According to Doris Wilson, the individual case management approach involves 'continuous control by a judge, who personally monitors each case on an *ad hoc* basis and ensures that the case moves at an appropriate

[165] See e.g. ABA Report, above n. 145, Standards 12-3.2, 12-2.6, 12-2.7.

[166] Karen Blöchlinger, 'Primus Inter Pares: Is the Singapore Judiciary First Among Equals?' (2000) 9 *Pacific Rim Law and Policy Journal* 591 (footnotes omitted).

[167] Ibid.; Doris I. Wilson, above n. 148.

[168] Doris I. Wilson, above n. 148.

pace'.[169] It is at this individual level that judges have a more active role in shaping and controlling the proceedings, sometimes giving rise to concerns about judges' suitability as managers, and about the boundaries of judicial activism.[170]

Individual case management in North American systems have recognised that benefits may be achieved through controlling cases by either time or events. For example, one Canadian report has described case management as a 'comprehensive system of management of the time and events in a law suit as it proceeds through the justice system, from initiation to resolution'. The two essential components of case management systems are the setting of a timetable for pre-determined events and the supervision of the progress of a case through its timetable.[171]

These different elements are addressed by the United States' Federal Judicial Center in its 'Manual for Complex Litigation'.[172] This Manual is designed for civil litigation, but some of its principles may be applicable to criminal trials. The Manual notes that limits on time and evidence should generally be set at a pre-trial conference to enable the parties to plan before the trial begins.[173] The Manual notes that excessively lengthy litigation may be curtailed by limiting the number of witnesses or exhibits (in relation to a particular issue or in general); controlling the length of examination or cross-examination of witnesses; limiting the total time allowed to each side for examining witnesses; and, narrowing the issues in the trial, by order or stipulation.[174]

The Manual notes that judicial intervention may become necessary if 'evidence exceeds reasonable bounds and does not contribute to resolving the issues presented',[175] and comments that one possibility is for judges to limit or bar the examination of witnesses whose testimony is unnecessary or cumulative, or when the questioning is confusing, repetitive or irrelevant and might delay the trial.[176] Several US Federal Rules of Evidence are cited which permit the exclusion of relevant testimony if its probative value is outweighed by considerations of delay, waste of time, or needless presentation of cumulative evidence.[177] One mechanism

[169] Ibid.

[170] See e.g. Judith Resnik, 'Managerial Judges' (1982), 96 *Harvard Law Review* 374.

[171] Ontario Court of Justice, Ministry of the Attorney General, *Caseflow Management: An assessment of the Ontario pilot projects in the Ontario Court of Justice* (1993), cited by the UK Department for Constitutional Affairs, at http://www.dca.gov.uk/civil/interim/chap5.htm 1 October 2006.

[172] Federal Judicial Center, *Manual for Complex Litigation*, (4th edition, 2004) http://www.fjc.gov/public/pdf.nsf/lookup/mcl4.pdf/$file/mcl4.pdf 1 October 2006.

[173] Ibid. 147. [174] Ibid. 127. [175] Ibid. 147. [176] Ibid. 148. [177] Ibid.

suggested by the Manual is for courts to 'bar questions that are framed as arguments, rather than requests for testimony that the witness is competent to give'.[178]

In relation to limiting time, the Manual recommends that limits should generally be established prior to trial, but concedes that this will not always be possible. Such limits may grant a specified number of hours for examination-in-chief or cross-examination, restrict time for specific arguments, or impose limits for particular witnesses.[179] Further, the Manual recommends that once limits have been imposed, the court should grant extensions only for good cause, 'taking into account the requesting party's good-faith efforts to stay within the limits and the degree of prejudice that would result from the denial of an extension'.[180]

Some of these individual case management approaches are reflected in the development of case management techniques in the regulatory and judicial work of the international criminal tribunals, particularly – as will be seen – in the ICTY.

The willingness and capacity of judges to manage cases

What emerges from the literature is that the need to manage effectively an increasing load of cases is a problem common to all courts.[181] Different courts will adopt different measures, or tailor measures according to their needs.[182] According to one US case management expert, case management should ideally be a mutual process, where 'control' is rejected in favour of 'supervision' to avoid any implication that a dictatorial approach by the court is advocated. She reasons that court supervision of case progress does not supplant the responsibilities of legal representatives. Instead, 'it should create a system of joint responsibilities wherein the perspectives and judgment of each can be applied in an appropriate manner to decisions concerning the progress of individual cases and the caseload as a whole'.[183]

This more cooperative rather than coercive perspective typifies the characteristically 'hands off' approach to case management taken in many adversarial criminal justice systems, particularly the US. This consensual perspective should probably be the starting point for any case management activity, although for reasons discussed further below, tends to be an unsatisfactory answer to case management needs in complex international criminal trials, both because of the nature of the cases and because of a predisposed lack of prosecutorial restraint.

[178] Ibid. 149. [179] Ibid. [180] Ibid. [181] Dinah Shelton, above n. 153, 337.

[182] Doris I. Wilson, above n. 148.

[183] Maureen Solomon, quoted in ALRC Report, above n. 149, para. 6.8.

Because the typical approach taken by the common law judge to management of a particular case, it has been noted that increased judicial intervention involves a significant change or 'reorientation' of the judicial role.[184] Justice Hayne of the High Court of Australia has observed that judges have always had some power to control the course of a trial, but that recently they have become more willing to use these powers.[185] In England and Wales also, the power of judges to exercise some control in respect of complex cases is contemplated.[186] Murray Gleeson, the Chief Justice of the High Court of Australia, has commented:

> Judges, who in the past concerned themselves only with the just resolution of individual cases as they came up for trial, have found it necessary to become more interventionist in the management of court lists in the progress towards trial of cases, and in the conduct of litigation. Case management has been accepted by the judiciary, principally because there is no other practical method of coping with the expanding workload. It means that a substantial new responsibility has been taken on by judges. Instead of simply deciding each case in turn as it finds its way to the head of a queue, judges have assumed the management of the queue. Instead of allowing the lawyers for the parties to run cases at their own pace, judges have taken to directing more closely the conduct of trials.[187]

Justice Gleeson has further remarked that this relatively recent change to the judicial role has exposed judges to a greater degree of scrutiny, observing that the increase of judicial case management can 'sometimes conflict with the requirement of strict judicial neutrality', and that this has led to a demand for greater accountability.[188] The increased judicial control of proceedings has led some to observe that judges are not necessarily trained or equipped for such a managerial role.[189] In the United States, at least, there are training courses for judges which focus on the principles and practices of case management.[190]

[184] Doris I. Wilson, above n. 148.

[185] Kenneth Hayne, 'Judicial Case Management and the Duties of Counsel', address to the Readers of the Bar Practice Course, Brisbane, 24 Wednesday February 1999 http://www.hcourt.gov.au/speeches/haynej/haynej_bris.htm 1 October 2006.

[186] See, e.g., Archbold, above n. 143, 1–110ff.

[187] Murray Gleeson, 'Current Issues for the Australian Judiciary', speech delivered to the Supreme Court of Japan, Tokyo, 17 January 2000 http://www.hcourt.gov.au/ speeches/cj/cj_Japanj.htm 1 October 2006.

[188] Ibid.

[189] ALRC Report, above n. 149, paras. 6.4, 6.17.

[190] Roger A. Hanson and David B. Rottman, 'United States: So Many States, So Many Reforms' (1999), 20 *Justice System Journal* 121, 124–5; 127–9.

Case management in civil law systems

In civil law jurisdictions, the term 'case management' appears to be largely unknown. It is not a term that appears in the literature, nor is the concept explicitly enshrined in the codified provisions of these legal systems. However, many of the inquisitorial procedures (in which the judge has significant control over the course of proceedings) can be seen to resemble case management ideas consciously developed in common law courts as well as in international criminal law.[191]

Practically, the civil and common law legal systems have very different approaches to procedure, and the two systems rest on different philosophical foundations. In common law adversarial systems, criminal proceedings are largely party-driven, with the parties controlling the definition of the subject-matter of the dispute and also the presentation of evidence upon which decisions are based.[192] In the adversarial system, the involvement of the court in the presentation and taking of evidence at trial is much reduced.[193] The judge in the common law system traditionally rarely interferes in the questioning of witnesses by counsel and, apart from exercising the judge's inherent power to ensure fairness to the parties, he or she does little more in this part of the process than to act as 'an impartial referee between the parties'.[194] It is in this setting that the concept of case management has developed in the last several decades. The very nature of and motivation for case management techniques means a movement away from this traditional adversarial procedure, as

[191] A rare exception to this paucity of conscious reference in civil-law discourse to case management is an English writer, Jolowicz, who uses the term in relation to French civil procedure in the context of a comparative study of civil procedure (which is discussed further below): J. A. Jolowicz, 'Adversarial and Inquisitorial Models of Civil Procedure' (2003), 52 *International and Comparative Law Quarterly*, 281. For a discussion of civil-law procedure of relevance to this analysis, see generally, Craig M. Bradley, *Criminal Procedure: A Worldwide Study* (1999); Mireille Delmas-Marty and J. R. Spencer (eds.), *European Criminal Procedures* (2002); Nigel G. Foster and Satish Sule, *German Legal System and Laws* (2002); Christine van den Wyngaert (ed.), *Criminal Procedure Systems in the European Community* (1993).

[192] Felicity Nagorcka, Michael Stanton and Michael Wilson, 'Stranded Between Partisanship and the Truth? A Comparative Analysis of Legal Ethics in the Adversarial and Inquisitorial Systems of Justice' (2005), 29 *Melbourne University Law Review* 448, 452.

[193] Rudolf Schlessinger, 'Comparative Criminal Procedure: A Plea for Utilizing Foreign Experience' (1976), 26 *Buffalo Law Review* 363; C. Linke, 'The Influence of the European Convention of Human Rights on National European Criminal Proceedings' (1989), 21 *De Paul Law Review* 397; L. J. Fassler, 'The Italian Penal Procedure Code: An Adversarial System of Criminal Procedure in Continental Europe' (1991), 29 *Columbia Journal of Transnational Law* 251; Christoph Safferling, *Towards an International Criminal Procedure* (2001).

[194] A. T. H. Smith, above n. 151, 85. See generally also, the literature referred to in above n. 75.

concerns over the length of proceedings and their cost have been considered as necessitating greater judicial intervention.

In contrast, civil law proceedings are profoundly judicially driven and controlled, and are usually characterised by the existence at the commencement of trial of an extensive written dossier from which the court explores the case to determine the truth of the accused's involvement, if any, in the crimes alleged. This in turn enables trials to be comparatively shorter than party-driven adversarial trials, the length of which are – at least traditionally – determined by the scope of the case presented by the parties. It may be that the development of case management ideas in the common law system is a transplantation of civil law pre-trial and trial procedures into common law adversarial systems. This tendency has been noted by several commentators. Robert S. Thompson has commented that the practice of 'managerial judging', designed 'to move cases through overloaded calendars', is 'encouraging American judges to abandon their passive role in favor of the posture of a more active participant in the shaping of a case. . .'.[195] In the context of English civil procedure, J. A. Jolowicz has commented that the reduction in the parties' control over litigation, which is a corollary of case management practices, has meant that the adversarial system is beginning to more closely resemble the inquisitorial system.[196]

Although there is little or no explicit reference in relation to civil law procedure to case management *per se*, there are examples of the approach taken in these jurisdictions which belie inherent case management principles or practices. The following provides some select examples of techniques used in civil law jurisdictions that could be viewed as falling within the rubric of case management.

Germany

The German Code of Criminal Procedure contains several principles that are designed to ensure that criminal trials are dealt with expeditiously. For example, the principle of the 'unity' of the main proceedings (*Einheit der Hauptverhandlung*) is designed to ensure that trials are completed expeditiously by limiting lengthy interruptions.[197] Section 229 of the Code provides that certain interruptions in the trial process are permitted but specifies time limits for such interruptions.[198] The principle of 'concentration' (*Konzentrationsmaxime/Beschleunigungsprinzip*) aims to

[195] Robert S. Thompson, 'Decision, Disciplined Inferences and the Adversary Process' (1991), 13 *Cardozo Law Review* 725, 742. [196] J. A. Jolowicz, above n. 191, 288–9.

[197] Nigel G. Foster and Satish Sule, above n. 191, 343.

[198] German *Criminal Procedure Code*, section 229.

keep proceedings as short as possible. Nigel Foster and Satish Sule note that the time limits set for the various stages of criminal trials are shorter than for civil law proceedings, and observe that the driving force behind this principle is Article 6 of the European Convention on Human Rights (which requires that trials be conducted in a reasonable time).[199]

Sections 417 to 420 of the German Code of Criminal Procedure provide that an accelerated trial procedure may be used in certain circumstances. Upon an application by the public prosecution office, certain cases may qualify for an 'immediate hearing' if the case involves a simple factual scenario or clear evidence.[200] This procedure means that the main hearing can be held immediately or at short notice, and obviates the need for a decision to open main proceedings.[201] According to Foster and Sule, this accelerated procedure is designed 'to speed up the process in relation specifically to minor offences whereby the interim procedure is abandoned and the main trial is held immediately'.[202] This procedure could be viewed as a 'fast-track' for certain kinds of cases, and in this way is clearly a form of case management because, although it is not labelled as such, it is clearly a mechanism for ensuring that certain kinds of cases are dealt with expeditiously.

Belgium

The Belgian system, although substantially civil law in nature, has been described as 'mixed' in that it contains some adversarial elements.[203] In the trial stage of proceedings in Belgium there are two important inquisitorial features, more characteristic of civil law systems.[204] First, the judges play an active role in the proceedings. It is the judges, rather than the parties, who control the proceedings; the judges choose which witnesses will be heard, and witnesses are examined by the judge and the public prosecutor (and the accused or their counsel request to ask questions of the witnesses).[205] Second, criminal trials in Belgium are based on evidence presented in a pre-trial dossier.[206] As Christine van den Wyngaert notes, the Belgian method of conducting trials allows the actual trial to be conducted with much greater speed.[207]

199 Nigel G. Foster and Satish Sule, above n. 191, 343–4.
200 German *Criminal Procedure Code*, section 417.
201 German *Criminal Procedure Code*, section 418.
202 Nigel G. Foster and Satish Sule, above n. 191, 339.
203 Brigitte Pesquié (revised by Yves Cartuvels), 'The Belgian System', in Mireille Delmas-Marty and J. R. Spencer, above n. 191, 84.
204 Christine van den Wyngaert (ed.), above n. 191, 33.
205 Ibid.
206 Ibid. 34. There are some differences for 'assize court' cases.
207 Ibid.

France

In France there is a preliminary judicial investigation (*instruction preparatoire*), in which the *juge d'instruction* investigates the case so it is brought to a point where it can be tried.[208] The *juge d'instruction*, takes an active role in investigating the case, rather than simply responding to requests from the parties. There is also a *Chambre de l'instruction* which has wide powers to control and correct the investigations of the *juge d'instruction*.[209] In France offences are classified into either *crimes*, *délits* or *contraventions*, and this classification determines which procedures will apply.[210] *Crimes* (the most serious offences) are judged by the *cour d'assises*. The presiding judge at the *cour d'assises*, has an active role, for example to dismiss evidence that might compromise the 'dignity of the trial' or protract the proceedings unnecessarily.[211]

In comparing the French system with English law, Jolowicz comments that 'case management' was introduced into France in 1935.[212] Before 1935, according to Jolowicz, French civil procedure 'had nothing inquisitorial about it' and the court's role was 'essentially passive'.[213] Under the code of civil procedure of 1806, French civil law, 'like the common law system[,] . . . led to practical disadvantages – adjournments, delays, deliberate use of dilatory tactics, and inadequate preparation of the *instruction* for the final audience'.[214] Jolowicz notes that by the end of the nineteenth century these problems had been reported upon by commentators, but nothing was done until 1935, when a judge was appointed to 'follow' proceedings, in an attempt to make parties conduct their cases more efficiently.[215] However, these changes were apparently ineffective, as the judge had little power and could not make binding orders: '[t]here was to be no departure from the traditional notion that the litigation belonged to the parties and the judge under this procedure had no power in relation to the *instruction*. . .'.[216] It was not until 1965 that substantial changes were made to civil procedure which gave the judge greater control over the proceedings.[217]

Case management in international criminal law

The development of case management in the domestic criminal law context, whether in its inherent system-oriented form in civil law

[208] Valérie Dervieux (revised by Mikaël Benillouche and Olivier Bachelet), 'The French System' in Mireille Delmas-Marty and J. R. Spencer, above n. 191, 239–40.
[209] Ibid. 243. [210] Ibid. 219. [211] See French *Code of Criminal Procedure*, Article 309.
[212] J. A. Jolowicz, above n. 191, 286. [213] Ibid. 290. [214] Ibid. [215] Ibid.
[216] Ibid. [217] Ibid.

jurisdictions or its conscious evolution in common law systems, is prevalent also in the international criminal law context. In chapter one, I referred to the differing experience, background and approaches of judges in international criminal courts and tribunals, the process of judicial appointment producing mixed benches of experienced judges, diplomats and academics (some of whom have never sat on a Bench or possibly never appeared in court). A traditional common law judge will be less interventionist than their civil law counterpart. Experience also plays a large part in the confidence of such judges to intervene in or control the proceedings in the face of experienced advocates, particularly in complex cases the scope of which can be difficult to grasp.

However, it is surprising to note that, although only just over a decade old, modern international criminal law has developed a considerable body of practice and procedure for the management of cases. In particular, the ICTY has – due to the sheer size and complexity of cases before it, the lack of any benchmark experience and the limits placed by its financiers on the length of its mandate – been forced in a very short space of time to find ways to manage its prodigious cases.[218] Therefore, although there is little literature dealing specifically with case management principles and the term 'case management' does not appear to be widely used or even defined in the international context, the rules and practice of the international criminal tribunals (particularly the ICTY) have made a considerable contribution to case management principles, some of which might well benefit complex domestic case management practice.

The framework for best case management practice in international criminal law

Looking forward from the *Milošević* trial to the future case management of complex international criminal trials, it is useful to first consider case management principles and nomenclature as they have evolved in the international criminal law context, then to set a framework in which to consider case management practice that has developed from the *Milošević* experience and, finally, to reach conclusions about how to develop best practice in the case management of these trials.

[218] Reference to the nature of such cases is made in the context of developing technology to manage international criminal cases: see e.g., David Pimentel, 'Technology in a War Crimes Tribunal: Recent Experience at the ICTY' (2004), 12 *William and Mary Bill of Rights Journal*, 715, 717–21; Henry H. Perritt, Jr., 'Cyberspace and State Sovereignty' (1997), 3 *Journal of International Legal Studies* 155.

As discussed in relation to case management in common law systems, there are ostensibly two forms of case management. The main division in the literature appears to be between individual case management and court-wide caseflow management (or differential case management). There has been no evolution in the nomenclature relating to case management in international criminal law and, as is clear from the jurisprudence, little conscious discussion of case management models. It is therefore appropriate to consider how to frame the case management issues under consideration to facilitate a clear and consistent discussion of the issues in future. Court-wide or systematic approaches to case management often give one judge or chamber responsibility for an entire case from start to finish, so that there is continuity and judges can implement procedural timelines and other case management measures. Because of the size and complexity of cases, the length of pre-trial preparation and the trial itself, and the delineated pre-trial/trial structure of the procedural rules, this judge-specific continuity regrettably rarely occurs in international criminal law jurisdictions. Indeed, in the ICC there is an entire Chamber dedicated to pre-trial management of all cases before it.[219] Caseflow management (or differential case management) is also less relevant to the management of international criminal trials because of the limited number of them in any court or tribunal's docket (compared with a national court system) and the difficulty involved in distinguishing them for 'tracking' purposes. They are all more or less large and complex. Of course, as the subject-matter of this book asserts, the trials of senior level accused are inherently more complex, as are the joined trials of numerous accused. However, a system of dividing cases into tracks or streams of like cases for like treatment would have little, if any, impact on the issues that make international criminal trials long and complex and meriting case management attention. What is needed is a well-considered and rational approach for these particular kinds of cases, coupled with a willingness for innovation and – at times – radical reactivity by a court to ensure the trial can be conducted within the fair and expeditious trial framework of international criminal law.

It is therefore my argument that for complex international criminal trials, the individual case approach to case management is the appropriate and applicable analysis within which to develop the measure of best practice for the conduct of such trials. The broader management of the case docket (notably determining which cases are readied for trial and in which order) should be relatively simple administrative decisions in an

[219] See ICC Statute, Part 5.

international criminal court or tribunal that can be determined, *inter alia*, on the basis of the number of cases on the docket, the length of time from the filing of the indictment, and whether the accused is provisionally detained. That is not to suggest that important pre-trial work should not be undertaken. Most of the proposed case management approaches to trial considered in this chapter, and future reforms discussed below, will be more effective if implemented or prepared during the pre-trial process, indeed some will only work in this way. Furthermore, a range of important pre-trial actions, discussed in respect of the ICTY regulatory framework above, will streamline the case and render both the case and the parties more amenable to meaningful case management at trial.

As stated in the opening of this chapter, I employ two different terms to describe two different kinds of case management within the rubric of international criminal law cases: 'micro' and 'macro' case management approaches, both of which operate within the context of the management of an individual case.[220]

By 'micro' case management, I am referring to the detailed intervention by a chamber in the structure and scope of a party's case. For example, selection of particular witnesses or categories of witnesses which the chamber considers repetitive, cumulative, insufficiently relevant, insufficiently credible or overly prejudicial. Another example might be limiting the number of witnesses that may testify on a specific incident, involving judgements about the sufficiency of evidence to prove an aspect of a party's case or the case strategy of that party. A further example, available under the ICTY Rules but rarely yet used is the availability under Rule 73*bis* to limit the number of counts, crime sites or incidents in respect of which evidence may be presented by the prosecution. All of these micro case management approaches carry with them inherent risks and complexities in an adversarial criminal law system.

220 There is very little mention of this nomenclature in common-law case management literature or practice. One exception is the United States Family Court Steering Committee in Florida, which refers to 'micro' and 'macro' case management. In the context of providing recommendations on the characteristics of a model family court, the Steering Committee has recommended a two-tiered approach to case management: (1) macro case management, which consists of caseflow monitoring (this may involve screening cases and allocating them to different time tracks, as well as the collection and review of aggregate data for evaluation of the progress of cases in a division), and (2) micro case management, which represents a 'coordinated team approach to addressing each family's litigation' (Family Court Steering Committee, *A Model Family Court for Florida: Recommendations of the Florida Supreme Court's Family Court Steering Committee* (June, 2000), http://www.floridasupremecourt.org/pub_info/documents/ModelFamilyCout2000.pdf at 1 October 2006.

By 'macro' case management, I am referring to more global forms of intervention available to a chamber to control the scope of a party's case. The most obvious example, and the technique which has yielded the greatest success thus far, is imposing limits on the time in which a party may lead evidence. Other examples include limiting witness numbers overall, as opposed to specific witnesses, witness categories and witnesses by location; encouraging the use of written testimony in lieu of oral evidence; allowing a more flexible approach to the introduction of documentary evidence than is typical of adversarial criminal law systems (for example, by not requiring a party to necessarily introduce and authenticate each document through a witness).

Generally speaking, the evaluation of case management decisions and approaches largely depends on the ends they are designed to and do actually achieve. An assessment that a 'good' case management decision has been made or procedure applied will hinge upon how 'good' is defined – that is, whether certain objectives have been met. This raises perennial theoretical questions about the purpose of criminal trials, the balance between 'justice' and 'truth', and the interests of the various participants (including the accused, victims, the international and local communities). In the context of international criminal trials, case management practices that ensure judgements are rendered in a timely manner may also enhance public perception of international courts and the enforceability of international law. At the same time, any case management practice must conform to the fundamental requirement that the trial be fair.

In the literature addressing this topic, much of which stems from the US experience of case management, any discussion of an evaluation of case management techniques tends to come from a practical viewpoint. The frequently cited goals of case management are to reduce delay, to ensure the efficient disposition of cases, to reduce the costs of litigation, to ensure that there is equal access to court services.[221] Implicit in these goals is the idea that fairness and the interests of justice will be best served by ensuring that trials are conducted expeditiously. It has also been recognised that case management is not an end in itself, but simply a mechanism for reaching these broader goals.[222] Others, however, have

[221] See, e.g., National Center for State Courts, above n. 14; Norma Shapiro *et al.*, above n. 157, 611–612; Holly Bakke and Maureen Solomon, above n. 147, 17; David C. Steelman, 'What Have We Learned About Court Delay, "Local Legal Culture", and Caseflow Management Since the Late 1970s' (1997), 19 *Justice Systems Journal*, 145; ABA Report, above n. 145.

[222] Federal Judicial Center, *Manual for Complex Litigation* (1995 edition), para. 20, extract available at http://www.lectlaw.com/files/lit11.htm at 1 October 2006.

expressed concern that too much of an emphasis on case management may in fact diminish the quality of justice.[223]

The National Center for State Courts in the US has stated that case management was originally developed to reduce the overall time taken to resolve cases and thus alleviate court congestion. While it argues that case management techniques, by reducing case timelines, should reduce both attorney time and the costs to litigants, it concedes that whether these goals are in fact achieved is an open question.[224] Similarly, David C. Steelman has suggested that even when successfully implemented, case management techniques by themselves 'can probably never be viewed as a full and final solution to court delay' as expectations and legal culture may need to be changed.[225]

While designed to reduce the time lawyers and judges spend on cases, thus reducing the overall time and cost of litigation, it is by no means clear that case management in common law systems has achieved these goals. Richard L. Marcus, for instance, suggests that case management may give rise to unnecessary expense and activity:

> For a long time there has been a question about whether case management "works," in the sense that it reduced the expenditure of both time and money on litigation. Under these circumstances, there is continuing reason to worry that the tradeoffs might not be worth the cost. But it is worth noting that this critique is not based on the inherent desirability of freedom of action by lawyers, but the concern that curtailing the freedom of action actually increases overall costs of litigation.[226]

Part of the problem of evaluation, it seems, is that there is no single or clear way to measure case management. Different factors (such as time or expenditure) could be selected, but it is difficult to compare these across different cases or courts given the unique circumstances of each case. Furthermore, it is difficult to evaluate the 'quality of justice' delivered as this is largely dependent on how 'justice' is defined and which values are prioritised.

Some case management guidelines and standards specifically address the issue of how to evaluate case management progress. For example, the American Bar Association's Standards relating to speedy trials contains a

223 See, e.g., Judith Resnik, Managerial Judges'.
224 National Center for State Courts, above n. 147.
225 Steelman, 'What Have We Learned About Court Delay', 158.
226 Richard L. Marcus, 'Reining in the American Litigator: The New Role for American Judges' (2003), 27 *Hastings International and Comparative Law Review* 3, 27.

provision about monitoring and accountability, which states that each jurisdiction should organise procedures which monitor the performance system in relation to the goals of case management.[227] Similarly, the Michigan 'Caseflow Management Guide' suggests that the establishment of time guidelines will 'define the outer limits of delay and provide a basis for measuring the effectiveness of the caseflow management system'.[228] Further, the guide states that setting standards and goals is futile unless there is a system set up to monitor performance and to compare performance with the standards.[229]

Apart from such technical, or practical, monitoring systems, some commentators have hinted at the broader difficulties of evaluating case management techniques. Douglas G. Smith, for example, has suggested that it is difficult to evaluate comparative procedural law due to the varying goals which may be sought.[230] He contends that the different values that may be served through litigation influence how different measures will be appraised.[231]

There is always some degree of uncertainty in any comparative analysis concerning what procedures lead to what advantages and to what degree. Furthermore, not all commentators agree on what constitutes an 'advantage' in the case management context. To a certain extent, this determination depends on the way in which one ranks a hierarchy of values that might be served through litigation.[232]

The difficulty experienced by domestic courts in measuring the success of (individual and flow) case management exists to a far lesser extent in international criminal law. The reason for this is probably the similarity of these cases, in comparison to the variegated and more numerically prolific case-loads of domestic court systems. The difficulty in international criminal courts and tribunals lies in determining what are the appropriate management approaches to these cases. The cases themselves are long, complex, and expensive, and there is little margin for error in the fair trial process – although there is a good deal of error nonetheless. Case management approaches might, as suggested in some of the literature, achieve success in expediting a case but adversely impact on aspects of the fair trial paradigm. Assessing the effectiveness of particular decisions and imposed systems is difficult, although in the international

[227] See ABA Report, above n. 145, Standard 12-3.3.

[228] Michigan State Court Report, above n. 145, 11.

[229] Ibid. 26.

[230] Douglas G. Smith, 'Structural and Functional Aspects of the Jury: Comparative Analysis and Proposals for Reform' (1997), 48 *Alabama Law Review* 441, 455.

[231] Ibid.

[232] Ibid.

criminal trial context it is possible to measure the effects of case management more easily – again, because of the lesser number of cases, their likeness and the more apparent effect on their length and complexity.

Detailed or micro management of a party's case in international criminal law (because it is to some extent party driven) risks interference with that party's capacity to establish an aspect of their case, possibly creating a strong ground of appeal and potentially affecting the fairness of the trial. Interestingly, as will be seen, where this approach was taken in the *Milošević* case, it was not anywhere near as effective as the macro case management approaches adopted. Macro case management allows a more global setting of boundaries for the conduct by a party of its case – particularly by setting overall time limitations – and the precedent set in the *Milošević* case seems to have been generally accepted (certainly on appeal) as not violating the fair trial principle. It is my argument, based on a detailed review of the *Milošević* case, other international criminal law cases, as well as a logical process of analogy between the operation of case management processes in national law systems and the particularities of the common/civil law dichotomy as it operates in international criminal law, that forms of macro case management will generally yield safer results because they will respect the adversarial nature of the proceedings while enabling a court to interfere in the conduct of the case to render its conclusion fairly and within a reasonable time.

However, I also believe that the development of some micro case management procedures in international criminal law is critical to the future success of these trials as both fair and expeditious. As that system of law comprehends and embraces more the fundamental civil law approach to case management, the idea that judicial control of a case extends to analysing the content and nature of a case and taking more responsibility for determining how the parties should conduct their cases, greater application of micro case management measures will become more acceptable and less likely to offend the fairness of the trial. It will be necessary for the future viability of international criminal courts and tribunals to become more robust and proactive in this area, an approach that must always be tempered by the overriding need for fairness.

Case management in the ICTY

While the Nuremberg and Tokyo trials adhered very closely to the adversarial or common law approach, the ICTY and other international criminal courts and tribunals – and particularly the ICC – have adopted what Judge

May described as a 'more nuanced approach'.[233] Even so, the negotiations among the four Allied powers that led to the Nuremberg trials spawned the first example of international criminal procedure. As Brigadier General Telford Taylor (chief prosecutor for subsequent Nuremberg trials) stated:

> It is important to keep clearly in mind that we are applying international penal law and that we should not, and cannot, approach these questions solely from the standpoint of any single judicial system. International law has made substantial strides in the development of both substantive and adjective law, and in both fields international law must derive from a variety of legal systems, including both civil and common law.[234]

However, it was not until the ICTY was created and its Rules of Procedure and Evidence were themselves created and thereafter copiously amended, that truly *international* criminal procedure and case management began to develop.[235]

Case management regulations at the ICTY

The important case management provisions are contained in Rules 65*ter*, 73*bis*, 73*ter* and 90 of the ICTY Rules, and they are largely mirrored in the ICTR Rules and heavily borrowed from by the ICC,[236]

233 Richard May and Marieke Wierda, *International Criminal Evidence* (2002), 18.

234 Taylor quoted in Ibid., 25.

235 For a detailed discussion of this, see Geert-Jan Alexander Knoops, *An Introduction to the Law of International Criminal Tribunals: A Comparative Study* (2003); Daryl A. Mundis, 'From "Common Law" Towards "Civil Law": The Evolution of the ICTY Rules of Procedure and Evidence', above n. 1; Daryl A. Mundis, 'Improving the Operation and Functioning of the International Criminal Tribunals' (2000), 94 *American Journal of International Law* 759; Gideon Boas, 'A Code of Evidence and Procedure for International Criminal Law? The Rules of the ICTY' in Gideon Boas and William A. Schabas (eds.), *International Criminal Law Developments in the Case Law of the ICTY* (2002); Gideon Boas, 'Creating Laws of Evidence for International Criminal Law: The ICTY and the Principle of Flexibility' (2001), 12 *Criminal Law Forum* 41; Gideon Boas, 'Developments in the Law of Procedure and Evidence at the International Criminal Tribunal for the Former Yugoslavia and the International Criminal Court' (2001), 12 *Criminal Law Forum* 167.

236 It is unpersuasively argued by one commentator, at least, that the procedural law of the ICC is structured upon neither adversarial nor inquisitorial models, and that it will be free to construct a non-adversarial model of judicial intervention even at the investigatory stage: Claus Kress, 'The Procedural Law of the International Criminal Court in Outline: Anatomy of a Unique Compromise' (2003), 1 *Journal of International Criminal Justice* 603, 603–5. However, although the ICC Statute and Rules provide for some more particular procedural civil law aspects, in reality its structure is adversarial in nature and it will – unfortunately – experience the same constraints as the ICTY and ICTR, but with less flexibility to adjust its procedural approach: see Gideon Boas, 'Comparing the ICTY and the ICC: Some Procedural and Substantive Issues' (2000) XLVII *Netherlands International Law Review* 267.

Special Court for Sierra Leone, and the (now defunct) East Timor Tribunal.[237]

Rule 65*ter*, initially adopted by the plenary of judges in July 1998, has been substantially overhauled on several subsequent occasions in an attempt to expedite the pre-trial process.[238] The pre-trial judge, created to aggressively manage the case to trial, must be appointed within seven days of the initial appearance of an accused.[239] The concept of a pre-trial judge draws partly on the civil law tradition, in that the judge assumes a greater managerial role by supervising disclosure, trial preparation, and narrowing the issues in dispute during pre-trial conference.[240]

Another amendment made to Rule 65*ter* relates to the stringent requirements placed on the prosecution concerning its pre-trial brief. Rule 65*ter*(E) requires a summary of the evidence the prosecution intends to lead in respect of the alleged crimes and form(s) of responsibility with which the accused is charged. Also required is a list of admissions by the parties, a statement of matters not in dispute, as well as a statement of contested matters of fact and law between the parties.[241] The prosecution is further required to identify the points in the indictment to which each of its witnesses will testify, including specific reference to counts and relevant paragraphs in the indictment.[242] Concomitantly, the defence is required to set out, in general terms, the nature of the accused's defence, the matters taken issue with in the prosecutor's pre-trial brief and why.[243]

Rule 73*bis*(C) empowers judges to set the number of witnesses the prosecution may call[244] and, after having heard the prosecution, the time it has available to present its case.[245] The same case management tools apply to the defence under Rule 73*ter*. Although rarely used to their full capacity by judges in the ICTY, these provisions were employed to varying effect in the *Milošević* case, and subsequently in other complex trials before the ICTY. Rule 73*bis*(D) was included in July 2003 to provide for a Chamber to 'fix a number of crime sites or incidents comprised in

[237] See Rodney Dixon, Karim A. A. Khan, and Richard May (eds.), *Archbold International Criminal Courts: Practice Procedure and Evidence* (2003), 186–90.

[238] Adopted in July 1998 (IT/32/Rev13), and subsequently amended (IT/32/Rev17; IT/32/Rev20; IT/32/Rev21, and IT/32/Rev22). See Daryl A. Mundis, 'Improving the Operation and Functioning of the International Criminal Tribunals', above n. 235; Gideon Boas, 'Developments in the Law of Procedure and Evidence at the International Criminal Tribunal for the Former Yugoslavia and the International Criminal Court' (2001), 12 *Criminal Law Forum* 167.

[239] Rule 65*ter*(A).

[240] May and Wierda, *International Criminal Evidence*, 43–4.

[241] Rule 65*ter*(E)(i).

[242] Rule 65*ter*(E)(i)(c).

[243] Rule 65*ter*(F).

[244] Rule 73*bis*(C).

[245] Rule 73*bis*(E).

one or more of the charges in respect of which evidence may be presented by the Prosecutor' and in June 2006, the judges sitting in plenary amended Rule 73*bis*(D) and created a new paragraph (E), in an apparent attempt to create a mechanism for greater judicial control of the scope of the prosecution case.[246]

Perhaps because of the radical nature of this provision and the status of international criminal law case management to date, Rule 73*bis*(D) was, until very recently,[247] never exercised by the Tribunal. However, this did not prevent the judges of the ICTY, sitting in plenary in June 2006, from amending Rule 73*bis*(D) and adopting a new paragraph (E) of the same rule. These amendments provide for the judges first to 'invite the Prosecutor to reduce the number of counts charged in the indictment' (paragraph (D)), then to 'direct the Prosecutor to select the counts in the indictment on which to proceed' (paragraph (E)). The material difference in these amendments appears to be the broader approach to focusing the prosecution's indictments, by dealing with a reduction of counts, which may be constituted by many locations and hundreds or thousands of individual charges. However, the formulation of the amendments appears tentative and almost meaningless. It invites the prosecution to reduce its indictment – an already existing power – and then *directs*, it to *make a selection*, a nugatory or even contradictory formulation that the Prosecutor has said she considers nothing more than 'advisory in nature'.[248] While ICTY President Pocar travelled to the Security Council days later touting this as an example of the measures which will have 'a

246 IT/247, 'Amendments to the Rules of Procedure and Evidence', 6 June 2006.

247 See *Prosecutor v. Milutinović et al.*, 'Decision on Application of Rule 73*bis*', Case No. IT-05-87-T, 11 July 2006, in which the Trial Chamber at the pre-trial conference utilised the pre-existing provisions to exclude three crime locations from the indictment, although preserved its final determination as to whether the prosecution could lead evidence on the affected crimes until later in the case. See also *Prosecutor v. Šešelj*, 'Request to the Prosecutor to Make Proposals to Reduce the Scope of the indictment', Case No. IT-03-67-PT, 31 August 2006 (the treatment of the issue in this case had not been determined as at the completion of this manuscript).

248 The President merely makes a vague reference to the amendments being made in response to increasing awareness 'that the length of trials starts with the complexity and breadth of the indictments, leading to a lengthy presentation of the parties' cases': 'President Pocar updates Security Council on Tribunal's mission and completion strategy', ICTY Press Release, LM/MOW/1084e, 7 June 2006. The Prosecutor was direct and clear in her view of the amendments: 'In view of the checks and balances contained in the Statute, and particularly the duties and responsibilities of the Prosecutor under the Statute, such directions by the Chambers can only be interpreted as purely advisory in nature': 'Tribunal's Prosecutor addresses Security Council on completion strategy progress', ICTY Press Release, AM/MOW/1085e, 7 June 2006.

fundamental impact on the efficiency of the Tribunal's trials',[249] nothing in the content of the provisions or the President's speech to the Security Council answers the concerns already existent in respect of the previously formulated Rule 73*bis*(D). Furthermore, neither the new provisions contained in Rule 73*bis*(D) nor the provisions of Rule 73*bis*(E), dealing with a reduction of counts in an indictment, have been effectively utilised.

These pre-trial and pre-defence provisions encompass civil law concepts in which it is the court that determines the nature and scope of the case and determines what evidence is to be tested.

In its earlier years, the ICTY operated more like a stereotypical common law court. This focus has already shifted considerably. In fact, the system of case management and criminal procedure developed by the ICTY has been described as a 'truly mixed jurisdiction',[250] or as a 'third way'.[251] The recent amendments are examples of the shift towards granting judges far greater control over not just the conduct of proceedings, but also control over the quantity and content of the evidence to be presented by the parties. They raise questions as to how effectively existing powers of judicial control have been used by judges to expedite trials.[252] Before recent amendments, the judges were already empowered to control significant aspects of the proceedings to ensure an expeditious trial. Rule 90(F) requires a trial chamber to exercise control over the mode and order of interrogating witnesses and presenting evidence 'so as to make the interrogation and presentation effective for the ascertainment of the truth . . . and avoid needless

[249] Ibid.

[250] Mundis, 'From "Common Law" Towards "Civil Law": The Evolution of the ICTY Rules of Procedure and Evidence', above n. 235, 767.

[251] Boas, 'A Code of Evidence and Procedure for International Criminal Law? The Rules of the ICTY', above n. 235, 26. A number of other scholars write about the mixed common/civil law approach of the international tribunals, and the tendency of the ICC toward a more civil-law (or at least less common law) approach: see e.g., Geert-Jan Alexander Knoops, above n. 235; Rodney Dixon, Karim A. A. Khan, Richard May (eds.), above n. 237; May and Marieke Wierda, above n. 233; Claus Kress, 'Procedural Law', Gregory P. Lombardi, 'The ICTY at Ten: A Critical Assessment of The Major Rulings of The International Criminal Tribunal Over the Past Decade' (2003), 37 *New England Law Review* 887; Máximo Langer, 'From Legal Transplants to Legal Translations: The Globalization of Plea Bargaining and the Americanization Book in Criminal Procedure' (2004), 45 *Harvard International Law Journal* 1; James Cockayne, 'The Fraying Shoestring: Rethinking Hybrid War Crimes Tribunals' (2005), 28 *Fordham International Law Journal* 616; Michael A. Newton, 'The Iraqi Special Tribunal: A Human Rights Perspective' (2005), 38 *Cornell International Law Journal* 863; Larry D. Johnson, 'Closing an International Criminal Tribunal while Maintaining International Human Rights Standards and Excluding Impunity' (2005), 99 *American Journal of International Law* 158.

[252] See discussion on the UN Expert Group Report in chapter 1.

consumption of time'. Furthermore, Rule 90(H) gives trial chambers considerable control over the cross-examination of witnesses. Interestingly, the Nuremberg and Tokyo tribunals limited the time allowed parties to cross-examine. For example, in the RuSHA case,[253] the prosecution were given thirty minutes to cross-examine each defendant and ten minutes per defence witness.[254] Judge May referred to Rule 90 of the ICTY Rules as giving judges an express power to control cross-examination, so as to 'prevent abuse and to ensure that proper use is made of the opportunity to cross-examine'.[255] Some Trial Chambers have exercised these powers to limit cross-examination and to focus the evidence which would be admitted into the proceedings. A provision added to the Rules in April 2001, Rule 90(G), provides that a Trial Chamber 'may refuse to hear a witness whose name does not appear on the list of witnesses compiled pursuant to Rules 73*bis*(C) and 73*ter*(C)'. Therefore, the judges may now not only set the witness list but, where a party seeks to present a witness not previously agreed to, they may refuse that evidence. Generally, chambers have required a showing of both 'good cause', and that the 'interests of justice' have been met, by a party wishing to add a witness or a document not previously on their pre-trial lists. Good cause has normally been satisfied by a showing of relevance and importance of the potential evidence to the case, as well as showing that diligence has been exercised in obtaining and bringing such proposed evidence to the attention of the Chamber at the earliest time practicable. In the *Milošević* case such procedure was utilised liberally.[256]

All these provisions give ICTY judges substantial power over the conduct of proceedings and enable them to direct and control the preparation for and conduct of trial. Used effectively, these powers may have the effect of narrowing the facts in issue at the pre-trial stage and controlling the scope of the case, including the amount of evidence received during a trial and the form that evidence takes.

Learning from the *Milošević* case

The case management procedures considered, attempted or discarded in the *Milošević* case, were the foundation for developing case management

[253] *United States v. Greifelt, Creutz, Meyer-Hetling, Schwarzenberger, Huebner, Lorenz, Brueckner, Hofmann, Hildebrandt, Schwalm, Sollmann, Ebner, Tesch, and Viermetz*, U.S. Military Tribunal, Judgement, 10 March 1948 ('*RuSHA* Judgement'), in *Trials of War Criminals before the Nuernberg Military Tribunals under Control Council Law No. 10* (1951), vol. V.

[254] See May and Wierda, *International Criminal Evidence*, 148 (note 25).

[255] Ibid. 148.

[256] See, e.g., *Prosecutor v. Milošević*, 'Decision on Prosecution Request for Agreement of Trial Chamber to Amend Schedule of Filings', Case No. IT-0254-T, 18 April 2002, 3.

practices in complex international criminal trials. As discussed earlier in this chapter, some of the regulatory changes at the ICTY (often mirrored at least in the ICTR) evolved out of experiences or expressed ideas during *Milošević*. The following discussion concerns the approach taken in these trials post-*Milošević*. Some of these approaches show the positive lead shown in the *Milošević* case which is being emulated in trials recently commenced. It also reveals some inappropriate judicial activity that appears to be motivated by lessons learnt during the *Milošević* trial but inappropriately applied in other cases. Finally, it reveals some differing approaches to case management that appear reactive to approaches taken in *Milošević* and appropriately remodelled for cases with different circumstances.

(a) The *Orić* case In an important decision by the Appeals Chamber in July 2005, the Trial Chamber's limitation of the number of witnesses and time allocated to the defence was considered.[257] The Appeals Chamber held that some of the Chamber's topical restrictions on proposed witnesses (such as those on the general historical and political background of the Balkan conflict) were 'defensible as a reasonable exercise of the Trial Chamber's Rule 73*ter* responsibility'.[258] However, it held that other restrictions were unreasonable.[259] This case involved various restrictions by the Trial Chamber on the time and scope of the Defence case: time, number of witnesses, and subject-matter of proposed witness testimony. The *Orić* defence had stated its intention to call 73 witnesses and estimated this would take 249 hours of evidence-in-chief. The Trial Chamber had rejected this and ordered that Orić would be restricted to a maximum of thirty witnesses.[260] In relation to the Trial Chamber's overall restriction on witnesses and time, the Appeals Chamber referred to the equality of arms and stated that this gave rise to a principle of basic proportionality (rather than a strict mathematical equality) between the parties.[261] It noted that when reviewing the Trial Chamber's exercise of power under Rule 73*ter*, as well as considering whether the time allocated was reasonably proportional (relative to the time allocated to the Prosecution), it was also relevant to consider whether the time given to the defence was objectively adequate, given the rights of the Accused under Article 21 of the ICTY Statute.[262] The

257 *Prosecutor v. Orić*, 'Interlocutory Decision on Length of Defence Case', Case No. IT-03-68-AR73.2, 20 July 2005 ('*Orić* Appeals Decision'), paras. 5–6. 258 Ibid., para. 6.

259 Ibid.

260 See *Prosecutor v. Orić*, 'Decision on First and Second Defence Filings Pursuant to Scheduling Order', 4 July 2005, Case No. IT-03-68.

261 *Orić* Appeals Decision, above n. 257, para. 7. 262 Ibid. para. 8.

Appeals Chamber held that the time allocated to the defence by the Trial Chamber was 'not remotely proportional' and held that it should recalculate the allocation of time and witnesses accordingly.[263]

The measures the Trial Chamber sought to introduce in this case are an example of a fairly aggressive individual case management programme, not in itself objectionable. However, the Trial Chamber had not implemented a similar case management plan with respect to the prosecution case. This threatened the equality of arms between the parties because, as the Appeals Chamber held, there was such a discrepancy in the time and witness numbers allowed the two parties, that the exercise of judicial discretion by the Trial Chamber was clearly unfair.

A persistent refrain in the *Milošević* trial had been concerns regarding the equality of arms, particularly in respect of the equal treatment given to the parties. In that trial, the parties started from a very different context and resource base. The accused was appearing *pro se* while in detention, whereas the prosecution was an institution with substantial resources to conduct its case. The Trial Chamber paid considerable attention to ensuring that the principle of equality of arms was not qualitatively violated such that the fairness of the trial was called into question. In *Orić*, the Trial Chamber was clearly inattentive to this critical issue of fairness. The extraordinary discrepancy between the treatment of the prosecution and defence in the allowance for the length and scope of their cases shows a profound misunderstanding of one of the important lessons to be learnt from consideration of these issues in the *Milošević* case. The equality of arms is a critical principle that must be assiduously attended to by a Chamber seeking to restrict particularly the defence in the presentation of its case. The Appeals Chamber rightly intervened to adjust the imbalance in this case.

(b) The *Prlić* case Another example of individual case management flowing from the experience of the *Milošević* case came in the *Prlić* proceedings. In that case, the pre-trial judge had ordered the prosecution to submit an electronic table of witnesses and exhibits, to be filed at the same time as its pre-trial brief. This table included an overview of the witnesses the prosecution intended to call and the exhibits to be introduced through each witness, which in turn related back to the relevant paragraphs of the indictment. One of the features of complex international criminal law cases, painfully experienced in the *Milošević* trial, is the

[263] Ibid. paras. 9–11.

volume of documentary evidence and courts invariably have difficulty managing the scope of this form of evidence, as well as regulating its relevance in the trial context. The *Prlić* order provided for the Chamber and defence to have advance notice of which exhibits will be tendered through particular witnesses, facilitating a better picture of the type and amount of evidence led in the case.[264]

Of greater significance, on the first day of the *Prlić* trial, the Chamber issued the first comprehensive order under Rule 73*bis* dealing with the management of a 'mega trial'.[265] Unlike in the *Milošević* case, which pioneered many of the case management approaches developed recently in international criminal law, the *Prlić* Trial Chamber endeavoured at the commencement of the trial process to set some boundaries on the scope and extent of the case. It first stated that, 'taking the view that it would be unreasonable for this trial to continue for longer than three years, it is appropriate for the Chamber to set out the manner in which it expects the trial proceedings to be conducted'.[266] The Chamber ordered that the prosecution would have 400 hours to present its case-in-chief (which would include evidence-in-chief and re-examination). The defence were told they would, in principle, be limited to an equal amount of time to cross-examine witnesses (including cross-examination by all six accused).[267] The Trial Chamber subsequently ordered that this limitation would be enforced, that in principle the defence would rotate the order of cross-examination, and that if the testimony of a witness concerned the responsibility of one of the accused in particular, the time for cross-examination may be allocated differently.[268] Importantly, the Appeals Chamber endorsed this case management approach, holding that 'the Trial Chamber adopted a sufficiently flexible approach', which preserved the 'right of cross-examination by each of the Defence counsels and complies with the right to cross-examine witnesses as stipulated under Article 21(4) of the Statute'.[269] In a further statement, the Appeals Chamber hit on one

264 *Prosecutor v. Prlić et al.*, 'Order on Guidelines for Drawing up the List of Witnesses and Exhibits', Case No. IT-04-74-PT, 30 November 2005.

265 *Prlić* Order, above n. 86. *Prlić* was the first so-called 'mega trial' (joined trials of a number of senior level accused which are of substantial scope) to go to trial. The other two 'mega trials' are *Milutinović et al.* (the Kosovo leadership case) and *Popović et al.* (the Srebrenica case).

266 Ibid. para. 2. 267 Ibid. paras. 5–6.

268 *Prosecutor v. Prlić et al.*, Hearing, 8 May 2006, Transcript, 1475-86.

269 *Prosecutor v. Prlić et al.*, 'Decision on Joint Defence Interlocutory Appeal Against the Trial Chamber's Oral Decision of 8 May 2006 Relating to Cross-Examination by Defence and on Association of Defence Counsel's Request for Leave to File an *Amicus Curiae* Brief', Case No. IT-04-74-AR73.2, 4 July 2006, 4.

of the persistent refrains in the fair and expeditious trial rubric, and one under scrutiny in this book, by holding that:

> [T]ime and resource constraints exist in all judicial institutions and that a legitimate concern in this trial, which involves six accused, is to ensure that the proceedings do not suffer undue delays and that the trial is completed within a reasonable time, which is recognized as a fundamental right of due process under international human rights law.[270]

In a clear application of time management techniques developed in the *Milošević* case, the Chamber ordered that a system for monitoring the use of time would be established by the registry, which would be responsible for recording time used (a) by the Prosecution for its examination-in-chief; (b) by each of the Defence for cross-examination; (c) by the Prosecution for re-examination; (d) by the Judges for putting questions to witnesses; and (e) for all other matters, including procedural matters.[271] The Chamber attached guidelines to its order dealing with the presentation of and challenge to evidence, standards of admissibility of evidence and other matters.

The *Prlić* orders are an example of the application of developed individual case management ideas, reflected in the regulatory structure of the ICTY and clearly developed in large part in response to the development and experience of case management issues in the *Milošević* case. If applied throughout the trial process, it is a sign that the ICTY is serious about seeking to contain the scope and length of complex international criminal trials before it, particularly in the more complex of trials.

(c) The *Milutinović* et al. case Other Chambers have ordered the application of similar case management procedures at the late pre-trial or early trial stage, in an effort to control the scope of the case (particularly that of the prosecution).[272] Interestingly, the Trial Chamber hearing the *Milutinović* Kosovo leadership case (the other co-accused on the initial *Milošević* Kosovo indictment), initially took a novel case management approach to dealing with the scope and conduct of that trial. It utilised the

[270] Ibid. [271] Ibid. para. 6.

[272] See, e.g., *Prosecutor v. Martić*, 'Decision Adopting Guidelines on the Standards Governing the Presentation of Evidence and the Conduct of Counsel in Court', Case No. IT-95-11-T, 13 April 2006; *Prosecutor v. Martić*, 'Decision Revising Time Available to the Defence for Presenting Evidence and Incorporated Scheduling Order', Case No. IT-95-11-T, 7 September 2006; *Prosecutor v. Jelisić*, Hearing, Case No. IT-95-10-T, 7 September 1999, Transcript, 1063; *Prosecutor v. Krajišnik*, Case No. IT-00-39-T, 23 April 2004, Transcript, 2652.

provisions of Rule 73*bis* to fix the number of crime sites or locations, by cutting three locations from the indictment.[273] This case management measure had been foreshadowed by Judge Robinson early in the *Milošević* trial and was subsequently included in Rule 73*bis* in July 2003. The *Milutinović* Decision was the first time this procedure had been exercised.[274] It is difficult to ascertain its effect, if any, on the overall length of the trial. This is so for two reasons. First, the ruling explicitly provided for the possibility that these crime locations might, pursuant to Rule 73*bis*(F), be successfully added back into the case on application of the prosecution during the course of its case, a possibility expressly acknowledged by the Chamber in refusing the prosecution certification to appeal the ruling.[275] Second, no expression of the effect of the decision on the overall scope and conduct of the prosecution case was included in the ruling and no limitation on time was initially made, such that it would be clear the overall time available to the prosecution to lead its case was being reduced.

This latter point about time-limits was in notable contrast to the macro case management approach taken in the *Milošević* trial, and followed in several cases since then. The Presiding Judge of the *Milutinović* case, Judge Bonomy, who was a judge sitting on the *Milošević* trial, decided at the outset of the trial to endeavour to avoid the imposition of time limitations and trust counsel 'to keep this case within bounds', while recognising that 'it may be necessary, as we move along, to make orders. . .'.[276] The Chamber logically also declined to impose limits on the length of cross-examination,[277] another potentially time-consuming part of a trial process with six accused. The approach taken, therefore, appears to be a micro case management approach mixed with a degree of laissez faire, in which the court will keep watch on the parties and determine if and when other limits on the conduct and scope of the case will be made.

On 9 October 2006, however, the Trial Chamber imposed time limits on the conduct of the prosecution case. Interestingly, although it acknowledged that good-faith efforts were being made by the parties to examine

[273] *Prosecutor v. Milutinović*, 'Decision on Application of Rule 73*bis*', IT-05-87-T, 11 July 2006.

[274] The Trial Chamber in the *Šešelj* case embarked upon a consideration of whether and to what extent Rule 73*bis* might be used in this way: see, *Prosecutor v. Šešelj*, 'Request to the Prosecutor to Make Proposals to Reduce the Scope of the indictment', Case No. IT-03-67-PT, 31 August 2006. No decision had been taken by the Chamber as at the completion of this manuscript.

[275] *Prosecutor v. Milutinović*, 'Decision Denying Prosecution's Request for Certification of Rule 73 *bis* Issue for Appeal', Case No. IT-05-87-T, 30 August 2006.

[276] *Prosecutor v. Milutinović*, Pre-Trial Conference, Transcript, 359.

[277] See, *Prosecutor v. Milutinović*, 'Order on Procedure and Evidence', IT-05-87-T, 11 July 2006.

witnesses efficiently and expeditiously, 'the Chamber is of the view that fixing temporal limitations based upon its experience of the trial so far would be conducive to ensuring that the conduct of the case is both fair and expeditious'.[278] The initial approach of the Chamber had some interesting and innovative aspects to it, which required considerable and constant attention by the court to determine whether the trust placed in the parties would have a material beneficial effect on the length of the trial while conforming to proper standards of fairness. The change of heart by the Chamber may have been the measure of time taken by the defence in cross-examination. In its account of time used in the trial, it was apparent the defence were using well over 200 per cent of the time taken by the prosecution in examination-in-chief and re-examination.[279] Of greatest interest in the case management approach in *Milutinović* is the apparent need, even where the parties are disciplined and cooperative, to engage in coercive case management methods. It is apparent that, on the experience thus far, in complex international criminal cases the courts need to set firm limits to the scope and length of the case. The returns this has started to yield in the short period of time since *Milošević* pioneered or contemplated a range of case management methods shows that best practice in this area is developing fast and is an encouraging sign for the fair and expeditious conduct of these proceedings.

Conclusion

There are important lessons to be extracted from the management of the *Milošević* trial and the reaction of other international criminal trials to case management issues that arose in that case. As I have discussed over this and the last chapter, the *Milošević* trial typified a body of issues that one would expect to see and which one does see increasingly in the criminal trials of senior officials for serious violations of international humanitarian law.

Different case management approaches were tried by the Trial Chamber in *Milošević*, in an attempt to expedite the trial while ensuring that a fair trial was had by the accused. As we have seen, endeavours to micromanage the parties' cases – limiting the number of witnesses on particular areas of the indictments, categories of evidence or the witness list overall – had a very limited impact on the expedition of the trial, as well as

[278] *Prosecutor v. Milutinović*, 'Decision on use of Time', IT-05-87-T, 9 October 2006, 5.
[279] Ibid. 4.

raising questions about the balance of the adversarial model operative in international criminal justice. Witness numbers tended to be amorphous and difficult to control. This evidenced the unmanageably broad nature of the case and the difficulty the parties themselves had in structuring and presenting their cases, as well as the Trial Chamber's difficulty in controlling them. For example, although the Chamber ordered at one stage that only one witness per 'incident' should be led in respect of the crime base of the Kosovo indictment, that clearly did not occur and was never enforced by the Trial Chamber during the proceedings. An express and written order to the prosecution to limit itself to four witnesses per municipality for Kosovo (one of which could be a *viva voce* witness) was equally not respected and no attempt was made to foreclose to the prosecution the right to call additional witnesses. Witnesses not on the initial witness lists were copiously added by both the prosecution and defence. The accused ignored numerous orders (oral and written) to comply with disclosure and other obligations.

Two important lessons flow from this. First, this form of micro case management is difficult to enforce and may, if not cautiously implemented under a carefully constructed regulatory framework, threaten the currently delicate adversarial structure of international criminal courts and tribunals. What would happen if the prosecution had only brought one witness on a particular incident in the *Milošević* Kosovo indictment and the Trial Chamber then acquitted for lack of evidence? Presumably this would be a strong appeal ground for the prosecution. Once that is extrapolated into all the crime base areas in the indictment it might be argued that the Trial Chamber had created an impossible task for the prosecution and all acquittals were potentially the fault of the Chamber for managing the prosecution out of its right and obligation to lead evidence on crimes charged. The same is true but more egregious in respect of an accused. What if the Chamber refused evidence on matters pleaded in the prosecution case and then subsequently convicted? Again, the accused would be entitled to consider that a strong case exists on appeal. More importantly, in that situation, the Chamber could well violate the accused's right to confront the case against him and to present a defence in full equality. The development of greater micro case management approaches needs to be done carefully and the structure must be right. Any reductions by the Chamber of the scope of the prosecution case should be done in the pre-trial phase, allowing for careful consideration of the impact of such judicial interference and for appropriate adjustments to be made by the parties. These are the areas in which determining best practice for the conduct of international criminal trials require consideration of the impact of any action on the fairness – as well as the expedition – of such trials.

As discussed earlier in this chapter, it may well be that as international criminal law develops and possibly takes on an infrastructurally greater civil law character, these forms of micro case management will be more workable. In particular, a change in culture is required to accept the intervention on a profound level of judges in the scope and structure of a party's case, and a stigma must evolve around judges and parties unwilling or unable to engage in the case management process in this way. This may be difficult to achieve in circumstances where the prosecutor investigates, prepares and presents a case, because of the sense of ownership by the prosecution in all aspects of the case and decisions about its scope, content and strategies for its presentation. These interrelated points (the willingness of judges to intervene and the prosecutor's self-perceived role) was underscored in relation to the tentative amendments to Rule 73*bis*, which provided for a chamber to invite and/or direct the prosecution to select counts in an indictment on which to proceed. The Prosecutor was able to respond by telling the Security Council it would be considered nothing more than an 'invitation' to consider the number of counts in the prosecution's indictment, in itself an indication of the lack of desire on the part of the ICTY Prosecutor to be a partner in reducing the scope of cases and making international criminal trials more manageable.

This judicial timidity and prosecutorial bullishness is exactly the area in which international criminal courts and tribunals must mature. It is possible that amendments to the constitutional instruments of the international criminal courts and tribunals is required to effectuate profound change in this respect. It is also possible that, as has occurred in the development of international criminal law procedure over the past decade, changes will evolve out of genuine and well-considered regulatory activity and judicial decision-making by the courts themselves. However such changes are achieved, they are clearly important to the development of the capacity of these courts to deliver justice within the framework of international criminal trials: that they be fair and reasonably expeditious.

The second lesson to be taken from this is simply the importance of judges making appropriate case management decisions and enforcing them. Despite the compulsory powers available to courts, it is clear even from consideration of the domestic common law experience of case management that there is a measure of consensual or cooperative problem-solving between the court and parties involved in any case management approach. However, a court needs to be able to set realistic goals and must be in a position to sanction parties for non-compliance. Such sanctions would include disallowing the presentation of witnesses or documentary evidence, where a party had failed to comply with timetabling or disclosure orders; penalising a party for wasted time; or, in the circumstances where consideration is being given to reducing the scope of the prosecution's case, an enforced removal of charges or counts from an indictment where the prosecution refuses to present a sufficiently restrained and manageable case. Because case management decisions can impact on core fair trial issues this has to be done carefully. In this sense, good case management entails a court considering the full range of consequences flowing from its case management decisions, including what will flow from non-compliance and enforcement of threatened sanctions. This is complicated in a complex international criminal trial context, because of the nature of these cases and particularly in cases involving difficult or manipulative accused, but it is important to develop coherent case management practices in order to achieve best practice in the conduct of these trials.

This is an area in which the Trial Chamber in *Milošević* did not achieve best practice. Beyond non-enforcement of some of its orders, the Chamber used equivocal language and appeared to change direction in its case management approach without considering the full impact of doing so. It shifted from macro case management techniques relating to overall witness numbers and time, to micromanagement techniques, which were not respected and never redressed. While this is understandable in the first trial of such magnitude dealing with these issues on this scale for the first time, it clearly had a deleterious effect on the overall management of the case.

The risk elements involved in case management exist, but are far more intellectually and doctrinally manageable, the more general the form of case management becomes. Therefore, giving the parties a limitation in time to present their case gives greater flexibility to them in the crafting and presentation of a case. As the Trial Chamber in the *Milošević* trial held, equality of time between the parties does not always achieve fairness, the proper test being 'whether the Accused has been given a reasonable and adequate opportunity to present his case'.[280] This is an area that needs careful attention by a court. Limiting the time the prosecution has to present its case is a justifiable way in which to limit the scope of a case, especially where it had exercised inadequate restraint in the breadth of its

[280] *Milošević* Severance and Time Decision, above n. 28, para. 25.

indictment against an accused. In trials of former heads of state and other senior officials in command positions, the temptation will always be great for the prosecution to indict for all relevant crimes, which can be extraordinarily broad. The *Milošević* trial exemplifies this. The *Krajišnik* case (of a Bosnian Serb political leader) and the *Prlić* case (of six senior Bosnian Croat military and political superiors) further exemplify this. The *Hussein* trial before the SICT and *Lubanga* before the ICC are probably good examples of restrained prosecution, although clearly a plethora of other problems attach to these cases.[281] It is clearly critical that a court exercise great control at the stage of reviewing indictments and in the pre-trial preparation of these cases. Courts should also be given greater control (foreign to domestic adversarial systems) over the scope and presentation of the prosecution case at the pre-trial stage and, importantly, the judges should use those powers effectively. Enforced reduction of the prosecution case – if carefully implemented – will be a crucial future form of micro case management of international criminal trials of this nature. Limitation of the scope of the indictment and range of criminal conduct charged would focus the parties and allow a case to address more adequately the criminal conduct of an accused, instead of spending 80 per cent (or some other substantial amount) of the case on crime base matters considerably removed from the accused's actual responsibility. The manner in which this could be undertaken is taken up in discussing reform and future developments in case management approaches to these trials in chapter 5.

The *Milošević* trial lasted four years and, if not for the death of the accused, would have lasted at least another half a year. It was, therefore, a case that could not be defined as expeditious. The trial was, however, overall a fair trial. The many factors that lead to this conclusion are also discussed throughout this book and explained in greater detail in the conclusions chapter.

More radical case management approaches will develop as international criminal law and its institutions develop their practice and procedure. Severance in the *Milošević* trial is an example of radical case management considered. Other techniques will arise and be tried in such trials. Experience so far shows that this will often be more in the nature of tactical

[281] See, e.g., Michael J. Frank, 'Justice for Iraq, Justice for All' (2004), 57 *Oklahoma Law Review* 303; Michael P. Scharf and Curtis F. J. Doebbler, 'Will Saddam Hussein Get a Fair Trial?' (2005), 37 *Case Western Reserve Journal of International Law* 21 (recorded debate); Human Rights Watch, 'The Former Iraqi Government on Trial: A Human Rights Watch Briefing paper', 16 October 2005.

interventions or reactions to individual challenges, the particularities of the trial of high-level accused inevitably throwing up unusual or unexpected problems. However, eventually a degree of predictability and a capacity to respond will emerge in complex international criminal trials. This will in turn affect the court's ability to ensure that fairness and expedition are achieved.

Case management in international criminal trials is in its infancy, although significant steps have been taken already – most notably in techniques developed in the *Milošević* trial and the progeny of like and reactive contrary orders made in subsequent complex trials – to develop case management approaches and principles specific to this system of law. The very essence of good case management is innovation coupled with a careful attention to the preservation of established legal principles. What is best practice is something that will develop and solidify over time. As already stated, it is apparent that a crucial aspect of good case management of such complex trials is to attend to the scope and preparation of a case at the earliest possible stage. The emphasis on the adversarial system in international criminal law creates complexities itself in the degree and manner of intervention in which a court can engage when dealing with these issues. While it is argued in this book that fairness must be the pre-eminent concern of a court, international criminal trials must see an appreciable improvement in expedition or risk losing the support of the international community for the institutions conducting these trials. With such complex cases, the more involved from the outset the judiciary are the more likely a case is to be well structured, fair, and manageable. However, within the framework of international criminal law as it has developed, the experiences drawn from the *Milošević* trial, in case management approaches attempted, considered, discussed or abandoned, give an experiential basis that will be valuable to the development of this important area.

4

Representation and Resource Issues in International Criminal Law

The issue of self-representation is becoming a persistent and critical refrain in the trial of senior (in particular) political and military officials for serious violations of international humanitarian law. In chapter 1 I discussed the development and application of the principle in the common and civil law systems, and in regional human rights courts, and foreshadowed its emergence and treatment in international and criminal courts and tribunals. The issue was of crucial importance in the *Milošević* trial. It threatened the trial's fairness, and adversely impacted on its expeditiousness. The critical issues surrounding self-representation in complex international criminal trials were developed more fully and analytically in this trial than in any other to date. Following a detailed discussion of the issue in *Milošević*, a comprehensive analysis of the emergence of self-representation in international criminal proceedings across the international criminal courts and tribunals is undertaken. An analysis of the proceedings which have dealt with problems related to self-representation reveals a range of approaches which have emerged to deal with different facts in different cases. The proliferation and importance of self-representation necessitates consideration of how to approach this issue in future international criminal trials.

The *Milošević* trial is also an important case in the development and understanding of representation and resource issues in international criminal law. The ICTY went to great lengths to provide resources to an accused who never declared himself indigent. These resources, and approaches to supporting the accused in the conduct and presentation of his defence (sometimes against his stated will), will be considered. The assignment of *amici curiae*, and extraordinary development of their role from 'friend of the court' more into the realm of *de facto* defence counsel, will be discussed in the context of the developing use and treatment of the *amicus curiae* as a quasi-representation model for self-represented accused. The special arrangement for Milošević to have privileged access and communication with legal associates not assigned as defence counsel will also be analysed, as will the considerable resources made available to him to conduct his defence from the confines of detention.

Self-representation in international criminal law – limitations and qualifications on that right

On 2 September 2004 – over two years into trial, after completion of the prosecution case and commencement of his defence case – the Trial Chamber imposed court-assigned defence counsel on Milošević, after having upheld on several occasions the accused's right to represent himself. In doing so, the Chamber made an important legal leap in the development of a critical aspect of how an accused's right to a fair trial is to be interpreted in international criminal law. The precedential nature of the Chamber's decision and subsequent reasoning had significant consequences for the conduct of that trial and for other senior level accused before international courts and tribunals. One of the curious similarities between the trials of such accused across the different tribunals is the increased determination of these accused to represent themselves. This appears to be in part related to an issue already touched on in this book – the personality type of these accused. The desire to speak on their own behalf, a mistrust of others to represent their understanding of events, the wish to utilise the forensic trial process as a political podium from which to attack the judicial process and the political powers and forces which reduced them from positions of power and leadership to detention and trial, all appear to be factors motivating this phenomenon. In the ICTY alone, Milošević, Šešelj, Krajisnik, and Prlić have sought to represent themselves, and others have expressed interest in doing so. At the ICTR, Baryagwiza and Ntahobali have done likewise, as have Norman and Gbao before the SCSL and Hussein before the SICT had expressed his wish to do so. This has raised significant questions about the nature and scope of the 'right' to self-representation and its impact on the ability of a court to achieve fairness and expedition in international criminal trials. It is clear, at least from the experience of the ICTY in *Milošević* and *Krajisnik*, that a lack of experienced and detached legal representation has caused considerable trial difficulties and delays. Although Milošević in some (although certainly not all) respects performed well as counsel in his own defence, attempts by Krajisnik to do likewise led the Trial Chamber to intervene because he was violating witness protection orders in the process of cross-examining witnesses against him and clearly lacked the necessary skills to undertake the task in an acceptably competent manner.

The purpose of this discussion is to analyse the state of law concerning the right to self-representation in international criminal law, and in particular the limits imposed on that right and how they are exercised. The interpretation of the relevant fair trial provisions to allow self-representation has given rise to the potential for abuse by some accused and challenged fairness and expedition in those trials. A court confronting such a scenario must balance what are often described as an accused's minimum guarantees with the overall requirements that a trial be fair and, as either a separate or related part of that paradigm, that the interests of justice be served. Recent jurisprudence shows that international criminal courts and tribunals are increasingly faced with such difficulties and have developed different approaches to accommodate competing interests and rights. In this section, these procedures and their validity and impact on the rubric of a fair and expeditious trial are considered.

A clear view developed in this chapter is that firm and principled action is required to deal with the adverse effect of self-representation on fairness and expedition. This has spawned a number of different approaches by international criminal courts and tribunals. I will consider the practical difficulties associated with imposing defence counsel on unwilling accused before returning, in the conclusion of this chapter and in chapter 5, to discuss remedies and possible future approaches to the problems posed.

While the international criminal courts and tribunals are influenced both by the common law and civil law systems of criminal justice, they are procedurally neither. It is apparent that their structure is inherently adversarial in nature, but they are also informed in a significant way by the civil law approach to a number of important matters of evidence and procedure.[1]

At least seven decisions in three international criminal courts and tribunals have explored the question of whether an accused has an absolute right to self-representation and how that right can be limited. Other cases in these jurisdictions also shed light on the issue.

[1] See generally, comments made by the Presiding Judge of the Trial Chamber in the *Milošević* case, Judge Robinson: 'If you want a correct description of [the system of international criminal justice], you'd have to say it is primarily or essentially adversarial. So that when you say that the case is the accused's, even that has [. . .] to be changed, in my view. The case is the accused's in some respects, but in other respects, because we have introduced strong elements from the civil law tradition [. . .] the case also belongs to the Court. It is also Court driven, judicially driven, in some respects' (*Prosecutor v. Milošević*, Hearing, Case No. IT-02-54-T, 10 November 2004, T. 33252–3).

The Milošević *Decisions – defining the limits of the right to self-representation*

Early history

The *Milošević* case is a rich source of law and practice concerning the right of an accused to self-representation under international criminal law, as well as the limitation or curtailment of that right. The issue of self-representation in that case has a long and complex history. Milošević informed the Trial Chamber in writing,[2] as well as orally during his initial appearance for the Kosovo Indictment in July 2001,[3] that he did not wish to be represented by a lawyer.

During a hearing on 30 August 2001, the Trial Chamber held that the accused was entitled to represent himself. The Trial Chamber rejected the Prosecution's suggestion that it should assign a defence counsel to the accused over his objections:

> We have to act in accordance with the Statute and our Rules which, in any event, reflect the position under customary international law, which is that the accused has a right to counsel, but he also has a right not to have counsel. He has a right to defend himself, and it is quite clear that he has chosen to defend himself. He has made that abundantly clear.[4]

Scharf and Rassi are critical of a conclusion reached by the Trial Chamber that the right to self-representation amounted to a rule of customary international law. They correctly point out that, given the contrary widespread practice of civil law countries, this proposition would be difficult to conclude.[5] Furthermore, as noted in chapter 1, while there are strong indications from many common law countries that the right to self-representation is protected, even in those countries there is either a gradual erosion of that right or strong pockets of judicial and legislative disharmony with the proposition that the right should be protected with absolutism. Furthermore, the international law precedent shows a contradictory practice. All of this, along with the clear position in a large number of civil law countries, indicates that an assertion that the right amounts to a customary international law principle must be wrong. Finally, it should

[2] *Prosecutor v. Milošević*, Written Note by the Accused, Case No. IT-99-37-I, 3 July 2001, Registry pp. 3371–2.

[3] *Prosecutor v. Milošević*, Hearing, Case No. IT-02-54-T, 3 July 2001, T. 1-2.

[4] Ibid T. 16-18.

[5] Michael P. Scharf and Christopher M. Rassi, 'Do Former Rogue Leaders Have an International Right to Act as Their Own Lawyers in War Crimes Trials?' (2004) 20 *Ohio State Journal on Dispute Resolution* 1, 14.

be noted that the comments cited above are the comments of a single judge of a three-Judge trial bench made during a status conference, and the two subsequent reasoned decisions of the Trial Chamber make no claim to the effect that the right to self-representation amounts to a principle of customary international law.

Following a further application from the prosecution in November 2002, and subsequent filings and oral submissions, the Trial Chamber again ruled that the accused may continue to represent himself, stating:

> Defence Counsel will not be imposed upon the Accused against his wishes in the present circumstances. It is not normally appropriate in adversarial proceedings such as these. The Trial Chamber will keep the position under review.[6]

Zappalà is critical of the Trial Chamber's early efforts to accommodate the right of the accused to represent himself. He argues that 'the cooperation of an accused should never be considered a condition for the trial to proceed'.[7] In this respect, and in light of subsequent events, Zappalà's point is persuasive. Interestingly, he bases his view purely on a reading of Article 21(4)(d) of the Statute, which, he says, provides two distinct rights: 'on the one hand the right to the assignment of legal assistance, on the other the right to free assistance', and argues that counsel could have been assigned on the basis that it was necessary, in the interests of justice, to ensure a proper administration of justice.[8]

Milošević – First Reasoned Decision of 4 April 2003

On 4 April 2003, the Trial Chamber issued its 'Reasons for Decision on the Prosecution Motion Concerning Assignment of Counsel', following some five months after its November 2002 oral ruling. This was the first reasoned decision of the Trial Chamber concerning the question of self-representation in the *Milošević* case. Unlike in the First *Šešelj* Decision (which followed one month after this decision), the Trial Chamber held that '[a] plain reading of [Article 21(4)(d) of the Statute] indicates that there is a right to defend oneself in person and the Trial Chamber is unable to accept the Prosecution's proposition that it would allow for the assignment of defence counsel for the Accused against his wishes in the present circumstances'.[9]

6 *Prosecutor v. Milošević*, Oral ruling, Case No. IT-02-54-T, 18 December 2002, T. 14574.

7 Salvatore Zappalà, *Human Rights in International Criminal Proceedings* (2003), 64.

8 Ibid. 63 and footnote 108.

9 *Prosecutor v. Milošević*, 'Reasons for Decision on the Prosecution Motion Concerning Assignment of Counsel', Case No. IT-02-54-T, 4 April 2003 ('First *Milošević* Decision'),

The Trial Chamber then spent a considerable number of pages on US law, and the Supreme Court case of *Faretta*[10] in particular, relating to the right to self-representation. It also analysed some of the international law jurisprudence, noting Judge Gunawardana's opinion in the *Barayagwiza* decision[11], and the ECtHR *Croissant*[12] decision and Human Rights Committee decision in *Hill.*[13] Interestingly, the Chamber noted that the *Hill* case had a special significance because it dealt with Article 14(3)(d) of the ICCPR, the instrument on which the rights of the accused were based in the Statute.[14] The Chamber found that it was 'appropriate to be guided by the ICCPR and the Human Rights Committee's interpretation of it, which confirms the right to self-defence and rejects the imposition of defence counsel on an unwilling accused'.[15] This was a position it would later qualify and rightly emphasise the unpersuasive nature of the *Hill* precedent.

The Trial Chamber also found practical reasons for its decision not to impose defence counsel on the accused:

> If such counsel were appointed, the Trial Chamber would have to take one of two courses: should the Accused (as, judging by his submissions, is likely to be the case) refuse to instruct him or her, the Trial Chamber could either: (a) not allow the Accused to make submissions and question witnesses, thereby effectively preventing the Accused from putting forward any defence; or, (b) it could allow him to make submissions and question witnesses, in which case, the defence counsel could do no more than the *Amici Curiae.*[16]

Footnote 9 *(cont.)*
para. 18. The Chamber went on to refer to the adversarial nature of proceedings before the ICTY.

10 *Faretta v. California*, 422 US 806 (1975) ('*Faretta*'). This is the most robust case asserting an accused's right to self-representation, applying even in circumstances where the effect of electing that right may adversely affect the fairness of the trial proceedings.

11 *Prosecutor v. Barayagwiza*, 'Decision on Defence Counsel Motion to Withdraw', Case No. ICTR-97-19-T, 2 November 2000 ('*Barayagwiza* Decision'). See, discussion of this case in this section below.

12 *Croissant v. Germany* (1992) A237-B Eur Court HR (Ser A) ('*Croissant*'). See, discussion of this case in chapter one.

13 *Michael and Brian Hill v. Spain*, Human Rights Committee, Communication No. 526/1993, UN Doc CCPR/C/59/D/526/1993, 2 April 1997 ('*Hill*').

14 Report of the Secretary-General (S/25704), 3 May 1993, para. 106, presented pursuant to paragraph 2 of Security Council Resolution 808 (1993), and approved by Security Council Resolution 827 (1993) ('Secretary-General's Report'). See also, *Prosecution v. Milošević*, 'Reasons for Decision on Assignment of Defence Counsel', Case No. IT-02-54-T, 22 September 2004, footnote 44 ('Second *Milošević* Decision').

15 First *Milošević* Decision, above n. 9, para. 37.

16 Ibid. para. 38.

These concerns would return to haunt the *Milošević* case, following the eventual Appeals Chamber's Decision of 1 November 2004. Finally, however, in an important qualification that would resonate consistently through decisions of all international criminal courts and tribunals to deal with these issues, the Trial Chamber held that 'the right to defend oneself in person is not absolute'.[17] It concluded that the accused had a right to defend himself in person 'in the present circumstances', but that 'there may be circumstances [. . .] where it is in the interests of justice to appoint counsel', and that the Trial Chamber would keep the position under review.[18] In particular, given the unpredictability of an issue such as health, the Trial Chamber allowed for the position to be reviewed in light of a change in circumstances.[19] The position with respect to the accused's health did indeed prompt the Trial Chamber to revisit its ruling and to ultimately impose defence counsel on the accused against his express objection.

Removing the right to self-representation

Because the Trial Chamber determined that it was the medical condition of the accused that caused it to revisit Milošević's election to represent himself, it is necessary to consider this issue as a preliminary step to analysing the Chamber's decision.

(a) Health of the Accused As early as 26 March 2002, the issue of Milošević's health had been raised. In a submission from the '"SLOBODA" ("Freedom") Association, The National Committee for the Liberation of Slobodan Milošević',[20] demands were being made for the examination of the Accused by medical experts, suggestions already emerging as to the seriousness of his medical state.

The health of the Accused had crippled the progress of the trial since the time the Trial Chamber issued its first reasoned decision allowing the accused to represent himself, in April 2003. Already early in the trial, medical reports produced at the request of the Trial Chamber noted that the Accused had a severely increased blood pressure and

17 Ibid. para. 40. 18 Ibid.

19 Ibid. para. 41: 'A Trial Chamber has indeed an obligation to ensure that a trial is fair and expeditious; moreover, where the health of the Accused is in issue, that obligation takes on special significance'.

20 See reference in *Prosecutor v. Milošević*, 'Prosecution's Position in Relation to Management of Trial Proceedings and the Regime for Presentation and Admission of Evidence With Comments on Issues Concerning the Accused's Health', Case No. IT-02-54-T, 5 April 2002, paras. 3, 39ff.

severe cardiovascular risk which demanded careful monitoring by a cardiologist coupled with a reduction of his workload.[21] Subsequently, whenever his blood pressure became elevated, Milošević was required to rest and the trial had to be adjourned to await his recovery. From August 2002 (only six months after the commencement of the trial) up until September 2003, Milošević's condition led the treating cardiologist to recommend that the Trial Chamber reduce its in court regime, eventually down to three days per week[22] – a regime that remained in place until the time of his death.

As a result of Milošević's medical condition, the trial was adjourned on thirteen separate occasions during the prosecution case, amounting to a loss of some sixty-six trial days.[23] This equals an astonishing twenty-two sitting weeks under the three-day-per-week regime the court had been forced to sit, or around six actual sitting months of trial. Furthermore, the Trial Chamber noted that from the close of the prosecution case on 25 February 2004 until 17 June 2004, Milošević's medical condition caused his doctors to recommend that the accused rest and not work on a total of fifty-one week-days.[24] Subsequent even to that, the commencement of his defence case had to be adjourned five times,[25] so that instead of opening on 8 June 2004 it finally began on 31 August 2004.

Milošević's medical condition led the Chamber to seek expert medical reports from the treating cardiologist and another expert cardiologist, both of whom reached the same conclusions: (1) the Accused had severe essential hypertension, (2) in the situation at the time of review, Milošević was not fit enough to defend himself, and (3) should he continue to represent himself, the progress of the trial would be delayed significantly. Both doctors were at one in concluding that a hypertensive emergency, a potentially life-threatening condition, could develop.[26]

An aspect of the ill-health of the accused that became important for case management purposes was the conclusion that he was, at least at one identifiable point, failing to follow his prescribed medication regime. In its reasoned decision assigning counsel to Milošević, the Chamber referred to findings by the doctors that the most likely explanation for the resistant nature of the accused's hypertension was his failure to adhere to his prescribed treatment regime.[27] This, as well as the presence of an unprescribed substance, was confirmed by blood tests carried out on Milošević and reviewed by a toxicologist and the treating cardiologist, as well as a

[21] Second *Milošević* Decision, above n. 14, para. 53, footnote 113. [22] Ibid. para. 53.
[23] Ibid. para. 56. [24] Ibid. para. 59. [25] Ibid. [26] Ibid. para. 60.
[27] Ibid. para. 61.

non-treating expert cardiologist.[28] While the Trial Chamber stated that it was 'concerned to note that irregularities in the medical findings relating to non-adherence to the prescribed medical regime and the drugs found in the blood and in the possession of the Accused', it stated expressly that it did not base its decision to impose counsel 'on the Prosecution submission that the Accused has wilfully manipulated the trial timetable through these and other means'.[29] These were matters which would continue to plague the trial process to the death of Milošević and its untimely end.

(b) Second Reasoned Decision of 22 September 2004 Following a period of substantial briefing and oral argument on the question of imposing counsel, the medical condition of the accused and other possible solutions to achieve a fair and expeditious trial (including considering severance of indictments), the Trial Chamber determined that the medical condition of the Accused required it to impose defence counsel on Milošević. On 2 September 2004, the Chamber issued its oral ruling to this effect.[30] In the subsequent written reasons, the Trial Chamber delivered what remains a seminal decision in international criminal law on the right to, and limitations of, self-representation.

The Trial Chamber based its competence to impose counsel on an unwilling accused on its overarching obligation to ensure a fair trial, as defined in Articles 20 and 21(4) of the ICTY Statute.[31] The Chamber, stating that it is well established that the Statute was to be interpreted as a treaty in accordance with Article 31 of the Vienna Convention on the Law of Treaties,[32] determined that the main issue was 'the ordinary meaning of the provisions of Article 21(4)(d) in their context and in light of the object and purpose of the Article and the Statute as a whole'.[33] The minimum guarantees contained in Article 21(4), including the right of an accused 'to defend himself in person or through legal counsel of his own choosing', are mere elements of this overarching requirement of a fair trial. The Chamber reasoned that, whether by way of self-representation or legal assistance, the purpose of this provision is to secure the accused's right to a defence – itself a prerequisite for a fair trial.[34] The Chamber held that references to defence 'in person' or

[28] Ibid. See also Medical Reports of Professor Tavernier, 29 July 2004 and 27 August 2004; Medical Reports of Dr. van Dijkman, 20 and 30 August 2004.

[29] Ibid. para. 67.

[30] Ibid. para. 1, at which the full text of the oral ruling is set out.

[31] Ibid. para. 32.

[32] Vienna Convention on the Law of Treaties (1969), 1155 UNTS 331, Part III. See Second *Milošević* Decision, above n. 14, para. 31 (for precedent on the treatment of the Statute as a treaty).

[33] Second *Milošević* Decision, above n. 14, para. 31.

[34] Ibid. para. 33.

'through legal assistance' of an Accused's own choosing, are simply means whereby the minimum guaranteed right to 'defend himself' may be exercised.[35]

The Chamber considered that, 'if at any stage of a trial there is a real prospect that it will be disrupted and the integrity of the trial undermined with the risk that it will not be conducted fairly', then it had a duty to implement a regime to avoid that.[36] Where self-representation has such an impact, the Trial Chamber considered it appropriate to assign counsel to conduct the defence case.[37]

This analysis is of particular importance as it is the first time a Chamber of the ICTY has sought to define a hierarchical regime in respect of the principle of a fair trial and that principle's interaction with the so-called 'minimum guarantees' set out in Article 21 of the Statute, guarantees which are the embodiment of the human rights fair trial regime found in various forms in all the relevant regional and international human rights treaties.[38]

The minimum guarantees, where their expression or effect interferes with the accomplishment of the fair trial right, must yield, and a court must fashion a response that gives efficacy to the overarching fair trial right. The Chamber went further, however, in defining the status of the minimum guarantees:

> There are other cases in which the enjoyment of a right under Article 21(4) of the Statute must yield to the overarching right to a fair trial: for example, where the exercise of the right to self-representation becomes an obstacle to the achievement of a trial without undue delay, which is a specific right or minimum guarantee designed, *inter alia*, to maintain the integrity and fairness of the process. Should a trial not be conducted expeditiously, *i.e.*, without undue delay, the risk of unfairness will arise requiring the Trial Chamber to consider how that risk may be avoided.[39]

The Trial Chamber appears here to confuse the principle of a trial without undue delay (which concerns the time taken for a case to be brought to trial) and the expedition of a trial (the time a commenced trial takes to conclude). The Chamber in fact appears to be intending to refer to the latter proposition. If so, its analysis is consistent with a persistent refrain in the jurisprudence of the ICTY, that a trial must be fair *and*

[35] Ibid. [36] Ibid. para. 33. [37] Ibid.

[38] For a detailed discussion of the relevant fair trial rights, their interpretation and application in international criminal law, see chapter 1 of this book.

[39] Second *Milošević* Decision, above n. 14, para. 33.

expeditious.[40] What the Chamber appears to suggest here is that expeditiousness is a component of the fair trial principle. Although at times throughout the Second Reasoned Decision, the Chamber itself reverts to familiar language (the need to 'ensure that the trial of the accused is fair *and* expeditious'),[41] the boxing of all other elements exclusively under the fair trial label is novel. In fact, it is probably an undesirable approach to the paradigm of international criminal trials. No doubt, a failure to achieve expedition in the trial process will, at times, cause unfairness. However, an underlying premise of this book is that expeditiousness is an important but less critical aspect of an international criminal trial. Best practice in the conduct of these trials is achieved only when they are both fair and expeditious, but the values to be attributed to these principles is not the same. It is unlikely, therefore, that conflation of the principles of fairness and expeditiousness will serve the process of understanding and applying these principles in the context of self-representation let alone a broader application.

Of further interest is the fact that the Trial Chamber chose to largely ignore the 'interests of justice' as a legal basis for its ruling. Whereas the ICTR in *Barayagwiza*,[42] the SCSL in *Norman*,[43] and the ICTY in the *Šešelj* Decision[44] all based the right to impose counsel (in those cases a standby counsel) on the requirement that the interests of justice be met, the Trial Chamber in the *Milošević* Second Reasoned Decision gives little attention to this principle:

> [i]n light of the history of the case and the conclusions that the Trial Chamber had reached, the Chamber was of the opinion that it was necessary

40 See Second *Milošević* Decision, above n. 14, para. 65; *Prosecution v. Milošević*, 'Decision on Interlocutory Appeal of the Trial Chamber's Decision on the Assignment of Defence Counsel', Case No. IT-02-54-AR73.7, 1 November 2004 (Appeal *Milošević* Decision'), para. 17; *Prosecution v. Milošević*, 'Decision on Prosecution's Motion for Judicial Notice of Adjudicated Facts and Documentary Evidence', Case No. IT-02-54-AR73.6, 20 January 2004, paras 19–20; *Prosecution v. Blagojević*, 'Public and Redacted Reasons for Decision on Appeal by Vidoje Blagojevic to Replace his Defense Team', Case No. IT-02-60-AR73.4, 7 November 2003. 41 Ibid. para. 34 (*my*).

42 *Barayagwiza* Decision, above n. 11, concurring and separate opinion of Judge Gunawardana.

43 *Prosecutor v. Norman et al.*, 'Decision on the Application of Samuel Hinga Norman for Self Representation under Article 17(4)(d) of the Statute of the Special Court', Case No. SCSL-04-14-T, 8 June 2004 ('*Norman* Decision'), para. 28.

44 *Prosecutor v. Šešelj*, 'Decision on Prosecution's Motion for Order Appointing Counsel to Assist Vojislav Šešelj with his Defence', Case No. IT-03-67-PT, 9 May 2003 ('First *Šešelj* Decision'), para. 20. The Chamber in Šešelj placed the obligation to ensure a fair trial under the requirement that a court act in the interests of justice.

> to relieve the Accused of the burden of conducting his own case with a view to stabilising his health to ensure, so far as possible, that the trial proceeds with the minimum of interruption in a way that will permit the orderly presentation of the Accused's case and the completion of the trial within a reasonable time *in his interests and the interests of justice: in other words, to secure for the Accused a fair and expeditious trial.*[45]

The Chamber appears to find that the interests of justice are subsumed within the 'overarching' fair trial right, although it does not resolve this matter expressly. Its interpretation, however, is neat and again ties in nicely with the proposition that a criminal court, properly applying its discretion, should be able to calibrate crucial aspects of the conduct of the trial within the overall requirement that the accused receive a fair trial. This is a better approach also because while the 'interests of justice' is a nebulous and not easily definable concept, the right to a fair trial is a more concrete principle with more meaningful and graspable component parts and with a more detailed jurisprudential foundation. Furthermore, untoward emphasis on *elements* of the human rights guarantees in the international criminal trial process presents the risk that a court will be required to ignore the obvious and critical requirement that the trial had by an accused is fair in its conduct and conclusion. The law on self-representation in the US reflects such a farcical state of affairs. As Judge Reinhardt's opinion in *Farhad* makes clear, by focusing too closely on a right that should form part of the fair trial regime (the Sixth Amendment right interpreted to entitle self-representation), the US Supreme Court in *Faretta* effectively elevated that right over the overarching requirement that a criminal trial be fair. In US law, at least in circumstances material to this analysis, an accused may have a right – admittedly by their own actions – to an unfair trial. This is a perverse conception of justice fortunately avoided in the evolving practice of international criminal jurisdictions.

Finally, and of relevance in part because of the unusual ruling of the ICTY Appeals Chamber on the Trial Chamber's decision to impose counsel upon Milošević, it is worth focusing on the modalities put in place by the Trial Chamber to effectuate its ruling. In a separate order following its ruling imposing defence counsel, the *Milošević* Trial Chamber issued an Order on Modalities, in which it set out the way in which imposed counsel was to operate, and the Accused's role:

(1) It is the duty of court assigned counsel to determine how to present the case for the Accused, and in particular it is their duty to:

[45] Second *Milošević* Decision, above n. 14, para. 66 (*my italics*)

   (a) represent the Accused by preparing and examining those witnesses court assigned counsel deem it appropriate to call;
   (b) make all submissions on fact and law that they deem it appropriate to make;
   (c) seek from the Trial Chamber such orders as they consider necessary to enable them to present the Accused's case properly, including the issuance of subpoenas;
   (d) discuss with the Accused the conduct of the case, endeavour to obtain his instructions thereon and take account of views expressed by the Accused, while retaining the right to determine what course to follow; and
   (e) act throughout in the best interests of the Accused;
(2) The Accused may, with the leave of the Trial Chamber, continue to participate actively in the conduct of his case, including, where appropriate, examining witnesses, following examination by court assigned counsel;
(3) The Accused has the right, at any time, to make a reasonable request to the Trial Chamber to consider allowing him to appoint counsel; and
(4) Court assigned counsel is authorised to seek from the Trial Chamber such further orders as they deem necessary to enable them to conduct the case for the Accused.[46]

The modalities by which counsel were to act distinguishes the *Milošević* approach from the approach taken in most other international criminal law cases.[47] Instead of utilising the mechanism of standby counsel, the Chamber clearly removed the accused from the control panel of his case, and required imposed defence counsel to take responsibility for the conduct and presentation of the defence case. This was done on the basis that, 'if the Accused was permitted to continue to represent himself, it was inevitable that his health would suffer, that his life could be at risk, and that he was unfit to continue to represent himself. The Chamber found that at the very least the trial would continue to be interrupted frequently to enable him to recover sufficiently to proceed'.[48]

[46] *Prosecution v. Milošević*, 'Order on the Modalities to be Followed by Court Assigned Counsel', Case No. IT-02-54-T, 3 September 2004.

[47] The only other example of a similar procedure being followed is in the Second *Šešelj* decision, discussed below.

[48] Second *Milošević* Decision, above n. 14, para. 63. An interesting aspect of this Decision was that, despite finding in its initial oral ruling, and in the written decision, the most likely reason for the resistant nature of his condition, was that Milošević had failed to

This was an approach which confronted more directly circumstances in which a court determines that the fairness of a trial is threatened by the continuing self-representation of an accused. In the First *Šešelj* decision and the *Norman* decision, standby counsel ostensibly played a role of understudy to the accused, with the possibility that, should circumstances such as obstruction occur, they would step up and take full control of the defence case. In these cases the Chambers held that, unless circumstances required it, the right of the accused to self-representation remained untouched. Therefore, while supporting the proposition that it is competent to impose counsel on an unwilling accused, the circumstances of those cases do not amount to an imposition of counsel in fact. The Trial Chamber in *Milošević* gave genuine effect to the role of defence counsel (who would be required to act in the best interests of the accused), while making it possible for the accused to be involved, to the extent that such involvement was consistent with the conduct of a fair trial, and always allowed him the possibility of requesting that counsel of his own choice be assigned to represent him.

Appeals Chamber decision of 1 November 2004

It took the Appeals Chamber just over one month to rule on the Trial Chamber's decision imposing defence counsel, holding that, 'although the question is close', it could not conclude that the Trial Chamber abused its discretion in imposing defence counsel upon Milošević,[49] but that the 'sharp restrictions' the decision placed upon Milošević's role 'were grounded on a fundamental error of law: the Trial Chamber failed to recognize that any restrictions on Milošević's right to represent himself must be limited to the minimum extent necessary to protect the Tribunal's interest in assuring a reasonably expeditious trial'.[50]

In its decision, the Appeals Chamber found that the Trial Chamber's restriction on Milošević's right of self-representation was not proportionate to the Tribunal's interest in an expeditious resolution of the case, and referred in support of this position to a principle of 'proportionality'.[51] The Appeals Chamber relied upon an unusual assortment of authorities in support of this principle, with a variety of subject-matter unrelated to

Footnote 48 *(cont.)*

adhere to his therapeutic regime – which included toxicological evidence that he was not taking medication he was prescribed to keep his blood pressure in check, and that he was taking an unprescribed substance. Despite these findings, the Trial Chamber expressly noted that it did not base its decision on this conduct of the accused, but rather on his medical condition, which dictated that counsel be imposed in the manner just explained.

[49] Appeal *Milošević* Decision, above n. 40, para. 15. [50] Ibid. para. 17. [51] Ibid.

assignment of counsel. Indeed, this assortment of decisions is – with one relevant exception – based on domestic administrative or constitutional law issues that have no bearing on an international criminal trial and the determination of defining and maintaining a fair trial for an accused.[52]

The Appeals Chamber itself set out the standard of appellate review in its decision:

> A Trial Chamber's exercise of discretion will be overturned if the challenged decision was (1) based on an incorrect interpretation of governing law; (2) based on a patently incorrect conclusion of fact; or (3) so unfair or unreasonable as to constitute an abuse of the Trial Chamber's discretion. Absent an error of law or a clearly erroneous factual finding, then, the scope of appellate review is quite limited: even if the Appeals Chamber does not believe that counsel should have been imposed on Milošević, the decision below will stand unless it was so unreasonable as to force the conclusion that the Trial Chamber failed to exercise its discretion judiciously.[53]

The Appeals Chamber, although it is not explained, appears to apply this principle of proportionality when dealing with a Trial Chamber's exercise of discretion, as an application of broad principles of public international law. Whether or not different considerations apply to the exercise of a lower court's discretion in criminal law matters is not discussed. The Trial Chamber's discretion, as exercised, was found to be so unreasonable as to force the conclusion that it failed to exercise that discretion judiciously.

The Appeals Chamber further held that 'the excessiveness of the Trial Chamber's restrictions' were apparent for three main reasons: '(1) the

52 The authorities referred to are: *Elloy de Freitas v. Permanent Secretary of Ministry of Agriculture, Fisheries, Lands, and Housing*, 1 AC 69 (1998) (Privy Council), dealing with whether the appellant acted in violation of statutory restrictions prohibiting civil servants from publishing their political views on any matter to anyone, in a public place; *McConnell v. Federal Election Comm'n*, 540 US 93 (2003), in which the US Supreme Court considered whether the Bipartisan Campaign Reform Act of 2002 violated the US constitutional guarantee of freedom of speech and association; *Chassagnou v. France* (2000) 29 EHRR 615, where the ECtHR considered a challenge based on proportionality by a French landowner required under French law to automatically transfer hunting rights over his land because it did not meet a certain size; *The Edmonton Journal v. Alberta*, CarswellAlta 198 [1989], in which the Supreme Court of Canada upheld the principle that a restrictive ban imposed on publication by certain legislation did not (as required) impair the right to freedom of expression as little as possible and went much further than necessary to protect privacy; and *Prosecutor v. Limaj et al.*, 'Decision on Fatmir Limaj's Request for Provisional Release', Case No. IT-03-66-AR65, 31 October 2003, in which the ICTY Appeals Chamber held that, when interpreting Rule 65(B) and (D) of the ICTY Rules (concerning provisional release), the general principle of proportionality must be taken into account.

53 Appeal *Milošević* Decision, above n. 40, para. 10.

medical reports relied on by the Trial Chamber explicitly rejected the notion that Milošević's condition is permanent; (2) there was no evidence that Milošević had suffered from any health problems since late July; and (3) Milošević made a vigorous two-day opening statement without interruption or apparent difficulty'.[54] However, the Appeals Chamber's reasoning is contradicted by the medical and other evidence relied upon by the Trial Chamber in reaching its decision, as well as the Appeals Chamber's own recounting of the facts which led it to hold that the decision of the Trial Chamber to impose defence counsel on an unwilling accused was legally sound.[55] The Appeals Chamber affirmed the Trial Chamber's imposition of defence counsel, but reversed its Order on Modalities, holding:

> On remand, the Trial Chamber should craft a working regime that minimizes the practical impact of the formal assignment of counsel, except to the extent required by the interests of justice. At a minimum, this regime must be rooted in the default presumption that, when he is physically capable of doing so, Milošević will take the lead in presenting his case – choosing which witnesses to present, questioning those witnesses before Assigned Counsel has an opportunity to do so, arguing any proper motions he desires to present to the court, giving a closing statement when the defense rests, and making the basic strategic decisions about the presentation of his defense. But this presumption is just that: a presumption. Under the current circumstances, where Milošević is sufficiently well to present a vigorous, two-day opening statement, it was an abuse of discretion to curtail his participation in the trial so dramatically on the grounds of poor health. The Appeals Chamber can hardly anticipate, however, the myriad

54 Ibid. para. 18.

55 See the health and history sections of the Trial and Appeals Chamber decisions, and other findings, including: that the accused suffers from two chronic cardiovascular conditions, severe essential hypertension and hypertrophic heart disease, which have been and continue to be exacerbated by the conduct of his own defence and are therefore unlikely to resolve while he takes any active role in the conduct of his own defence – the very reasons the doctors opined that the accused is not medically fit to represent himself, and which are unlikely to have resolved in any material way since the end of July 2004; the medical findings that the effect of Milošević's chronic conditions is that it resurfaces periodically and persistently, not that his blood pressure is at permanently dangerous levels – and, therefore, it is entirely consistent with his medical condition that he is at times fit to present his case (not to mention that the accused had some 6 months since the end of the Prosecution case in which to prepare the text of his opening statement); and, the finding, at footnote 42 of the Decision on Interlocutory Appeal, that trial litigation 'is an extraordinarily demanding profession', which is presumably consistent with the rationale for the Trial Chamber dramatically reducing the accused's role.

> health-related difficulties that may arise in the future, or use this occasion to calibrate an appropriate set of responses to every possible eventuality. It is therefore left to the wise discretion of the Trial Chamber to steer a careful course between allowing Milošević to exercise his fundamental right of self-representation and safeguarding the Tribunal's basic interest in a reasonably expeditious resolution of the cases before it.
>
> The Appeals Chamber stresses the following point: in practice, if all goes well, the trial should continue much as it did when Milošević was healthy. To a lay observer, who will see Milošević playing the principal courtroom role at the hearings, the difference may well be imperceptible. If Milošević's health problems resurface with sufficient gravity, however, the presence of Assigned Counsel will enable the trial to continue even if Milošević is temporarily unable to participate. The precise point at which that reshuffling of trial roles should occur will be up to the Trial Chamber.[56]

Although it upheld both the legal principle that a Chamber is competent to impose defence counsel on an unwilling accused, as well as the exercise of the Trial Chamber's discretion to do so in this case, the consequence of the ruling was to remove the lynchpin of the Trial Chamber's decision – the control of the defence case by counsel. On the basis of the Appeals Chamber decision, even an uncooperative accused, refusing to communicate with or instruct imposed counsel, can have control of the conduct of his case, imposed counsel in effect being relegated to a standby counsel role. In the context of the *Milošević* case, the Appeals Chamber decision had the effect of returning the accused to full control over the preparation and presentation of his case – the very thing that the Trial Chamber had sought to disallow on the basis of medical advice that Milošević was not fit to conduct his own defence and that to continue allowing him to do so risked killing him. Milošević, following the Appeals Chamber ruling, resumed the conduct of his own case in full and, some sixteen months later, died as a direct result of the cardiovascular condition with which these matters are concerned.

In relation to its broader application to international criminal law cases concerning self-represented senior level accused, the Appeals Chamber decision creates real challenges for the fledgling attempt to effectuate the imposition of counsel. It does so in a manner that is, in law and principle, unconvincing and will need careful attention in future work in this important area. This is a matter that will be reflected on further below.

[56] Appeal *Milošević* Decision, above n. 40, paras. 19–20.

Self-representation issues arising in other international criminal courts and tribunals

The *Milošević* case is the most significant precedent for consideration of the right to self-representation and its limitations and qualifications. But it is not the only case in which senior accused have asserted the right to self-representation in ways that threatened the fairness and expedition of the trial, and courts and tribunals have responded to these threats in different ways. As discussed at the commencement of this section, something of an industry has emerged in these cases, with accused using the right to self-representation to disrupt or manipulate proceedings and to politicise the forensic trial process. This section considers those cases before international criminal courts and tribunals where accused have elected to represent themselves, which will set the basis for later consideration of possible reform and future approaches to self-representation that will assist in achieving best practice in the conduct of complex international criminal trials.

The Special Court for Sierra Leone

(a) The *Norman* Decision In a decision in June 2004, the Special Court for Sierra Leone (SCSL) considered a late application by one of the accused, Samuel Hinga Norman, to represent himself.[57] Having been represented by counsel since his incarceration in March 2003, Norman sought to dispense with the services of counsel by a letter addressed to the Principal Defender on the day the trial was to commence.

The main issue considered by the Trial Chamber was the scope of the right to self-representation, as set out in Article 17(4) of the SCSL Statute (which reproduces the same language as Article 21(4) of the ICTY Statute). The Chamber held that, 'as a matter of statutory construction, Article 17(4)(d) does guarantee to an accused person, first and foremost, the right to self-representation'.[58] However, the Chamber went on to find that, 'having regard to the statutory purport and intendment of Article 17(4)(d)', that right is not absolute but is qualified. This interpretation, the Chamber found, 'is amply corroborated by the qualifying clause of Article 17(4)(d), which provides "[. . .] and to have legal assistance assigned to him or her, in any case where the interests of justice so require" '.[59]

The Trial Chamber formulated the question for its consideration as follows:

> [t]he question to put here is whether the attendant consequences that would flow from our granting the request [. . .] would, in the overall

[57] *Norman* Decision, above n. 43. [58] Ibid. para. 8. [59] Ibid.

> interests of justice, be consistent with the statutory guarantees to a fair and expeditious trial to be reserved by the Court to the accused particularly where, as in this case, his detention has been as long as over one year.[60]

The Chamber considered that, as a co-accused, the accused Norman should not be permitted to exercise 'his qualified right to self-representation', to the detriment of the rights of his two co-accused to a fair and expeditious trial.[61]

The Trial Chamber made reference, in its decision, to the *Milošević* case, noting that the Trial Chamber, in its First Reasoned Decision, had also held that the right to self-representation is not absolute and that there may be circumstances where it is in the interests of justice to appoint Counsel. The Trial Chamber noted that the material distinction between the *Norman* case and the *Milošević* case was that the latter had been permitted to exercise his right to self-representation in circumstances where he had indicated his intention to do so from the outset and was being tried without co-accused who would be prejudiced by the exercise of the accused's right.[62]

The Chamber held that the role of defence counsel 'is institutional and is meant to serve, not only the interests of his client but also those of the Court and the overall interests of justice'.[63] Interestingly, in reaching this conclusion, the Chamber stated that it was guided by the opinion of Judge Reinhardt in the US Court of Appeals case *Farhad*, where that judge stated that permitting self-representation regardless of the consequences threatened to divert criminal trials from their clearly defined purpose of providing a fair and reliable determination of guilt or innocence.[64]

Finally, the Trial Chamber set out six factors to be considered in the determination of the issue before them: that the right of counsel is predicated upon the notion that representation by counsel is an essential and necessary part of a fair trial; that the right to counsel relieves the burden on the trial judges of explaining and enforcing basic rules of courtroom protocol and assisting the accused; given the complexity of such trials, there is a high potential of complexities and intricacies typical of evolving international criminal law, which risk unfairness to the accused; there is a public interest, national and international, in the expeditious completion of the trial; there is the high potential for further disruption to the Court's

60 Ibid. para. 12. 61 Ibid. para. 14.

62 Ibid. paras 19–20. The Trial Chamber of the SCSL also referred to the ICTY decision concerning the right to self-representation in the First *Šešelj* Decision, and the ICTR in the *Barayagwiza* Decision. 63 *Norman* Decision, above n. 43, para. 23.

64 Ibid. para. 25.

timetable and calendar; there is a tension between giving effect to the accused's right to self-representation and that of his co-accused, to a fair and expeditious trial as required by law.[65]

The Trial Chamber ultimately held that it:

> [could not] allow the integrity of its proceedings to be tarnished or to be conducted in a manner that is not in conformity with the aspirations, or the norms of the judicial process. As a matter of law, it is our duty as a Chamber at all times, to protect the integrity of the proceedings before us and to ensure that the administration of justice is not brought into disrepute. This we can achieve by ensuring, amongst other measures, that persons who are accused and indicted for serious offences such as these, are properly represented by Counsel because this safeguard is very vital in ensuring that the overall interests of justice are served and of the Rule of Law, upheld.[66]

The Trial Chamber subsequently issued a Consequential Order assigning standby counsel,[67] stating that 'Standby Counsel will provide legal assistance to the Accused and ensure the safeguard to his right to a fair and expeditious trial'.[68] When Norman subsequently failed to appear in court, his right to self-representation was revoked and the standby counsel previously appointed were designated as 'court-appointed counsel' to represent him in the proceedings.[69] The Trial Chamber held that Norman's deliberate absence from the Court warranted, in the interests of justice, the revocation of his right to self-representation, and that in accordance with Rule 60 the trial would continue in his absence.[70]

(b) The *Gbao* Decision Of peripheral interest is another decision of the SCSL, in which the Appeals Chamber considered an appeal from the Trial Chamber's decision to refuse an application by the Accused Gbao to withdraw the assignment of his counsel to him, on the basis that he no longer recognised the legitimacy of the SCSL.[71]

The relief sought by the defence was summarised by the Appeals Chamber as being (i) that the accused be accorded his right not to have

[65] Ibid. para. 26. [66] Ibid. para. 28. [67] *Norman* Decision, above n. 43. [68] Ibid. 3.

[69] *Prosecutor v. Norman et al.*, 'Ruling on the Issue of Non-Appearance of the First Accused Samuel Hinga Norman, The Second Accused Moinina Fofana, and the Third Accused, Allieu Kondewa at the Trial Proceedings', Case No. SCSL-04-14-PT, 1 October 2004, para. 23; *Prosecutor v. Norman et al.*, 'Consequential Order on the Role of Court Appointed Counsel, Case No. SCSL-04-14-PT, 1 October 2004. [70] Ibid., para. 22.

[71] *Prosecutor v. Sesay et al.*, 'Gbao – Decision on Appeal Against Decision on Withdrawal of Counsel', Case No. SCSL-04-15-AR73, 23 November 2004.

counsel representing him; (ii) that the Trial Chamber be ordered to consider alternative measures for the protection of the integrity of the proceedings and the fairness of the trial such as the appointment of standby counsel; or, (iii) that the Trial Chamber reconsider its decision having heard counsel for the defence and prosecution and in the light of the findings of the Appeals Chamber.[72] The Appeals Chamber held that the issue before the Trial Chamber was correctly determined as being an application by the accused to have assignment of counsel withdrawn and not, as argued by the defence on appeal, a question of whether the accused was in effect electing to represent himself.[73] It was declared that the 'overriding considerations in the circumstances that arose were the interests of justice and fair hearing',[74] although it did not explain how it was that those principles were to be applied in the circumstances.

The Appeals Chamber quoted the Trial Chamber's determination of the matter on the basis of the interests of justice:

> It is clear from examining all of the circumstances of this case that the interests of justice would not be served by allowing Mr. Gbao to be unrepresented before the Court. The Trial Chamber accordingly takes the position that it must safeguard the rights of the accused and the integrity of the proceedings before the Court by insisting that Mr. Gbao should continue to be represented by the Counsel that have represented him throughout these proceedings. We hold in this regard that an accused person cannot waive his right to a fair and expeditious trial whatever the circumstances.[75]

Of residual interest to the question of the right to self-representation, the Chamber held that the provisions of Article 17(4)(d) – the same as those found in the Statutes of the ICTY and ICTR – dictate that the rights an accused has in regard to the conduct of his defence are: '(i) to defend himself or herself in person; or (ii) to defend himself or herself through legal assistance of his or her own choosing; and (iii) to have legal assistance assigned to him or her, in any case where the interests of justice so require'.[76] The first two are said to be within the choice of the accused, however 'the law does not recognise a right "not to have counsel assigned" to an accused who has refused to exercise the choice available to him under (i) and (ii).[77]

The Appeals Chamber of the SCSL has, therefore, established for that jurisdiction a right to assign counsel to an accused who does not properly elect to represent himself or to have counsel. So in the circumstances of

[72] Ibid. para. 56. [73] Ibid. paras 53–4. [74] Ibid. para. 55. [75] Ibid. para. 46.
[76] Ibid. para. 57. [77] Ibid. para. 58.

this case, where the accused did not recognise the legitimacy of the SCSL and did not wish to be represented by counsel (and so in effect boycotted the proceedings entirely) the court could assign counsel or insist on assigned counsel continuing to represent the accused, even *in absentia*, in 'the interests of justice and a fair hearing'. This reflects the basic principle that an accused cannot be allowed to frustrate the proceedings by an act of obstruction – whatever form that obstruction takes. This principle, although treated differently under the facts of different cases in different jurisdictions, and in particular articulated differently as relating to the fair and expeditious conduct of a trial or in the interests of justice, is ostensibly universal in its recognition.

The ICTR

(a) The *Barayagwiza* Decision In a decision by a Trial Chamber of the ICTR in the *Baryagwiza* case,[78] the accused instructed his lawyers 'not to represent him in any respect during the trial'.[79] The ICTR has a provision, Rule 45(I) of its Rules of Procedure and Evidence, which states that 'Counsel will represent the accused and conduct the case to finality [. . .] Counsel shall only be permitted to withdraw from the case to which he has been assigned in the most exceptional circumstances'. This is a provision which is not part of the regulatory structure of the ICTY or SCSL. The accused had refused to attend his trial, and the Chamber had determined that it would proceed in his absence, requiring his lawyers to attend court, even though the accused had instructed them not to participate in his defence and not to attend court on his behalf. The accused did not express a lack of confidence in his counsel or that they were incompetent, but rather refused to participate in the trial process because he considered that the ICTR was anti-Hutu and that he would not receive a fair trial. The Chamber held that it was consistent with the ICTR Statute and human rights law to proceed in the accused's absence and his arguments for withdrawal of counsel did not constitute 'exceptional circumstances' under Rule 45(I).

In a concurring and separate opinion, Judge Gunawardana stated that it was in the interests of justice to ensure that the accused was represented, despite his application and the application of counsel to withdraw. He went on to suggest that 'it would be useful to consider the established procedure adopted in the United States of appointing standby counsel, by the

[78] *Prosecutor v. Barayagwiza*, 'Decision on Defence Counsel Motion to Withdraw', Case No. ICTR-97-19-T, 2 November 2000. [79] Ibid, para. 2.

Court'.[80] It was suggested that the accused's counsel could be assigned as standby counsel, thus relieving them of the difficulty placed upon them by the accused's position and ensuring the accused, who had absented himself from the trial, could be represented. Judge Gunawardana referred to Article 20(4)(d) of the ICTR Statute as 'an enabling provision for the appointment of a "standby counsel"' and stated that 'in any event, the Court has the inherent power to control its own proceedings, which in this case, could be achieved by such an appointment'.

Neither the *Barayagwiza* nor the *Norman* decisions include any real analysis of applicable law at an international or domestic level. Some reference is made to US Supreme Court case law, without any comparative analysis or consideration of the transposition of the standby counsel concept under domestic US law to an internationalised criminal court with different jurisdictional considerations and cases inevitably larger and more complex in nature. In the case of *Norman*, reference is also made to two ICTY decisions. In neither case is any depth given to its analysis; no comparative law research is undertaken to determine the appropriateness of considering, let alone applying, selective domestic legal provisions or mechanisms to international criminal law cases subject to different jurisdictional and subject-matter considerations; and no real analysis of the practical ramifications is set out.

(b) The *Ntahobali* Decision A form of standby counsel was appointed by the ICTR in the *Ntahobali* case. In this case, the accused Ntahobali submitted a motion for the withdrawal of his counsel, on the ground that he no longer had confidence in them and there had been a complete breakdown of communication.[81] Ntahobali expressed a desire to represent himself pending the assignment of new counsel of his choice from a list provided by the Registry.[82]

The Trial Chamber noted that, under Rule 45(H) of the ICTR Rules of Procedure and Evidence, it may instruct the Registrar to replace an assigned counsel if satisfied that exceptional circumstances exist and good cause has been shown warranting the withdrawal of counsel, provided that the request was not designed to delay the proceedings.[83]

The Chamber held that these conditions had been satisfied, and decided to grant the Accused's request to withdraw his counsel. The

[80] Reference is made to the Supreme Court case of *McKaskle v. Wiggins*, 465 US 168 (1984).

[81] *Prosecutor v. Nyiramasuhuko and Ntahobali*, 'Decision on Ntahobali's Motion for Withdrawal of Counsel', Case No. ICTR-97-21-T, 22 June 2001, para. 9.

[82] Ibid. para. 2.5. [83] Ibid. para. 12.

Chamber noted that Ntahobali had firmly reiterated that if his request were granted, he wished to exercise his right to represent himself pursuant to Articles 20 and 20(4)(d) of the ICTR Statute and Rule 45(F) of the Rules pending the assignment of new counsel.[84] The Chamber granted Ntahobali's requests, but because of the seriousness of the charges and the prosecution's submissions about the accused directly cross-examining victims of rape,[85] decided to exercise its inherent powers to appoint a 'duty counsel' to assist the accused in the conduct of his defence. This was considered to be in the interests of justice under Rule 44 *bis*, and was only to be until the assignment of new counsel.[86]

This is the only time that a 'duty counsel' in such a form has been employed in international criminal law and appears to be a form of standby counsel, appointed for a limited period to protect the accused and the court from the potential consequences of self-representation.

The ICTY

(a) The First *Šešelj* Decision In a decision on 9 May 2003, a Trial Chamber of the ICTY in the *Šešelj* case[87] imposed standby counsel on the accused. The Chamber held that the wording of Article 21 of the Statute does not on its face exclude the possibility of imposing on an accused the assistance of assigned counsel where the interests of justice so require. It held that the need may arise for unforeseeable reasons to protect an accused's interests and to ensure a fair and expeditious trial.[88] The Trial Chamber referred to the *Milošević* First Reasoned Decision, which had held that the right to defend oneself in person is not absolute and that there may be circumstances where it is in the interests of a fair trial to appoint counsel.

The *Šešelj* Trial Chamber commented on the approach in US courts, stating that there, as in other common law jurisdictions, an accused is entitled to conduct his own defence and interference with this right is limited.[89] The Chamber referred to *Faretta*, in which the US Supreme Court recognised that a court may appoint standby counsel at the outset of trial 'even over objection by the accused' to aid the accused and to be available to represent him in the event that termination of his self-representation is necessary.[90]

The Trial Chamber held that it was in the interests of justice to assign standby counsel to the accused. It interpreted Article 21 of the ICTY

[84] Ibid. para. 18. [85] Ibid. para. 8. [86] Ibid. para. 20.
[87] First *Šešelj* Decision, above n. 44. [88] Ibid. 3. [89] Ibid. 5. [90] Ibid. 6

Statute, and the jurisprudence of the ICTY and the ICTR, as leaving open the possibility of assigning counsel to an accused on a case-by-case basis in the interests of justice.[91] According to the Trial Chamber in the *Šešelj* Decision, the phrase contained in Article 21(4)(d) of the ICTY Statute – 'in the interests of justice' – potentially has a broad scope, including the right to a fair trial, which is not only a fundamental right of the accused, but also a fundamental interest of the Tribunal related to its own legitimacy.[92] Of particular importance to the issue as it arises in senior leadership cases, the Chamber considered that in the context of the right to a fair trial, the length of the case, its size and its complexity all need to be taken into account. The complex legal, evidential, and procedural issues that arise in a case of this magnitude may fall outside the competence even of a legally qualified accused, especially where that accused is in detention without access to all the facilities needed. Moreover, the Tribunal has a legitimate interest in ensuring that the trial proceeds in a timely manner without interruptions, adjournments, or disruptions.[93]

The Chamber referred to and distinguished the circumstances under its consideration from the *Milošević* case. It also reviewed some of the available ECtHR and domestic law jurisprudence, with particular emphasis on US law relating to standby counsel, and referred favourably to the ICTR *Baryagwiza* Decision. The accused Šešelj, it was held, portrayed a clear attitude and actions indicative of obstructionism on his part.[94] It noted remedies used by the *Milošević* Chamber to ameliorate the problems associated with an unrepresented accused (including, as discussed earlier in this chapter, the appointment of *amici curiae* and legal associates), but determined that the best response to the circumstances of its case was to impose a standby counsel.[95]

The Trial Chamber went on to define the role that standby counsel would play, including assisting in the preparation of the defence case during the pre-trial phase whenever so requested by the accused; assisting in the preparation and presentation of his case at trial whenever so requested by the accused; receiving copies of all court documents, filings, and disclosed materials that are received by or sent to the accused; being present in the courtroom during the proceedings; being engaged actively in the substantive preparation of the case and to participate in the proceedings, in order always to be prepared to take over from the accused at trial; addressing the Chamber whenever so requested by the accused or the

[91] Ibid. para. 11. [92] Ibid. para. 21. [93] Ibid. [94] Ibid. paras. 23–6.
[95] First *Šešelj* Decision, above n. 44, para. 27.

Chamber; offering advice or making suggestions to the accused, in particular on evidential and procedural issues; in the event of abusive conduct by the accused, putting questions to witnesses, in particular sensitive or protected witnesses, on behalf of the accused if so ordered by the Trial Chamber, without depriving the accused of his right to control the content of the examination; and, in exceptional circumstances, taking over the defence from the accused at trial should the Trial Chamber conclude that the Accused is engaging in disruptive conduct or conduct requiring his removal from the courtroom under Rule 80(B).[96]

It is difficult to see how standby counsel is to interact effectively in a complex international criminal law case, with an uncooperative accused who does not recognise the legality of the court and is intent on presenting a political case to the public through the mechanism of a criminal court. If an accused manifests a clear intention to challenge the legitimacy of the court (as Barayagwiza, Šešelj and Milošević expressly have), and further manifests an intention to use the forensic process to highlight their extracurricular goals, then it is unclear how a standby counsel could effectively ensure that the accused receive a full and adequate defence. Is a court meant to interject every time an accused strays or misuses an opportunity to lead or cross-examine a witness and insist that standby counsel take over that process? How is counsel to prepare for that task? If the court's imposition of a standby counsel – as was initially determined in *Šešelj* and *Norman* – is to leave 'absolutely untouched' the 'accused's right to defend himself', it is entirely uncertain how counsel is to operate. He is being asked, as it were, to wear half a hat. It is my assertion that it is more consistent with the objective of a fair trial to give counsel control over the presentation of the defence case so that they may focus on representing the accused's best forensic interests. In fact, this is exactly the outcome of both the *Šešelj* and *Norman* cases. After flirting with the standby counsel representation model in these cases, the conduct of the accused forced the courts to remove entirely the right to self-representation and impose counsel.

(b) The Second *Šešelj* Decision On 21 August 2006, three years after the First *Šešelj* Decision, the new Trial Chamber preparing for trial in the *Šešelj* case determined that the time had come to impose defence counsel, abandoning the more tentative mechanism of standby counsel.[97] The

96 Ibid. para. 30.

97 *Prosecutor v. Šešelj*, 'Decision on Assignment of Counsel', Case No. IT-03-67-PT, 21 August 2006 ('Second *Šešelj* Decision').

Chamber recounted in excruciating detail the litany of repugnant statements by Šešelj in court, in his written submissions and in his publications, as well as his utter lack of respect for the Tribunal and decorum and, more importantly, his efforts to breach witness protections and breach other important rules and orders.[98]

Unlike Milošević, who was far more cunning and cautious in his obstructive behaviour, Šešelj was a clear example of bullish and obstructive behaviour. It was hardly difficult for the Chamber to determine that the trial would have been intolerably interrupted by his unacceptable disrespect, rudeness, and aggressiveness – characteristics he had not even managed to contain in the brief hours he spent in court during the pre-trial preparations for his case. What is surprising is the time it took for the Chamber to impose counsel.

In doing so, the Trial Chamber dealt with the distinctions between the *Šešelj* and *Milošević* cases and why the Appeals Chamber decision in the latter, to the effect that the accused should be left in control of his case, was distinct from Šešelj.[99] The Chamber concluded:

> While it is clear that the conduct of the Accused brings into question his willingness to follow the 'ground rules' of the proceedings and to respect the decorum of the Court, more fundamentally, in the Chamber's view, this behaviour compromises the dignity of the Tribunal and jeopardises the very foundations upon which its proper functioning is based.
>
> . . .
>
> The conduct of the Accused as a whole – obstructionist and disruptive behaviour; deliberate disrespect for the rules; intimidation of, and slanderous comments about, witnesses – leads the Chamber to conclude that there is a strong indication that his self-representation may substantially and persistently obstruct the proper and expeditious conduct of a fair trial.[100]

Of some interest is the legal test the Chamber set itself to determine whether imposition of counsel was warranted in the circumstances. The Chamber stated that it must determine whether the conduct of the accused 'warrants the imposition of restrictions on his right to represent himself in the interests of justice' and, if so whether imposing counsel is

[98] Ibid. Part III. *Šešelj* has published books entitled 'Genocidal Israeli Diplomat Theodor Meron', 'In the Jaws of the Whore Del Ponte', and 'The Lying Hague Homosexual, Geoffrey Nice' (para. 30). He has written to the Tribunal in one submission stating 'you, all you members of the Hague Tribunal Registry, can only accept to suck my cock' (para. 48), amongst many other obscene and improper statements.

[99] Ibid. para. 80.

[100] Ibid. paras. 77, 79.

in the interests of 'a reasonably expeditious trial'.[101] The reliance on the interests of justice is an unfortunately (although no doubt conveniently) nebulous principle, although it is clearly favoured in the consideration of representation issues by international criminal courts and tribunals. A preferable approach is to speak in terms of a fair trial. Although the principle of a fair trial is not wholly concrete, it is more comprehensible and has been considered at some length and detail in international criminal and human rights jurisprudence, such that it provides a more solid basis for assessing the appropriateness of a court's determinations. The interests of justice, on the other hand, tends to get thrown into judicial reasoning when there is an intuitive sense that a proposition is correct but the court has difficulty explaining why.

(c) The First Appeals Chamber *Šešelj* Decision The Appeals Chamber in the *Šešelj* case overturned the Trial Chamber's ruling imposing counsel on the ground that the Trial Chamber had not explicitly warned the accused that his conduct might have the effect of the court removing his right to act in his own defence before actually doing so.[102] The Chamber in its Second Decision had set out *Šešelj*'s extraordinary and grossly inappropriate conduct in painful detail. The Trial Chamber had clearly put the accused on notice of its concern and the possibility that he would not be allowed to appear *pro se*. It had appointed standby counsel in its First Decision with a specific brief to act as *Šešelj*'s assigned lawyer should the accused's behaviour mandate such a course of action. The Appeals Chamber also admitted coming to the question of warning in respect of the removal of the right to self-representation as an issue of first impression.[103] Nonetheless, the ruling was made sending the Trial Chamber's apparently well- reasoned case strategy into disarray.

The Appeals Chamber held that, in reference to Rule 80(B) of the ICTY Rules, a specific warning is required to be given by a Trial Chamber before it takes measures, and those measures are to be specific in nature and in response to obstruction caused by the accused. This approach taken by the Appeals Chamber appears to build a legal principle around a discrete Rule regarding in-court obstructive behaviour,[104] without elucidating in any detail how the provision which concerns a specific type of obstruction

[101] Ibid. para. 72. The latter point of the Chamber is quoted from the *Milošević* Appeals Decision, above n. 40, para. 17.

[102] *Prosecutor v Šešelj*, 'Decision on Appeal Against the Trial Chamber's Decision on Assignment of Counsel', Case No. IT-03-67-AR73.3, 20 October 2006 ('*Šešelj* Appeal Decision').

[103] Ibid., paras. 22–6.

[104] Ibid.

under the ICTY Rules is applied broadly to an accused's right to appear *pro se*. In doing so, the Appeals Chamber in effect elevates the right to elect to self-representation further than it did in the *Milošević* Decision, without providing any premise in legal principle for doing so and apparently without consideration of competing important legal objectives or practical ramifications for doing so in the context of the *Šešelj* case.

(d) The Second Appeals Chamber *Šešelj* Decision The treatment of these issues in the *Šešelj* case was, however, to become more complicated. Following the Appeals Chamber ruling, the Trial Chamber immediately reinstated the terms of the First *Šešelj* Decision (in effect reinstating standby counsel) and it delayed the scheduled commencement of the trial to enable adjustments to the representation regime and its effect on the conduct of the trial to be made.[105] Šešelj objected to standby counsel being reinstated and sought certification to appeal that ruling. The Trial Chamber denied his application on the basis that it did no more than reinstate the position prior to the imposition by the Trial Chamber of counsel on the accused.[106] Following this ruling, Šešelj continued to engage in repetitive and profound acts of obstruction, which drew specific and detailed warnings from the Trial Chamber – presumably in compliance with the warning requirements mandated by the First *Šešelj* Appeal Decision. Šešelj also commenced a hunger strike in response to the Chamber's imposition of standby counsel.[107] The Trial Chamber, again articulating in some detail the accused's obstructive behaviour and its warnings to him, then issued a decision removing Šešelj's right to represent himself and ordering the standby counsel to take over the conduct of his defence,[108] a decision which the Chamber then certified for appeal.[109] The trial then commenced.

The Appeals Chamber subsequently reversed the Trial Chamber on the basis that, following the First *Šešelj* Appeal Decision, it had re-imposed

105 *Prosecutor v Šešelj*, 'Order Concerning Appointment of Standby Counsel and Delayed Commencement of Trial', Case No. IT-03-67-PT, 25 October 2006 ('Decision Reinstating Standby Counsel').

106 For a procedural history of these matters, see *Prosecutor v Šešelj*, 'Decision on Appeal Against the Trial Chamber's Decision (No. 2) on Assignment of Counsel', Case No. IT-03-67-AR73.4, 8 December 2006 ('Second *Šešelj* Appeal Decision'), paras. 5–6.

107 Ibid., para. 8.

108 *Prosecutor v Šešelj*, 'Reasons for Decision (No. 2) on Assignment of Counsel', Case No. IT-03-67-PT, 27 November 2006.

109 *Prosecutor v Šešelj*, 'Decision on Application for Certification to Appeal Order of 25 October 2006', Case No. IT-03-67-PT, 30 November 2006.

standby counsel, although it acknowledged that it was not in fact lawfully seized of that issue on appeal:

> If the Appeals Chamber was to ignore the background to the Impugned Decision and apply the applicable law and the standard of review to the Impugned Decision, it would find no error on the part of the Trial Chamber in ordering the imposition of assigned counsel . . . There is no doubt that in light of the behaviour exhibited by Šešelj that the Trial Chamber was entitled by the terms of the Appeal Decision to impose assigned counsel upon him.[110]

Having declared that the decision which was the actual subject of appeal was lawful, the Appeals Chamber identifies the matter uppermost in its contemplation – the 'collision course' on which the Trial Chamber's ruling re-imposing standby counsel placed Šešelj and itself (most obviously his hunger strike).[111] The Appeals Chamber also acknowledges that Šešelj had not satisfied the formal requirements entitling his appeal on the merits to be heard before it, but seems to intimate that, because he placed himself on a hunger strike, this justified the exceptional measure of the Chamber allowing the appeal to proceed.[112]

In effect, Šešelj ostensibly blackmailed the Appeals Chamber into hearing his appeal and, it would seem, obtaining relief:

> The Appeals Chamber decision to . . . [consider the appeal] . . . should in no way be construed as evidence of the Appeals Chamber rewarding Šešelj's behaviour, rather it is recognising that he does have a right to appeal the Impugned Decision and that resolution of this issue is of utmost importance to Šešelj and to the interests of the Tribunal. It is also recognition of the fact that after 28 days of refusing to take food and medicine, Šešelj's condition is such that he is simply unable to do more to comply with the Practice Direction, albeit due to his own actions.[113]

Rewarding Šešelj for his behaviour is exactly what the Appeals Chamber did. It capitulated to him and the very obstructionist tactics that led the Trial Chamber to impose counsel in the first place. So apparently unconvinced of its own justification is the Appeals Chamber that much of its written reasoning is spent defending the grounds for even considering the

[110] Second *Šešelj* Appeal Decision, para. 20. The Appeals Chamber attempts to justify this endeavour by suggesting that the appeal before it could not be fully understood without contemplation of all the relevant procedural history, but fails to explain why its contemplation of relevant facts that form part of the history of the matter before it give it lawful authority to determine an issue not on appeal. [111] Ibid. [112] Ibid., paras. 13–14.
[113] Ibid., para. 15.

appeal, apologising for not being more explicit in its First Decision about the scope left for the Trial Chamber to exercise its discretion with respect to standby counsel and, finally, stating:

> In light of the decision of the Appeals Chamber, *and in interests of fairness to Šešelj*, the Appeals Chamber nullifies the opening of the proceeding in this case and orders that the trial restart. Due to the current health condition of Šešelj, the Appeals Chamber orders that his trial should not open until such time as he is fully able to participate in the proceeding as a self-represented accused.[114]

Gone – and in one sentence – is the legal foundation articulated in previous decisions on self-representation, including the Appeals Chamber's own precedent in the *Milošević* case that exercise of the right to self-representation and limitation or qualification of that right must be in the *interests of justice*, a proposition that contemplates far broader interests than the mere question of fairness to an accused.

This decision is clearly not in the interests of justice, nor in the interests of ensuring a fair trial – in fact it is likely to render it virtually impossible for the Trial Chamber to be able to deliver such a result, and the ruling renders uncertain when the trial will even be able to start and on what terms. Even were the interests of fairness to the accused the only applicable test justifying the overturning of a sensible and well-founded exercise of trial court discretion, this decision is clearly concerned with the sole aim of persuading an intransigent accused, with an extraordinary history of manipulation and abuse of the court (as well as its officers and its processes), to suspend a dangerous and embarrassing hunger strike, a goal apparently achieved[115] – for the moment.

It is difficult to know whether to treat this decision as an aberration, specific in its findings to the accused and his particular circumstances, or whether this is to set broader precedent for the exercise by a Trial Chamber of its discretion, either to appoint standby counsel or to impose defence counsel on an obstructionist accused. It is difficult to see how an accused in such a trial could be more wilfully obstructive and abusive of a court and the forensic trial process. If applied to its fullest, this decision risks derailing the crucial balance between respect for an apparent right of an

[114] Ibid., para. 29 (emphasis added).

[115] See, ICTY Press Release, RH/MOW/1134e, 8 December 2006: 'Šešelj informed the Tribunal that his decision was made in view of the Appeals Chamber's decision issued today, as well as commitments from the Registry to facilitate many of his requests concerning arrangements for his defence', available <http://www.un.org/icty/pressreal/2006/p1134-e.htm> 10 December 2006.

accused to represent himself in international criminal law and the exercise of discretion by a trial chamber to limit that right where obstruction threatens the fairness of the trial or the interests of justice. The degree to which this and the First Appeal Decision interfere with the Trial Chamber's exercise of discretion is also a disturbing factor. It is hoped that this Decision will be seen in time as itself overstepping the boundary of appropriate appellate interference in the trial court's conduct of its case, violating the Appeals Chamber's own stated test for doing so and, consequently, not be seen as good appellate law. In my view, that is certainly how it should be considered and international criminal courts and tribunals should apply previously established legal principle in dealing with these issues. Until this question is resolved, however, it raises many questions and concerns about how to manage a manipulative and obstructionist accused in the context of a complex international criminal trial.

(e) Self-representation in the *Krajišnik* case The accused Krajišnik, on 24 May 2005, stated his intention to conduct his own defence.[116] The following day, he informed the Trial Chamber during the hearing that his defence team was unable to assist him in establishing the truth and that he had made the decision 'very unwillingly' to represent himself.[117] The Trial Chamber issued a provisional ruling on 26 May 2005 to the effect that representation by counsel would continue but allowed the accused, 'as an exception to the usual regime, to supplement counsel's cross-examination with his own questions'.[118] On 22 July 2005, the Trial Chamber denied the accused's request to represent himself and, on 18 August 2005, issued its written reasons.

The Trial Chamber found that Krajišnik's request to represent himself was equivocal and was essentially driven by a desire on his part to achieve financial and structural improvements to his defence team.[119] The Trial Chamber supported a process of negotiation between the accused, his defence team and the Registry, and noted in its decision that defence resources had increased and the organisation of the defence team had improved since the original application was made.[120]

The Chamber, which was guided strongly by the US case law in its consideration of the issue, held that 'the preliminary inquiry [is] to determine whether the request is unequivocal, informed and intelligent'.[121] It was not

[116] *Prosecutor v. Krajišnik*, 'Reasons for Oral Decision Denying Mr Krajišnik's Request to Proceed Unrepresented by Counsel', Case No. IT-00-39-T, 18 August 2005 ('*Krajišnik* Decision'), para. 1. [117] Ibid., para. 2. [118] Ibid., para. 3. [119] Ibid., para. 10.
[120] Ibid., paras. 12–20. [121] Ibid., para. 3, citing *Williams v. Bartlett*, 44 F 3d 95, 100–1.

persuaded that Krajisnik's request was unequivocal, but furthermore considered it to be 'uninformed – especially as to the financial and practical consequences of such a decision' and 'unintelligent' in the sense that the Accused 'did not have a rational appreciation of the burden of conducting a large criminal case from the confines of the UN detention centre'.[122] The Chamber referred to the dangers involved in the accused cross-examining witnesses on his own behalf, the damage done to his own case, and breaches of protective measures granted witnesses in the brief period in which he did so.[123] In *dicta* relevant to the overall impact of allowing self-representation in complex international criminal trials, the Chamber stated as follows:

> The Chamber should also not fail to remark upon the fact that a criminal case of the present magnitude, which has been experienced as a great strain even by learned defence counsel, would certainly collapse if put into the hands of Mr Krajišnik, who in his limited cross-examination of witnesses between May and July inadvertently revealed details of protected witnesses and was frequently cautioned by the bench for his improper questions and misunderstandings of procedure; and this is to say no more, and no less, than that the Accused does not know, and has no reason to know, how to run a criminal defence case. If his request were honoured, he would end up receiving a very poor defence, which would only serve to bring the international criminal process into disrepute.[124]

Although the application was rejected on the grounds that it was 'equivocal' and 'unintelligent', the Trial Chamber did consider what its decision would have been had the application passed this initial test. The Chamber noted that, pursuant to ICTY case law, 'the assertion of a right to self-representation will succeed or fail depending on the factual context',[125] and that a relevant factor is the potential disruption to proceedings that self-representation may cause. Once a factual assessment is made, the legal determination as to the acceptability of any disruption 'taking into account the general interest in an expeditious trial and the accused's right to self-representation' is then made.[126] The Chamber relied on a line of US cases, which held that the request by an accused to represent himself made after the commencement of trial is less likely to be accepted by a court.[127] It considered the possibility of appointing standby counsel but

[122] *Krajišnik* Decision, above n. 116, para. 8. [123] Ibid. paras. 8, 34. [124] Ibid. para. 34.
[125] Ibid. para. 24. [126] Ibid. para. 31.
[127] See *Zuppo v. Delaware*, 807 A 2d 545 (2002); *Robards v. Rees* (1986) 789 F 2d 12; *US v. Lawrence* (1979) 605 F 2d 1321; *US v. Dunlop* (1978) 577 F 2d 867; *US v. Dougherty* (1972) 473 F 2d 1113; *US v. Denno* (1965) 348 F 2d 12.

considered that a long adjournment would be required and this would not serve the interests of the trial process.[128]

The Trial Chamber concluded that allowing the accused to take over the conduct of his defence would mean considerable disruption to the trial proceedings and, in the context of Krajisnik's case, 'the case would certainly collapse'.[129]

The Supreme Iraqi Criminal Tribunal

The Statute of the Iraqi Special Tribunal was promulgated by an Order of the Coalition Provisional Authority (occupying armed forces) on 10 December 2003,[130] and established the Tribunal as an independent entity made up of Iraqi judges, nominated and appointed by the Governing Council or the Successor Government, after consultation with the Judicial Council.[131] In October 2005, the provisional Statute was revoked and replaced by a Law establishing the Iraqi High Criminal Court,[132] establishing the Supreme Iraqi Criminal Tribunal (SICT)[133] as an ostensibly civil law system.

Article 20 of the original statute contained a guarantee of the right to defend oneself in person or through counsel of one's choosing but the revised rules only stipulate the latter right. The revision (Article 19(4)(d)) was one of a number of changes made when the National Assembly restated the Tribunal's statute, a formality designed to legitimise what had been an American creation under Iraqi law.[134]

128 *Krajišnik* Decision, above n. 116, para. 35. 129 Ibid., para. 34.

130 'Coalition Provisional Authority Order Number 48: Delegation of Authority Regarding an Iraqi Tribunal', CPA/ORD/9 Dec 2003/48 (2003).

131 For information about the Iraqi Special Tribunal, how it is structured and will operate and the revocation of the initial Statute and transition to the Iraqi High Criminal Court (including rebuffing the notion that the tribunal should be international in nature), see generally Michael J. Frank, 'Justice for Iraq, Justice for All' (2004) 57 *Oklahoma Law Review* 303; Michael P. Scharf and Curtis F.J. Doebbler, 'Will Saddam Hussein Get a Fair Trial?' (2005) 37 *Case Western Reserve Journal of International Law* 21 (recorded debate); Human Rights Watch, 'The Former Iraqi Government on Trial: A Human Rights Watch Briefing paper', 16 October 2005, <http://hrw.org/backgrounder/mena/iraq1005/> at 1 October 2006; Diane Marie Amann, ' "The Only Thing Left is Justice": Cherif Bassiouni, Saddam Hussein, and the Quest for Impartiality in International Criminal Law' in David E. Guinn (ed.), *Coming of Age in International Criminal Law: An Intellectual Reflection on the Work of M. Cherif Bassiouni* (forthcoming); Eric Stover, Hanny Megally and Hania Mufti, 'Bremer's 'Gordian Knot': Transitional Justice and the US Occupation of Iraq' (2005) 27 *Human Rights Quarterly* 830, 838–43.

132 Law No, 10 (2005), Law of the Iraqi Higher Criminal Court, 18 October 2005.

133 In Arabic: المحكمة الجنائية العراقية العليا

134 Article 19(4)(d) provides that the accused is entitled to the following minimum guarantee: 'To be tried in his presence, and procure legal counsel of his choosing; to be informed of

When the Iraqi National Assembly first re-promulgated the statute, it was speculated that the defence would file a pre-trial motion asserting that Hussein had a right to represent himself before the court, the argument being that fundamental human rights law as contained in the ICCPR (to which Iraq is a party) required that Hussein be allowed to represent himself despite the express wording of the Statute.[135] However such an argument was never made.

In view of the international jurisprudence on the right to self-representation and the increasing tendency to qualify the right in practice, the removal of the right to self-representation might be viewed as a dramatic and unfortunate move. Scholarly opinion appears to be divided as to whether this is a sensible or regrettable move on the part of the Tribunal.[136] However, the reality is that the SICT is not an international tribunal but rather a civil law criminal court and the mandatory imposition of counsel on accused persons being tried for serious offences is a common feature of civil law criminal systems. The change is therefore hardly surprising.

Practical difficulties of imposing counsel on uncooperative accused

In light of the *Milošević* Decision on Interlocutory Appeal, is it in practice possible to effectuate the imposition of counsel on an uncooperative and manipulative high level accused in an international criminal trial?[137]

his right to ask for legal assistance in case he does not have sufficient means to pay for it; and of his right to receive assistance that allows him to procure legal counsel without financial burden.'

135 M. Scharf in 'Experts Debate the Issues #1, Does Saddam Hussein have a right to represent himself before the Iraqi Special Tribunal like Slobodan Milosevic has done at The Hague?', Case School of Law Grotian Moment, 22 September 2005, http://www.law.case.edu/saddamtrial/entry.asp?entry_id=8 at 1 October 2006.

136 For support for this approach, see Michael P. Scharf and Christopher. M. Rassi, above n. 5. But see William A. Schabas, 'Experts Debate the Issues #1, Does Saddam Hussein have a right to represent himself before the Iraqi Special Tribunal like Slobodan Milosevic has done at The Hague?', Case School of Law Grotian Moment, 22 September 2005, http://www.law.case.edu/saddamtrial/entry.asp?entry_id=8 at 1 October 2006.

137 There is some scholarly opinion that, although the right to self-representation is limited, it may only be so limited in restricted circumstances where more clear and 'traditional' methods of obstruction are employed by an accused: see, e.g., Göran Sluiter, 'Fairness and the Interests of Justice: Illustrative Concepts in the *Milošević* Case' (2005) 3 *Journal of International Criminal Justice* 9, 13. Such a view, however, naively misunderstands the more subtle forms of manipulation that an accused such as Milošević is able to bring to bear on the trial process and, by doing so, threaten seriously its expeditiousness and fairness. Sluiter's view that a very long trial would have had no impact on fairness being attributed

The view accepted by all international criminal courts and tribunals which have dealt with this issue is that there is a right, at international law, to self-representation. Apart from the unlikely view expressed early on in the *Milošević* case that the right is derived from customary international law, the legal basis for this view has never been clearly articulated. Given the wide divergence in the approach taken by the civil and common law systems, it is unlikely that any general principle of international law exists reflecting this right. It may be that the best interpretation of the source for such a proposition lies in a plain reading of the relevant statutory instruments based, as they are, on Article 14(3)(d) of the ICCPR (which itself is clearly reflective of customary international law), which stipulate that there is a right (in some form) to defence in person.

It is equally clear from the international law jurisprudence on this issue, that this right is not absolute. Different courts and tribunals have described differently the basis upon which the right can be limited or qualified, whether in the interests of justice or to help secure a fair (and expeditious) trial, although the factors which lead these courts to their conclusions tend to reflect similar considerations.

An accused has a right to a fair trial or, more properly put, the court has an obligation to see that everything that is reasonable is done to ensure that a fair trial is had by an accused. An argument made by assigned counsel on behalf of Milošević on appeal, but not dealt with by the Appeals Chamber, was that the Trial Chamber gave the fair trial consideration broader meaning than the right of an accused (and only an accused) to a fair trial. In counsel's view, 'the only type of unfairness contemplated by the Statute is unfairness to the Accused'.[138] However, this is inconsistent with the jurisprudence of the international criminal tribunals.[139] A court's

Footnote 137 *(cont.)*
to Milošević ignores the very real potential for a trial to go on for so long that it is unmanageable for all, including the accused, and become unfair. C.f. the radically opposing view of Michael Scharf, 'Self-Representation versus Assignment of Defence Counsel before International Criminal Tribunals' (2006) 4 *Journal of International Criminal Justice* 31, where he opines that the likelihood that former leaders accused will be disruptive coupled with the unique need for complex international criminal trials to be orderly, militate in favour of imposing defence counsel on such accused.

138 *Prosecution v. Milošević*, 'Appeal Against the Trial Chamber's Decision on Assignment of Defence Counsel – Corrigendum', Case No. IT-02-54-AR73.7, 29 September 2004, para. 67.

139 For example, the Appeals Chamber of the ICTY has held that there is a 'responsibility of [a] Trial Chamber to ensure that the trial is fair, and secondly, the right of [an accused] to a fair trial': *Prosecutor v. Prlić et al.* 'Decision on Appeal by Bruno Stojić Against Trial Chamber's Decision on Request for Appointment of Counsel', Case No. IT-04-74-AR73.1, 24 November 2004, para. 21.

duty to ensure that a trial is fair has been interpreted as including concerns which go beyond just those of the accused.[140] The Trial Chamber in the *Milošević* Decision gave a broader application to the right to a fair trial, insisting that the many component parts which make up that right can be either emphasised or set aside if the effect of doing so is to ensure that the trial is fair overall.

Another consideration expressed by international criminal courts and tribunals in dealing with the right to self-representation is the interests of justice. A number of the decisions on representation issues discussed above have stated that where the insistence by an accused on representing himself has the effect of compromising the interests of justice, a court has a duty to qualify or remove the operation of that right so as to ensure that the interests of justice are met.[141]

In the relatively short time span in which modern international criminal law has existed and evolved, a small but coherent body of jurisprudence has emerged which expresses some general principles for the treatment of the issue of self-representation. This jurisprudence establishes that a qualified right to self-representation exists; that there are limits and boundaries to this right, which are considered and applied by the dictates of ensuring a fair trial and/or that the interests of justice are adhered to; in the exercise of this right the dignity of the court must be preserved; there will be different and varied responses taken by courts to ensure these principles are complied with, but the right may be taken away by a court in the proper and proportional exercise of its authority.

Examples of the circumstances in which it is permissible to impose defence counsel on an accused, which can be gleaned from the cases considered above, are: (1) where an accused refuses to participate at all in his trial; (2) where an accused appears with other co-accused and the exercise of his right would impact adversely on a fair trial being had by them; (3) where the accused is being obstructionist, including breaching protective measures orders, acting in flagrant disregard for the rules of the court and otherwise rendering the conduct of proceedings unmanageable;

[140] See, e.g., *Norman* Decision above n. 43, para. 25, in which the Chamber refers to the separate opinion of Judge Reinhardt in the Farhad case, supporting his view that a defendant could not waive his right to a fair trial and that this right implicates not only the interests of the accused but also the institutional interests of the judicial system; and First *Šešelj* Decision above n. 44, para. 21, in which the Tribunal Chamber stated that 'the Tribunal has a legitimate interest in ensuring that the trial proceeds in a timely manner without interruptions, adjournments or disruptions'.

[141] As discussed above, this is the basis upon which the *Norman*, *Šešelj*, and *Barayagwiza* decisions proceeded.

(4) where the accused is medically unfit to conduct his own defence; (5) where the accused seeks to represent himself after the commencement of the trial; (6) where self-representation is elected in an equivocal, uninformed or unintelligent manner, and (7) where allowing an accused to conduct his own defence would unreasonably prolong the trial or threaten its conclusion. These are factual scenarios under which international courts and tribunals have acted to remove or qualify the accused's right to self-representation. The principles set out by those courts clearly indicate that any range of circumstances might trigger a court's duty to interfere with the accused's right, either where the exercise of the right compromises the fairness of the trial or the interests of justice.

The experience of the ICTY in the *Milošević* case is that, where you have an intransigent accused, and one who appears motivated not just by a desire to mount a forensic case but to assert a political position,[142] it is difficult to implement an effective regime to ensure that the trial is fair. The Trial Chamber took some three years to impose counsel. In the few weeks that regime was allowed to operate it was clearly fraught with practical problems, stemming from a reluctance of witnesses to cooperate with assigned counsel and a carefully orchestrated campaign – at least by supporters of the accused but more likely undertaken on his instructions – to obstruct the presentation of evidence in his defence on the basis that his right to represent himself had been taken away.[143] Witnesses persistently refused to attend the trial or answer questions until Milošević had been given back control of his case. This caused considerable concern that the path adopted by the Trial Chamber of imposing counsel might have the

[142] Reference has been made throughout the trial to the accused using the forensic process as a platform to making political speeches See, e.g., *Prosecutor v. Milošević*, Initial Appearance, Case No. IT-02-54-T, 3 July 2001; *Prosecutor v. Milošević*, Status Conference, Case No. IT-02-54-T, 30 October 2001; *Prosecutor v. Milošević*, Hearing, Case No. IT-02-54-T, 10 November 2004, where references made by the Prosecution, T. 33293; *Prosecutor v. Milošević*, Pre-Defence Conference, Case No. IT-02-54-T, 17 June 2004, in which the Chamber made reference to the accused not being permitted to use Defence witnesses to make speeches, T. 32115–16.

[143] See, e.g., *Prosecutor v. Milošević*, Hearing, Case No. IT-02-54-T, 15 September 2004, submissions by court assigned counsel, T. 32858–63; *Prosecutor v. Milošević*, Hearing, Case No. IT-02-54-T, 10 November 2004, submissions by the prosecution, referring to the accused being implicated in the refusal of witnesses to testify in such circumstances: 'I had in mind the question that was asked of the accused by His Honour Judge Bonomy in direct terms on an earlier hearing whether he wanted the witnesses to attend. He declined to give a straight yes to a simple question and gave a coded answer that may easily have been relied upon by witnesses, and I made this quite clear in the Appeals Chamber, as guiding them that they should engage in the obstructive course of conduct that they collectively then pursued.'

effect of there being few defence witnesses willing to testify. The Trial Chamber's regime was, however, given little opportunity to develop, with the Appeals Chamber in effect reversing the Trial Chamber's strategy and returning Milošević to the control of his case.

The surprising decisions by the Appeals Chamber to overturn the imposition by the Trial Chamber of defence counsel on Šešelj twice reveals a considerable reluctance on the part of the appellate court for the ICTY and ICTR to allow Trial Chambers to manage the issue of self-representation on grounds of well-reasoned legal principle and pragmatism, although the consequences of these decisions on broader legal principle remain unclear.

The other alternative path taken by international criminal courts and tribunals to imposing defence counsel is the use of standby counsel. The purpose behind this model appears to be to impact as minimally as possible on an accused's election to represent himself, at the same time as maintaining a lawyer fully versed in the proceedings, able to assist the accused (at his or her request or at the behest of the court) and who is in a position to step in and run the case in the event that the court revokes self-representation for whatever reason. The *Norman* case in the SCSL and the *Šešelj* case before the ICTY initially took this path before finally abandoning their initially diffident position and imposed counsel. The practical effect of the Appeals Chamber decision in the *Milošević* case is probably to have 'downgraded' imposed defence counsel to a standby counsel role. Although the standby counsel model has clearly worked effectively in the US, large and complex international criminal trials present many differences and difficulties, and the transposition of the standby counsel model from domestic to international criminal law appears to have been a more or less pointless, frustrating and expensive exercise – except to the extent that in those cases that employed this model it prepared the practical and theoretical path towards imposed counsel.

Mechanisms have been trialled by courts to ameliorate the effects of self-representation where the exercise of that limited right interferes with the accomplishment of a fair trial, even if it does not entirely vitiate that right. Many different tools were utilised to bolster the accused's representation resources in the *Milošević* case, including allowing for privileged communication with unassigned 'legal associates', to assist the accused outside of the courtroom in the preparation of his cross-examination of prosecution witnesses, and preparations for the presentation of his defence;[144] the provision of significant facilities at the court and United

[144] Second *Milošević* Decision above n. 14, para. 64.

Nations Detention Unit; the creation of a *pro se* legal liaison office to assist Milošević in the administrative aspects of the preparation and conduct of his defence; and, most significantly and innovatively, the development of what I have termed hybrid *amicus*/defence counsel. This latter innovation, which evolved incrementally and apparently without a conscious intent to metamorphose the *amicus curiae* role, presents an interesting alternative for the future conduct of international criminal trials. It has many of the benefits of assigning a standby counsel without evoking the conflictual relationship that has invariably emerged where standby counsel has been used (in international tribunals as in the US). This form of *amicus* can function as a 'friend of the court' with a brief to move as close to acting as counsel for the accused as is feasible and possible. *Amicus* has the protection of the court as its 'friend' and appears less likely (at least in its operation in the *Milošević* case) to offend the accused as much as imposed or standby counsel.

Other representation models are possible. The utilisation of the 'McKenzie friend' model is used in some common law courts, where the accused may be assisted in court by a person (not necessarily legally qualified) who can assist them in organising the presentation of their case.[145] Finally, in common law courts, the trial judge is generally obliged to assist a self-represented accused during the trial process as far as is appropriate.[146]

Many of these scenarios are forms of hybrid representation. Where they are achieved by the cooperation of an accused and within the fair trial structure, they may have a positive effect on the trial process and therefore contribute to best practice of such trials in an imperfect scenario. However, they may also cause confusion and give rise to abuse by manipulative accused and their application and management are clearly complex matters.

Whether a court seeks to implement a paradigm of imposed or standby counsel, in all the international criminal law cases examined there were problems in implementation and effectuation. In circumstances in which

[145] For England and Wales, see *McKenzie v. McKenzie* [1970] 3 All E.R. 1034; *R v. Leicester City Justices and Another ex parte Barrow* [1991] 3 W.L.R. 368; *Izzo v. Philip Ross & Co* [2002] B.P.I.R 310; *Re O (children) and joined cases* [2005] EWCA Civ 759. For Australia, see *Smith v. The Queen* (1985) 159 CLR 532 at 534; (1985) 71 ALR 631; *R v. E J Smith* (1985) 159 CLR 532; *New South Wales Bar Association v. Livesey* [1982] 2 NSWLR 231; *Re B* [1981] 2 NSWLR 372; *Dodd (No 2)* [1985] 2 Qd R 282; *R v. Burke* [1992] 56 A Crim R 242; *Schagen v. R* (1993) 65 A Crim R 500. For New Zealand, see *Mihaka v. Police* [1981] 1 NZLR 54; *R v. Mitchell* (1992) 9 CRNZ 537; *R v. Frederick Hill* [2003] NZCA 4.

[146] See, *e.g.*, P. J. Richardson *et al.* (eds.), *Archbold: Criminal Pleading, Evidence and Practice* (2003) ('Archbold'), 4–41, 4–42.

standby counsel is imposed, it is unclear how it is that counsel is to step in and take over the conduct of the defence where the court determines that this should occur. It is a simple enough exercise to imagine standby counsel making discrete legal submissions; examining or, less controversially, cross-examining witnesses on discrete areas that it can be identified are consistent with the accused's best forensic interests. In light of the Appeals Chamber ruling in the *Milošević* case, the same role was ostensibly played by assigned counsel there. However, the *Milošević* experience suggests that where an accused is truly uncooperative, just how counsel is to step in and conduct an affirmative defence is unclear. In the *Blagojević* case, great courage was shown by counsel, Michael Karnavas, in remaining as an unwanted counsel for an accused who capriciously sought his removal.[147] Although he had a long history of cooperation with and instruction from the accused before they fell out (upon which he was clearly at an advantage in knowing what the accused's lines of defence were), it is an example of how counsel might remain and represent an unwilling and uncooperative accused.[148] What happens, however, if witnesses refuse to cooperate, or the testimony a witness could give is based on the personal knowledge of the accused who will not communicate with, or give instructions to, counsel and he is not in a position to do more than ask a handful of general questions?

The answers to these difficult questions are critical to the future conduct of fair and expeditious international criminal trials. After consideration is given also to crucial issues relating to resources and facilities for an accused in a complex trial of this nature, I will return in the conclusion to consider how these issues might be addressed in future.

Resources and Facilities Available to Milošević

Resource issues are of considerable importance and complexity in international criminal trials of senior level accused. In the *Milošević* case, as

147 See *Prosecution v. Blagojević*, 'Public and Redacted Reasons for Decision on Appeal by Vidoje Blagojevic to Replace his Defense Team', Case No. IT-02-60-AR73.4, 7 November 2003.

148 In contrast, assigned counsel in the *Milošević* case sought desperately to escape their role as imposed counsel after it became apparent that Milošević would not only not cooperate, but that he would call their professional integrity into question: see *Prosecution v. Milošević*, Assigned Counsel's Motion for Withdrawal with Annex A, Case No. IT-02-54, 8 November 2004; *Prosecutor v. Milošević*, Decision on Assigned Counsel's Motion for Withdrawal, Case No. IT-02-54-T, 7 December 2004. The Trial Chamber refused counsel's application.

in a number of other high level cases in which accused have elected to represent themselves, these resource issues have impacted considerably on the conduct of the proceedings. This section considers the effect of these issues on the conduct of the *Milošević* trial and its broader impact on the conduct of complex international criminal trials in a fair and expeditious manner.

The use of amici curiae *in international criminal law*

The role of *amici curiae* in international criminal law

(a) Definition *Amicus curiae* literally means 'friend of the court'. The friend of the court is recognised in many legal systems and increasingly in international proceedings. In such cases, a non-party to the dispute provides the court or tribunal with its 'special perspectives, arguments, or expertise on the dispute, usually in the form of a written *amicus curiae* brief or submission'.[149] While the development and role of *amicus curiae* in national legal systems has a long history, it is not the purpose of this study to analyse the role of *amicus* in these contexts. For the purpose of the critical analysis of this book, I will review the development and use of *amici curiae* in international criminal law proceedings and give considerable attention to the *Milošević* case, where the Trial Chamber developed an innovative representation model out of the traditional *amicus curiae* role.

(b) *Amicus curiae* at the ICTY and ICTR Rule 74 of both the ICTY and ICTR Rules of Procedure and Evidence state: 'A Chamber may, if it considers it desirable for the proper determination of the case, invite or grant leave to a State, organization or person to appear before it and make submissions on any issue specified by the Chamber'. This rule confers on chambers an explicit power to appoint *amici curiae*. Both Tribunals have used this power in a broad range of circumstances relating to substantive and procedural issues. Example includes the deferral proceedings in the *Tadić* case, in which the Federal Republic of Germany appeared as *amicus* and the Federal Republic of Yugoslavia's appearance as *amicus* in the *Erdemović* deferral

[149] *Aguas Argentinas S.A. and Others v. Petition for Transparency and Participation as Amicus Curiae*, International Centre for Settlement of Investment Disputes ('ICSID'), Case No. ARB/03/19, 19 May 2005. See also Lance Bartholomeusz, 'The *Amicus* Curiae before the International Courts and Tribunals', (2005) 5 *Non–State Actors and International Law* 211.

proceedings.[150] The power has also been used in proceedings concerning the failure to execute a warrant;[151] in jurisdictional proceedings concerning whether the ICTY was 'established by law';[152] on questions relating to the protection of victims and witnesses;[153] the ICTY's power to address subpoenas to sovereign States and their high government officials, and the appropriate remedies for non-compliance;[154] evidence issues related to sexual

[150] See Rodney Dixon, Aga Khan, and Richard May (eds.), *Archbold International Criminal Courts: Practice, Procedure and Evidence* (2003), 379–84; Ascensio Hervé, 'L'*amicus curiae* devant les juridictions internationals', (2001) 105 *Revue générale de droit international public*, 4; *Prosecutor v. Tadić*, 'In the Matter of a Proposal for a Formal Request for Deferral to the Competence of the International Tribunal Decision of the Trial Chamber on the Application by the Prosecutor for a Formal Request for Deferral to the Competence of the International Criminal Tribunal for the Former Yugoslavia in the Matter of Dusko Tadic (Pursuant to Rules 9 and 10 of the Rules of Procedure and Evidence)', Case No. IT-94-1-D, 8 November 1994; *Prosecutor v. Erdemović*, 'In the Matter of a Proposal for a Formal Request for Deferral to the Competence of the International Tribunal Addressed to the Federal Republic of Yugoslavia in the Matter of Drazen Erdemović', Case No. IT-96-22-D, 29 May 1996; *Prosecutor v. Mladić and Stanišić*, 'In the Matter of a Proposal for a Formal Request for Deferral to the Competence of the Tribunal Addressed to the Republic of Bosnia and Herzegovina in Respect of Radovan Karadžic', Case No. IT-95-5-D, 16 May 1995.

[151] The ICTY has permitted some *amicus* participation in Rule 61 proceedings For example, in Rule 61 proceedings concerning Karadžić and Mladić, the Tribunal invited to the hearing a Special Rapporteur of the UN Commission on Human Rights and a member of the Commission of Experts established by Security Council Resolution 780 (1992): *Prosecutor v. Karadžić and Mladić*, 'Review of the indictments pursuant to Rule 61 of the Rules of Procedure and Evidence', Case Nos IT-95-5-R61; IT-95-18-R61, 16 July 1996, para. 2. In the same proceedings, however, permission to appear as *amicus* was refused to the Republic of Croatia and Human Rights Watch: see *Third Annual Report*, UN Doc. No. A/51/292, 16 August 1996, para. 65.

[152] In the *Tadić* case, the US Government successfully intervened in relation to this important question of general international law on the basis of 'its special interest and knowledge as a Permanent Member of the UN Security Council and its substantial involvement in the adoption of the Statute of the Tribunal': see Rodney Dixon, Aga Khan and Richard May (eds.), above n. 150, 698.

[153] Professor Christine Chinkin was permitted to file an *amicus* brief for the purposes of the preliminary status conference relating to the appropriate principles in international criminal proceedings concerning witness confidentiality and witness anonymity: *Prosecutor v. Tadić*, 'Decision on the Prosecutor's Motion Requesting Protective Measures for Victims and Witnesses', Case No. IT-94-1, 10 August 1995, para. 10.

[154] The Trial Chamber invited requests to participate as *amicus curiae* and specified the questions to be addressed. It received a number of requests from individuals, mainly distinguished international law professors, and some NGOs such as Juristes sans Frontières and Lawyers Committee for Human Rights. The Trial Chamber granted leave to 13 applicants to make written submissions, amongst whom seven were allowed to participate in the hearing: see, *Prosecutor v. Blaskić*, 'Decision on the Objection of the Republic of Croatia to the Issuance of Subpoenae Duces Tecum', Case No. IT-95-14, 18 July 1997, paras 7, 8, 10 and 12. On appeal, the Appeals Chamber extended a similar invitation for *amici* to

violence trials,[155] and the question of whether to compel testimony by war correspondents before a war crimes tribunal.[156] The ICTR has even permitted the Belgian Government to intervene as *amicus* on the scope of Common Article 3 of the Geneva Conventions and Additional Protocol II.[157] It has also permitted *amicus* submissions on the exercise of prosecutorial discretion in respect of sexual offence charges not pleaded in the *Akayesu* case, which had the unusual effect of causing the prosecution to seek amendment of its indictment *during the trial* to reflect the concerns set out in the brief.[158]

ICTY practice suggests that requests to participate will not be granted where a chamber considers that they will not be useful. For example, in the *Tadić* case, an organisation called Courtroom Television Network sought leave to oppose a Defence motion to curtail press access to the forthcoming trial. The Chamber rejected the request on the basis that the Network's views would not contribute sufficiently to the issue in question.[159]

While the distinction in the role between a party and *amicus curiae* has not always been clear in practice in the ICTY, the ICTR distinguished

Footnote 154 *(cont.)*

participate, to which five States responded with *amicus curiae* briefs: see, *Prosecutor v. Blaskić*, 'Judgement on the Request of the Republic of Croatia for Review of the Decision of Trial Chamber II of 18 July 1997', Case No. IT-95-14, 29 October 1997, para. 17. For more details about participation in these proceedings, see e.g, Juristes sans Frontières, 'Juristes sans Frontières, Le Tribunal pénal international de La Haye: le droit l'épreuve de la "purification ethnique"' (2000), 235–77.

155 In the Furundžija case, the Trial Chamber accepted an *amicus* brief from a coalition of women's groups about the credibility of a rape victim's evidence as witness and about appropriate protective measures for the witness Proceedings had been re-opened because of the Prosecutor's late disclosure of evidence that, after being raped, the witness had received medical, psychological or psychiatric treatment or counselling: see *Prosecutor v Furundžija*, 'Judgment', Case No. IT-95-17/1, 10 December 1998, paras. 35, 107.

156 In the *Brđanin* case, the Appeals Chamber permitted written and oral *amicus* participation on behalf of 34 media companies and journalists' associations.

157 *Prosecutor v. Semanza*, 'Decision on the Kingdom of Belgium's Application to File an *Amicus Curiae* Brief and on the Defence Application to Strike the Observations of the Kingdom of Belgium Concerning the Preliminary Response by the Defence', Case No. ICTR-97-20-T, 9 February 2001, para. 10. Belgium complained that the ICTR had interpreted these provisions too restrictively.

158 In the ICTR *Akayesu* case, the accused had not initially been charged with crimes of rape or other sexual violence. During the trial evidence emerged about the accused's prominent role in mass rape in Rwanda. Subsequently a coalition of international and Rwandan NGOs concerned with international human rights and women's issues were granted leave to submit an *amicus* brief that urged the prosecutor to amend the indictment to bring charges of rape and sexual violence against the accused. Following acceptance of the brief, the Prosecutor did amend the indictment: *Prosecutor v. Akayesu*, Case No. ICTR-96-4-T.

159 *Prosecutor v. Tadić*, 'Order Denying Leave to Appear *Amicus Curiae*', Case No. IT-94-I-T, 3 May 1996.

clearly between the two when it held that an *amicus* could not present witness evidence – this could be done only through the prosecution or the defence.[160] The issue of the impartiality of an *amicus* arose in the *Bagosora* case. The defence had argued that the Belgian Government's appearance to make submissions on questions of law 'would create an unacceptable disequilibrium in the proceedings in favour of the Prosecutor, as the Belgian Government could not be considered a neutral party'. The Trial Chamber held that 'the general definition of *amicus curiae* does not call for impartiality on the part of the filing party. Rather it takes into consideration that such briefs are filed by an entity, not party to the case, but one with strong interests in or views on the subject matter before the court'.[161]

(c) *Amicus curiae* in the Special Court for Sierra Leone Rule 74 of the SCSL Rules of Procedure and Evidence is identical to the *amicus* provision in the ICTY and ICTR Rules.

The SCSL has used this rule in proceedings involving Charles Taylor, the former President of Liberia. Taylor applied to the SCSL to quash the Court's indictment against him and to set aside the warrant for his arrest on the grounds that he was immune from any exercise of the Court's jurisdiction.[162] In considering the application, the Court invited Professors Diane Orentlicher and Philippe Sands to make written and oral submissions as *amici curiae*. Philippe Sands made submissions about a head of state's immunity from indictments of international or national courts; on whether the SCSL was an international court; on whether it was lawful for the SCSL to issue the indictment and circulate the arrest warrant while Taylor was a serving head of State, and on the effect of Taylor's subsequent status as a former head of State. Professor Orentlicher addressed two questions: whether the indictment was invalid because it violated the procedural immunities accorded serving heads of State under international law, and whether Taylor had substantive immunity as a former head of state from prosecution for the specific crimes charged. The Court referred in detail to the briefs and explicitly adopted Sands's conclusions that the Court was an international court 'with all that implies for the question of immunity of a serving head of State'. The African Bar Association also submitted an *amicus* brief late in

160 *Prosecutor v. Bagosora*, 'Decision on the *Amicus Curiae* Application by the Government of the Kingdom of Belgium', Case No. ICTR-96-7-T, 6 June 1998. See also Lance Bartholomeusz, above n. 149, 249–51.

161 Ibid.

162 *Prosecutor v. Taylor*, 'Decision on Immunity from Jurisdiction', Case No. SCSL-2003-01-I, 31 May 2004.

the proceedings, which the Court accepted, but in its judgement only referred briefly to its contents.[163]

(d) *Amicus curiae* in the International Criminal Court The ICC's Rules of Procedure and Evidence explicitly provide for the use of *amici curiae* at trial and on appeal.[164] Rule 103 ('*Amicus curiae* and other forms of submission') provides:

1. At any stage of the proceedings, a Chamber may, if it considers it desirable for the proper determination of the case, invite or grant leave to a State, organization or person to submit, in writing or orally, any observation on any issue that the Chamber deems appropriate.
2. The Prosecutor and the defence shall have the opportunity to respond to the observations submitted under sub-rule 1.
3. A written observation submitted under sub-rule 1 shall be filed with the Registrar, who shall provide copies to the Prosecutor and the defence. The Chamber shall determine what time limits shall apply to the filing of such observations.

Rule 103 is substantially similar to Rule 74 of the ICTY, ICTR, and SCSL Rules, although it emphasises that *amicus* participation may be appropriate at any stage of the proceedings. The Rule grants chambers a broad discretionary power either to invite or, in the case of spontaneous submissions, to grant leave to, *amici curiae* to submit their observations. Competence to submit observations is not limited: 'States, organizations and persons' may be invited or may apply for leave to submit observations. The term 'organizations' is not qualified, clearly leaving the door open for the involvement of non-governmental organisations, mixed-membership organisations, and public intergovernmental organisations. The term 'persons' is also not qualified by either the adjectives 'natural' or 'legal', leaving it to the Court to invite or accept submissions from individuals and corporations or other legal persons. The only criterion for inviting or granting leave to submit observations is whether the Court considers it 'desirable for the proper determination of the case'. The range of issues upon which observations may be invited or accepted can be legal or factual and appears to be entirely within a Chamber's discretion. The prosecution and defence have a right to respond to the observations.[165]

[163] See Lance Bartholomeusz, above n. 149, 253–4.

[164] Rules of Procedure and Evidence, Official Records of the Assembly of the States Parties, 1st session, 3–10 September 2002, Doc. No. ICC ASP/1/3 (part II-A), 9 September 2002.

[165] See, Lance Bartholomeusz, above n. 149, 242.

(e) Conclusion Although the use of *amici curiae* and the subject-matter on which they may brief differ in the experience of international criminal tribunals, the nature of their involvement in the trial or appeal process is generally consistent with the traditional employment of *amici curiae* in domestic legal systems as friends of the court. As will be seen, the *amicus* role was greatly expanded upon in the *Milošević* case.

Role of *amici curiae* in the *Milošević* case

Early on in the trial, while the Trial Chamber upheld Milošević's entitlement to self-representation it held that, in light of that entitlement and its duty to ensure that the trial is fair and that the rights of the accused are fully respected, the registrar should appoint *amici curiae* to assist it in the proper determination of the case.[166] The Trial Chamber stressed that the role of the *amicus curiae* would not be to represent the accused, but to assist the court by (1) making submissions properly open to Milošević by way of preliminary or other pre-trial motion; (2) making any submissions or objections to evidence properly open to him during the trial proceedings and cross-examining witnesses as appropriate; (3) drawing to the attention of the Trial Chamber any exculpatory or mitigating evidence on Milošević's behalf, and (4) acting 'in any other way which designated counsel considers appropriate in order to secure a fair trial'.[167] The registrar complied with the Chamber's order by appointing Steven Kay QC, Branislav Tapušković, and Mischa Vladimiroff as *amici curiae* in the case.[168]

The Trial Chamber early on evinced an approach to broadening the role normally attributed to *amicus curiae.* On 23 November 2001, the Trial Chamber ordered the three *amici* to make submissions or objections on the evidence presented which would be properly open to Milošević and reiterated that they were to act 'in any other way they consider appropriate in order to secure a fair trial'.[169] In an unusual twist in the trial, on 10 October 2002, Mr. Vladmiroff's appointment as *amicus curiae* was terminated as a result of media interviews in which he commented on the

166 *Prosecutor v. Milošević*, Status Conference, Case No. IT-99-37-PT, Transcript, 15-18, 30 August 2001. 167 Ibid.

168 *Prosecutor v. Milošević*, 'Decision by the Registrar', Case No. IT-99-37-PT, 6 September 2001.

169 *Prosecutor v. Milošević*, 'Order Inviting Designation of *Amicus Curiae*', Case No. IT-01-51-PT, 23 November 2001. The Registrar responded by formally appointing the three *amici* already identified in his Decision of 6 September: *Prosecutor v. Milošević*, 'Decision by the Registrar', Case No. IT-01-51-PT, 27 November 2001.

case and expressed views as to the outcome of the trial.[170] Soon thereafter, the Trial Chamber appointed Timothy McCormack as *amicus curiae* dealing in particular with international law issues.[171] Over the course of the trial, the *amici curiae* were invited to brief the Chamber, or requested the Chamber for permission to brief it, on a number of areas.[172]

In an important step in the developing role of *amicus* in the *Milošević* case, on 27 June 2003, the *amici curiae* requested clarification from the Chamber on their role in relation to motions under Rule 98*bis*(A) for a judgement of acquittal at the conclusion of the prosecution case, as well as their engagement and role – if any – during the defence case. The Trial

[170] *Prosecutor v. Milošević*, 'Decision Concerning an *Amicus Curiae*', Case No. IT-02-54-T, 10 October 2002.

[171] *Prosecutor v. Milošević*, 'Order Appointing *Amicus Curiae*', Case No. IT-02-54-T, 22 November 2002.

[172] On 11 January 2002, the *amici curiae* were invited by the Chamber to draw to its attention any defences, such as self-defence, which may be open to Milošević. They were also invited to make submissions as to the relevance, if any, of the NATO air campaign in Kosovo (*Prosecutor v. Milošević*, 'Order Concerning *Amici Curiae*', Case No. IT-99-37-PT, 11 January 2002). The Trial Chamber ordered Professor McCormack to prepare written submissions on self-defence as it arose in the Kosovo part of the case, including an analysis of the applicable law, the history and growth of this form of defence, and its status in customary international law: *Prosecutor v. Milošević*, 'Order to an *Amicus* to Prepare Written Submissions', Case No. IT-02-54-T, 11 December 2002. On 21 July 2003, the Trial Chamber extended this brief, ordering Professor McCormack to prepare written submissions on self-defence as it arose in the Croatia and Bosnia parts of the case: *Prosecutor v. Milošević*, 'Order to an *Amicus* to Prepare Written Submissions', Case No. IT-02-54-T, 21 July 2003. Much later, on 1 July 2005, the Trial Chamber issued an order instructing him to make written submissions on self-defence as it arose during evidence led in the defence case: *Prosecutor v. Milošević*, 'Order to *Amicus Curiae* to Prepare Written Submissions', Case No. IT-02-54-T, 1 July 2005. On 25 April 2005, Professor McCormack requested permission to make written submissions on the legal test to be applied for criminal responsibility under Article 7(1) of the Statute and in particular the joint criminal enterprise and the legal test to be applied for criminal responsibility under Article 7(3) of the Statute: *Prosecutor v. Milošević*, '*Amicus Curiae* Observations *Proprio Motu* on the Desirability of Submissions on the Alternative Bases of Individual Criminal Responsibility Alleged in the Case and on the Issue of Trials *in Absentia*', Case No. IT-02-54-T, 25 April 2005. On 26 October 2004, the Trial Chamber had denied a similar request: *Prosecutor v. Milošević*, 'Order on *Amici Curiae* Observations on Relevant Issues of International Criminal Law', Case No. IT-02-54-T, 26 October 2004. On 1 July 2005, having received the submissions by the assigned counsel and the prosecution, the Trial Chamber granted the *amicus curiae*'s request and ordered him to make written submissions on these matters: *Prosecutor v. Milošević*, 'Order on *Amicus Curiae* Observations *Proprio Motu* on the Desirability of Submissions on the Alternative Bases of Individual Criminal Responsibility Alleged in the Case and on the Issue of Trials *in Absentia*', Case No. IT-02-54-T, 1 July 2005. Regrettably, the death of Milošević meant that these briefs were never concluded and filed in the case.

Chamber responded by ordering the *amici* to file a motion under Rule 98*bis*, if they deemed fit.[173]

On 6 October 2003, the Trial Chamber issued an order giving further instructions to the *amici curiae*, authorising them to receive such information as the accused may provide to them and to act in any way to protect and further the accused's interests.[174] This was an important order, as it extended the role of the *amici* well beyond any traditional role normally played by them. It ostensibly encouraged the development of their role into a form of *de facto* defence counsel. Although the Chamber did not explain the motivation, reasonings, or limits of its order, it is apparent that attempts were being made to support Milošević as much as possible in the conduct of his case. It is possible the Chamber wished to encourage the accused to make use of the services of *amici curiae* but knew that forcing them upon him would create vehement opposition. This order was made well before the imposition of defence counsel upon the accused but appears to be an early indication that the Chamber was concerned that the level of in-court and out-of-court legal assistance Milošević was receiving might be insufficient.

The Trial Chamber never expressly articulated its expansion of the role of *amici curiae* in the context of the *Milošević* trial, but it certainly encouraged such a role that, after almost two years of trial, was to be tested on appeal. The Trial Chamber had granted a request by the *amici curiae* to certify an interlocutory appeal of the Chamber's decision granting the accused three months in which to prepare his defence, some twenty-one months less than Milošević had requested.[175] The *amici curiae* sought to appeal the decision. The central question considered by the Appeals Chamber was whether the appeal had been properly brought by the *amici curiae*, when Rule 73 entitled only 'a party' to bring an appeal, a definition that did not include reference to *amicus curiae*. The Appeals Chamber held that 'the *Amici* do not act as representatives of the Accused at trial, but solely as assistants to the Trial Chamber' and they could not therefore be

[173] *Prosecutor v. Milošević*, 'Order on *Amici Curiae* Request Concerning the Manner of Their Future Engagement and Procedural Directions Under Rule 98 *bis*', Case No. IT-02-54-T, 27 June 2003. It also noted that the appointment of Mr. Tapušković would end at the conclusion of the prosecution case and that Ms. Gillian Higgins (who had worked as a legal assistant to Steven Kay) would be appointed as his replacement.

[174] *Prosecutor v. Milošević*, 'Order of Further Instruction to the *Amici Curiae*', Case No. IT-02-54-T, 6 October 2003.

[175] *Prosecutor v. Milošević*, 'Decision Granting Request by the *Amici Curiae* for Certification of Appeal Against a Decision of the Trial Chamber', Case No. IT-02–54-T, 25 September 2003.

considered 'a party'.[176] However, it went on to hold that, in view of the 'identity of interests between the *Amici* and the Accused with respect to the issue presented in this appeal' and the alignment between the arguments of the *amici curiae* and the accused's oral statements during argument on the issue, Milošević's interests were not infringed and the Appeals Chamber decided to consider the appeal on its merits.[177] Judge Shahabuddeen dissented, arguing that the appeal should have been dismissed on the basis that an *amicus curiae* was not a party and therefore not entitled to use Rule 73 to bring an interlocutory appeal.[178] However, it appears that – despite Judge Shahabuddeen's dissent – the Appeals Chamber tacitly supported the expanded role developed by the Chamber for *amici curiae* in the *Milošević* trial.[179]

Actual assistance provided to the accused by the *amici curiae*

It can therefore be seen that the nature and role of *amici curiae* in the *Milošević* trial differed from the traditional concept of an *amicus curiae.* Almost immediately upon the *amici curiae* being assigned in the case they assisted the accused in many respects, acting more as an uninstructed *de facto* defence counsel. For example, on 19 October 2001, they submitted a brief in support of the accused's challenge to jurisdiction, making the additional argument that the International Court of Justice should be called upon to determine whether or not the Tribunal had jurisdiction to try Milošević.[180]

On 20 February 2002, *amici curiae* filed a brief in response to the prosecution's application to tender a large number (123) of Rule 92*bis* witness statements (testimony in written form). The *amici curiae* expressed concern about the hearsay evidence contained in the statements as well as the substantive content of the evidence relating to alleged crimes, and argued that the accused be permitted to cross-examine these witnesses.[181]

[176] See *Prosecutor v. Milošević*, 'Decision on the Interlocutory Appeal by the *Amici Curiae* Against the Trial Chamber Order Concerning the Presentation and Preparation of the Defence Case', Case No. IT-02-54-AR73.6, 20 January 2004, para. 4. [177] Ibid. para. 5.

[178] Ibid., Separate Opinion of Judge Shahabuddeen.

[179] On 5 February 2004, the Trial Chamber referred to the ruling of the Appeals Chamber as authority for the position that the *amici curiae* had standing and thus could present a motion for judgement of acquittal under Rule 98 *bis*, a position that was not challenged: *Prosecutor v. Milošević*, 'Decision on Prosecution's Motion Under Rule 73 (A) for a Ruling on the Competence of the *Amici Curiae* to Present a Motion for Judgement of Acquittal Under Rule 98 *bis*', Case No. IT-02-54-T, 5 February 2004.

[180] *Prosecutor v. Milošević*, '*Amici Curiae* Brief on Jurisdiction', Case No. IT-99-37-PT, 19 October 2001.

[181] *Prosecutor v. Milošević*, '*Amici Curiae* Brief on Rule 92 *bis* Procedure', Case No. IT-02-54-T, 20 February 2002.

Furthermore, on 6 March 2002, they filed a brief on the provision of adequate facilities to allow the accused to prepare his defence.[182]

On 26 April 2002, *amici curiae* responded to a prosecution motion which sought a variation of their role to curtail cross-examination of witnesses by them on issues of fact.[183] The *amici* argued that the issue of cross-examination of witnesses should be dealt with by the Trial Chamber on a case-by-case basis. On 18 November 2002, the *amici curiae* also filed observations on the imposition of defence counsel on the accused and argued that counsel should not be imposed on him, a matter taken up in detail later in this chapter.[184] On 27 September 2003, *amici curiae* also filed submissions in response to the order of the Trial Chamber concerning the implications of the accused's health.[185]

Of greatest significance, and evidencing just how far the *amici* had travelled in their role as *de facto* defence counsel, in March 2004 the *amici curiae* filed a motion for judgement of acquittal pursuant to Rule 98*bis*, thereby truly advocating on Milošević's behalf his acquittal of certain charges against him.[186] While a host of other submissions made show just how aggressively *amici curiae* took their role as one more and more aligned to the accused and his legal interests (and as encouraged by the Chamber),[187] the act of filing a judgement of acquittal application on

[182] *Prosecutor v. Milošević*, 'Brief on the Provision of Adequate Facilities to Allow the Accused to Defend Himself', Case No. IT-02-54-T, 5 March 2002. They argued that the administrative and/or security-related issues associated with Milošević's detention must not erode the minimum guarantees available to him in terms of the conduct of his own defence.

[183] *Prosecutor v. Milošević*, 'Response by the *Amici Curiae* to Prosecution's Motion for Variation of an Order of the Trial Chamber', Case No. IT-02-54-T, 26 April 2002.

[184] *Prosecutor v. Milošević*, 'Observations by the *Amici Curiae* on the Imposition of Defence Counsel on the Accused', Case No. IT-02-54-T, 18 November 2002.

[185] *Prosecutor v. Milošević*, '*Amici Curiae* Submissions in Response to the Order of the Trial Chamber Concerning the Implications of the Accused's Health dated 24 September 2003', Case No. IT-02-54-T, 27 September 2003.

[186] *Prosecutor v. Milošević*, '*Amici Curiae* Motion for Judgement of Acquittal Pursuant to Rule 98*bis*', Case No. IT-02-54-T, 3 March 2004.

[187] See e.g., *Prosecutor v. Milošević*, '*Amicus Curiae* Submissions on Self-Defence Arising in the Latter Stages of the Prosecution Case', Case No. IT-02-54-T, 8 July 2004; *Prosecutor v. Milošević*, '*Amici Curiae* Motion in Relation to the Accused's Disclosure Obligations and Request for Additional Time', Case No. IT-02-54-T, 16 July 2004; *Prosecutor v. Milošević*, '*Amici Curiae* Submissions on the Trial Chamber's Further Order on Future Conduct of the Trial Relating to Severance of One or More Indictments Dated 21 July 2004', Case No. IT-02-54-T, 27 July 2004; *Prosecutor v. Milošević*, '*Amici Curiae* Submissions on the Trial Chamber's Further Order on Future Conduct of the Trial Relating to Severance of One or More Indictments Dated 21 July 2004', Case No. IT-02-54-T, 27 July 2004; *Prosecutor v. Milošević*, '*Amicus Curiae* Observations *Proprio Motu* on Relevant Issues of International Law', Case No. IT-02-54-T, 25 August 2004; *Prosecutor v. Milošević*, '*Amicus Curiae*

his behalf was of greatest significance. The application succeeded in reducing the number of allegations against Milošević by over one thousand, although it did not cause a reduction in any of the sixty-six counts against him.

The future for the innovative use of *amicus curiae* in complex international criminal trials

This formulation and development of the role of *amicus* created, incrementally, a case management methodology for self-represented accused in complex international criminal trials which may have currency for future trials of this nature. By taking the traditional *amicus curiae* role and developing it into a hybrid *amicus*/defence counsel, the Chamber created a way of supporting the accused in the preparation and (particularly) representation of his or her case, while maintaining the basic characteristics of self-representation. This was particularly important in the *Milošević* case, but will be equally important with other high level accused in similar circumstances. The reason for this is, in part, the particular personality of such accused, which are characterised by a manipulative approach to the trial process. As can be seen from the *Milošević* trial, but also other such trials where issues of self-representation have arisen, the personality and capacity for mischief of such accused creates extraordinary case management complexities. The hybrid *amicus*/defence counsel role is innovative but it is also controversial. While such use of *amicus curiae* has not been considered in any detail in the literature, it has been subject to some scholarly criticism.[188] For example, Zappalà argues that the solution 'is not entirely persuasive', focusing on a purist analysis of the role of *amicus curiae* in an adversarial criminal trial structure.[189] Zappalà's concerns are (1) that the judges should need no assistance in ensuring a fair trial, one of the grounds upon which the Chamber decided to appoint an *amicus*; (2) the Chamber's request to the Registrar to appoint an *amicus* was considered ambiguous because this is the procedure normally reserved for the assignment of defence counsel, and (3) adversarial criminal trials consist of a debate

Footnote 187 *(cont.)*
Observations *Proprio Motu* on the Desirability of Submissions on the Alternative Bases of Individual Criminal Responsibility Alleged in the Case and on the Issue of Trials *in Absentia*', Case No. IT-02-54-T, 25 April 2005.

[188] See *e.g.*, Jarinde Temminck Tuinstra, 'Assisting the Accused to Represent Himself: Appointment of *Amici Curiae* as the Most Appropriate option' (2006) 4 *Journal of International Criminal Justice* 47.

[189] Zappalà, above n. 7, 63–4.

between two parties before an impartial arbiter, and an *amicus* cannot properly be considered a 'party'.[190]

However, good case management requires innovation. While international criminal tribunals are ostensibly adversarial in nature, there are strong overlays of the civil law system and they represent, importantly, a *sui generis* system of law, the interpretation and definition of which is not undertaken within the confines of the common law adversarial model of criminal justice. The concerns expressed by Zappalà would be well placed in such a context. However, in the context of complex international criminal trials, this hybrid *amicus*/defence counsel appears to be a more appropriate model. One issue that does trouble the development of such a practice is a concern that it may encourage intransigence in the approach of high level and manipulative accused to the trial process. A criticism of the *Milošević* Trial Chamber was that it allowed Milošević to represent himself at all let alone for such a long period. One conclusion which flows from my contention about how to deal with self-representation issues in these trials is that this use of *amicus curiae* is counterproductive, because it is preferable for a court to exercise greater restriction on accused who wish to represent themselves rather than expending resources to create what might be viewed as a façade for the proceedings to continue while bolstering the defence process.[191] Whether the development of the *amicus* role contributes to best practice in the conduct of such trials depends at least in part on a consideration of the prevailing circumstances in each case. As with all procedural issues in complex international criminal trials, it is difficult to formulate a hard and fast principle which can be applied appropriately in every case. This is particularly so when complexities and their solutions are in such early development.

However, it is clear that the hybrid *amicus*/defence counsel model was an important aspect of the Trial Chamber's management of the *Milošević* trial – particularly in circumstances where the Chamber had upheld the accused's right to represent himself. The complexity of international criminal trials of senior officials appears to justify the expansion of procedural law to service the greater rubric of a fair and expeditious trial.

190 Ibid. Zappalà himself acknowledges that some scholars, including Schabas would disagree that an *amicus* cannot be considered a party: see William A. Schabas, 'Article 67', in Otto Triffterer (ed.), *Commentary on the Rome Statute of the International Criminal Court* (1999), 857.

191 This would no doubt be a logical extrapolation of the position taken by Scharf and Rassi, 'Rogue Leaders'.

The provision of 'legal associates' in the Milošević *trial*

Another step taken by the Trial Chamber in the *Milošević* case to ensure adequate resources for the accused to prepare his case concerned the acceptance of legal assistance to Milošević which fell outside generally accepted practice in the Tribunal's management of legal counsel.[192] Early on in the trial, the Chamber realised that the Accused, if he were to represent himself, needed at least to have access to lawyers in whom he had trust and with whom he could communicate in a privileged manner. Milošević was clearly receiving some assistance from Serbia but was confronting defending himself against an enormous trial without material legal assistance in The Hague.

On 15 November 2001, the Trial Chamber issued an order noting that Milošević had requested the Registry to permit him to meet with lawyers Ramsey Clark and John Livingston and ordered that the two men be deemed to be 'legal advisors' to the Accused.[193] The Trial Chamber also ordered that Milošević be entitled to communicate fully and without restraint with them in accordance with Rule 67 of the ICTY Rules of Detention.[194]

During a hearing on 10 April 2002, Milošević identified Zdenko Tomanović and Dragoslav Ognjanović (both lawyers), as associates with whom he wished to communicate.[195] In an Order of 16 April 2002, the Trial Chamber noted that the accused was defending himself in person and that he had indicated that he did not intend to appoint counsel. The Chamber held that it would be in the interests of a fair trial for Milošević to meet and be able to communicate freely with persons for legal advice, and to be able to discuss and supply them with copies of documents subject to the Trial Chamber imposing protective orders. It consequently granted Milošević privileged communication with Mr. Tomanović and Mr. Ognjanović as

[192] For the procedure required for assignment of legal counsel at the ICTY, see Rules 44–6 of the ICTY Rules; 'Code of Professional Conduct for Counsel Appearing Before the International Tribunal', IT/125 Rev. 1, 12 July 2002; 'Directive on the Assignment of Defence Counsel', IT/73 Rev. 8, 15 December 2000. See also, Michael Bohlander, 'The Defence', in Gideon Boas and William A. Schabas, *International Criminal Law Developments in the Case Law of the ICTY* (2003), 35; Michaels Greaves, 'The Right to Counsel Before the ICTY and the ICTR for Indigent Suspects: An Unfettered Right?', in Richard May et al. (eds), *Essays on ICTY Procedure and Evidence in Honour of Gabrielle Kirk McDonald* (2001), 177.

[193] *Prosecutor v. Milošević*, 'Order', Case No. IT-99-37-PT and IT-01-50-PT, 15 November 2001.

[194] 'Rules Governing the Detention of Persons Awaiting Trial or Appeal Before the Tribunal or Otherwise Detained on the Authority of the Tribunal', IT/38/Rev.9, 21 July 2005 ('Rules of Detention').

[195] *Prosecutor v. Milošević*, Hearing, 10 April 2002, Transcript, T. 2797.

'legal associates'.[196] The Trial Chamber stated in its Order that the accused 'shall be entitled to communicate fully and without restraint' with the two named associates and that 'all correspondence and communications between them and the accused shall be privileged'. On 23 October 2003, the Trial Chamber issued an order appointing Branko Rakić as a third legal associate to Milošević.[197]

No clear definition of the role of legal associates was ever given by the Trial Chamber. There is also little concrete evidence of what these legal associates actually did in the trial. On 3 December 2004, the Trial Chamber issued an order refusing Milošević's application to add four witnesses.[198] According to this order, the application was based on a confidential memorandum by the *pro se* legal liaison officer, Evelyn Anoya, who attached a letter written by one of the associates, Mr. Ognjanović, seeking to add four witnesses to the defence list. This application was later granted. Therefore, it would appear that the legal associates made some applications to the Trial Chamber, albeit through an intermediary source. The transcripts of the hearing also reveal that the legal associates relayed information from the accused to the parties in the case, including the Trial Chamber, but also relayed information from the prosecution to the accused. For example, they informed Milošević of the issues relating to witnesses called by the prosecution.[199] They also informed the Court at one stage of Milošević's ill-health[200] and provided information relating to the defence witnesses to be called by the Accused.[201] They appeared to collect information on Milošević's behalf from the both the ICTY[202] and institutions back in Serbia.[203] At times, the legal associates appeared to also

[196] *Prosecutor v. Milošević*, 'Order', Case No. IT-02-54-T, 16 April 2002. By this Order, the two Legal Associates became bound by all existing Orders of the Trial Chamber, including the Order for Protective Measures Mr. Tomanović's power of attorney was filed with the Registry on 16 April 2002 and Mr. Ognjanović's power of attorney was filed on 22 April 2002.

[197] *Prosecutor v. Milošević*, 'Order Appointing Branko Rakić as Legal Associate to the Accused', Case No. IT-02-54-T, 23 October 2003. The conditions imposed with respect to the other two Legal Associates also applied to Branko Rakić. It also appears that Milošević had at least one additional associate in Belgrade, Momo Raičević, who appeared to be involved in sourcing of information and briefing witnesses (see, *Prosecutor v. Milošević*, Hearing, 22 September 2005, Transcript, 44547; 30 September 2005, 44973; 3 October 2005, 45045).

[198] *Prosecutor v. Milošević*, 'Order on Application by the Accused to Add Four Witnesses to his Witness List', Case No. IT-02-54-T, 3 December 2004.

[199] *Prosecutor v. Milošević*, Hearing, 11 June 2002, Transcript, 6673.

[200] *Prosecutor v. Milošević*, Hearing, 7 October 2003, Transcript, 27109.

[201] *Prosecutor v. Milošević*, Hearing, 9 November 2004, Transcript, 33197.

[202] *Prosecutor v. Milošević*, Hearing, 18 October 2005, Transcript, 45316.

[203] *Prosecutor v. Milošević*, Hearing, 19 October 2005, Transcript, 45472; see also 26 October 2005, 45744 and 26 April 2005, 38812.

act as translators.[204] Finally, it was clear they also reviewed exhibits provided to the defence by the prosecution.[205] Therefore, the legal associates acted in some respects and at different times as both investigators and defence lawyers, although they never appeared in court.

Resource issues in international criminal trials – Milošević and other senior level accused

An important aspect of representation in the *Milošević* trial, as in all complex international criminal trials, was the resources that are available to accused to conduct their defence.

According to a report prepared by the registry on 18 March 2002,[206] Milošević, upon his admission to the ICTY's Detention Unit, was provided with standard facilities available to the detainees such as the use of phone and/or mail. He was also told that he was entitled to meet with a maximum of five attorneys and/or law professors, in order to choose his defence counsel and was reminded that he could communicate on a privileged basis with two defence counsel. He personally met with two attorneys and two law professors. He submitted additional requests to meet with persons with whom he had previously consulted or was consulting for the first time but this was denied in line with the ICTY's detention policy. The report also stated that Milošević had been given an opportunity to communicate by phone with persons who could provide him with legal advice.[207]

Apart from receiving legal advice from Ramsey Clark and John Livingston, Milošević also received visits from Nico Steijnen and Jacques Verges regarding his application against The Netherlands before the European Court of Human Rights concerning deprivation of his liberty. While in the Detention Unit, Milošević was able to forward and to receive documents during the official working hours of the Tribunal, to receive mail and facsimile messages from legal advisers and to transmit and receive mail every weekday. He was allowed to communicate by phone with Clark and Livingstone and to receive scheduled visits by them anytime during the week between 9am and 4:45pm, times which were extended. According to the report, Milošević was also allowed to review video evidence on a VCR, which had been installed and connected to the television in his prison cell, and to use his own laptop computer and printer.[208] The registry report also stated that, while in court, the accused

204 *Prosecutor v. Milošević*, Hearing, 27 April 2005, Transcript, 38858.

205 *Prosecutor v. Milošević*, Hearing, 9 May 2005, Transcript, 39186.

206 *Prosecutor v. Milošević*, 'Registry Report on Practical Facilities Available to the Accused', Case No. IT-02-54-T, 18 March 2002. 207 Ibid. 208 Ibid.

was permitted to access a privileged phone line from his holding cell during the trial breaks. From this telephone, he could call his legal associates. With the assistance of a security officer, he was also able to send facsimile messages to his legal associates during the trial breaks. If urgently needed and with the assistance of a security officer, the accused could use the photocopying facilities during these breaks. Finally, if required, his holding cell at the Tribunal could be equipped with a TV/VCR. On 17 March 2003, the Trial Chamber issued an order pursuant to which the registrar was to provide Milošević with facilities, in a privileged setting, to confer with witnesses and others relevant to his defence; facilities, in a privileged setting, to review and work with documents and other material relevant to his defence; logistical support with regard to witnesses; and facilities to prepare for the presentation of his case. Pursuant to that order, the registrar created a *pro se* legal liaison office, staffed by several people to assist the accused in preparing and presenting his defence.[209]

All of these seemingly banal facts are important for an understanding of the sorts of efforts made to ensure that Milošević was adequately resourced to conduct his defence and help understand the anatomy of how a self-represented accused is *in fact* to prepare and conduct his defence.

In its first decision on the assignment of counsel, issued on 4 April 2003, the Trial Chamber considered the issue of adequate facilities for the accused.[210] The Chamber referred to its oral ruling of 24 April 2002 in which, having considered a brief by the *amici curiae*[211] and a registry report[212] on the matter, the Trial Chamber had found that, in accordance with Article 21 of the Statute, the accused had adequate time and facilities for the preparation of his defence, and that it was satisfied that 'all possible efforts were being made to assist him'.[213]

In its second decision on the assignment of counsel, the Trial Chamber referred to different ways in which it accommodated the accused, including the appointment of three legal associates of Milošević's own choosing; the expansion of the role of the *amici curiae* to undertake substantial work in the character of defence counsel; and ordering to the Registrar to provide the accused with adequate facilities to conduct his defence.

[209] See *Prosecutor v. Milošević*, 'Decision in Relation to Severance, Extension of Time and Rest', Case No. IT-02-54-T, 12 December 2005 ('*Milošević* Severance and Time Decision').

[210] First *Milošević* Decision, above n. 9.

[211] *Prosecutor v. Milošević*, 'Brief on the Provision of Adequate Facilities to Allow the Accused to Prepare his Defence, re-filed by the *Amici Curiae*', 5 March 2002.

[212] *Prosecutor v. Milošević*, 'Registry Report on Practical Facilities Available to the Accused', 18 March 2002 ('Registry Report').

[213] *Prosecutor v. Milošević*, 'Oral Ruling', 24 April 2002, Transcript, 3737–40

According to the Chamber's ruling, this decision had been fully implemented by the registrar.[214] The Trial Chamber went on to say that this showed it had gone to great lengths to accommodate Milošević's right to represent himself. Later, in a decision in December 2005, the Chamber reiterated the considerable resources that had been made available to the accused in the conduct of his case.[215]

There is little available information on the provision of resources to self-represented accused in the international criminal tribunals. While issues have been raised and discussed in various cases, including the *Šešelj* case[216] and the *Milutinović et al.* case,[217] the case law largely concentrates on the questions of principle involved in resources and representation. In the Special Court for Sierra Leone, however, the accused Norman submitted a request to the Trial Chamber for 'adequate and effective resources' to assist in the defence of his case.[218] The resources requested included a complete computer set, a personal telephone, a regular supply of stationery, an assistant and an investigator, a modification of the conditions of his detention, and a consideration of the quality and quantity of the food provided at the detention unit.[219] The Trial Chamber held that the accused could be provided with a desktop computer and printer (although due to security concerns the computer was not to be connected to the internet or Special Court network);[220] a stationary desk telephone within his cell which he could use at any time for the purpose of being in contact with his standby counsel;[221] the continued provision of stationery on request considered reasonable and proportionate to the requirements of representing himself on the understanding that the standby counsel had been appointed to assist in this process.[222] Other requests were denied.[223]

214 Second *Milošević* Decision, above n. 14, para. 61.

215 *Milošević* Severance and Time Decision, above n. 209, para. 21: 'To be added to the list of resources set out in the footnote [49] [of its 22 September 2004 Decision on assignment of counsel], two Counsel and their team have been assigned to assist the Accused in the preparation and presentation of his case, and the Registry has also created a *Pro Se* Legal Liaison Office, staffed by several people to assist the Accused in preparing and presenting his defence.'

216 See e.g., *Prosecutor v. Šešelj*, 'Motion for Trial Chamber II to Decide on all Status Issues Raised by Professor Vojislav Šešelj at Status Conferences', Case No. IT-03-67-PT, 28 March 2006.

217 See e.g., *Prosecutor v. Milutinović et al.*, 'Second Decision on Motions to Delay Proposed Date for Start of Trial', Case No. IT-05-87-PT, 28 April 2006.

218 *Prosecutor v. Norman et al.*, 'Decision on Request by Samuel Hinga Norman for Additional Resources to Prepare his Defence', Case No. SCSL-04-14-PT, 23 June 2004, para. 1.

219 Ibid. 220 Ibid. para. 12. 221 Ibid. paras 13–15. 222 Ibid. para. 16.

223 Ibid. paras 17–20.

When the Trial Chamber subsequently decided to revoke Norman's right to self-representation (discussed below), it also decided that the additional measures granted to Norman to assist him in the presentation of his case were to be revoked on the basis that he was no longer a *pro se* defendant.[224]

Little information exists about the manner in which international criminal tribunals deal in detail with the provision of adequate facilities to accused persons before them. This is largely because in the classical defence counsel representation model, these issues only tend to arise in respect of adequate remuneration for counsel to enable them to conduct a defence. However, the sorts of issues considered by the SCSL and, in particular, the ICTY in the *Milošević* case, show the difficulties experienced by international criminal tribunals in finding the right resource balance so as not to reward an accused for electing self-representation, while ensuring some measure of equality of arms with the prosecution and fairness to the accused.

Concluding comments on resource issues and the equality of arms

The issue of resources is a crucial aspect of ensuring equality of arms between the parties in an international criminal trial. The position at international criminal law is probably best described by Judge May:

> Although it is clear that the question of equality of arms cannot be reduced to an exact equation, there must, in the least, be an approximate equality in terms of resources. Any substantial inequality will call into question the fairness of the trial.[225]

An example of significant resource disparity can be seen in the size of the *Milošević* prosecution team, which had more than twenty lawyers and investigators working during its case-in-chief and considerable other resources at its disposal.[226] It is clear that no legally aided defence team (and not many privately funded defence teams) could boast these sorts of resources. This point was made by counsel assigned to Milošević in a hearing to determine whether more time should be accorded the accused for his defence.[227] The Tribunal made considerable efforts – at the expense

[224] *Prosecutor v. Norman et al.*, 'Ruling on the Issue of Non-Appearance of the First Accused Samuel Hinga Norman, The Second Accused Moinina Fofana, and the Third Accused, Allieu Kondewa at the Trial Proceedings', Case No. SCSL-04-14-PT, 1 October 2004.

[225] Richard May and Marieke Wierda, *International Criminal Evidence* (2002), 271.

[226] *Prosecutor v. Milošević*, 'Prosecution's Comprehensive Report Concerning Its Compliance to Date with Rule 68', Case No. IT-02-54-T, 20 February 2004.

[227] *Prosecutor v. Milošević*, Hearing, 8 December 2005, Transcript, 47230: 'No matter what the Prosecution say about their resources and claim this, that, and the other, it is apparent

of the international community – to provide Milošević with substantial resources in the conduct of his case, despite him never declaring himself indigent.[228] However, the broader question remains whether the disparity in resources between the prosecution and Milošević created an inequality and, as a result, whether this adversely affected the fairness of the trial.

It is often difficult to conclude with certainty whether, in a particular case, inequality in resources between the parties has caused unfairness. The question must be assessed in light of the overall conduct of the trial, including consideration of what resources were available to an accused, what was the scope of the case and how much material was there to assimilate in order to answer the prosecution case and mount a full defence, was reasonable time provided to an accused to prepare his or her case, and many other variable factors. Outcomes in the trial process may also help to answer the question. For example, a Chamber might conclude that the defence failed to address significant aspects of the prosecution case or address critical issues because of a lack of resources to do so, which could raise questions as to whether an accused has been given a fair opportunity to meet the case against him or her in that respect. As already discussed, the circumstances of the *Milošević* case and some other international criminal trials examined, posed serious questions about the fairness of the trial in terms of equality of resources. Conclusions about the adequacy of resources for the fairness of the proceedings are difficult to reach in this case, because the accused died and the case terminated before the overall effect of these matters could be measured.

There is no doubt, in light of the volume of material served on Milošević and the unequal resources available to the prosecution vis-à-vis the accused, that the potential existed for there to be an inequality of arms. The Chamber sought to address this in ways discussed already, and it must be remembered that Milošević chose to represent himself and thereby forego considerable professional assistance by instructed counsel in dealing with these issues (although the *amici curiae* and assigned counsel gave considerable uninstructed support to him). He also refused to avail himself of methods of presenting written evidence that would have allowed him to introduce a greater amount of defence evidence. In light of

Footnote no. 227 *(cont.)*

there is a vast body of technical expertise out there that is able to produce matters during proceedings and produce filings, research that is beyond the scope and resources of any Defence team. So there is an inequality in strength. That has to be taken into account in relation to time for the accused to present his Defence on the indictments, that that has to be factored in meeting the challenge mounted against him.'

[228] *Milošević* Severance and Time Decision, above n. 209.

the intransigence of the accused in these material respects, and the considerable efforts to which the Chamber went to encourage, caution, advise, and assist the accused in his case it is difficult to conclude that the obvious inequality of resources between the parties eventuated in unfairness and a violation of the obligation of the Chamber to give Milošević a fair trial.

Conclusion

How to achieve a fair and expeditious international criminal trial for complex cases involving high level accused is affected by a myriad of issues, not the least of which are questions related to resources and representation.

International criminal courts and tribunals have legal aid schemes, are funded to ensure that the rights related to adequate time and facilities and to representation are respected, all of which are essential to a fair and expeditious trial being accorded. However, it is apparent that high-level accused who are uncooperative and manipulative create profound challenges. In what circumstances should such accused be entitled to represent themselves, and to what degree of self-harm or harm to the trial process? Should considerable funds be expended by the international community supporting the choices made by these accused, or should rules be set and followed to conclusion, whatever that may be? When should counsel be assigned or imposed, and when should courts utilise innovative but contentious means to support the preparation and conduct of a defence case?

There are two materially distinct ways of dealing with these questions. The first approach is to determine that international justice requires a degree of flexibility in the treatment of such highly complex and difficult cases. The degree of unfairness caused by allowing self-representation without any additional assistance or simply imposing counsel and proceeding to the conclusion of trial whatever might arise, may be considered an overly harsh and absolutist response, itself compromising fairness in the trial process – or at least the perception of fairness. There is a fairness issue already created by the very scope and complexity inherent in these trials. Thus a self-represented accused in an international criminal trial is already at a significant disadvantage vis-à-vis a self-represented accused in a standard (or even complex) domestic criminal trial. This fact in itself justifies additional effort and resources being expended on resources for such accused. The nature of these trials and accused evokes potentially serious political implications for the international community and therefore for international criminal justice, also rendering these trials distinguishable from their domestic law analogues. Indeed, Scharf and Rassi focus in their article on the political implications of allowing former heads of state to conduct their own defence.[229] They analyse the *Milošević* case (although in the context prior to imposition of counsel) and express the view that given what they call grave implications (the perception that a former leader could appear a martyr and the effect on reconciliation in their countries), it may not be right to find that 'former rogue leaders have an international right to act as their own lawyer in war crimes trials'.[230]

The second approach is that, if a court has determined that the fairness of the trial militates in favour of the imposition of counsel to conduct an affirmative defence case – to take control of the preparation and presentation of that case – then an accused who will not communicate or instruct, let alone one who attacks, antagonises or seeks to impugn the professionalism of counsel, cannot be allowed to run the proceedings aground. Following this approach, the argument by assigned counsel in the *Milošević* case that the right to a fair trial is a right that only concerns the accused's interests – let alone his perceived interests – cannot stand. A court will, as part of its fundamental duty, have ensured the integrity of the proceedings before it, as well as the judicial process it represents. If counsel is assigned and the accused obstructs the presentation of favourable evidence or, as a result of that conduct counsel is unable to bring any further evidence, the accused has been given an opportunity to have a fair trial and the case may be closed and determined. The court's duty to ensure that the proceedings are fair would have been discharged in such circumstances – the accused would have been allowed to frustrate justice. It must be anticipated that in such circumstances judgement on a plethora of heinous crimes might be issued on the basis of little or inadequate evidence led by the defence. However, so long as the court has taken all reasonable measures to secure the accused's rights within the constraints of this approach, the court may be said to have provided a fair trial.

The not insignificant body of practice in international criminal trials to date shows that these are extremely complex questions. The facts of each case obviously differ and may dictate a different nuance in the approach taken. In *Norman*, before the SCSL, the accused was clearly seeking to fracture and obstruct the trial process – by requesting on the first day of a

[229] Scharf and Rassi, 'Former Rogue Leaders', 3–8. [230] Ibid.

co-accused trial (after one year of pre-trial representation) to act on his own behalf. The Court consequently dealt with the application on that basis, using a standby counsel model similar to that in the First *Šešelj* Decision. In *Baryagwiza*, the accused sought to dismantle the trial process by boycotting the proceedings and ordering his counsel to do the same. The ICTR, by ordering his counsel to attend the trial and represent their client (even uninstructed), were responding to the particular threat to the trial in that case. In *Krajisnik*, the Chamber interpreted, after lengthy questioning of, and negotiation with, the accused, that he was really using an election to represent himself to seek more resources and a better trial team structure, refused his 'equivocal' and 'unintelligent' request to represent himself and sought to broker a solution that would satisfy the Chamber that all had been done to ensure that the accused received adequate and sufficiently resourced defence counsel representation. In *Šešelj*, the Chamber initially perceived that the accused might obstruct the trial process and sought to put in place a standby counsel as insurance so the trial could proceed should he render the trial unmanageable. It subsequently determined that sufficient indicia of obstructionism had occurred warranting the imposition of counsel – although the Appeals Chamber ultimately frustrated these measures. Finally, in *Milošević*, the Trial Chamber accepted the accused's election to represent himself, interpreting the accused as having the right and capacity to conduct his own defence until, due to his medical condition and intransigence in accepting the assistance offered to him, the Chamber determined that he was no longer fit to defend himself and assigned defence counsel to act (even uninstructed) on his behalf. The ICTY was prepared to go to great lengths, and expend considerable resources paid for by the international community, to support the accused in representing himself until it perceived a direct threat to the life of the accused and/or the conclusion of the trial. Had the Appeals Chamber not intervened as it did, the Trial Chamber may – having imposed counsel – have been prepared (after an established unwillingness of any defence witnesses to attend court in the accused's defence in such circumstances) to close the trial and render judgement. As it turned out, the Appeals Chamber's reversal of the Trial Chamber's imposed representation model realised the Trial Chamber's initial concern for the accused and the future of the trial.

However, while each case is materially different in its facts, these cases all have similar indicia. They all concern manipulative accused of relative or significant seniority who do not respect the authority and legality of the court trying them and who use the forensic trial process as a political platform and/or as a means to exploit their personal interests – even if that is only to obstruct and derail the trial against them. It is my assertion that the appropriate way to manage the conduct of complex international criminal trials in these circumstances is, in accordance with the second approach just discussed, for courts to impose counsel in a dauntless way, clearly articulating the principle applied to the particular facts of that case.

The review of the different treatment of the issue in this chapter shows the effects of prevarication or fearfulness by international criminal courts and tribunals confronting this dilemma. The tentative measure of appointing standby counsel while allowing the accused to represent himself in the *Norman* case, was abandoned when he took the additional step of refusing to come to court. The Court revoked his right and imposed counsel. In *Šešelj*, the Trial Chamber appointed standby counsel and tremulously abided by the accused's election to represent himself while he heaped abuse and disrespect on the Tribunal and its officers in the most vile of ways, until finally summoning the strength to impose counsel upon him. In *Milošević*, the Trial Chamber having taken its time determining that imposition of counsel was required to ensure the fairness of the trial (and the maintenance of Milošević's health), again the Appeals Chamber effectively reversed the decision, the eventual consequence being the untimely death of the accused and an unconcluded trial.

Standby counsel has consistently been employed with the stated intention that counsel will not interfere with an accused's self-representation unless and until the court is satisfied that the appropriate circumstances arise, most notably an unacceptable obstruction of the trial process. Apart from being largely ineffective, it has also generally had the effect of creating considerable animosity between the accused and counsel and is no doubt expensive.

The lesson to be learnt from these cases, and in particular the *Milošević* and *Šešelj* cases, is that senior accused in complex international criminal trials should not be allowed to continue to represent themselves where there is sufficient evidence that self-representation will threaten the fairness of the trial or its reasonable expedition. In the relative plethora of such cases in international criminal law thus far, this has been the net effect of self-representation. International criminal courts and tribunals hearing such cases in the future should learn from these experiences and be more willing – more quickly – to impose counsel. A clear message to accused prone to such manipulation that the court will not tolerate interference with the forensic trial process in such a way that it threatens fairness and expedition will better serve the cause of justice and fairness.

Further principles and practical outcomes emerge from the jurisprudence discussed in this chapter that enable conclusions about future directions to be taken in these trials. First, issues relating to the adequacy of resources affect the equality of arms. The principle upon which courts are to proceed appears to be that there should be a reasonable amount of assistance given to an accused to process and consider the considerable quantity of evidence and disclosed material, so that they are in a position to prepare and present a defence. This is so even where such accused are duly represented. Clearly, the *Milošević* case stands as an extraordinary example of one man buried beneath a mountain of paper. However, the Chamber having made considerable resources available and given time for the accused to prepare and conduct his case, it was determined that the fairness of the trial had not been compromised. The litmus test appears to be that if an accused is able effectively to cross-examine and present coherent evidence that forensically challenges the prosecution case, a court is unlikely to conclude that the equality of arms has been compromised. It will be difficult to determine this as an ultimate question before the trial has concluded and all the evidence has been heard. In this, as in other areas of international criminal law, best practice suggests that a rational reduction in the scope of the prosecution case and the volume of material therefore presented for an accused to digest, will facilitate greater equality and therefore fairness. Best practice also suggests that competent counsel will far better manage these issues and present an effective defence than a self-represented accused.

In terms of representation models, clearly the standard defence counsel model is a preferable way for such trials to proceed. This is more likely to ensure adequate resources and skilled representation. To a significant extent, skilled representation should be encouraged and compelled. Where, however, an accused wishes to appear self-represented, there is now a developing body of law that will enable a court to determine whether such a choice is in the interests of a fair trial. It is argued that this will not often be the case and that respect for the principles by which international criminal proceedings are to be conducted will more often than not mandate the imposition of defence counsel. In this respect, the First and (particularly) Second *Šešelj* Appeal Decisions should be read as a circumstance-specific aberration and should not be followed as good law on this issue. In the *Milošević* decision imposing counsel, the Chamber stated that a fundamental aspect of the right to a fair trial is ensuring that the accused has the opportunity and facility to present a defence fully and effectively, and it took the additional step of stating that the overall right to a fair trial could be achieved at times by limiting individual guarantees that are constituent parts of that right. This is one area in which the formulation of the right to a fair trial has been interpreted in a nuanced manner to achieve overall fairness.

A preferable outcome, therefore, and one more likely to deliver a fair and more expeditious trial, is to curtail to a greater extent the circumstances in which self-representation will be allowed. These trials are simply so complex and challenging that the potential for mischief, disruption, delay, and ultimately unfairness – and possibly non-conclusion – is too great. However, it would be naïve to argue for absolutism in such complex and varied cases. Ultimately, the effect of different models used to deal with a self-represented accused does not appear to be profound. Whether a court accepting self-representation appoints a standby counsel ready to step in if the court revokes self-representation, or the hybrid *amicus curiae*/defence counsel, the real distinction is between allowing self-representation and imposing defence counsel on an accused. Where the court allows an accused to exercise the limited right to appear *pro se*, it will need to plan for the possibility that removal of that right is appropriate to achieve the goals of the international criminal trial. The achievement of best practice in the conduct of complex international criminal trials will be assisted by limiting, and normally refusing, self-representation, borrowing from the jurisprudence already developed and a clear understanding of the practical implications of this, as well as the potential impact on the principles of the criminal trial process. Complexities related to the lack of instructions, counsel's consideration of his or her ethical obligations in such circumstances and the extent to which, if any, such accused might be allowed to particulate in the presentation of their own defence, are matters that courts have to adjust to in the context of each particular case. A strong judicial hand in these issues early in the proceedings will do much to enhance the fairness and efficiency of complex international criminal trials.

5

Conclusions

The purpose of this book is to analyse what lessons can be learnt from the *Milošević* trial that would improve the fair and expeditious conduct of complex international criminal trials of senior political and military officials and, by doing this, determine best practice for the conduct of such trials. The primary challenge here is striking an appropriate balance between the often competing principles of fairness and expedition. It is apparent from the analysis in this book that the principle of fairness is composed of a myriad of complex rights, obligations, and interests. Perfection in these trials is impossible, and international courts and tribunals should not be expected to achieve this. Defining appropriate benchmarks can be extremely difficult; accomplishing these benchmarks may be even more difficult. The system of modern international criminal law is little more than a decade old. It lacks the infrastructure of domestic criminal law systems, which can rely on hundreds of years of development on which to rest their determination and application of such fundamental issues – issues which have not only legal implications, but also political, sociological, economic and historical ones. It is in this context that international criminal law must be judged, and it is in this context that consideration must be given to its development and future application in complex international criminal trials.

Courts and tribunals applying international criminal law have an obligation to ensure that a trial is fair, and they have an obligation to ensure that it is expeditious. How to characterise fairness and expedition in this context has been the preoccupation of this work and the conclusions in this chapter go some way towards establishing some concrete measures and determining how they might be achieved. The *Milošević* trial was one of the most complex criminal trials in history and one from which much can and has already been learnt in answer to these questions. Many of the cardinal issues discussed in this book emerged for the first time or were brought into sharp focus by the trial. The content of the issues, and the manner in which the Tribunal interacted with them, provide some basis for constructing criteria for best practice. Because international criminal trials are increasingly concerned with the senior political and military leaders in conflicts, this book is really a legal analysis of the future of international criminal law, which grapples with the questions raised by the protracted, complex, and at times incomprehensible nature of such proceedings. Each area of analysis in which the *Milošević* trial is discussed raises questions about what lessons can be learnt, what will be the impact for the future conduct of complex international criminal trials, and ultimately, whether it is possible to construct an international criminal legal regime in which fair and expeditious trials can be consistently conducted.

The *Milošević* trial lasted four years and one month and ended abruptly with the death of the accused months before its projected conclusion. It might have taken anything up to a further year to render the judgement in the case. In such circumstances, it is not possible to define the trial as expeditious. It is important, of course, to consider the context of a trial of this nature. As asserted throughout this book – and as borne out by a simple assessment of the nature and scope of these cases – international criminal trials are inherently more complex than domestic criminal trials. This is particularly true of cases involving senior level accused whose responsibility is incorporated into criminal conduct encompassing broad geographic and temporal allegations, and usually within the framework of organised, widespread, and systematic criminality. Therefore, it is important to acknowledge that these cases will be longer than even the most complex domestic trials. The international community, as well as victims, parties and courts must accept this and construct a framework for expedition within the rarefied context of international criminal trials.

Recognition of this fact, however, does not require acceptance of the inevitability of unduly long or open-ended trials. The analysis in this book reveals that there is a variety of ways in which a failure to ensure expeditiousness in the conduct of complex international criminal trials can also have a negative effect on their fairness. The longer a trial is allowed to run, the broader its scope, the more voluminous the evidence, the less manageable the trial becomes for all involved, particularly the accused. This can itself violate discrete fair trial rights (such as the right to trial without undue delay and the equality of arms) and may amount ultimately to an unfair trial. In considering the imposition of counsel on Milošević, the Trial Chamber defined the issue of expeditiousness itself as a fair trial issue. Although this approach, without careful elucidation, really serves to confuse the already complicated framework for the conduct of these trials, it is an example of the importance placed on the issue by a court that had endured years of complex trial work. It is in fact impossible to set exact limits to the length of complex international criminal trials, if only because this so obviously depends on the individual facts and particularities of each case. However, there will always come a point in such a lengthy trial where the failure to conclude proceedings risks two infelicitous outcomes: calling into question the fairness of the trial, and hazarding the loss of support by the international community for such trials and the courts that conduct them. Best practice in the conduct of these cases will see them concluding in a considerably shorter time-frame than the four plus years that the *Milošević* trial ran for.

Many of the same factors relating to the expedition of complex international criminal trials encompass the fairness of such trials. There are a number of constituent parts of the fair trial right, or 'minimum guarantees' as they tend to be described in the constitutional instruments of the international criminal courts and tribunals. The court must ensure that a trial is public (subject to legitimate and proportionate limitations); that an accused has adequate time and facilities to prepare a defence; that trial be given without undue delay; that an accused be allowed to confront witnesses and test the evidence against them, and that there be an equality of arms between the prosecution and the accused.

The interpretation of such rights in the context of international criminal law may differ from their origin and interpretation within the human rights regime. The application of these rights in the *sui generis* system of international criminal law is necessarily contextual, but this does not water down their significance or the requirement that they be adhered to within an established, consistent, and clear regime.

The greatest threat to the fairness of the *Milošević* trial was the inequality in resources between the parties. Despite the efforts made by the Trial Chamber and the ICTY as an institution, the resources available to the prosecution dwarfed Milošević. Sir Richard May, the first presiding judge of the *Milošević* trial, wrote in a different context that, while the question of equality of arms cannot be reduced to an exact equation, 'there must, in the least, be an approximate equality in terms of resources. Any substantial inequality will call into question the fairness of the trial.'[1] The sheer volume of material and capacity to cope with that material posed challenges to the fairness of the trial in respect of the accused. However, despite reference by Milošević during the trial to more than one million

[1] May and Wierda, *International Criminal Evidence* (2002), 271.

pages of disclosed material; his inability to read it all, let alone incorporate that material into his defence; and the insufficiency of time and resources given to him to cope, he clearly had considerable information on which to base his cross-examination of prosecution witnesses and was able to deliver a prepared and relatively effective defence case.

Furthermore, Milošević did show quite some ability in the mounting of a defence case. He led evidence or cross-examined at length on the involvement of KLA or NATO in crimes alleged or in responsibility for the displacement of civilians; he raised a sufficient case for the Trial Chamber to order extensive *amicus curiae* briefs from Professor McCormack on the international law of self-defence and its application to the evidence in the case; he led considerable evidence to assert that the Serbian army was not involved in various crimes alleged to have been committed by them in Kosovo; and he dealt with the political and constitutional structure and formal lines of authority in an endeavour to clear himself of responsibility. In this respect, he was clearly able to mount a vigorous forensic case, even if he also wasted considerable time on political points and (importantly) focused over 80 per cent of his time on the Kosovo part of the case against him (largely ignoring the Croatia and Bosnia indictments).

It is generally not possible to truly determine whether a fair trial has been given until it is over and all the relevant factors have been weighed and considered. However, consideration of all the factors suggests that the *Milošević* trial was, to the extent that it is possible to make such a determination, fair – although it is always possible that the Trial or Appeals Chamber may have determined otherwise. Yet, the factors which threatened that conclusion require attention if future complex international criminal trials are to meet the required standards of fairness, let alone achieve best practice. The human and financial resource implications of not rationalising these cases will inevitably threaten a trial's fairness, render it anything but expeditious and may inevitably lead to a lack of support from the international community for the conduct of such trials. The death of Milošević in custody prior to the conclusion of the trial and rendering of judgement could easily have exacerbated these concerns. When in hindsight the possibility existed for a two-year trial resolving the Kosovo indictment, and the outcome was a four-year trial without conclusion and an accused dead on remand, questions may also legitimately be posed concerning the conduct of the proceedings.

This chapter will now consider the key areas of analysis in the book, concrete lessons that can be learnt, and what reforms should be undertaken, to develop best practice in the conduct of complex international criminal trials.

The prosecution case must be focused, comprehensible and manageable

There are ways in which these trials can be reduced by appropriate conduct by the parties and appropriate control by the court. Reduction in the scope of a case should start with a restrained and realistic assessment by the prosecution of its case, in terms of what exactly it seeks to prove and how such proof will be presented. A clearer and more focused case will invariably affect favourably the fairness of the trial, if for no other reason than that the accused (and court) will comprehend better the prosecution case and the volume of issues and material will be less likely to offend the principle of the equality of arms.

All three indictments against Milošević were in material respects defective. These shortcomings could have had a profound impact on the final judgement in the case, although we will now never know. Considering the broader application of these concerns relating to the deficiency of indictments before international criminal courts and tribunals more generally, and considering the outcome of appeal cases like *Kupreškić*[2] and *Ntakirutimana*,[3] it is apparent that prosecutorial offices should act to address the content and satisfactoriness of indictments. My own experience from years of reviewing indictments before the ICTY, and from review for academic purposes of indictments in other international criminal courts and tribunals, is that sound drafting principles have not been consistently applied and not enough has been done to redress errors and defects that have occurred. Indictments remain largely poorly structured, incredibly long (sometimes even over 100 pages) and the process of amendment (forced by legal process or sought by the prosecution to add, remove or alter charges) has often served to layer error upon mishap. The future conduct of international criminal prosecutions should proceed from a fresh slate: indictments should be drafted with clarity of the criminal conduct charged, the accused's responsibility in it clearly particularised and defined, and nomenclature carefully and consistently employed. This in itself will save time both at the pre-trial stage and at trial, and it will be beneficial to the prosecution (which will be clearer

[2] *Prosecutor v Kupreškić*, 'Appeal Judgement', Case No. IT-95-16-A, 23 October 2001, where two accused were acquitted on the basis of defective pleading. This judgement is discussed in chapter two.

[3] *Prosecutor v Ntakirutimana*, 'Judgement', Case No. ICTR-96-10 & ICTR-96-17-TA, 21 February 2003, where acquittals on the basis of defective pleadings led to a genocide conviction being overturned.

about its case), the defence (which will know better the case it has to answer) and the court (which must adjudicate and determine the case). The effect will not only be beneficial for the expeditiousness of the trial, it will also materially impact on the trial's fairness, as the accused will be properly informed of the case at an early stage, enabling time for investigation and preparation and enabling a focus on the real issues.

Furthermore, the prosecution should cease the lamentable practice of 'throwing the book' at those it charges in international criminal proceedings. Charging almost every accused with every form of criminal responsibility, as is particularly the case with senior level accused, has the effect of broadening the scope of the case and therefore the length of proceedings, as well as reducing their clarity and potentially impacting upon fairness. Furthermore, at least in the *ad hoc* Tribunals, Trial Chambers are, thanks to an Appeals Chamber ruling in the *Blaškić* case, no longer at liberty to select the most appropriate form of responsibility on which to consider the accused's conduct, but must rather assess his role in respect of all forms of criminal responsibility before determining guilt or innocence.[4]

Furthermore, it is unnecessary and inappropriate to use a high-level accused like Milošević to try every conceivable crime, or even many such crimes over which they are said to have presided or participated in some manner. Despite the very legitimate concerns of victims and communities in seeing justice done, there are many reasons for prosecutors to exercise restraint. First, a criminal trial should be a forensic process involving determination of the criminal responsibility of an individual or individuals, and not a truth commission let alone a political exercise. Second, victims will not be served by the prosecution pleading an overly broad case in which it is unable to lead sufficient evidence in a reasonable time to cover all the crimes charged, or at worst, find itself unable to establish the accused's criminal responsibility, either because its case was insufficiently coherent or it spent so much time leading crime base evidence that it was unable to lead sufficient evidence going to the accused's criminal responsibility. This is exactly what happened in *Milošević*, where over one thousand allegations were dismissed at the judgement of acquittal stage, mostly because the prosecution had been unable to lead any evidence at all on the offences charged in the time available. Finally, the international community may perceive investment of time and money in such trials as disproportionate to the outcome (a real risk arising out of the *Milošević* trial, given its conclusion), compromising its commitment to the future of international

[4] *Prosecutor v Blaškić*, 'Judgement', Case No. IT-95-14-A, 29 July 2004, paras. 91–2

criminal justice and the fight to end impunity for such crimes – the very purpose behind the prosecutorial mandate. A better approach would be to choose crimes representative of the criminality of that accused and to focus clearly on the form and nature of that person's responsibility. It is possible to achieve the goal of establishing the widespread or systematised nature of a high-ranking accused's criminal conduct without trying him for everything, a point made by the Trial Chamber during the *Milošević* trial and later reflected in amendments to the ICTY Rules.[5] One of the crucial future reforms of international criminal practice will, therefore, be reducing and focusing prosecution cases against senior accused.

The required process of reform is not exclusively the responsibility of the prosecution. The *Milošević* Trial Chamber played some part in the trial proceeding on the basis of defective indictments. Even after it was aware that at least the Kosovo indictment contained material errors which could affect the outcome of the trial, the Trial Chamber did not intervene *proprio motu* to order the prosecution to remedy the defects. The role of the court is unclear in such circumstances. The adversarial character of international criminal tribunals may dissuade a court from intervening in the prosecution's accusatory instrument. It is my argument, however, that the court is obliged, if it sees such defects and considers that they are potentially harmful to either the fair or expeditious conduct of the trial, to intervene, even if only to order the parties to make submissions on the defined issues, following which it can rule. The adversarial nature of the international criminal trial process need not, and should not, act as an excuse for a court not intervening to ensure the case is adequately pleaded and prepared.

Had the prosecution in the *Milošević* case narrowed – or been forced to narrow – the focus of its indictments, it might have been better placed to define its case against the accused and prove it. Instead, it took well into the defence case before its principal case theory against Milošević (relating to his relationship with the idea of a Greater Serbia) was clarified. It was the breadth and vagueness of the prosecution indictments, and therefore more broadly the lack of clarity and focus in the conception of its case, that was a primary reason for the lack of expedition in that trial. This is not an experience of international criminal trials limited to *Milošević*.[6]

Careful attention should be paid by judges or chambers reviewing indictments prepared for confirmation, something which did not occur in

[5] See discussion in chapter 3 of this book.

[6] Examples of this include the *Blaškić*, *Krajišnik* and *Orić* cases. For a more detailed discussion of these issues, see discussion in chapter 1 of this book.

the early or even relatively recent history of the ICTY and ICTR and, as a result, regrettably defective and overly expansive indictments were confirmed. The process of reforming the approach to pleading, in respect of accuracy as well as scope, also requires regulatory action. Beyond the unilateral review of an indictment by a judge presented by the prosecution, an additional contested review procedure should be formally implemented, providing after initial appearance and preliminary disclosure for the defence to challenge the *prima facie* establishment of each and every charge in the indictment. This should, if properly implemented and adjudicated, provide greater certainty about the merit of an indictment, it will undoubtedly clarify error or confusion arising from the prosecution's accusatory instrument and it will provide a vehicle for early agreement on material facts and case management approaches to the scope of the pleaded case. This will, as a result, positively impact upon fairness and expeditiousness.

Another key reason for the length of the *Milošević* trial was an important decision by the Appeals Chamber joining the three indictments into one case, spanning three conflicts over eight years and encompassing over 7,000 charges in 66 separate counts against one man. The Appeals Chamber's reasoning was spurious, the consequences devastating for the expeditiousness of the trial. The Trial Chamber had determined that the trial would proceed on the Kosovo indictment alone, leaving the other two indictments to be prosecuted jointly later. Apart from identification by the Trial Chamber of the disparate and tenuous connectivity between events at the end of the Bosnia war in 1995 and the start of the Kosovo war in 1999 as a single transaction, the Chamber also considered joinder of the three indictments as a case management nightmare. Even the Appeals Chamber, in overturning the Trial Chamber ruling, acknowledged that there was potential for joinder to create an unmanageable case. The prosecution's zealous quest for joinder, justified largely by extra-legal concerns relating to victim representation and other political and historical interests, set the scene for an unmanageable trial. A valuable lesson to be learnt from this experience is that the prosecution should exercise restraint and common sense in its approach to such strategic issues and, where the prosecution fails to do this, courts should use a heavy hand to control the scope of proceedings so that they are manageably fair and expeditious. To the credit of the Trial Chamber in the *Milošević* case, that is exactly what it did. Regrettably, the Appeal Chamber's ill-advised and poorly reasoned decision overturning that ruling directly impacted on these crucial principles.

The future of case management in complex international criminal law cases

In chapter 3, the development of case management principles and practices were discussed in respect of common law and civil law domestic systems. Of considerable interest is the growing consciousness in adversarial criminal justice systems that courts must take an active part both in the pre-trial process and in the regulation of the scope and conduct of a case during trial. These propositions are complementary because the better-managed a case is in pre-trial the more focused it is likely to be at trial. For the future conduct of international criminal trials, it will be important for international courts and tribunals to focus on individual case management to reduce the scope of cases on the basis of their own particular complexities.

It is apparent that in the mere decade in which modern international criminal law has existed, considerable development of complex case management has already occurred. This has been a product of necessity, as well as a function of the merging of practices and practitioners of criminal law from different legal systems. My own experience working for the ICTY Rules Committee between 1998 and 2004 gave me clear and direct experience of this. Common and civil law judges and practitioners traditionally see material aspects of the case management paradigm differently and bring very different perspectives and experiences to the process of developing a *sui generis* system focused on the achievement of a fair and expeditious international criminal trial. Tensions clearly exist in perceptions as to what embodies an acceptable degree of intervention by a court in the preparation, conduct, and even content of the prosecution's case. Such tensions extend to the degree of judicial intervention or control of a case considered acceptable, the degree of flexibility in the trial process and admissibility of different kinds of evidence, the extent to which the defence should be required to disclose its case or indicate areas of dispute or to agree undisputed or non-critical parts of the case with the prosecution, as well as many other matters. The different legal cultures make agreement on these matters difficult. But they also expose the chauvinism inherent in any entrenched system of thought and behaviour. What is encouraging is the extent to which belief in the superiority of one's own system or practice can give way to a *de novo* consideration of issues when faced with the necessity of achieving conformity with the common belief that international criminal trials must be fair and expeditious.

The Milošević case represented the turning point in the development of these issues in international criminal law. The case was so broad and complex that it compelled the ICTY to consider and take radical action to try to contain and manage it. The action taken by the Trial Chamber, in turn, spilled over into other trials (before the ICTY and other international tribunals) and into the regulatory activities of the ICTY.

I have asserted, however, that although setting overall time limits on the parties' cases is a safer and sometimes preferable form of macro case management, it will not be enough to reduce sufficiently the length of complex international criminal trials and make them more manageable in the future. More radical case management approaches are needed for international criminal courts and tribunals to prove their ability to transcend real or perceived infrastructural adversarial limits imposed by their constitutional instruments or application of them. There must be a willingness in these institutions for the judges to define and grapple with some micro-management methodologies in conducting such cases. Rules 73*bis*(D) and (E) of the ICTY Rules may exemplify the future of case management of these trials, whereby courts have greater powers of intervention in the scope and conduct of the parties' cases, particularly that of the prosecution.

However, prosecution offices (particularly at the *ad hoc* Tribunals) have shown that they are not yet prepared to take responsibility for reducing and focusing their cases in a way that will impact substantially and favourably on their length and manageability. Judges will, therefore, have to intervene and judiciously exercise available powers to ensure cases are conducted in a reasonably expeditious manner. They will have to attend to the scope and nature of the case; limit witnesses and witness numbers where appropriate; foreclose on the parties leading tangential or irrelevant evidence; continue the procedure of setting global time limits; and develop nuanced case management approaches, macro and micro in nature, which answer challenges to both the fairness and expedition of the trial process. As concluded in chapter three, some degree of skilled and measured reactivity will be required by international criminal courts and tribunals to deal with complex cases of senior level and intelligent accused who are sometimes obstructive and mischievous in respect of the forensic purpose of their trials. Achieving a tough but balanced approached to these issues will go a long way to achieving best practice in the conduct of complex international criminal trials.

In chapter three, I foreshadowed specific case management reforms I consider essential to the future development of the fair and expeditious management of complex international criminal trials. The analysis of case management in this area of law thus far reveals a need for a solidified practice, consolidating macro case management approaches that are safer and have clearly worked with more radical micro case management procedures, which are implemented in a careful and principled manner.

The development of a pre-trial judge or chamber in international criminal courts and tribunals is a potentially valuable pre-trial case management mechanism. However, a reform that must also be made is for the chamber that is to hear the case to be appointed as the chamber managing the pre-trial preparation for the case as early as possible. This consistency of judicial control through the pre-trial stage to the trial has been identified as an important individual case management tool in common law systems dealing with these issues. It is also clearly important, particularly in light of the approach taken at the ICTY of pre-trial chambers deferring decisions on important issues relating to the form and admissibility of evidence until the case is transferred to a trial chamber,[7] that cases be transferred over as soon as possible.

Case management of complex international criminal trials should be separated into four distinct phases. The first phase concerns the stage of reviewing the indictment. As discussed in respect of reforming the presentation by the prosecution of these cases, a clear and diligent indictment review process must be established. The first stage of the process will invariably be undertaken by a single judge or chamber reviewing a proposed indictment for which the prosecution is seeking confirmation. This must be far more assiduously attended to by international criminal courts and tribunals than appears to have been the case in the past. The prosecution must be put to task on both the extent to which it has established a *prima facie* case, as well as the nature, content and structure of its case so that the court is satisfied that the legal elements are sufficiently determined such that the prosecution should proceed. Once the indictment is confirmed, the accused is in custody and preliminary disclosure has occurred (including provision to the accused of all material on which the pre-trial judge or chamber confirmed the indictment), the defence should be able to challenge the indictment on the same terms as the initial review process took place. This will allow for a thorough and contested process for testing the prosecution's accusatory instrument. It will serve to ensure the case gets off on a solid footing at the earliest stage of the pre-trial process and may have the collateral advantage of clarifying the case and its crucial issues early on – a benefit both to the parties and the court.

7 See, e.g., *Prosecutor v Prlić et al.*, 'Decision on Admission of Rule 92bis Witness Statements', Case No. IT-04-74-PT, 4 April 2006; *Prosecutor v Prlič et al.*, 'Decision on Admission of Rule 92bis Witness Transcripts', Case No. IT-04-74-PT, 4 April 2006.

The second phase would require the pre-trial judge or chamber to oversee a meticulous *inter partes* analysis of the indictment and the case. This process would, using procedures currently provided, for example, in Rule 65*ter* of the ICTY Rules, require a genuine review of what facts and propositions can be agreed upon or stipulated to in the indictment. While such provisions do exist in the *ad hoc* tribunals, an insufficient degree of judicial coercion has been brought to bear on the parties such that they are compelled to approach the exercise in good faith and to a meaningful end. This is where the experience and capacity of the judge is an essential ingredient to success. In the *Milutinović* trial, where the pre-trial judge (who also was to be the presiding judge of the trial) took a strong degree of control of the pre-trial process and pushed the parties for measurable outcomes, the state of the case, its content and framework were much clearer going into trial. The advantage of this is also to build up mutual respect and understanding in a complex trial environment. As discussed in chapter three of this book, the presiding judge was able to impose orders reducing (at least initially) the scope of the indictment under Rule 73*bis* and take – at least initially in the trial – a more consensual approach to other potentially coercive case management measures, on the basis that he had developed a relationship with the parties and had clear authority. The general response from the parties in these cases to forcing them to clarify a position, reduce the scope of the case, or accept the imposition of restrictions on their adversarial freedoms, is resistance. A strong judge who is well-prepared and understands the case and issues well, will be in a better position to break down the initial resistance to judicial intervention and develop a constructive discussion on the proposed measures. If that judge continues to be met with intransigence, then measures of compulsion will be well founded and difficult to countermand.

The third phase is the transition from the pre-trial process into trial preparation work. At this stage, the pre-trial judge or chamber should be examining the content of the proposed case in detail, examining witness numbers, the use of written testimony, adjudicated facts, discussing time limits on the case, and other case management measures that will prepare the case for trial. Some of these measures are macro in nature and some minor. For example, setting global time limits and witness numbers is a macro case management measure that still gives parties control of the form and content of their case, but limits the perimeters within which it is conducted. Selecting individual witnesses or categories of witnesses for deletion from the witness list, challenging the relevance of particular areas of evidence proposed, or deleting areas of the indictment, is more of a micro case management approach. The importance of approaching these issues early enough in the pre-trial stage is that the more consensual or suggestive work that can be done without the need for orders, the less likely it is that the adversarial structure of the proceedings will be threatened. Furthermore, when the court is required to issue orders on these matters, this can be done against the background of every effort having been made to first achieve agreement with the affected parties.

The fourth phase is the final trial preparation phase, which would normally culminate in a pre-trial conference. At this stage, all the trial procedures should be clarified, specific time limits set for the overall conduct of the prosecution case (if, as I would argue, that is appropriate), time for cross-examination and final decisions set, as well as the final position on trial procedures and the treatment of evidence in the case. This is the point at which orders for more invasive case management procedures, such as those set out in Rule 73*bis* of the ICTY Rules, should be made, reducing the number of crime sites or locations, or the number of counts in the indictment. However, the work for these orders should have started back in phase two and, although the prosecution may object to the proposed reduction in the scope of its case, the court would be in a position to proceed to order such reduction on the basis of a long and consultative process between the court and the parties. This should have the effect both of ameliorating the discontent the prosecution may feel about the orders, as well as allowing the parties time to consider the implications of such orders and prepare.

Regrettably, the terms of Rule 73*bis* of the ICTY Rules are inadequate and are not a good precedent for how such Rules should be formulated. While the approach of reducing counts or crime sites and locations appears to be a largely appropriate way of reducing these cases to some form of manageability, the nomenclature of the Rule is confusing and it reads as though the power to reduce counts is merely suggestive (an interpretation the ICTY Prosecutor has already given to the Rule[8]). This Rule, or similar provisions, should be cast in clear terms, providing chambers with coercive powers to reduce the scope of the prosecution case. As discussed in chapter three, there is danger in chambers engaging in micro

[8] The Prosecutor, just after implementation of the Rule, addressed the Security Council on the amendments: 'In view of the checks and balances contained in the Statute, and particularly the duties and responsibilities of the Prosecutor under the Statute, such directions by the Chambers can only be interpreted as purely advisory in nature': 'Tribunal's Prosecutor addresses Security Council on completion strategy progress', ICTY Press Release, AM/MOW/1085e, 7 June 2006.

management of a party's case in an adversarial criminal justice system. This is why the process must have been developed during the pre-trial phase, with negotiations and discussions in full candour with the prosecution and defence, so that the court is not acting in a manner which unfairly prejudices the prosecution's case.

Where the proceedings are adversarial, there will always be a balance between allowing the parties to construct and present their case freely and the court intervening to ensure that the trial proceeds in a fair and sufficiently expeditious manner. In this respect, it is clear not only that fairness and expedition are sometimes competing interests, but that different aspects of fairness can conflict, requiring international criminal courts and tribunals to attend diligently to the appropriate balancing of these interests.

Managing resource and representation issues in complex international criminal law cases

Many models of representation have emerged in the short existence of modern international criminal law. The standard defence counsel model, as well as legal aid schemes and the regulation of the appearance and conduct of counsel, have developed over the past decade in international criminal courts and tribunals. The evolution of defence counsel offices, trialled at the SCSL and developed furthur in the ICC's administrative and procedural structure, are signs of the development of a self-established international criminal defence bar. This is also a sign that international criminal law is becoming a well-rooted system of law with a future.

However, other representation models have emerged or are emerging which betray the true challenges facing international criminal law. The sheer size and complexity of these cases, and the rarefied environment in which this system operates, pose complexities that have called for innovative and sometimes radical consideration of the kind of legal representation that is available particularly to high level accused. It has also required that considerable resources be made available to these accused to counterbalance the significant resources available to prosecution offices and to address the complexities, scope and nature of international criminal trials. The *Milošević* case was the source of considerable trial and innovation in this area and techniques (relating to the provision of extraordinary resources or *de facto* legal assistance) were either created or developed by the Trial Chamber in an attempt to achieve the goal of conducting the trial fairly and expeditiously.

Self-representation was a profound procedural challenge to the *Milošević* trial and it is a spreading problem in international criminal law. Senior level accused, with the personality and the will to interfere with the smooth running of trials that are already complex, have increasingly followed Milošević's lead and chosen to defend themselves or use representation issues in other ways to obstruct the trial process. In the *Milošević* case, this absorbed considerable resources and energy and led the Trial Chamber to conclude that there were circumstances in which the right to self-representation, which it held was recognised in international criminal law, was subject to limitation and qualification. In international criminal law, following the *Milošević* Trial and Appeals Chamber decisions, and other decisions in the ICTY, ICTR and SCSL, there appears to be a clear legal proposition to the effect that the right to self-representation will be taken away or limited in circumstances where it threatens the overall fairness and expeditiousness of the trial. This will be so even in circumstances where individual constituent rights (or 'minimum guarantees') which make up that overarching right to a fair trial must be violated.

In this area, the *Milošević* trial once again provides a rich and detailed source of law for issues that go to the heart of best practice for the conduct of complex international criminal trials. Decisions in the *Šešelj* and *Krajišnik* cases before the ICTY and the *Norman* case before the SCSL are others. In future, international criminal courts and tribunals will undoubtedly be confronted with the complexities of representation and resources discussed and will be obliged to make difficult decisions about the balancing of rights and interests in determining the manner of representation, particularly where accused seek to wilfully manipulate or obstruct the trial process. The future trials of accused such as Šešelj will accentuate these issues. Again, much can be taken from the *Milošević* trial in determining how to weigh and conclude such issues.

Although different representation models have evolved in recent years to deal with accused who by their conduct or choices pose a challenge to a fair and expeditious trial (the adaptation of standby counsel, the imposition of defence counsel, and development and modification of *amicus curiae*), the real distinction to be drawn is between representation and self-representation. The strong position ultimately taken by the Trial Chambers in the *Milošević* and *Šešelj* cases, in imposing counsel on intransigent and manipulative accused, presents real challenges for the conduct of those trials as well as – crucially – their fair and expeditious conduct. However, the consequences of not taking a strong position may be the total derailment of the trial and an inability of the court to impose an effective and acceptable framework for the trial to proceed to conclusion – a conclusion borne out by the Appeals Chamber's intervention in the *Šešelj* case. An essential principle in the reform process when dealing with these issues for future complex international criminal trials, is for the court to enforce respect for the judicial institution, its officers and the forensic trial process. In the *Milošević* trial, as in others, the court has shown a considerable degree of leniency towards accused who show disrespect and who use the forensic trial process to peddle political views or threaten the good conduct of the trial. Clearly this has developed, in part, out of a concern over achieving the practical goal of keeping the trial moving. However, the *Milošević* case serves as an example of high level accused who are able to take advantage of the niceties of the trial process for inappropriate motives. International criminal courts and tribunals must ensure that less latitude is given to such accused and that the integrity of the trial process is preserved. This is an important aspect of a court ensuring the fairness and expedition of these trials.

The outdated common law/civil law divide: time for international criminal law to evolve

Much has been made by scholars and in the jurisprudence of the differences between the two major systems of law and the extent to which the international tribunals reflect them.[9] Judge Robinson has gone so far as to argue that 'if not properly resolved, tension between the legal systems may lead to unfairness'.[10] These matters have been discussed in different contexts throughout this book. It is apparent that international criminal law is infrastructurally adversarial but that it has many civil law overlays which can or do impact profoundly on the conduct of proceedings.

[9] See, e.g., Megan Fairlie, 'The Marriage Between Common and Continental Law at the ICTY and its Progeny, Due Process Deficit' (2004) 4 *International Criminal Law Review* 243; Salvatore Zappalà, *Human Rights in International Criminal Proceedings* (2003); Patrick L. Robinson, 'Ensuring Fair and Expeditious Trials at the International Criminal Tribunal for the Former Yugoslavia' (2000) 11 *European Journal of International Law* 569; Patrick L. Robinson, 'Fair but Expeditious Trials' in Hirad Abtahi and Gideon Boas (eds.), *The Dynamics of International Criminal Justice: Essays in Honour of Sir Richard May* (2005), 169; Mirjan Damaška, 'The Uncertain Fate of Evidentiary Transplants: Anglo-American and Contemporary Experiments' (1997) 45 *American Journal of Comparative Law* 839; Françoise Tulkens, 'Main Comparable Features of the Different European Criminal Justice Systems' in Mireille Delmas-Marty (ed.), *The Criminal Process and Human Rights: Toward a European Consciousness* (1995), 5.

[10] Patrick L. Robinson, 'Rough Edges in the Alignment of Legal Systems in the Proceedings at the ICTY' (2005) 3 *JICJ* 1, 4.

However, it is in fact time to abandon the preoccupation of international criminal courts and tribunals with this dichotomy and embrace the newly created system of international criminal law as a jurisdiction in its own right. Only then will the law makers and interpreters be free from the perceived constraints of principle and procedure derived from national legal precedent. Freedom from preoccupation with the common and civil law approach to legal and procedural problem-solving in international criminal law will facilitate a more clear application of principle developed in the context of that legal system and encourage lawyers and judges to look at these issues in their context, rather than through the lens of their own domestic legal experience. This proposed re-focusing is by no means intended to suggest that comparative law is not an important discipline and influence on the interpretation of the relevant law, nor that general principles of law are not a crucial source of international law in this discipline. But there has been an overinvestment in the common law/civil law dichotomy and its perceived impact on the fair and expeditious conduct of international criminal proceedings. This dichotomy and its anatomical relationship with fairness and expeditiousness was critically important in the early years of development of modern international criminal law, as can be seen from its emergence in key issues discussed throughout this book. But now is the time for international criminal law to unchain itself from these constraints, acknowledge that there is a strong foundation for the still-fledgling system of international criminal law, and one on which can be built a sound and permanent *sui generis* legal system.

An opportunity exists to develop a coherent and comprehensive body of law and procedure that is capable of succeeding in the prosecution of cases of a great size and complexity, in an environment at least partially removed from the narrow-mindedness of long-established domestic criminal law systems. This innovative approach may assist in the development of a long-standing international criminal justice system. It may even strike broader than that. In the process of developing laws and procedures for the conduct of these trials, large-scale comparative law research has been undertaken by international criminal courts and tribunals, and both judicial decisions and scholarly writing on these issues have made clear reference to the sources of this developing law, as well as discussing its adaptation and application. There is no impediment to the emergence of a degree of reciprocity, in which law makers and commentators from domestic systems of law look at the application of similar legal principles in international criminal law and reincorporate them back into their own systems. This organic relationship could benefit the development of both national and international systems, particularly in the area of complex litigation, which plagues law and policy makers in all jurisdictions.

The need to consider a new appellate jurisdiction for international criminal law

Several rulings by the Appeals Chamber during the *Milošević* case force consideration of the role and structure of an appeals court in international criminal law. Appellate jurisdictions of international criminal courts and tribunals should exercise judiciousness and restraint in interfering with the conduct of a case by a trial chamber, applying strictly their own tests for overturning decisions made by trial chambers in the exercise of their discretion and with the full context of the case in mind. Experience in the *Milošević* case shows just how failure to do so can have disastrous consequences, not just on the expeditious conduct of such trials but on their very viability. The Appeals Chamber's decisions in respect of joinder[11] and representation of the accused[12] in the *Milošević* case were poorly reasoned, exceeded the appropriate – or at least advisable – application of appellate review, and had a direct and injurious impact on both the fair and expeditious conduct of the trial. Add to these, decisions on the admission of written testimony pursuant to ICTY Rule 89(F)[13] (which prompted Judge Hunt in dissent to accuse the Appeals Chamber of putting politics over the interests of a fair trial) and adjudicated facts[14] (which was almost incoherent) – let alone the extraordinary decisions on imposing defence counsel in the *Šešelj* case – and a disturbing picture begins to emerge of an appellate jurisdiction overly zealous in its interference with the trial court's conduct of the proceedings, yet poorly equipped to do so.

This is not at all to suggest that an appellate review process will necessarily impact adversely on the trial management process, let alone fail to

[11] *Prosecutor v. Slobodan Milošević*, 'Reasons for Decision on Prosecution Interlocutory Appeal From Refusal to Order Joinder', Case No. IT-99-37-AR73, IT-01-50-AR73, IT-01-51-AR73, 18 April 2002.

[12] *Prosecution v. Milošević*, 'Decision on Interlocutory Appeal of the Trial Chamber's Decision on the Assignment of Defence Counsel', Case No. IT-02-54-AR73.7, 1 November 2004.

[13] *Prosecutor v. Milošević*, 'Decision on Interlocutory Appeal on the Admissibility of Evidence-in-Chief in the Form of Written Statements', Case No. IT-02-54-AR73.4, 30 September 2003.

[14] *Prosecutor v. Milošević*, 'Decision on Prosecution Motion for Judicial Notice of Adjudicated Facts', Case No. IT-02-54-PT, 10 April 2003.

protect or enhance the fairness of the proceedings. In many instances, appellate review can and will protect legitimate interests and correct egregious errors. However, a restrained approach that respects a trial court's intimate understanding of the intricacies of the case (its parties' conduct, the evidence led, the effect of impugned decisions on the myriad of case-related matters), and only interferes where a clear justiciable error has occurred, will better facilitate the management of such complex cases. As a principle, therefore, appellate bodies should exercise caution in interfering in complex case management processes that reach more broadly than a narrow issue of contention before it.

This issue, however, is much broader than the ICTY Appeals Chamber's inappropriate interference in the *Milošević* or *Šešelj* cases, or any other complex international criminal trial. There is a structural issue in respect of appellate jurisdictions in all international criminal courts and tribunals that should at least be raised and considered, even if not resolved. In chapter one of this book, I reflected on Judge Hunt's criticism of his own Appeals Chamber colleagues for what he described as 'destruction of the rights of the accused enshrined in the Tribunal's Statute and in customary international law', by reversing or ignoring well-considered precedent on the basis of an improper contemplation of the completion strategy.[15]

Such an explicit and unveiled attack on the judicial decision-making process of the Appeals Chamber by Judge Hunt gives rise to some concern. The appellate body of the *ad hoc* Tribunals, by virtue of its own holding, 'requires that the *ratio decidendi* of its decisions is binding on Trial Chambers'.[16] The rationale, as expressed by the Appeals Chamber, for this fundamental proposition, is that (1) the ICTY and ICTR Statutes establish a hierarchical structure in which the Appeals Chamber is given the function of settling definitively certain questions of law and fact arising from decisions of the Trial Chambers; (2) the Tribunal's mandate requires the assurance of certainty and predictability in the application of the applicable law; and, (3) the right of appeal is said to be a component of the fair trial requirement, which is itself a rule of customary international law and gives rise to the right of the accused to have like cases treated alike.

[15] See *Prosecutor v. Milošević*, 'Dissenting Opinion of Judge David Hunt on Admissibility of Evidence in Chief in the Form of Written Statements (Majority Decision Given 30 September 2003)', Case No. IT-02-54-AR73.4, 21 October 2003, paras. 20–2; *Prosecutor* v. *Nyiramasuhuko*, 'Decision in the Matter of Proceedings Under Rule 15*bis* (D), Dissenting Opinion of Judge David Hunt', Case No. ICTR-98-42-A15*bis*, 24 September 2003, para. 17.

[16] *Prosecutor v. Aleksovski*, 'Judgment', IT-95-14-1, 24 March 2000, para. 113.

However, if there is any merit in Judge Hunt's criticism that the Appeals Chamber is unduly influenced in its decision-making by the Tribunal's commitment to comply with the completion strategy, the basis for the Appeals Chamber's determination of its own supremacy should be scrutinised. Perhaps the fact that the President of the ICTY – responsible for all the political and administrative functioning of the institution, including its closure – is also the judicial President of the ICTY and ICTR Appeals Chambers, at least adds to the perception of potential conflict between the judicial and the political processes. Furthermore, while the value of certainty is high, it is unclear whether the appellate body for the ICTY and ICTR is deserving of the sort of confidence one generally expects of appellate bodies in national systems of law that apply the principle of *stare decisis.*[17] This reflection comes into focus when one considers the vehemence of Judge Hunt's criticism.

It should be considered whether it is unreasonable to expect appellate bodies as they are structured in the international criminal courts and tribunals to be able to effectively create consistent, reliable and high quality precedent in a relatively new system of law. For a start, these appellate bodies are simply a larger number of judges, who are not selected for service in the Appeals Chamber on the basis of any seniority or particular experience in the application of appellate law in their own jurisdictions. While this issue is analysed in the context of the ICTY, the same is true for all international criminal courts and tribunals, where judges are elected by a State political process, need not necessarily be (and most often are not) judges in their own national jurisdictions and are placed on the appeals bench by an internal decision which clearly does not necessitate appellate judicial or equivalent experience as a pre-requisite for service.

It is possible that the time has come to consider the creation of a separate appellate court (consisting of a Bench of highly experienced appellate judges from different jurisdictions) vested with jurisdictional powers over all standing and future international and internationalised criminal courts and tribunals. If such a system were to work, the selection and appointment of judges would have to be carefully considered and the politics which tends to dictate judicial appointment at the international level would have to be curtailed to ensure the requisite quality and expertise of an institution vested with such an important role in international criminal

[17] *Stare decisis* embodies the principle that a settled point of law established by binding precedent must be adhered to where the facts of a case are substantially the same. See *Black's Law Dictionary* (6th edn 1990).

law. Failure to ensure the appointment of highly qualified appellate judges to such a court would simply exacerbate in a dramatic fashion the existing concerns, rendering the solution far worse than the problem. However, were it possible to create an independent, high quality super-appellate international criminal jurisdiction, the international criminal courts and tribunals could then focus on their trial work, their Presidents could freely engage in the important political, diplomatic and financial negotiating work free of concern that they are mixing the judicial with the political and compromising the crucial perception that justice is being delivered purely on the basis of legal principle.

Of course, the mechanical, jurisdictional and practical details, as well as the funding for such an institution, are enormously complex issues. These issues would require considerable attention, all of which are clearly outside the scope of this book or the point I am seeking to make in this context, which is that the limited capacity of these appellate courts should be acknowledged and accepted by them and their political masters. If, as these courts have established for themselves, their decisions are to be binding and *stare decisis* is to operate as a legal principle in international criminal law, then care and restraint should be exercised so as to enable trial courts to get on with the task of trying these complex cases and so as not to give the impression (apparently given even to at least one former serving appellate judge of the ICTY) that politics and not law dictate the determination of issues going even to the fundamental fair trial rights of accused.

After *Milošević*: the future of complex international criminal trials

Is it possible to conduct fair and expeditious complex international criminal trials, particularly those involving high level accused? And, if so, how much fairness and how much expedition? This has been the preoccupation of this book.

The benchmarks for fairness have developed over the past ten years of jurisprudential and regulatory activity in international criminal courts and tribunals. The interpretation of what constitutes a fair trial, and what embodies the constitutive rights or 'minimum guarantees' that make up this right, has undergone a degree of solidification within the context of international criminal law, such that this is becoming clearer and the international community can have greater confidence that these important trials are being conducted within a definable and, more importantly, acceptable framework. The analysis of complex international criminal trials in differing contexts throughout this book provides discrete answers to how a fair – and expeditious – trial will be conducted. The *Milošević* trial has provided important lessons for how this goal is to be achieved.

It is important that sovereign states develop their own internal commitments to investigating and prosecuting international crime domestically, an underdeveloped avenue for the prosecution of violations of international humanitarian law, crimes against humanity and genocide. But it is more important that international criminal law continues to be administered by international criminal courts and tribunals more removed from the exigencies of domestic political concerns. These institutions are far from flawless. They are not, as idealists might argue, apolitical. They need time and opportunity to develop strong, consistent and reasoned general principles to underpin the construct of international criminal law. However, they are far more resistant to political influence because of the mélange of different legal and political cultures of judges and legal staff, and a trial will invariably be conducted before three independent judges from three different countries. That fact in itself lends greater protection to the goal of delivering justice independently and impartially. Political and social commitment to these institutions peaked with the creation of the ICC. In many ways the completion strategy and enforced wind-down of the ICTY has benefited the development of ideas and tools for the conduct of complex international criminal trials that will preserve fairness as perceived and defined in their contextual legal environment and make them more expeditious.

The *Milošević* trial originated or developed many of these mechanisms, but it was only the beginning of the burgeoning industry of international criminal law. It is crucial to the future of this important and fledgling area of law that not only the *ad hoc* or hybrid international courts and tribunals build on the lessons learnt thus far, but that the ICC pay close and conscious attention to what has been done at the ICTY, ICTR, SCSL and elsewhere, when building the pre-eminent international criminal jurisdiction of the future. If it succeeds in doing this, the legacy of the *Milošević* trial will be a positive one – it will be a future symbol of the challenge to impunity and an acknowledgement that it provided some of the framework and intellectual work product for future success.

Piecing together the indicia of investigation, pre-trial, trial and appeal activity discussed throughout this book starts to build a picture of what best practice in the conduct of international criminal trials might be: focused investigations that are lawyer-driven; indictments that are restrained, focused and subject to rigorous judicial scrutiny and include the opportunity for adversarial challenge; greater judicial intervention in and control over all aspects of the pre-trial and trial processes; strict and enforced case management, with an increasing but balanced disposition to be more radical and creative; ensuring adequate resources and representation for accused, including a willingness to limit or finesse particular aspects or constituent parts of the fair trial right to ensure overall fairness; stricter limitation on the right to self-representation; the informed, considered but strict imposition of time limits by a court on parties and the case; and an uncompromising attention to the forensic purpose of the trial process. The experience of the *Milošević* trial and other complex cases examined in this book provide a clear message for the future successful conduct of complex international criminal trials: all aspects of the process must be sedulously attended to achieve fairness and expeditiousness. If the experiences analysed are heeded and adjustments made to the conduct of future trials, then in the short time that modern international criminal law has existed and flourished, the prospect of conducting fair and expeditious complex international criminal trials will have been created virtually from the ashes of persecution and genocide.

If this occurs there is hope that future leaders will heed a warning that might save thousands, or millions, of people their lives and livelihoods: that the international community will no longer tolerate impunity. To this end, the *Milošević* trial will have offered some good for the future of humanity.

INDEX

Note: 1. Entries in **Bold** denote main entries.
2. References are to proceedings against Slobodan Milošević unless the contrary is indicated.
3. The following abbreviations are used in this Index:

ABAS	American Bar Association Standards
ACHP	African Charter on Human and Peoples' Rights
ACHR	American Convention on Human Rights
DB	Serbian State Security Service
ECHR	European Convention on Human Rights
ECtHR	European Court of Human Rights
FRY	Federal Republic of Yugoslavia
ICC	International Criminal Court
ICCPR	International Covenant on Civil and Political Rights
ICJ	International Court of Justice
ICL	International Criminal Law
ICT	International Criminal Tribunals
ICTr	international criminal trials
ICTR	International Criminal Tribunal for Rwanda
ICTY	International Criminal Tribunal for the Former Yugslavia
IMTFE	International Military Tribunal for the Far East
JNA	Yugoslav National Army
KLA	Kosovo Liberation Army
MUP	Serbian Ministry of Internal Affairs
NATO	North Atlantic Treaty Organisation
OPCD	Office of Public Counsel for the Defence
PDO	Principal Defender's Office
SAOs	Serb Autonomous Regions
SCSL	Special Court for Sierra Leone
SDS	Croatian Serbian Democratic Party
SFRY	Socialist Federal Republic of Yugoslavia
SICT	Supreme Iraqi Criminal Tribunal
VJ	Yugoslav Army
VRS	Bosnian Serb Army